THE LUST OF SEEING

THE LUST OF SEEING

Themes of the Gaze and Sexual Rituals in the Fiction of Felisberto Hernández

Frank Graziano

Lewisburg
Bucknell University Press
London: Associated University Presses

Associated University Presses
440 Forsgate Drive
Cranbury, NJ 08512

Associated University Presses
16 Barter Street
London WC1A 2AH, England

Associated University Presses
P.O. Box 338, Port Credit
Mississauga, Ontario
Canada L5G 4L8

The paper used in this publication meets the requirements of the American National Standard for Permanence of Paper for Printed Library Materials Z39.48-1984.

Library of Congress Cataloging-in-Publication Data

Graziano, Frank, 1955–
    The lust of seeing : themes of the gaze and sexual rituals in the fiction of Felisberto Hernández / Frank Graziano.
       p.   cm.
    Includes bibliographical references (p.   ) and index.
    ISBN 0-8387-5338-8 (alk. paper)
    1. Hernández, Felisberto—Criticism and interpretation. 2. Gaze in literature. 3. Sex in literature. 4. Narcissism in literature.
I. Title.
PQ8519.H34Z68   1997
863—dc20   96-12340
                                               CIP

For my fantastic daughter Jessica
(who may not read this book until she is eighteen)

*Ay, del que no marcha esa marcha donde la madre
ya no le sigue, ay.*
—José Lezama Lima

Contents

Acknowledgments

Preparation of *The Lust of Seeing* was significantly enhanced in 1991 by four months of research in Montevideo, Uruguay, under the auspices of a Fulbright research award. I most gratefully thank the Council for International Exchange of Scholars in Washington and the Fulbright Commission in Montevideo for this truly valuable personal as well as professional experience.

There are many Uruguayans to whom I owe my sincere gratitude. Foremost among them is Ana María Hernández de Elena, daughter of Felisberto Hernández, who granted me free access to Hernández's archives and who was generous with her time and kindness. Amalia Nieto, one of Hernández's widows, was likewise generous and accommodating, offering me access to the Hernández materials in her possession and a friendship that made my stay in Montevideo most meaningful.

In April 1993, my understanding of Hernández's work and world was furthered by the conference "Felisberto Hernández: An International Homage," which was cosponsored under my direction by the American University College of Arts and Sciences and the Embassy of Uruguay in Washington. I am sincerely grateful to Betty Bennett, dean of the College of Arts and Sciences, whose support made that conference possible. I was also fortunate on that occasion to converse at length with María Isabel Hernández Guerra (Hernández's first daughter) and Norah Giraldi Dei Cas (Hernández's biographer), both of whom significantly enhanced my understanding of Hernández's life and world.

My thanks are again due to Dean Bennett and to the American University for the fall 1993 research leave and accompanying stipend that accelerated completion of *The Lust of Seeing*. A portion of that leave was spent at the Bellagio Center, where the last chapter of the manuscript was drafted. I extend my most sincere appreciation to the Villa Serbelloni staff and to the Rockefeller Foundation for that experience beyond description. I am also indebted to the American University's Department of Language and Foreign Studies, which provided funds for the research assistants whose help greatly expedited the manuscript's development.

And finally, I gratefully acknowledge *Revista Iberoamericana* and the *Indiana Journal of Hispanic Literatures*, in which sections of the manuscript were published in earlier versions.

THE LUST OF SEEING

Introduction

So cleverly did his art conceal its art.
 —Ovid, in reference to Pygmalion

THE OPEN WORK

Between 1925 and 1931 Felisberto Hernández insinuated himself modestly into the world of letters with four tiny chapbooks published without covers. The first of these, *Fulano de tal* (So-and-so), emphasized with its title the tentativeness, the quasi-anonymity of the venture: a sparse book without covers by a narrator without identity *(fulano),* a text sketched in on the frontiers of the absence that it barely escaped. This collection of unrealized potential concludes appropriately with a section entitled "Prologue to a Book that I Could Never Begin," delineating not only the projection of ambiguity, an "exhibitionist modesty," and a metafictional *ars poetica* discourse into the future poetics that Hernández would derive from them, but also—as apparent in this prologue's first line—the extension of nebulous *fulano* nonidentities: "I plan to say something about somebody."[1] That this "somebody" turns out to be a prototype implied author derived from the author's own psychobiography is also signaled in the prologue to another unwritten book, *Filosofía del gangster* (Gangster philosophy), that the author proposed to dedicate to himself (*OC,* 1:147).

With the publication of *Libro sin tapas* (Book without covers) in 1929, the material absence of covers occasioned by impoverished production budgets was thematized and integrated into Hernández's poetics.[2] The collection's epigraph states: "This book is without covers because it is open and free [*libre*]: one can write before and after it" (1:79).[3] Hernández was here clearly under the influence of his friend and mentor Carlos Vaz Ferreira, to whom the book is dedicated.[4] In his *Lógica viva* (1910) and *Fermentario* (1938), Vaz Ferreira stressed writing as process and argued for "more amorphous" publications, or, as Hernández put it, for "the free and capricious forms that lips take as words come out of them" (1:99). Vaz Ferreira was himself following Henri Bergson's description of ideas that "follow the sinuous and mobile contours of reality." A relation between writer and reader is established as the reader's mind—"continually guided by a series of nascent movements . . . which translate symbolically the thousand successive directions of the thought"—is led across "a curve of thought and feeling analogous to that we ourselves [the writers] describe."[5] In pursuit of this line, Vaz Ferreira favored writings that evidenced their stages of fermentation ("the psychological fringe, the penumbra, the halo around absolute clarity") rather than presenting themselves as crystalline works purged of subjectivity, as definitive and definitively closed.[6] In lieu of a prefabricated idea adorned with words, writing as a means of creative discovery captures "the movement of an idea in formation" (1:184).

Insofar as Hernández is concerned, these ideas-in-the-making are formalized into narratives through a generative mechanism of association. Ideas and emotions cluster around a given memory, image, or theme, and the narrator registering "everything with a strange simultaneity" allows the emerging sensations to form "a rhythm amongst themselves" (1:111). "The tune is the mood groping for its logic," as Robert Penn Warren once put it.[7] Text production serves as a means of inventory, organization, and self-exploration as the narrator probes "secrets that have gathered without my knowing" (1:49), searching for "unexpected connections" (2:59) and endeavoring to "join together those that have some affinity, however vague" (1:71), because "I must make poetry of that confusion" (3:196). "I worked almost as though in a dream, letting things come to me, waiting for them and observing them with a deep and childlike interest" (1:38).[8] The writer proceeding by these dreamy poetics is, in Robert Frost's dictum, the happy discoverer of his ends: "I am inventing something and I still don't know what it is" (3:169). He pursues the "mystery," he traces the footprints at the moment that they make their impressions in the sand, and he allows the text to assume an autodefinition discovered in the process of its creation: "I wasn't looking for anything and knew that I would find something" (1:163).[9]

Throughout his career Hernández pieced together a fiction with fragments excavated from "what he doesn't know." The "mystery" retrieved from unknown or partially explored quarters of his own psyche were then, in a process of "downloading" onto the text, purged from the self as they were objectified by writing. In Hernández's case, as in many others, the obsessive haunting of ideas, of images, of memories, of fears and desires, is neutralized as it is textualized, liberating the author to pursue his generative quest of self-exploration into other unknowns, other fictions. The intrapsychic overload occasioning the "need to get rid of oneself, as it were, through signs and gestures" is sometimes represented in Hernández's canon by ideas that get "in one's blood" or "under one's skin," by external ideas that intrude, are incorporated, and for better or worse become a part of the self.[10] Advertising provides the paradigm for this barrage, with its capacity to penetrate and internally circulate represented clearly enough in an early Hernández text: "They are always coming up with new ways to get their advertisements into our blood" (1:194). When the incorporation of extraneous ideas or imagery is further developed in "Canary Furniture Company"—where advertisers actually inject their commercial announcements into potential customers with huge hypodermic needles—the trope speaks more directly to the inability to shut down one's thoughts, to get something off of one's mind, to quiet the omnipresent, internal harangue of one's echoing obsessions.[11] Writing becomes the means by which the voices are silenced, the "getting rid of oneself" by unloading onto the text. Following Nietzsche, Roland Barthes summarized the process most succinctly: "I write because I do not want the words I find: by subtraction." Barthes is yet closer to Hernández and the alien interior voice "injected" into language when he remarks that "This book consists of what I do not know," of "things which utter themselves only by the voices of others."[12]

On many occasions—particularly in the early and then again in the final texts—the poetics of the unknown and its "mystery" become a metafictional thematic concern of central importance to Hernández. "I think that my specialty is in writing about what I don't know" (1:190) relates one narrator, and elsewhere, "I don't think I should only write about what I know, but also about the unknown [*lo otro*]" (1:23).[13] Excavation of *lo otro* is fruitful because "speaking about something that does not exist one comes to a better understanding of things that do exist."[14] The unknown is made manifest through a fiction with a seemingly unelaborated surface—"like someone who relates something strange that he has just found out, with the simple language of improvisation or even with the language that comes to me naturally, full of repetitions and imperfections" (3:214)—but Hernández's spontaneity is something of a sleight-of-hand. The surface might be "a little clumsy and seem improvised" (3:67), the texts might be composed of "words that come out to be heard like grotesque and timid men going out to dance for the first time" (2:132), but the clumsiness is always strategic. Hernández's deceptive textual surface must give the impression of spontaneity and even carelessness ("my uglinesses will always be my richest form of expression") (3:214), but the calculated imprecision was earned through endless revision of his manuscripts. As Hernández remarked to one of his daughters, "Spontaneity requires great elaboration."[15] In a passage read most fruitfully as an *ars poetica* statement, a Hernández narrator notes: "I must give the impression of carelessly carrying some mysterious aspect of myself that was elaborated in an unknown life" (2:98). This elaborated spontaneity and the poetics of "giving an impression" underscore a congruity of style and theme when one recalls the Hernández narrators who—like Pygmalion—allow the impression to displace reality as they reify their own projections.[16] The production of the text, in other words, evidences a poetics of concealment that is represented again in the themes that the text explores, the "form" and the "content" thereby dialoguing to generate the artifact, the fiction, that this interaction constitutes through its "happy disorder" (3:18).

Beyond the presence of ideas in formation as desired by Vaz Ferreira, beyond the associative pursuit of the mysteries intrinsic to *lo otro*, what is written before and after Hernández's text without covers, like any text, includes not only the clever additions that latecomers (the author himself, readers, critics) might append to the work's formal boundaries but also, and most importantly, an entire baggage of cultural history inscribed in the ideas, the psychology, and the words with which the narrative is composed. A text is bounded, its intertextuality is not. Closure holds jurisdiction over a narrative's unfolding toward its conclusion, over the linear artifact with a beginning and an end, but never over the uncontainable, polysemous, endlessly potential discourse bound between a book's covers. While the two ends of a text are nobly defended, the field between them "would remain open and mysterious" (1:160), vulnerable to escapes and invasions. Characterized by a "menacing imprecision" and a "delay in closing," Hernández's book remains a book without covers (1:93).

The "coverlessness" establishing an intertextual arena is complemented in Hernández's canon by an "unfinished" quality that similarly predisposes these texts to an interplay of voices and associative relations. The tentative, open-ended, and structurally inconclusive qualities are evident enough in the fluidity with which one Hernández text flows into the other. Rather than strictly defined narratives one discovers, in most cases, "the mobility of diverse attempts" that evidence a constant, "interminable intertextual circulation."[17] Roberto Echavarren similarly observes that Hernández's narratives "do not have denouements, but only interruptions. They are the model of some compulsion to repeat, machines that rehearse the same error, the same extravagance."[18] The repetition is paradoxically coupled with the sparsity of the text and the absences that punctuate it, with the narrator speaking—in the extreme instances—only to textualize what he does not know and to record his silence. "I don't remember whatever it was that I was going to tell you," writes Hernández in a letter to his longtime lover Paulina Medeiros, "but consider it said."[19] What is articulated stands in as a monument of what the author did or could not express, "as though the textual space were nothing more than an allusion to something ultimately unspeakable."[20] The reader is invited to participate in the construction of this textual monument to the unutterable by filling in the voids with his or her own interruptions, by "injecting" his or her own discourse into the unfinished text in formation: "I will ask that you interrupt the reading of this book as many times as possible: perhaps, almost surely, what you think in these intervals will be the best part of this book" (1:149). The narrator recruits the reader as an accomplice in what Jean-Philippe Barnabé describes as a "voluntary and tenacious blurring of the structural coherence."[21] The architectonics of well-structured, beginning-middle-end narratives fall by the wayside as Hernández's poetics privilege an accumulating intertextual repetition, a layering of voices, an evasive but flirtatious relation with the unutterable, and a relentless rehashing of the themes that index Hernández's obsessions. The forfeiture of strict structural coherence in Hernández's narratives displaces each text's richest and most resonant meaning to its mutual interrelation with the other texts around it, texts that are equally "unfinished" and—like the injected advertisement and the readers' interruptions—are accepted as intertexts by the narrative, whose loose structure readily accommodates them within "the false clarity of some dreams" (3:190). Hernández's fiction, like Marcel Proust's, "is a palimpsest in which several figures and several meanings are merged and entangled together, all present together at all times, and which can only be deciphered together, in their inextricable totality."[22]

One intent of the "unfinished" text is to "move its mystery" (1:173) through "the intimate silence of others" (3:146).[23] The narrator understands that each reader rewrites the text as he or she uses it as a mirror, but this textual mirror reflects selectively and the narrator necessarily remains blind to the content of these multiple self-readings. As Proust put it, "Every reader is, while he is reading, the reader of his own self." Furthermore, "The writer's work is merely a kind of optical instrument which he offers to the reader to enable him to discern what, without this book, he would perhaps have never perceived in himself."[24] The reader, in turn, offers his or her "optical instrument"—the reading eye—to the writer who anticipates it, thereby conferring upon writing the interpersonal meaning and function that motivates production of the text, without which the *author* would remain unaware of his own "mysteries." Hernández fiction thematically engages the concept of implied reader and actively explores the recognition—later central to poststructuralist theory—that "there is not, behind the text, someone active (the writer) and out front someone passive (the reader)."[25] Rather, for Hernández the text "is that Moebius strip in which the inner and outer sides, the signifying and the signified sides, the side of writing and the side of reading, ceaselessly turn and cross over, in which writing is constantly read, in which reading is constantly written and inscribed."[26]

If the reader is told too much, if the text clogs its potential resonance by writing through to "completion," then the mystery is undermined, the Möbius curl is undone and flattened: "The idea dies and thought arrives dressed in black to build to measure a coffin with golden handles" (1:184). Hernández prefers the spare and indecorous use of words to elicit "something that had nothing to do with words; but the words served to mutually attract us toward one another's silence" (1:175). The words serve as points of contact between writer and reader; their poetry is not in the decorum of the text's surface but rather in the energetic "mystery" sparked by consolidating two silences. These are words under which "unknown silences wait to again awaken their extinguished resonance of memory" (1:175).[27] Words "full of intentions" (2:46) reactivate static ideas and emotions; a sympathetic, unspoken relation is established; and the abyss between individual solipsisms is bridged.[28] For Bergson—who influenced Hernández via Vaz Ferreira—the words themselves ultimately disappear in the course of this improvised harmony between writer and reader, as "there is nothing left but the flow of meaning which runs through the words, nothing but two minds which, without intermediary, seem to vibrate directly in unison with one another."[29]

The written word is static and mute until the reader invests it with his or her vision: "We project names, faces, voices into those inanimate black marks on the page."[30] These voices, however, are themselves silent, are products of a synesthesia that we perceive in a nonauditory manner like the voices of thoughts and dreams. If one were able to peer inside a brain, Bergson speculated, one would "be in the situation of the spectator seeing distinctly all that the actors were doing on the stage, but not hearing a word of what they were saying." Witnessing this pantomime, "he would be like a person who could only know a symphony by the movements of the conductor directing the orchestra."[31] The wand or words mobilize a silent world of "ideas" or "memories" or "mysteries"; the conductor's gestures, the signs on the page, orchestrate the reader's accompaniment. This mute harmony is thematized throughout Hernández's canon through the treatment of silent film, of silent stages (the glass showcases of *The Hortensias*, for example), and of silent musical performance (such as the "Schubert of the tunnel" in "Except Julia"). "Black marks on the page" orchestrate an internal composition accompanied by moving visual images—a series of "stills" that produce the illusion of movement—but "the film of my memories is silent" (2:30). The textual music must be added as it is in film, in the dimly lit parlors of many Hernández stories, and in the showcase gallery of *The Hortensias*, but its emotional cueing is nevertheless silent.

Umberto Eco's analysis of narratives as works open "to a continuous generation of internal relations" complements contributions made by intertextuality theorists to describe this textual field of possibility as "a braid of different voices, of many codes, at once interlaced and incomplete," as "saturated with other people's interpretations," "permeated with intentions," adhering simultaneously to various sign systems.[32] In a passage underlined by Hernández himself in a copy of Alfred North Whitehead's *Modes of Thought*, we learn that one's "immediate imaginative experience" can be "enormously increased" through "the aid of a common language, the fragmentary past experiences . . . as enshrined in words."[33] One of Hernández's narrators, under the "immense force of other people's thoughts," remarks, "These words, that seem to have passed through many mouths and been in very different voices, that have crossed through the times and places of others, now present themselves to claim a meaning that I would never have granted them" (3:54). The entire canon insistently attests that for Hernández "literature is not a means of expression, a vehicle, an instrument, but the very locus of his thought," and further, that "it is not he who is thinking his language, but his language which is thinking him and thinking outside him."[34] As Hernández himself expressed it in notebook fragments, "Words are proud and are patient in expressing themselves, not for me, but for the mission that they have to accomplish"; and again: "The greatest anguish was feeling that in my own head there were words that didn't belong to me, and that those words composed thoughts planned by a foreign master" (3:200). The author's voice overlaps with the voices of his narration; the reader sets the fiction in motion by introducing his own fictions; the themes framed by the text's formal closure resonate beyond it into the history of their expressions and distortions; the language "permeated with intentions" speaks for itself. Literary narrative is thereby something of a mixed metaphor negotiating reconciliation between a palimpsest and a chamber of resonance, between Narcissus mesmerized by representation and Echo bound bodiless to the discourse of the other.

Hernández's before-and-after epigraph of the *Book Without Covers* epitomizes his entire canon's demonstration that a text's boundaries are merely formal, that the before and the after are intertextually inscribed *within* the text. The extraordinary resonance that Hernández's fiction generates through its deceptively modest surface owes a great deal to intertextual permeations and circulations, to an infusion and overlapping of thematic echoes released by and then multiplying the minimalist voice that dared to evoke them. A deluge of motifs emerges from a common nexus seemingly too flimsy to accommodate any one of them, and the themes summoned forth all forfeit their respective definitions as the narrative subtly exploits the resonance of their interaction. When in his peculiarly acute manner Hernández treats such archetypal themes as the gaze, the mother, the mirror, and the fragmented self and body, he situates his text without covers in an unfinished discursive continuum always in the process of becoming, always rehearsed and reinscribed, always original because it always returns to origins.

The present study is situated on these permeable borders where textuality and intertextuality negotiate their interrelation. My intent is to elucidate Hernández's canon by considering it in relation to the psycho-cultural continuum to which it is integral, but this approach must not be misunderstood as a confusion of the author with the narrative voices of his texts or as a suggestion that Hernández was familiar with, influenced by, or responding to the cultural phenomena to which I relate his canon. Hernández was, in fact, rather culturally isolated, partly due to limited resources in Montevideo and, later, in the Uruguayan provinces where substantial periods of his formative years were spent, and partly due to his autodidactic, eclectically selective, and self-defensive temperament, which filtered out most potential influences and neutralized—"felisbertized"—those few that permeated his protective barriers. Hernández's fourth wife, Reina Reyes, observed that he defended himself from all external influences that might modify him, and Medeiros referred to him as a "literary illiterate," partially because his formal education was minimal. "I didn't study philosophy in the University, Hernández notes, but rather across from the University. In this café."[35] He read with no great depth or breadth, often abandoning books before concluding them, and he naïvely overvalued the local intellectual heroes of his era (taking, for instance, Vaz Ferreira "as indisputable model"), receiving world literary and intellectual trends "by osmosis" through these masters' interpretations.[36] This quasi-hermetic cultural enclosure in which Hernández lived was rehearsed in his later years by the dimly lit basement, "damp and gloomy," where he reflected and wrote on what he had at hand: his body, his memories, his language, his obsessions.[37]

Hernández's treatment of themes and archetypes prevalent in Western cultural traditions results not from his erudition or self-conscious participation in the preoccupations of high culture, but rather from a groping—as relentless as it was calculated—through the "confusion" and "mystery" woven inextricably into the fabric of what it means to be human. His genius was achieved precisely when "he found in his work the locus of language in which it would be possible to explode his individuality and become dissolved in the idea."[38] The autonomous individual or collective expressions (in actions, in artifacts) of such "ideas" inherent in cultural traditions and in the languages that carry them are most thoroughly understood when considered in relation to one another and to the psychology generating them. "Understanding involves a system of layering of meanings, one layer forming the context by which the other layers take on significance."[39] The Hernández "layer" is the one in question here, but the realization that these layers are not static, that filtration, osmosis, erosion, and upheaval are far more characteristic of textual sedimentations than of their stolid geological counterparts, leads one to view "the text itself as a system of internal energies and tensions, compulsions, resistances, and desires."[40] The volatility of those internal relations is indebted not only to the psychology that bore them, but also to the cultural history that collects subjective experience, objectifies it as it imbeds the many layers into a palimpsest, and returns the composite to each individual who speaks or picks up a pen. "The powerful fiction is that which is able to restage the complex and buried past history of desire as it covertly reconstitutes itself in the present language."[41]

My intent in the chapters that follow is to excavate the layers of this palimpsest insofar as the themes of Hernández's canon are concerned, deriving from this analysis a greater understanding of the poetics in question and also of the larger issues—predominantly psychosexual—that gain exemplary representation in these fictions. In considering the strata of interrelations in Hernández's works, I hope to avoid clumsy criticism's tendency to neutralize the ambiguity—Hernández's "mystery," "confusion," "imprecision"—upon which the entire enterprise is based. Analysis of texts like those of Hernández benefits little from what Tzvetan Todorov referred to as "translation," the term here denoting the reduction of an overdetermined text to a definitive "meaning" that "explains" it. The Hernández text rather elicits an "amazement of incomprehensibility without offering justifications" (3:208). One perceptive reader, Saúl Yurkievich, recognized early on that the strangeness of Hernández's texts must be respected, that the "clarification" of their imprecision is analogous—as Hernández himself put it—to neutralizing the absurd and fantastic content of a dream (2:36).[42] If the "system of internal energies and tensions, compulsions, resistances, and desires" is provisionally frozen as an expository convenience, if the confusion is tamed and precision exacted "to restage the complex and buried past history of desire as it covertly reconstitutes itself in the present language," then this must be done with the understanding that the restoration of volatility and ambiguity is a necessary condition of the text's meaning, and that the critic's "interruption" must ultimately be silenced so that the narratives themselves can again speak with and against this new voice added to their choir. Otherwise, as Jacques Lacan would put it, one has nothing but the punctuation without its text.

THE NORMALIZED FANTASTIC

The fantastic quality of Hernández's fiction is derived not from a supernatural reality populated with extraordinary beings but rather from the insistence of the exception as the rule, from the premise that "there is now only one fantastic object: man."[43] Like Franz Kafka, and like the decadents of late romanticism writing under the influence of E. T. A. Hoffmann, Hernández exploits the elasticity of probability, normalizing strangeness through narrators and protagonists whose abnormalities are to varying degrees destigmatized and socialized.[44] The uncanniness generated by strangeness made normal is then redoubled by an assault on the opposite front: the normal is estranged as the text "presents or re-presents a weird, refracted world, transformed through the mind of the perceiver and his or her unconscious projections into the world."[45] The "disquieting strangeness of everyday life" in these texts results precisely from the Hernández narrators' "allying the common with the exceptional to the point of demonstrating that they can be one and the same."[46] This strategy of the fantastic has been succinctly summarized by Hugo Verani, who observes how "through a subtle alteration in perception the familiar becomes strange and the unusual habitual with disquieting naturalness; two mutually exclusive orders tend toward a deliberately ambiguous coexistence, resulting in strange resonances."[47]

The normalization of strangeness is particularly evident on the few occasions in which Hernández uses a third-person narrator, notably in *The Hortensias*, or in which the narrator is an observer rather than a protagonist, as in "Except Julia." In both cases an "atmosphere of complicity" provides that "the absurd is accepted not only by the protagonist . . . but also by the narrator and the other participants."[48] The narrator's nonchalant acceptance of the exceptional as commonplace serves to disseminate the protagonist's peculiarities beyond his private rituals and across the textual reality as a whole, with the social milieu—constructed by that narrator— generally in tacit compliance. Horacio's passion for dolls (the exceptional) is generalized into a social phenomenon through mass production (the commonplace), and this transition from private madness to public product normalizes the perversion. A fantastic quality is generated precisely because the narrator's perceptions are synchronized with Horacio's, because socialization of Horacio's fantasy is taken for granted. What the reader experiences as fantastic ambiguity or "confusion" is for the narrator "indifferentiation," which is to say indifference to discriminating between his own identity and that of his protagonists, and between subjective belief systems and social reality.[49] It is almost as though the protagonist were speaking through the narrator, as though Horacio had contracted a third-person mouthpiece (as he has contracted Facundo to fabricate the dolls and specialists to design the scenes) to construct an ambience in which his obsessions make supreme sense. Such othering of discourse—one's voice, another's mouth—recalls the relation that any writer has with his or her characters, of course, and this more so in the case of an author like Hernández, who is self-consciously "split into writer and spectator of his own eccentricity."[50] The synchronization of narrator and protagonist in *The Hortensias* provides that Horacio—like the implied author of Hernández texts generally—is both written and writer.

The socialization of abnormal behavior in Hernández's work is quintessentially psychoanalytical because it recognizes that psychopathology is a question of context and measure, of interpretation and degree, rather than of a given act's inherent sanity or insanity. Hernández narrators demonstrate a clear realization that even the most bizarre human behavior shares a continuum with its complements in the range of sanity, as is most apparently evidenced in the similarity of psychotic delusions and normal dreams.[51] The competing demands of human psychic and social realities—of the private and the proper—are constantly renegotiating a compromise to keep one within the realm of normalcy, or, that failing, to "normalize" the behavior that slips over the edge. If one acts in society on the aggressive and sexual impulses that ethics, law, and decorum confine to one's private psychic life, then society applies its ostracizing qualifiers, "criminal" and "mad," unless one limits the expression of forbidden impulses to sublimations—literary fictions in the present case—that concretize and socialize fantasies without violating the norms defending civilization. Fantastic literature such as Hernández's, what Todorov calls the generalized fantastic, is characterized precisely by this diversion. Like dreams and fantasies it implicitly subverts the inhospitable order forbidding one's desires, it redesigns social reality to accommodate them, and it disavows both the subversion and the redesign, taking its actions for granted and presuming absolute objectivity and universality of this private kingdom catering to its needs. The Hernández text constructs a milieu into which the forbidden fantastic aspects of daily human existence are integrated and then permitted to cast their hue over the social reality inclined elsewhere to exclude them.

Also psychoanalytical, and later deconstructive, is a manner of reading and writing in pursuit of traces that sketch in the mysterious underside, "the sense of objects . . . covering themselves with shadows" (1:43). While reading, for example, Hernández searches for the "mystery" at moments when an author unwittingly reveals something of which one could not be proud, something not readily remembered or repeated (1:167). The psychoanalyst's perspective is further established in statements such as, "I wanted to rebel against the injustice of excessive insistence of what is most conspicuous without being most important" (1:129) and, "I found myself with a mystery that aroused another quality of interest in things that were going on" (1:29). Under the influence of the Polish psychologist Waclaw Radecki, who advanced a psychology of cognition and perception based in part upon a *foco* (focal point) of attention surrounded—like a bull's-eye—with a peripheral *franja* (fringe), Hernández developed his poetics through exploration of the periphery, through reconception of the *franja* as a new *foco*, through restitution of the seemingly inconsequential detail to the foreground.[52] In this enterprise of tracking down the unnoticed or unacknowledged, of "discovering, lens in hand, the micro-structure of life," Hernández recalls José Ortega y Gasset's "dehumanization": "The procedure simply consists in letting the outskirts of attention, that which ordinarily escapes notice, perform the main part in life's drama."[53] The "outskirts" in Hernández's case are complemented by a pronounced interest in the hidden and forbidden realm *under* skirts (3:152, for example) and in matters that ordinarily escape notice because they are kept "under the rug": "If Colling's story were a rug that unrolled as we walked and my eyes were attracted by its plot [*trama* = weft/woof and plot], design, and color, one could also say that there were other things that attracted one's attention, and they were something like bulges moving under the rug" (1:57). While the fiction entertains by mobilizing its narrative resources, these "other things" squirm under the surface to dominate the text thematically and to generate its fantastic quality.

The Hernández narrator's concern with psychoanalytic interpretation is not therapeutic, but quite the contrary utilizes ubiquitous spying and self-spying to reinforce delusion, to strengthen private myth and ritual, and to give "the fantastic being: man" a forum for his forbidden inner theater. The gesture of writing and recording his history, of archiving his distorted perceptions, necessarily socializes him, but that formal step forward is accompanied by an ironic two-step backward as the resultant text boasts protagonists prone to entrench themselves in their abnormalities, to defend the barriers between themselves and normalcy, and to subvert the order as though they were upholding it. The prototypical Hernández narrator is unswervingly faithful to his own vision "and does not make the least effort to explain it."[54] Like any competent narcissist, he avoids adaptation and instead modifies the world to conform to himself, constructing a pseudo-community, scripting roles for other players, imbuing objects with special self-referential meanings, and celebrating his treasured peculiarities. "Sometimes they are on the verge of falling into truth but they get nervous, they have life, they have a preservation instinct, they have doubt and mystery, and because they see everything through their condition, they are saved" (1:90). The salvation of Hernández's protagonists is in an inward retreat to the fantastic beings who they are, insulated by their private realities and protected by the masks melded to their faces. These protagonists espouse an existential perception of reality as meaningful only because it lacks inherent meaning; it is reorganizable by whatever design one wishes to impose. They have an affinity with Francis Bacon's ideal of "a person totally without belief, but totally dedicated to futility."[55] In Hernández's narratives this person is one who plays "a great aesthetic role: getting involved in progress after knowing it was useless" (1:210) and who delivers himself to "a trap of entertainment even though he knows it's a trap" (1:73).[56] His voice breaks when he remarks, "I love my . . . illness more than life" (2:72) because the "illness" "is my life, I always feel it and need to always feel it" (1:183). The obsession is yet more irresistibly voluptuous, more thrilling, because its relentless pursuit seems to terminate in a vague but always imminent doom: "I cannot so easily renounce such an immense desire" (1:175); "although I suspected it would come to a bad end, I couldn't stop myself" (2:68). Pathology before life, passion before reason, obsession before moderation—the text tracks characters "who are not governed by anyone" and who "blindly obey their passion" to the precipice where their balancing act, perpetually off-balance, normalizes the fantastic.[57] It is for this reason that "the fantastic is not a disintegration of the world but a disintegration of the psyche," a disintegration *integrated* by and into the text cohering it.[58]

The fantastic quality of Hernández's fiction is further generated by two interrelated narrative perspectives, the first of which is characteristic of the quasi-autobiographical texts *Por los tiempos de Clemente Colling* (Through the times of Clemente Colling), *El caballo perdido* (The lost horse), and *Tierras de la memoria* (Lands of memory). In these texts the narrator of "memories" speaks in a Proustian manner from an adolescent perspective, with shifts of register setting the immediate past, the present past, in dialogue with memories from "a more distant temporal plane."[59] The adolescent voice is both undermined and underscored by metafictional intrusions thematizing it. In one typical instance of such an interruption, the adult narrator bemoans his complex relation to the adolescent who necessarily constitutes a part of him (and his narrative voice), but who at the same time is necessarily elusive and alien (2:38).

The other perspective—characteristic of the texts in *Nadie encendía las lámparas* (No one lit the lamps)—is a mature one that preserves the adolescent naïveté by encoding perceptions with a boyish innocence, insecurity, and vulnerability. These interact in various configurations with a daring—and also boyish—fascination for the "violation" of secrets. This "special simplicity" on the part of the narrator is due to "something in me that remained childlike," and consequently, he says, "I found the dimension of the unknown that interests me" (1:169–70). In the cases of both the adolescent narrator and the mature but boyish narrator, Sigmund Freud's definition of the *unheimlich* (uncanny, literally "unhomely") is signaled, since the uncanny "is in reality nothing new or alien, but something which is familiar and old-established in the mind and which has become alienated from it only through the process of repression."[60] The "unhomeliness" indexes a property essential to Hernández's poetics, "the fundamental propensity of the familiar to turn on its owners, suddenly to become defamiliarized, derealized, as if in a dream."[61] Each of the two perspectives pays homage to this revisitation of familiar, but estranged, material; the repressed returns loaded with negotiations between the man who writes and the boy who speaks. The boyish narrations of *No One Lit the Lamps* as much as the memory-based fictions preceding them dredge up and elaborate "something which is familiar and old-established in the mind," and the uncanny resonance that they thereby generate then flows quite naturally into Hernández's archetypal themes—animism, omnipotence of thought, dissociation, the fragmented body, the double, and the effacement of the distinction between reality and fantasy, to mention only those noted by Freud—which in turn make their respective contributions to uncanniness. The frequent use of prosopopoeia (take, for example, the Hortensia doll as representation of the absent mother or dead wife) is similarly "an invocation, an attempt to bring back something that was presumably once present but no longer is present."[62] The text moving forward drags its past in tow, but the "things" it manages to lug to the surface are always othered ("because I reconceived them as another person") (1:49) and "deformed" (2:126) by secondary revision. "What you call the spirit of past times," Goethe noted, "is after all nothing but your own spirit, in which those times are reflected."[63]

For the Greeks, the past was kept present through the goddess Mnemosyne (= memory), who is mother of the Muses (= reminders). Mnemosyne represents cultural memory, in which "the factual and the symbolic, the historical and the mythical, 'real' events and 'imaginary' happenings are all tangled up inextricably."[64] By transforming the memory of a past lived experience into a present textual fiction, Hernández participates in perpetuation of this inextricable tangle of cultural memory that, simultaneously, has him ensnared in its (feminine) web. When Hernández as "sonneteer of the quintas" registers his recollections of experiences in the parlors of spinsters, to cite one simple example, these personal memories and the texts elaborating them carry the baggage of cultural memory that evokes an entire ambience—physical environment, attitudes, customs, gestures—pertaining to life on the fringes of high-society Montevideo in the early decades of this century. The influence—in the strict sense of *flowing into*—that Mnemosyne-type memory has on Hernández's work is yet more pronounced when one considers the thematics of water. Mnemosyne's link is direct: one drinks from her well to remember. The Muses, for their part, may originally have been water spirits with the powers of prophecy and later inspiration, both associated with the "speaking" of flowing waters. Still water (inside the Hortensia dolls, for example) and flowing water (of the flooded house, for example) are associated with memory in Hernández's canon, and, as we shall see later, are likewise interrelated in differing ways with the female body and its powers. Most importantly in the present context, water and memory for the Greeks extended into the poetics of the Lethe, from which the dead drank to forget beyond recall all that they had known and to thereby dissociate definitively from the world of the living. The streams of the world then carry "the memories that Lethe has washed from the feet of the dead" to Mnemosyne's well; the poet who drank there "recollects the deeds which a dead man has forgotten."[65] Water in Greek mythology, as throughout Hernández's canon, is thus linked not only with women and memory but with death, dissociation, and the internalized discourse of the other. Hernández is this poet at the woman-well, haunted internally by a choir of voices resonating in the chambers of his solipsism. As in "Canary Furniture Company," the uncanny return to the forgotten familiar results from a liquid "injection" that incessantly speaks inside him, that circulates through him, that mobilizes the mouth and the pen in an effort to silence himself-as-another.

THE DURATION OF UNCERTAINTY

As a counterpoint to the polysemous "open work," Umberto Eco posited the traffic sign, which is restricted to a single interpretation.[66] A street sign, for example, designates the name of a given right-of-way, and there the reading ends without complication. Pursuing Eco's trope into the fantastic, however, a variant analogy suggests itself. On occasion a neighborhood wise guy rotates a street sign, creating confusion and consequently triggering an interpretive sequence in the mind of a driver partially but not thoroughly familiar with a given intersection. The driver reckons: "Based on my experience, I am on X Street, but that sign, which indicates Y Street, undermines my relative certainty." The rotated sign confounds expectations, making way for a new cognitive state that—like the fantastic as Todorov describes it—"occupies the duration of this uncertainty."[67] The sign begins to "spin" when invested by the thought of the subject reading it and by the history—the convention—that endows it with special relevance in relation to its referent. An a priori belief, a traditional conviction that the name X refers to one street and no other, is suddenly challenged; an interlude of confusion opens in which the driver must sort through the competing versions and then proceed by the letter (conceding that the roadway must be Y Street, because it is written) or by imposing his will to overthrow the letter and reestablish his historic conviction as it was before subverted by the altered sign.

That, precisely, is what one encounters in the normalized fantastic quality of Hernández work: a "spin" is put on common signs viewed from a particular angle, evoking the traditions they carry, projecting the narrator's history (memories, obsessions, conventions) on and into them, and investing them constantly with the dynamics of their competing variations—the world (or word) as it is, the world as it should be, the world as I perceive it. In another passage underlined by Hernández in *Modes of Thought*, Whitehead notes that "Language is expression from one's past into one's present. It is the reproduction in the present of sensa which have intimate association with the realities of the past."[68] When language functions to subvert rather than to uphold one's "intimate association with realities of the past" (by imposing "Y" on a street historically called X, by normalizing aberration) the borders of the fantastic are delineated. As the driver or reader struggles "to bring back something that was presumably once present but no longer is present," he or she enters the realm of Freud's *unheimlich*, where the "reproduction"—always elaborated and usually distorted—makes the familiar unfamiliar.

One fine example of this "duration of uncertainty" that is central to the fantastic is found in *The Lost Horse*. A boyish narrator on one of his missions of erotic (re-)discovery returns à la Freud to the mysterious aspects of something once familiar: "Something known . . . and something unknown were confused together in that woman" (2:10). The "woman" in question is a sculpture, or—stressing the maternal erotics of the forgotten familiar—a "bust." The boy begins to touch it, but he experiences "confusion" when for a moment the sculpture seems to be a real woman ("who had something to do with Celina") to whom he would owe more respect. The obstacles of doubt and decorum are ultimately overcome ("I felt the pleasure of violating something serious") and the fondling continues, but the narrative stresses the confusion that the boy experiences as the result of the competing versions—sculpture, real woman—which enrich his ritual as much as they interrupt it. Ultimately, as Echavarren recognized, "what the child pursues is not the statue, nor even a 'real woman,' but rather a latent conglomerate, 'unknown,' that the statue evokes, the 'confusion' that the statue arouses."[69] The essence of Hernández's fantastic agenda resides in the process of "making poetry of that confusion" (3:196), with the "poetry" and the "confusion" coalescing as related by-products of the dialectic between objects and the subject's projective recreation of them. In the hands and imagination of Hernández's boyish Pygmalion, Celina's sculpture hovers in suspended animation between stone and flesh, with its dual identity ("I have had the virtue of being able to be hard and soft at the same time," as it is worded at 1:89) dramatizing the fantastic text's facility for reconciling opposites.[70]

In normalized fantastic literature the reader enters the hazy frontier opened by the overdetermined sign and participates in the interplay of possibilities. The rotated street sign, like the sculpture, registers an emerging mutation—X Street now *seems* to be Y Street—while experience dictates that the street still *is* X Street despite the misleading indication. The two competing meanings interact dialectically, and the resultant "confusion" delivers a syncretic third (the latent conglomerate that the statue arouses) that glosses the text with the uncertain and uncanny qualities characteristic of the fantastic. The universal, Saussurean arbitrariness of signs then adds its customary assault at the certainty afforded by linguistic conventions. This is particularly relevant in our street-sign case, "since the proper name, unlike other words, has no meaning, but, like other words, has a capacity for designation."[71] The name X Street "was chosen by chance among many" (1:162); it could as well have been named Y (or Z or N) Street with no necessary change to its physical constitution.[72] But in the driver's experience, on the maps, among the neighbors, in the real estate titles, the name X comes to dominate reality. The roadway *is*, *must be*, X Street, as though platonically preconceived to be so, as though X were inherent to its nature. The street sign in its proper place "gives us a finger to point with, . . . to pass surreptitiously from the space where one speaks to the space where one looks, . . . to fold one over the other as though they were equivalents."[73] When the street sign is rotated, however, "The text points in one direction," as Michael Riffaterre says, "while it looks in the other." The closure is reopened by ambiguity and competing meanings, by the overdetermined responses that they elicit, by the "confusion" and "mystery." Living with the rotated street sign or with the fantastic text requires that one accommodate the constant dialectics of *seems* undermining *is* and of simultaneous but contradictory messages posed against the backdrop of all alternatives' ultimate improbability.

The displacement of certainty by the "true seeming" quality characteristic of Hernández's fiction has a scientific precedent in the quantum theory of physics introduced in the late 1920s. Empirical "facts" presumed to be inviolable were gradually demoted as quantum physics proposed that "nothing *was* apart from how it *appeared*, and nothing *appeared* except as it was *observed*."[74] Hernández reasons along these lines when he reminds himself to be attentive to appearances that challenge our fixed ideas (3:146) and to "look for *facts* that yield to poetry and mystery and that surpass and confuse explanation" (3:196). He was, according to his first daughter, infuriated by acceptance of preconceived ideas because he held a deep suspicion of the absolute (but specious) truth that common sense presumes for our ungrounded certainties.[75] Since his realm is art rather than science, Hernández thematizes not only appearance and reality in their relation to human observation but also the defiance of empiricism by objects that "take advantage of the general confusion" (1:74) to carry out their own animistic sideshow "while I was distracted" (1:97).

Hernández's pronounced distrust of "certainties" ossified by dogma and underwritten by transcendental authority was also perhaps evidenced by his enthusiasm for the film *Lawrence of Arabia*. To the dictum "It is written," the renegade Lawrence, who "can't want what he wants," offers a defiant response: "Nothing is written." This meets with Sherif Ali's reply, "For some men nothing is written unless they write it."[76] Ali never mentioned how they write it, but Hernández, who also "can't want what he wants" and for whom likewise "nothing is written," writes his version of reality quite purposefully with the imprecision of dreams, with "a quality of confusion like that of an old film" (1:165).

On the surface the imprecision and the perpetual automutations of ambiguity are generated by tense choice—the subjunctive, the conditional—in league with the poetics of the "unfinished" and with the frequent repetition of *seems* and similar locutions. "I don't remember if," "I don't know why," "without my realizing," "as if," "perhaps," "I'm not sure," "without intending," "I vaguely supposed," "I would like to believe": all of these feints evidence "a narrator who insists upon adopting an ingenuous attitude" and who "deliberately wears the mask of naïveté."[77] The passive, ingenuous narrative tone softens the already malleable surface that is spoken from the edges of an anonymity, itself situated in a void, a no-place.[78] This "halo of indefiniteness" in which Hernández envelops his narratives is "a deliberate move to 'open' the work"; it enhances ambiguity, keeps the multiple relations of narrator, text, and reader in the constant flux of "confusion."[79] "Without these [seems] locutions," remarks Todorov of the pre-Kafka fantastic, "we should be plunged into the world of the marvelous, with no reference to everyday reality. By means of them, we are kept in both worlds at once."[80] These two worlds in the fantastic according to Hernández are not the natural and the supernatural but rather the world evoked by the everyday object (street sign, sculpture) and the same world "othered" when it is mobilized by the subject projecting "the contradiction of his desires" (1:95).

The seems locutions, complemented by the subjunctive and the conditional, also contribute to the Hernández text's dreaminess, to the slow-motion, nostalgic, cinematic quality that, as in Proust, is achieved by patiently evoking the past with a fiction that has the texture of memory. This softening, lulling effect sometimes gains direct expression, as it does, for example, when the screech of a trolley car is recalled in Clemente Colling. The actual sound of the wheels grinding on the tracks is first recorded as "a deafening noise," but once elaborated by memory "that noise is diminished, pleasant, and in turn evokes other memories" (1:24). This metafictional interlude identifies the associative mechanism that connects memories as it produces its text, and it does so in the context of the "two worlds" whose competition "opens" the work: first memory of the noise itself, and then a second-level memory—the memory of text production—through which the noise is elaborated to suit the tone of the fiction reconstructing it. The softening effect that processes the noise or humanizes Celina's sculpture also casts a calming but ominous hush over the parlors of El Prado; its melancholy tone is almost tangible, almost as visible as dust in the lamp-lit air. On occasion human movements are similarly relaxed to the dreamy, liquid quality of an elegant ascent up a staircase (1:24) or to the slow-motion replay of one's life as almost an accumulation of cinematic movements (1:156).

Conspicuous among the pervasive "halo of indefiniteness" in Hernández's work is a single instance in which ambiguity yields to an assertion of absolute conviction. As the short text in question ("Elsa") progresses, the narrator is overtaken by a "fever to affirm" that the eponymous young lady will cease to love him. The otherwise ubiquitous poetics of uncertainty are jettisoned as the narrator succumbs to the compulsion: "I have the conviction, I categorically affirm, I absolutely believe . . . I affirm again that . . . very soon [Elsa] will stop loving me" (2:140). Lest the reader harbor any lingering doubts, the unflinching conviction is reiterated in expanded form at the text's conclusion: "In summary, I want to go on record as having the conviction, of affirming categorically, and of absolutely believing that Elsa is different from other girls in that none of the others love me, while Elsa will stop loving me very soon" (2:141). The passage is noteworthy because its categorical affirmation defends a possibility as yet unrealized—a presumption emerging from fear—and is therefore itself grounded in an inarticulated *seems* construct ("Based upon the evidence, it seems as though Elsa will stop loving me"). "Elsa" is even more revealing, however, because the catalyst for its presumptuous and insistent forecast is the preoccupation with being stranded, precisely, in lovelessness. Read in the context of the "confusion," the "halo of indefiniteness," the "true seeming" in the canon around it, "Elsa" argues, in effect, that "Everything in the world is uncertain, with one exception: that I am not or will not be loved." This fear of imminent lovelessness is as fundamental to Hernández's *seems* poetics as the categorical denial of ambiguity in "Elsa" is atypical.

The collective success of maneuvers fostering fantastic ambiguity in Hernández's work is perhaps evidenced by the "confusion" of his critics themselves. Even when approached by readers more inclined to understand it than to dismiss or assault it, Hernández's peculiarly resistant canon "escapes all classification" and readily accepts definition only by default, only in terms of what it is not.[81] Witness, for example, Saúl Yurkievich, maintaining that Hernández's work "does not tip the scale to one side or the other," that it is "neither realism nor surrealism . . . neither in reason nor in madness," and that "There is not an order . . . nor a disorder. . . . There is a constant proximity, a tangency . . . with the absurd without entering in it decidedly." Everything in Hernández is tangency, Yurkievich concludes, everything indecisive and in suspension.[82]

One factor contributing to Hernández's evasive fictions is the "unfinished" quality that catalyzes a dynamic relation between the reader, the manifest text, and something "menacingly imprecise" that stands between the reading and closure (1:93). Whatever is missing in the "unfinished" text is defined and made conspicuous by the same narrative that thematically exploits these—its own—shortcomings. An analogous maneuver is described in "Irene's House" when the narrator relates that Irene took objects in her hands with such spontaneity that "it seemed that the objects had an understanding with her, that she had an understanding with us, but that we couldn't have an understanding [directly] with the objects." Irene stands as an interpretive intermediary between the protagonist and these objects in the same way that the Hernández narrator—an ambiguous narrator—is positioned between the text's cloudy referent (what-is-missing) and the reader. The inability to remove those strata of ambiguity—to bypass the dubious mediator—reemphasizes the fictional essence of the texts, for there is no access to the "memory" or the ostensible events upon which it is based without passing through the fiction that invents them in order to represent them. The conditions for the normalized fantastic are ideal, for each of these fictions is a simulacrum in Jean Baudrillard's sense of the term: a genuine replica without an original.

Hernández's plays with such denial of direct access are perhaps best exemplified through the themes of love and lovelessness mentioned above. Nowhere in his canon is there anything that even vaguely resembles a love scene or explicit sexual content, but in compensation for this specific (or, one might say, specified) absence there is a general panerotic quality that maneuvers in nuance and imbues the text with a muted sexuality.[83] At one level Hernández's paneroticism can be understood as a simple sublimation—"he wrote the story because she no longer loved him" (2:126)—with an inversely proportional, "corrective" relation established between the sublimating text and the cruel reality that fuels it: "I write better and better about what happens to me: too bad what happens to me gets worse and worse" (2:129).[84]

At another level more apropos of the normalized fantastic, the eroticism apparent but always implicit in texts like *The Hortensias*, "The Usher," or "Except Julia" is made manifest in an "erotic haze" that "serves to deny that reality is not in accord with fantasy."[85] Horacio with his dolls, the usher with his projecting eye light, the tunnel owner with his objects and his harem all enact their obsessions in this erotic haze that buffers them from the impositions of reality and that buffers the reader from the resolution and closure (one might even say the sexual contact) always out of range. An erotic haze is further enhanced by the peculiarity of a compromised narrator (in *The Hortensias*) or a cast of characters (in, for example, "The Crocodile," "The Balcony," or "Except Julia") who nonchalantly comply with a protagonist's eroticized rarities. "Mystery" as a quality "so important to sexual excitement that the two are almost synonymous" rolls across the textual surface when one character's subjective fantasy subsumes the narrative milieu as a whole, when private ritual becomes public drama, and when that out-of-whack ambience moves its "confusion" beyond its margins and into the social reality reintroduced with each reading.[86]

The fantastic qualities of vague eroticism and explicit "incompletion" are further reinforced by the ritual postponements typical in Hernández's work. The moment of consummation, the moment when the *seems* yields to the *is*, when doubt yields to certainty, when the erotic haze concretizes into sexual union, is always indefinitely postponed. The piano cannot be played *yet*, the secret cannot be revealed *until* . . . , the dinner can only begin *when* . . . , the news can only be revealed *after* . . . This postponed, unconsummated, imminent, intended, ritualized, and as-if quality in Hernández is reminiscent of the decadents' struggle "to render what is most inexpressible in thought, what is vague and most elusive in the outlines of form," including "the subtle confidences of neurosis, the dying confessions of passion grown depraved, and the strange hallucinations of the obsession which is turning to madness."[87] Here, as in Hernández's case, the obsession is turning to madness but is not there *yet*, with its text suspended on the threshold.

POTENTIAL SPACE

D. W. Winnicott has described an intermediate area of experience between fantasy and reality, a "potential" or "transitional" space "to which inner reality and external life both contribute."[88] This "resting-place" for those weary of "the perpetual human task of keeping inner and outer reality separate yet interrelated" has as its essential feature what Winnicott terms "transitional objects," the paradigm of these being the security blanket, the teddy bear, the doll—all characterized by "a tendency on the part of the infant to weave other-than-me objects into the personal pattern."[89] Potential space generally and transitional objects in particular are characterized by "*paradox, and the acceptance of paradox*: the baby creates the object, but the object was there waiting to be created. The baby both created it and found it."[90] The toy or blanket has objective qualities in the world at large irrespective of its possessor, but in the child's experience these coalesce with and to some degree are dominated by the function that the object assumes in the child's subjective fantasy—thus, the "creation." In the potential space of play "the child gathers objects or phenomenon from external reality and uses these in the service of some sample derived from inner or personal reality." The child manipulates the environment into his or her service and "invests chosen external phenomena with dream meanings and feelings."[91]

Adults likewise find relief from the strain of negotiating a balance between inner and outer realities by repairing to an unchallenged intermediate area "in direct continuity with the play area of the small child who is 'lost' in play."[92] To cite a simple example from the canon in question, a narrator sitting across a café table from a friend excuses himself momentarily to write in his notebook. He remarks, "What I want, really, is to rest my eyes—they bother me less when I'm writing—my face and my soul" (3:142). Were he not writing, he continues, he would be obliged to transform into a social self accommodating "ideas that he [the friend] has made of me," and "because it takes a lot of effort to rise to the heights where his illusions have placed me, I prefer to hide my eyes and my face in this paper and to leave my friend behind through this flight of signs" (3:142).[93] While Hernández aspired to transform "what I live into what I write" (3:172), he simultaneously used what he wrote and the process of writing to retreat from what he lived. When an aggressive in-law remarked to him, "You write those things because they didn't give you some good beatings when you were young," Hernández replied, "On the contrary, because they gave me too many."[94] The protective flight into signs becomes yet more significant in another passage where the narrator remarks, "I had the sensation of having gone to that little town to rest as if my misery had given me a vacation" (2:117). The "little town" is "some place in my self" where memories, associated in the text with the mother and grandmother, are guarded. This nexus of overlapping potential spaces—that of flight into signs, fugue into memory, and repair into the maternal sphere of protection—delineates the psychological locus from which much of Hernández's fiction emerges.

A fictional text is characterized by the acceptance of paradox as much as a transitional object is, but the text goes further to emphasize its fictionality while simultaneously representing its story as true.[95] Literary fiction goes unchallenged precisely because it "cannot be subjected to the test of truth; it is neither true nor false, to raise this question has no meaning; this is what defines its status as 'fiction'."[96] Texts in the genre of the normalized fantastic, as we have seen, exploit fiction's exemption from tests of truth, always probing its elasticity and manipulating the judgment of verisimilitude that the reader holds in reserve. Winnicott's description of a potential space of repose between fantasy and reality, between symbol and symbolized, where paradoxes are "to be accepted and tolerated and respected . . . and not to be resolved," bears an uncanny resemblance to Hernández's fiction as described above.[97] Normalized fantastic literature is possible only in the "neutral area of experience which will not be challenged," or which will not be challenged yet. It is a supreme expression of the transitional area where the self reconstitutes its alienated parts, negotiates a balance between subject and object, and celebrates the blurriness of borders.[98] What the reader experiences as "uncanny" during Todorov's "hesitation" is the simultaneity of opposing registers—me/not me, subject/object, present/past, interior/exterior, attraction/fear, fantasy/reality. The dichotomy of these pairings is absorbed in paradox; the inherent contradiction, the textuality "lost in play," is reconciled beyond the laws of logic.[99]

Winnicott's concept of potential space is also suggestive in relation to Hernández's literal and figurative treatment of confines. We have already seen the intertextual arena established by the "coverless" text as an open work: a field of discursive possibility is more or less bound by the narrative constituting it but nevertheless remains open, like a framed mirror, "to a continuous generation of internal relations." Hernández represents the mind itself as a defined space of opposing relations—a kind of racket-ball court—with ideas bouncing back and forth (as do the reader's ideas confronting the "spinning" sign) between "two walls in my head" (1:135).[100] The borders of temporal expanses are also provisionally sketched in to delineate the duration of an uncertainty. The opening and eventual closure of the many ritual postponements in Hernández's canon are a case in point, while an alternate play on demarcation of time periods is represented through interacting perspectives in the memory-based texts: "I throw myself voraciously into the past thinking about the future, about what shape these memories will take" (1:49). The amorphous past is retrieved and gradually assumes the shape of the text that it generates, but the reactivation of the repressed material embedded in memories integrates Freud's *unheimlich* into the process and thereby reopens the space one had presumed to be filled and closed.

Also typical of Hernández's work are what might be described as "emotional spaces," such as the dreamy dissociation in which one wanders upon leaving a movie theater, still negotiating the transition between the fictional world on the screen and the reality that intervenes abruptly (2:206). The emotional space spanning the distance between a hope and its disappointment gains most frequent expression, these instances usually featuring an optimistic impulse opening the way and an implacable reality rudely foreclosing it (1:80 and 1:141, for example). Hernández's emotional spaces are generally eroticized and prolonged in a manner reminiscent of Proust's goodnight-kiss ritual at the opening of *Swann's Way*. The drama of the mother's withheld kiss affords an indulgence in the deliciousness of erotic waiting even to the degree of "hoping that it would come as late as possible, so as to prolong the time of respite during which Mamma would not yet have appeared."[101] The luxury of longing in this exquisite realm of idealized desire is experienced with immense satisfaction before the event itself—which can only seem meager in relation to its anticipation—intervenes and closes the parentheses. The same holds true for Hernández, and in relation to the insistent presence of the absent mother that Hernández holds in common with Proust we find in the former's work an anticipation of the secrets guarded behind closed doors and a corresponding desire—almost a compulsion—to penetrate spaces that are forbidden. A physical locale—the contiguous room, the area behind a partially opened door—thereby coincides with the emotional space opened by the desire to penetrate and closed by that desire's satisfaction or its slow demise in frustration.

The space between an eroticized hope and its fulfillment (or—in most cases—its disappointment) is in Hernández canon often the result of an amorous opportunity enshrouded in "confusion." The narrator is never quite certain if his readings of reality are accurate, so every move, particularly those as delicate as an adventurous amorous advance, must be rehashed with Raskolnikovian thoroughness. Such is the case with the caressing of Celina's "bust" as described above, and then again with Celina herself as the narrator's imaginary love affair terminates harshly with a pencil cracked down across his knuckles (2:18). In "Mamma's Tree" the opening and closure of an eroticized space is even more explicit. The protagonist's cousin, a fat, rude, and dominating girl named Eva, orders him to tie her shoes. The eroticized emotional arena opens as he kneels to fulfill her request. In this prolonged, momentary interim the mystery dominating the scene yields to obsession: was Eva's demand an indirect invitation for him to kiss the knee peering out from the opening in her kimono, or has he miscalculated? The pressure is on: "I'm finishing the knot and have to decide"; the window of opportunity is about to slam closed while the protagonist wallows in his duration of uncertainty, but then the space is reopened—"Fortunately he saw the other shoe, also untied. He would think it through better while he tied the other knot." As the clock ticks the girl (like the mother in Proust) participates in extending the emotional space—"Make the knot a little tighter, dear"—so that the ritual can be repeated on both feet. The protagonist, now on borrowed time, measures the erotic space before him, tallies his calculations, and finally consummates his desire ("he sunk his lips into the knee and awaited the consequences"), closing down the emotional space opened by longing and the textual space in which the episode unfolds (2:187–88). Both spaces are framed on one side by the desire to kiss the knee and on the other by the kiss itself, but their meaning—and here the "spin" that generates the text's resonance—is dominated by the unacknowledged unilaterality of the negotiations. The boy deliberating on whether or not to kiss the knee dialogues not with the girl herself but rather with an internalized representation of her discourse, with his own construct of what she might be thinking or desiring.[102] The actual girl (or her feet) contribute to framing the duration and rhythm of the encounter, but in the boy's calculations a representation—a useful prop—displaces the girl and consigns the matter, for better or worse, totally to his better judgment.

This "disappearance" of the other into the subject's interpretations leads quite directly to the Hernández narratives built around transitional objects. The balcony of the story by the same title is a clear example; it exists in itself as an architectural structure, but this objectivity is largely disavowed by delusions of the daughter who perceives the balcony as her lover. The balcony's inherent constitution as a transitional space—neither inside nor outside, part of the house *(heimlich)* but exterior to it *(unheimlich)*—reinforces its function as a transitional object.[103]

In "Except Julia" transitional objects are likewise central. The story develops around a ritual in which objects displayed in a dark tunnel are handled by characters who attempt to tactilely determine what they are holding. The things in themselves—among them a plucked chicken in a button box (2:78)—are metamorphosed as they assume special fetishistic meaning, function, and value in the ritualized world of the tunnel owner. The girls who are also touched in the tunnel are transformed similarly: their subjectivity is disavowed (except Julia's) as the ritual reduces them to anonymous faces whose identity is in the hands of the tunnel man. In all cases—the balcony, the tunnel objects, Celina's sculpture, the showcase displays—things become transitional as they are divested of their objectivity and, thus "emptied," are filled with private meanings enacted in rituals.

Such is most patently the case in *The Hortensias*, where the transitional object par excellence—the Hortensia dolls—indexes a subjective investment in objects so profound that it terminates finally in reality being subsumed by fantasy. The dolls are entangled in Horacio's obsession from the beginning, but their presence in the earlier stages is restricted to that of a fantasy within a reality; the distinction between one realm and the other is still defended. Horacio enters the potential space of his showcase gallery and celebrates the brinksmanship "of the obsession which is turning to madness," but he initially reserves the capacity to exit the ritual confine (defined and contained quite clearly with doors, curtains, and glass) and to recognize Hortensia's essence as a simulacrum, as an inert reproduction of his wife. As the narrative progresses, however, "the dialectic of reality and fantasy collapses in the direction of fantasy."[104] The boundaries can no longer be defended; Horacio's entire experiential field comes to be dominated by transitional objects (the dolls) as emblems of a reality encompassed by fantasy. If a clinical patient "became terrified of department store mannequins feeling that they were living people," Horacio provides an inverted complement in his fearful retreat from humans to mannequins.[105] What Horacio and the patient have in common, along with the tunnel owner in "Except Julia" (himself "the grand object of the tunnel") (2:79), is ultimate absorption into their own deliria. Inert objects come alive around them while, reciprocally, they become progressively more wooden. Completion of this exchange of roles, of the subject as his own ultimate transitional object, is the conclusion that Hernández suspends in the potential space of uncertainty.

1

Narcissus and Hernández

In the third book of *Metamorphoses* Ovid develops the most complete and thematically complex version of the Narcissus myth by engaging Narcissus's fate with the parallel fate of Echo. The text begins with verses establishing lineage, relating how the river-god Cephisus embraced the river nymph Liriope with his winding stream and took her by the force of his waters. Liriope was impregnated during this river-rape and gave birth to Narcissus, whose identity is consequently glossed from the start with implications of eroticized water. As he grew into his teens Narcissus's beauty was fascinating to male and female suitors alike, but in his haughtiness and pride the boy slighted those who sought his love and devastated them with his mocking rejection.

The nymph Echo was one of these rejected suitors. Earlier Echo had cunningly used her verbose harangues to distract and detain Juno, so that nymphs on the mountainside—who were making love to the adulterous Jove—would have time to escape. In retaliation for the trickery, Juno revoked Echo's capacity to speak, confining her discourse to partial mimesis, to repeating the last few words spoken by others. In integrating Echo's fate with that of Narcissus, Ovid links the motif of repetition or duplication in its auditory form (echo) with the visual form (reflection) that would come to fascinate Narcissus once he discovered his image in the pond.

On one occasion Echo pursues Narcissus through the secluded countryside, taking advantage of his separation from companions during a deer hunt. A pseudodialogue is exchanged (Narcissus speaking, Echo miming), which concludes when Echo attempts an embrace and Narcissus responds with his characteristic rejection: "Take your hands off me. I would die before I let you possess me." (The) Echo comes back with: "Possess me." Echo's strategic repetition inverts the intent of Narcissus's rejection; it repeats his negative insult as an affirmation, defending the letter of the other's word while the spirit (escaping the rigor of Juno's penalty) expresses Echo's own desire. Echo speaks her own mind by strategically repeating, but nevertheless she is spurned and ultimately devastated by the rejection. She dries out and withers away until only her bones and voice remain, then only her voice alone because "they say that her bones were turned to stone."[1]

One of the many other suitors whom Narcissus had scornfully rejected raised his hands up to the heavens and prayed, "May he himself love, and not gain the thing he loves!" The goddess Nemesis—"the scourge of mankind"—heard this love-lost prayer and granted its wish by casting the curse on Narcissus that resulted in his demise at the pond.[2] Narcissus approached the silvery, undisturbed surface of the water, and, as it is worded in an irresistible Old English translation, "as he stooped lowe / To staunche his thurst, another thurst of worst effect did growe."[3] Having caught a glimpse of his reflected beauty, Narcissus fell desperately in love. He initially did not realize that the object of his love was a reflection ("He thinkes the shadow that he sees, to be a lively boddie") and he presumed this misconstrued "lively boddie" to be not his own but another's. Narcissus is transfixed; he attempts to hug, to kiss, the image that eludes him; he pines in desperation and despair. His amorous rapture delays his recognition of the image on the water for what it is, but finally he makes the fatal realization:

> It is my selfe I well perceyve, it is mine Image sure,
> That in this sort deluding me, this furie doth procure.
> I am inamored of myself, I doe both set on fire,
> And am the same that swelteth too, through impotent desire.
> What shall I doe? be woode or woo? whome shall I woo therefore?
> The thing I seeke is in my selfe, my plentie makes me poore.

Having recognized *himself* as the object of his love Narcissus turns back to the reflection, sick with longing. "There is no satisfaction or enchantment over the fact that the beauty of reflection is his own, but rather a despair so deep that he wishes he were dead since the stranger whom he thought he saw does not exist."[4] Narcissus's frustrated love—now self-love detoured through the reflection—is thereby situated beyond the range of satisfaction, and it is perhaps for this reason that the insight of self-recognition is readily abandoned, "remains short-lived and clouded by Narcissus's lament that he might be separated from his beloved."[5] "Oh, whither do you flee?" Narcissus laments when his tears fall on the water, disturbing the image. "Stay here, and desert not him who loves thee, cruel one! Let me still gaze on what I may not touch, and by that gaze feed my unhappy passion."

The grieving Narcissus tears open the upper fold of his tunic and he beats his bare chest red. When he witnesses himself in this pathetic condition he can bear no more and succumbs to his self-destructive, love-lost fate, wasting away in his reflection, consumed by his unconsummated passion. Finally Narcissus "drooped his weary head" and death "sealed the eyes that marvelled at their master's beauty." Even after his reception in Hades he continued to gaze upon himself in the still waters of the Styx. No body was found for the funeral pyre, but in its place grew a yellow flower with a circle of white petals at its center.

The complex of themes emerging from Ovid's version of the Narcissus myth is adapted and elaborated brilliantly in the fiction of Felisberto Hernández. One of the thematic threads unifying Hernández's entire canon can be described as a "narcissistic confusion," the confusion that results when one's own image is alternately perceived as an object and as a dissociated extension of the self.[6] For many Hernández characters as much as for Narcissus, the dialectics of identity are negotiated between the self and its "reflections," that last term including all self-representations projected onto and then retrieved from the world at large. When pushed to the extreme—as, for example, in *The Hortensias*—such projections result in a fetishistic fascination with an objectified and vivified image or idea, a "lively boddie," closely associated with the self. The intermingling of the subject's identity with his own reified projections then contributes on the rebound to clouded ego boundaries and to the corresponding themes of dissociation. Hernández's preoccupation with animism, the double, the multiplication of reflections, and the fragmented body figure prominently among these themes, each treating in its respective manner the self's disintegration before the world-as-mirror. The Hernández character—like Narcissus—resists recognizing that the object of his love is a projection of himself, because such an acknowledgment would lead to "a despair so deep that he wishes he were dead." These characters rather resort to the gaze to "feed their unhappy passion," to alleviate the frustration of their solipsistic longings, and to contrive a compensation for the inaccessibility of an imaginary love object representing the self. That narcissistic agenda is as obstinately defended as it is futile. The impossibility of consummating (projected) self-love necessarily delivers this entanglement of desire, the gaze, projection, and dissociation to its woeful conclusion in direct, vicarious, or symbolic self-destruction.

Hernández narratives also share with Ovid's Narcissus myth the scripting of supporting roles for objectified women participating in monological, narcissistic productions. In the cases of both Narcissus and Horacio of *The Hortensias*, the key female players are partially or fully incapacitated women (the silenced Echo for Ovid, the inert dolls for Horacio) who live for nothing other than to be possessed.[7] They are passive interlocutors in a pseudo-dialogue characterized by a male speaking and a female receiving or miming, and—as evidenced by the advertisement for Hortensia dolls that promises "a silent love"—they are perhaps manifestations of "a male fantasy of the dream-woman as dumb."[8] This dumb woman is certainly the one who lip-syncs her lines in Hernández's "silent film" of memories. But if indeed "the male imagination constructs a mute ideal," built into the ideal is the surreptitious, feminine power to transcend the very silence that is imposed.[9] These fantasy women are dumb but they are not stupid; they "add something of their own" that complicates their presumed passivity and puts a "spin" on the monologue constructing them (*OC,* 2:145). Echo, to cite the paradigm, transforms Narcissus's negation into an affirmation merely by selectively returning his own words to him. Her strategic reversal enacted through the words "Possess me" establish her as a mirrored acoustic image, an inversion of Narcissus and his discourse. This trope is then extended—echoed—in the thematics of reflection off the pond.

As we shall come to understand in the pages that follow, the Hortensia dolls likewise function as mirror images of negated desires projected by Horacio and returned to him as affirmations. Like Echo, the doll's "discourse" and "gestures" assume enhanced meaning precisely because the dolls are handicapped, and because they are caught in the interpretive orbit of a male protagonist pursuing self-love through the manipulable objects that he constructs. The dolls, when they are filled with water, further accommodate the maternal and eroticized-water themes evoked by Ovid's treatment of the Narcissus myth. Bound by the thread of sight, Narcissus is unable to free himself from the eroticized, reflecting water, just as his mother Liriope, herself a river nymph, was "imprisoned" by water during her rape by the river-god. Narcissus's conception as the result of the flow and flood of those waters then introduces a third "imprisonment": an internal one enveloped by the fluids of mother's womb. Narcissus in the womb is imprisoned in solitary confinement until birth; Narcissus at the pond likewise until death. The womblike water of the Hortensia dolls flows in all of these directions, mingling the eroticized reflection and death themes that will concern us in chapter 3 with the maternal and oedipal themes treated in chapter 5.

The predominating motifs of the literary canon and of Hernández's psychobiography itself coincide not only with the mythological Narcissus, but also with the essential features of clinical narcissism. Prominent among patients diagnosed as narcissists are fantasies of grandiosity alternating with extreme insecurity, the latter accompanied by an intense need for tribute; exploitative interpersonal relationships and the incapacity to accept romantic partners as independent subjects; and a tendency to construct a self-oriented or self-referenced living fiction in which objectivity is manipulated by projections cast on and into it.

These narcissistic traits as manifest in Hernández's personality are particularly resonant and ambiguous when one considers that Hernández's fantasies of artistic grandeur were as firmly grounded in reality as they were in fantasy. Hernández always believed that he was an innovative, grossly undervalued fiction writer, and it turns out—if international critical assessment can be trusted—that this is precisely what he was. Hernández's and his characters' insistence of their superiority in this perspective is something like the mad Nietzsche's "delusional" belief that he was a great philosopher. While there is no doubt that Nietzsche was, in his last years, insane, his stature as a great philosopher is equally indisputable. The delusion coincides with the truth and yet remains a delusion. One recalls Jean Cocteau's remark that "Victor Hugo was a madman who believed he was Victor Hugo."[10] The fantasies of Nietzsche and Hernández regarding their accomplishments are "true," but they are nevertheless hyperbolic representations, obsessively attended, and interpretable as fantasies in context of the respective symptomologies with which they are inextricably entangled. My intent, in any case, is not to diagnose Hernández, to assess the propriety of his self-image, or to pass moral judgment on his actions. I rather wish to come to an understanding of how his apparent narcissistic personality traits, be they pathological or otherwise, engendered and informed the unique body of literature that he authored.

GRANDIOSITY AND INSECURITY

The third revised *Diagnostic and Statistical Manual of Mental Disorders (DSM-III-R)* notes that narcissists are "preoccupied with fantasies of unlimited success, power, brilliance, beauty or ideal love," that they have a "grandiose sense of self-importance," and that they feel unjustly misunderstood, expecting recognition of themselves as "'special' even without appropriate achievement."[11] This "undue sense of uniqueness" and these "feelings of entitlement" are, however, accompanied by competing feelings of inferiority and unworthiness, a "marked propensity to criticism," fragile self-esteem, and "morose self-doubts."[12] Otto Kernberg similarly observes in narcissists "a curious apparent contradiction between a very inflated concept of themselves and an inordinate need for tribute from others."[13]

Those who knew Hernández personally make frequent reference to his grandiose self-perception, his insecurity, or the two presenting simultaneously or in alternation. According to his second daughter, Ana María Hernández de Elena, Hernández "knew he was 'chosen' for a specific artistic, poetic, philosophical mission" and he had "a commitment and intention to open a new path for art and thought." "He considered himself to be ahead of his time," and he commented—much like the analysands with "a distinct secret sense of waiting to be found"—that "fifty years will pass before I'm recognized."[14] Hernández's friends likewise comment on "his clear awareness of his artistic worth" and his intellectual superiority, but they add that this elation was always coupled with the frustrated conviction that his astonishing talents were misunderstood or dismissed by others.[15] One Hernández narrator, voicing the author's own "long *via crucis* as someone misunderstood," remarks, "I felt that my entire life was something that others were incapable of understanding" (2:71).[16]

The fantasies of unrecognized grandiosity are in one sense undermined and in another serviced by the reality in which Hernández experienced them. Unknown even in the reduced cultural milieu of Montevideo, unread, dismissed by critics, wandering from pension to pension, demeaned by petty, arrogant superiors in his menial employments—all of these rude realities devastated the narcissist's inflated sense of self, while at the same time it reinforced the essential narcissistic features of being misunderstood, of having a unique gift and mission incomprehensible to popular opinion, of guarding a secret asset that constitutes and guarantees one's unacknowledged superiority. These dynamics, represented throughout Hernández's literary canon, are particularly central to "The Usher," in which the protagonist (like his author) is in one register a demeaned failure—with a life "like a mouse under old furniture" (2:59)—but in another is "superior," "proud," because of the secret power "that compensated for my misfortunes" (2:60). The guarded, empowering asset in the usher's case is the capacity to "penetrate a world closed to all others" thanks to light projecting from his eyes. This carefully developed trope pays homage to the "chosen" author's penetrating lucidity, of course, and is further associated with the narcissistic projection by which the world is interpreted and transformed in light of one's I/eye. "The eye controls the self," as one observer put it, "the vision makes up the personality of the 'I'."[17] But despite the great powers that "vision" holds in reserve, the usher and other protagonists are handicapped in a manner directly derived from Hernández's own "inadaptation before a world he perceived as hostile."[18]

The insecurity occasioning this mild but chronic paranoia also resulted in Hernández's "inordinate need for tribute from others." Even Hernández's reading habits evidence an indirect expression of this need. Amalia Nieto, Hernández's second wife, remarks that "Felisberto read above all to find affinities between what he had written and the texts of famous authors." If he browsed the masterpieces of world literature, it was not "in search of inspiration but rather to corroborate the validity of his own writing." Reading the masters was "a justification of himself in the work of others."[19] The masterpieces are mirrors in which Hernández discerns traces of himself, paying tribute to his own fictions by measuring their merit against the officially accepted canon of great literature.

Paralleling this indirect means of reinforcing self-worth are many explicit demonstrations of Hernández's persistent need for homage and reassurance from others. José Pedro Díaz has described on more than one occasion how Hernández was "always tortured by his notorious sense of insecurity." Hernández had little need of a coterie of disciples but evidenced instead the need "to feel surrounded by people of recognized importance who gave him their approval."[20] Established senior figureheads, notably the philosopher Carlos Vaz Ferreira and the poet Jules Supervielle, provided the unwavering approval, applause, defense, and reassurance that Hernández "always searched for and perhaps never found completely."[21] In exchange for their endorsement this Supreme Court of literary judgment was inordinately idealized, exalted, and apotheosized by Hernández; the phrase "jury of the Gods" (1:79) describes the arrangement precisely. Hernández kept his masters at "mythological heights . . . without tolerating the slightest criticism of them."[22] His "exaggerated admiration" of Supervielle (whom he referred to as "my Giant") was so jealously guarded that it occasioned a separation between Hernández and Paulina Medeiros when the latter exhibited traces of irreverence during and following a visit to the master.[23]

But Hernández's dependency relation and what presents as humility before awesome figureheads is ultimately more self-referential than its innocent naïveté would suggest. Exaltation of a Vaz Ferreira or a Supervielle doubled back to satisfy Hernández's own narcissistic need for tribute by establishing the indisputability of the criteria by which he himself is favorably judged. If these (inflated) masters honored him from their Parnassian heights, then must he not be truly worthy of praise? To complement the circularity of that feat, the mirror we have seen in the masterpiece then turns up again in the masters themselves, since, as Kernberg put it, "Idealized people, on whom these patients seem to 'depend,' regularly turn out to be projections of their own aggrandized self concepts."[24] Projected qualities—indisputable greatness, superior artistic and intellectual accomplishment, stature and recognition—recycle back to the self negotiating a delicate balance between profound insecurity and fantasies of grandeur.

Any newcomer to Hernández studies is greeted at the entry by a gallery of phrases, most of them culled from letters, that the "inordinate need for tribute" has anthologized into the dogma defending Hernández's intrinsic literary worth. In 1925 Vaz Ferreira provided one of the cornerstones: "Perhaps there are not ten people in the world who find [Hernández's work] interesting, and I consider myself one of the ten." (Hernández implicitly responded many years later when he remarked in a letter, "I feel the need for the pleasure of vanity and vanity among people who can satisfy it for me, and who aren't so few.")[25] Supervielle later added that Hernández had "the sensibility of what will someday be classic," while Ramón Gómez de la Serna dubbed Hernández "the great sonneteer of memories and quintas."[26]

A litany of such quotations—repeated endlessly in letters, conversations, and promotional brochures—buffered Hernández from the daily reality that menaced his insecurity. His extraordinary talents were authorized and guaranteed, and anyone suspicious was welcome to have a look at the verifying documents. Like all narcissists, however, Hernández nevertheless always harbored the suspicion that there must be some mistake, that the whole affair was some kind of hoax, that somehow he would be revealed as a fraud, that eventually the masters would come to their senses and reject him. Juan Carlos Onetti described the young Hernández as "so sincerely insecure," and late in his career Hernández was still haunted by the same preoccupation of unworthiness, aggravated by the attending fear of imminent rejection.[27] On the occasion of a homage to him at the "Amigos del Arte" in the early 1940s, Hernández expressed "an immense happiness" but also a "terror" that his fatal flaw would be revealed and that "it would be discovered that the whole thing was a great mistake" (3:216). He calculated that if he could "deceive" Vaz Ferreira and Supervielle over such a long period of time, then it must be by virtue of some merit; but he nevertheless feared that if he allowed himself to believe in that merit, or in the masters' faith in that merit, then he would somehow magically provoke a change in opinion that would doom him (3:217). Noteworthy in these ruminations and in their superstitious conclusion is the narcissist's secret will to omnipotence as it confronts his situation's dramatic fragility; even a thought—his own all-powerful thought—could devastate the foundation upon which his very identity is constructed. He would have to be cautious and on guard even from himself, for one presumptuous belief could magically provoke his masters to abandon him.

In a letter from the same period Hernández again expresses the fear that "someday an unexpected error will be discovered by the people who appreciate my work with such noble generosity, and they will discover that they had been defrauded" (3:217). This obsessive concern with a trick or fraud or deception (of the admirers, of himself) sets the tone for introduction of a greater fear, ultimately a "fear of the truth" (3:218), a truth—as in the literary texts—that has been invaded by fantasy. When Supervielle introduced him at the Sorbonne on 17 April 1948, Hernández again took the opportunity to publicly reiterate his unworthiness, remarking that the occasion must be the result of some confusion or mistake and that the great poet Supervielle had taken Hernández's name and some data to invent the character who he had now propped up before the audience. The invention of this Hernández character was due to Supervielle's "love for animals," and Hernández accordingly dehumanized himself into a rabbit pulled by its ears from a hat during Supervielle's performance of marvelous tricks (3:219).[28] Any measure of success, Hernández as narcissist feared, owed little to the intrinsic worth of his writing (which he simultaneously inflated) and everything to some outrageous mistake, to a misperception or misrepresentation that would be imminently revealed, or to a strategic deception maneuvered on his behalf by the masters. At the Sorbonne it is Supervielle's magic that makes him appear out of the black nothingness of the hat to squirm, unworthy, before his audience.

Hernández's shaky conviction in the merit of his writing put him in a precarious position before unfriendly criticism. He awaited assessment of his work with an anxiety bordering on dread, and when negative criticism did surface—as it did, for example, in the imposing opinion of Emir Rodríguez Monegal in 1945—he overvalued the assault and suffered each word profoundly. "Adverse criticism paralyzed him"; Hernández would literally hide from public view and felt as though all creative energies drained from his body.[29] His excessive sensitivity to criticism made negative feedback not only injurious and demoralizing but also capable of exiling him and of demeaning his self-image to the subhuman status of the masters' thinglike invention. A passage in "My First Concert" pushes the process yet further, for here *imagined* ridicule deflates and dehumanizes the artist—"I began to contract like a worm"—who is victim of nothing more than his own insecurity (2:101).

An oversensitivity to criticism was complemented in Hernández's character by a more general tendency to mood swings often triggered by seemingly inconsequential stimuli. One moment Hernández was in an agitated, vibrant, extroverted state and in the next he was withdrawn, inert, disinterested, and drowsy, with the shift owing to nothing objectively identifiable. Such oscillations between affective extremities, "with quick flare-ups and subsequent dispersal of emotion," parallel the narcissist's broader swings between the poles of grandiosity and insecurity.[30] Hernández was "incredibly polarized" and "a solitary person decidedly arbitrary in the area of feelings," says Medeiros. His blind passion yielded readily to absolute rejection, and his holding court as a showman doubled as a strategy for withdrawn isolation, behind the masks of his face, in "the solitude that he loved."[31] At social gatherings Hernández would "tell funny and picaresque stories about a varied cast of characters: Galicians, Andalusians, drunks, Turks, madmen," but at the same time he was ill disposed to nontheatrical contact with other guests, even to the simple matter of greeting them.[32] "When he did not know someone well or felt insecure before someone he resorted to telling stories. . . . He dressed himself in the clothes of stories so that his personality wouldn't be seen and no one could endanger his emotions."[33] The narrator of the "Diary of Shamelessness" ("Diario del sinvergüenza," literally "Diary of the Shameless One") anguishes over this point, relating how his "artificial person" insistently treated others "in a not very natural manner," utilizing a "cordiality full of jokes" to evade more genuine contact (3:188). Concern for this showmanship that fills the space of contact and buffers the players leads the narrator to probe for an understanding of why "it takes so much for him to come out of himself" and why his relationships are unnatural, forced, cowardly, and characterized by an inability to listen to or understand others. Due to "some unknown difficulty in relations" (3:188), Hernández was "always contradictory" and "with different masks he hid the dark depths of his ego."[34] As Norah Giraldi Dei Cas put it, "Felisberto appeared before others as though performing a theatrical work: his own life."[35]

Hernández also holds in common with clinical narcissists a preoccupation with idealism. Medeiros describes him as a fanatical "survivor of 'pure art'" who privileged this urge toward an aesthetic ideal as the organizing principle for his life and thought.[36] On aesthetic grounds Hernández here shares turf with his fantastic precursors ("We are decadent, since this decadence is nothing but the ascending march of humanity toward ideals which are reputed to be inaccessible"), but in Hernández's case there seems to be insufficient recognition that the ideal is a utopian fantasy.[37] At the same time, Hernández's aspiration toward purism was exploited to trivialize and dismiss troublesome mundane realities—measured now against the grandeur of the ideal—and to thereby pardon failures in everyday life or justify dubious values or beliefs. In the name of his "theory of uncontaminated art" he subordinated "concepts of moral order that hindered him," permitting his depreciation of "domestic obligations" and of the liberal politics that he "ingenuously considered at odds with his art."[38]

The (disappointed) quest for an ideal, fueled and frustrated by the attending fantasy of being endowed and "chosen" for unique accomplishment, is often linked in the clinical literature to the narcissist's relation with his mother (herself a representative, among other things, of the inaccessible). "The difficult situation of dependency" and the "mysterious, semiconjugal tie that united Felisberto with his mother" are of thematic interest in chapter 5, where oedipal aspects of Hernández's fiction are explored.[39] My comments here will therefore be limited to those pertinent to understanding the pathogenic mother as she relates to the development of narcissistic traits in Hernández's personality.

"Mothers of narcissistic patients have difficulty in letting their children separate."[40] Described as "authoritarian and absorbing," Hernández's mother "exercised definitive influence over Felisberto," dominating him with her unsatisfiable demands, sabotaging his marriages in order to monopolize his affection, imbuing him with her idealized image rather than nurturing, or permitting, his development as an independent subject.[41] As described by Hernández's first daughter, Calita (as the mother was known) was "an extremely dominant woman," herself "dominated by a single idea, that was to take possession of the world and believe that it belonged to her, above all the world of those people close to her." This "terrible, terrible" woman, the daughter reiterates, "was the type of person who felt that she was on this planet to direct the lives of everyone, especially her family."[42] Under Calita's "direction" Hernández found himself incapable of separating as an autonomous, independent, free-willed subject, and his four marriages and two extended relationships were consequently undermined. At forty-five years old, to illustrate the extent of Calita's "permanent control" over him, Hernández interrupted his fellowship tenure in Paris partially because his mother "always wrote with insistence and anxiety," urging his speedy return to Montevideo.[43] In his mid-fifties he was still complaining, in this case to his fourth wife, "I want to be alone with you, but she [the mother] won't let us."[44]

Kernberg describes the mother of the narcissist as overinvesting herself in the child's life, as fulfilling her own needs at the child's expense. In all cases studied by Masud Khan, as well as in Hernández's case, an additional commonality emerges: "The father was alive and around in the child's experience" but nevertheless "he was not registered as a significant presence or person."[45] Hernández—a first child, like many narcissists—was born when his mother was eighteen years old, and her doting affection for him was, in part, a means of escape, of evading family contact. According to his sister, Hernández was "our mother's favorite" and always remained "a child attached to his mother, for whom he professed an unhealthy love."[46]

The monopoly of mother's charms that Hernández enjoyed as a boy, particularly for his first three years until the next child (Deolinda) was born, would later return to haunt him as a man. The "debt" would have to be repaid with interest: Calita's total dedication demanded a total, lifelong response that exhausted Hernández emotionally, incapacitating him for sustained romantic relationships. After the death of his father this affective drain was then compounded by a financial one. Because he had drawn excessively from the revenues, Calita's husband Prudencio had been forced to leave a construction partnership that he had formed with his brothers. Calita enjoyed fabricating the illusion of social status through an ostentation well beyond the family's means, and her husband's humble finances were finally exhausted by the "intense social life that she [Calita] loved."[47] When Prudencio died in 1940 something of this same scenario was replayed between Calita and her son Felisberto, the former deploying guilt to tap into her son's meager resources (for modest living expenses now, the social pretenses already in her distant past) and the latter forfeiting any semblance of economic stability in an attempt to accommodate her endless demands.

The narcissist's mother tends to invest her dreams in the firstborn son, even to use him "as a kind of 'object of art'," a creation that "perfects" her, an adornment that distinguishes her.[48] Such is evidenced in Hernández's case by the precocious piano career that Hernández commenced under his mother's guidance when he was nine. From Calita's lower-middle-class perspective, music, and particularly piano music, was a symbol of the Montevideo elite, which took its social and cultural cues from Europe. Calita wanted to invest in her son "a different culture, like that of the upper classes in their parlors and mansions." Studying the piano, "the privileged instrument in the parlors of the great families of that era," implied the dream of someday playing in the company of this elite, of breaking through the barriers of exclusivity and gaining access to their homes, of being among them as the focus of their attention. Calita herself was incapable of realizing that dream, but she was "obsessed with the good intention" of using music instruction as a social-climbing device for her children. Her firstborn and favored son Felisberto would be entrusted with the piano—the dominant symbol of social accomplishment—but he would also bear the corresponding responsibility for the financial and social transformation of the family in accord with his mother's fantasy.[49] The stakes were high and so, consequently, was the price for failure.

As Kernberg describes them, the mothers of narcissists function more or less adequately on the surface, but also manifest "a degree of callousness, indifference, and nonverbalized, spiteful aggression."[50] The cold, mute sensuality evidenced by the dolls of *The Hortensias* is suggestive in this context, as it is also in light of Khan's remark that "The mother lavished intense body-care on the infant-child but in a rather impersonal way."[51] The narcissist experiences a resultant "terrifying passivity" (projected and represented by the Hortensia dolls' inertia) in relation to a mother "perceived as dangerously malignant, malicious, and all-powerful."[52] The vacuousness of this power, however, is revealed by the ways in which it manifests itself, and the narcissist—Hernández—ultimately feels not so much frightened as "disappointed and betrayed" by a doting mother incapable of meeting his needs while she tirelessly demands that he strive to please her.[53]

In Hernández's case a sense of betrayal, anxiety, and the resultant inability to separate from the mother are partially the consequences of an extended traumatic episode that Hernández experienced at the age of five. Around 1907 Prudencio Hernández, Felisberto's father, found temporary employment in the construction of a military barracks in Maldonado, and his wife, Calita, accompanied him. The family was residing at the time in the house of Deolinda Arecha de Martínez, the aunt who had raised Calita and filled the role of grandmother for the children, so Felisberto and his younger sister were left in Deolinda's care during their parents' absence of more than a year. The separation from his overprotective mother at the age of five was in itself significantly stressful for the young Hernández, and the fear of betrayal that it engendered made a significant contribution to his later inability to deliver himself—as a secure, trusting, autonomous subject—to the marriages that invariably failed. In a parallel but more severe case from the clinical literature there similarly had been "a long early childhood separation from the mother (over a year) and, after the reunion, a locking together in a guilt-ridden close symbiotic bond." As a consequence, this patient was totally incapacitated for normal relations with women other than the mother: "When he wanted to marry, he felt his mother would not allow it; he fell ill immediately after the wedding and was taken home by his mother to be nursed, deferring the honeymoon and leaving his wife stranded."[54]

Aggravating the absence of Hernández's mother was her replacement by the stern, possessive, and authoritarian Deolinda, who assumed what must have seemed to her a compensatory obligation. Given Calita's lenient overprotection, "it was the grandmother who frequently imposed her authority and punished the children."[55] Deolinda would find fault with Hernández's behavior, would scold him, and would strike him, but she then often held her formal punishment in reserve until an unspecified future moment when she could attack the boy by surprise. "I'll beat you with the whip," Deolinda would say to him, "but I'm not going to tell you when."[56] The whippings generally came in the early morning hours: before he had awakened Deolinda would burst in, tear back the sheets, and bring the whip down on his startled body.[57] The unannounced moment of punishment and the inability to defend himself kept the boy perpetually terrorized, particularly at night, because falling asleep always carried the possibility of being violently awakened by Deolinda.

The perpetual threat of imminent, unannounced abuse was further aggravated by confusion and helplessness, since the young Hernández never understood why his behavior inspired Deolinda's violence nor how he might modify it to win her approval.[58] The boy also, of course, had nowhere to turn for appeal or consolation. As Hernández related it to Reina Reyes later in his life, Deolinda's punishments were expressions of a greater, sadistic pleasure that Deolinda derived from frightening him. Cruel jokes and tricks, such as the casting of strange, phantasmal shadows on his bedroom wall or the placing a frog on his bare stomach while he slept, index the severity of her behavior.[59] Deolinda's emotional inconsistency—one moment abusing him with punishments or cruel jokes, and the next pampering him or smothering him with affection—seems also to have made an indelible imprint at a crucial stage of Hernández's psychological development, as evidenced for example in his mood swings from the overtly romantic to the coldly withdrawn. What remained constant in the boy's experience with Deolinda and the man's with other women was the inability to account for the changes that his behavior somehow inspired. Amidst that "confusion" Hernández developed the reflexes of a hair-trigger defense system activated to cover the odds, and his body, just in case. When Deolinda spoke to the boy "he covered his head with his hands."[60]

The destabilizing interlude of a year under Deolinda's domination was a traumatic formative experience that contributed to Hernández's lifelong fearfulness and insecurity, to his concept of women, to his need for approval and reassurance, and to his quasi-paranoid inability to genuinely trust those with whom he was intimate. As one of the early texts worded it, Hernández has "a long history against those who guide or who have my life in their hands" (1:192). The hands trope takes more of a maternal tone in The Lost Horse, where Celina "had my innocence in her hands, as my mother had earlier" (2:21). Hernández's split mother imago derives from one hand being unaware of, indifferent to, or incapable of controlling what the other hand is doing with that innocence. The splitting of the mother imago and, in turn, of all women in Hernández's psychobiography and literature is more than likely a byproduct of an arbitrarily violent surrogate mother incongruous with and suddenly displacing the overprotective mother to which the boy was accustomed.

At the same time, however, that dichotomous depiction is to some degree contrived; neither the doting mother nor the sadistic great aunt are monolithic, and the emotions that they elicit in the boy, the man, and the canon are more complex than one can account for with the simple, clean cleavage of the mother imago into polarized good and bad halves. As evidenced by her representation in The Lost Horse, for example, the grandmother may have represented for the children a pillar of strength, security, and stability, despite her inconsistencies and violent outbursts. The troubled matrimony of Hernández's parents ("the Hernández home lacked stability") created the need for such a force, as did the complicated demeanor of Calita herself, who besides being overprotective is described as "authoritarian," "strange," and "sometimes bitter and dominant."[61] Deolinda's inconsistency itself may have had positive effects on Hernández's development: the doting mother was permissive but suffocating, while the explosive Deolinda operated in outbursts between which the young Hernández could find greater developmental latitude, greater freedom for the formation of an autonomous identity. In all cases, when the split mother is reintegrated the composite yields an imago more volatile and complex than Calita or Deolinda ever were on their own. The loving—even smothering—mother conceals an ominous lining, and Hernández's own intense attraction to her and to the series of lovers constructed from her prototype was itself lined with fear of separation alternating with a fear of absorption, repressed anger, a vague sense of ominous dread, and an incapacity for basic trust.

Instructive in this context is D. W. Winnicott's case presentation concerning a boy obsessed with string. When the parents entered the boy's room they would find that with string "he had joined together chairs and tables; and they might find a cushion, for instance, with a string joining it to the fireplace."[62] The boy, Winnicott realized, "was dealing with a fear of separation, attempting to deny separation by his use of string."[63] His "maternal identification based on his own insecurity in relation to his mother" became apparent during the boy's analysis, and Winnicott observed that his "preoccupation with string could develop into a perversion" if left untreated or if unsuccessfully treated.[64] Another boy patient similarly expressed his anxiety of separating from his mother through string rituals. He would take the exposed string trailing out of a tangle and make "a gesture which was as if he 'plugged in' with the end of the string like an electric flex to his mother's thigh." The string here, as in the previous case, was "used as a symbol of union with his mother."[65]

One can then trace a path—a path well traveled in Hernández's fiction—from the loss or feared loss of the mother to the feared fragmentation of the self. Once one's identity is tied up with the mother her loss constitutes a loss of a part of the self. The pieces begin drifting and must be tethered, connected, tied down. Horacio's playing with dolls (one of the string boys "has a number of teddy bears which to him are children. No one dares to say that they are toys") is a ritual of union which holds his pieces together in the absence of the mother, an absence that, like a baby, he gradually learns to accept and exploit.[66] The dissemination and interconnection of fragments rehearses the subject's "falling to pieces," while at the same time the string or the doll rituals attempt to take control, enact a ceremony in the potential space of repose where the fear of mother's absence is neutralized. The string boy's play "was of a self-healing kind" because exercises in "the sense of loss itself can become a way of integrating one's self experience."[67] Hernández's obsessive quest to recapture a memorial past likewise evidences a positive effort to confront the anxiety of absence, to integrate a fragmented experience, to connect the loose ends of recollection and thereby to preserve the past, embalming the dead in narration. Despite the relative success of those efforts, however, Hernández remained "tied up" with his mother throughout his life. The string has the qualities of a rubber band. In the case of one of Winnicott's analysands (and in the case of Hernández), "All attempts to get him placed away from his mother failed because he regularly escaped and ran back home."[68]

The grandiose self-ideal developed in an effort to satisfy the mother's fantasies (and, in Hernández's case, to forestall the grandmother's violence) often juxtaposes sharply with the accomplishments (humbled by measure against the ideal) that the narcissist can actually achieve. Something of this dissymmetry between mother's fantasy and son's reality is revealed by the circumstances concerning the publication and reception of Hernández's books. Each work of "pure art" was conceived as the messianic instrument that would catapult Hernández into fame and fortune and deliver him— along with the baggage of his mother—from his gloom and destitution. The reality, however, was crueler: the books generally went unnoticed, Calita undermined what she at once demanded by depreciating her son's literary talent, and Hernández nursed a progressively dwindling hope, rekindling what he could of the dream with each new book's publication.[69] In the copy of *The Lost Horse* that he inscribed for Calita in January 1944, Hernández wrote: "For my mother, because in this book I feel so close to her that I plan to pass with her into posterity: the two of us will go on the lost horse toward our destiny, and our feet will never touch the earth."[70] Here the son, humbled by life, poorly received, and incapable of coping with daily responsibilities (let alone his domineering mother's continuing demands) arrives glorified on a white steed as the prince of his mother's dreams, galloping her off (though they are lost) toward a posterity that more than compensates them for the transitory misfortunes that they have unjustly suffered. When reality again intrudes to disappoint that fantasy, hope is postponed until the next occasion. Meanwhile the private myth of unimaginable glory firmly binds mother and son, the latter "transformed into an organ or an instrument for the satisfaction of the mother's unconscious needs."[71] During his piano concerts—to take that "instrument" literally—

Hernández the showman frequently played Schumann according to a school-teacher, according to a recently retired colonel, according to a child just beginning lessons. Given his subordinate posture before others, his susceptibility to living out imposed versions of his life, one can understand Hernández himself in this same pattern of variations: Hernández according to Vaz Ferreira, according to Supervielle, according to his mother.

In another clinical case closely paralleling Hernández's situation, an analysand's "covetous mother" imagined that her son "would undo their misery through great deeds." This son—like Hernández as a precocious piano player, as "chosen" author of "pure art," and as the master of fate suggested in the book dedication—was his mother's "knight errant" and "the golden larva, the unborn hero, who, if he did not shatter mythic function with personal needs, would soon be delivered into a world of riches beyond fame and imagination." The mother invested herself in her son as a mythical object rather than as a subject; "she did not actually attend to the real him, but rather to him as the object of her dreams." Khan summarizes much the same in reference to other analysands: "The child was treated by the mother as her 'thing-creation' rather than as an emergent growing person in his or her own right."[72] Consequently Khan's patient lived, as did the Hernández described by his wives and lovers, "primarily inside a myth he shared with his mother," and he seemed to "empty himself compulsively of his true self needs in order to create an empty internal space to receive mother's dream thoughts." This patient as a mythological object, as an "emptied" self, experienced additional symptoms familiar to readers of Hernández, among them the perception of the body as "a depersonalized object." The mother cathects and invests in "something very special" in the child, but not in the child as a complete person. The child, consequently, "learns to tolerate this dissociation in his experience of self and gradually turns the mother into his accomplice in maintaining this special created-object."[73] These dynamics between mother and son governed Hernández's perception of his relations with the masters who "mothered" him, as is evident in the Sorbonne comment indicating that the real Hernández has been displaced by a "character" created by Supervielle. Hernández modeled his own self-representation on patterns established by his mother, and his work as an author drawing heavily from autobiography reveals the fictional self and the devalued actual subject intermingling and negotiating a relation: "His existential despair was continually flung into mythic narrative, a symbolic order where the real is used to populate the fantastic."[74]

When the probability of long-awaited recognition was waning, intermingled reality and fantasy gained exemplary expression in a letter sent to Reina Reyes on 11 August 1954. The document is noteworthy for its comprehensive representation of the narcissistic traits already summarized—grandiosity, insecurity, need for tribute, idealization, and maternal overprotection—as well as of others (exploitative interpersonal relations and paranoia) that will concern us shortly. The fictional narrative comprising the letter details an imaginary new procedure for awarding the Nobel Prize. Since a windfall of fame and fortune "upset the life and work of someone unaccustomed to them," the Nobel Prize—according to this imaginary procedure—would not be announced until after the laureate's death.[75] Rather than troubling the laureate's delicate sensibilities with the problems of riches, the award would be used to fund a team of specialists, "primarily psychologists," who would move to the laureate's country and dedicate themselves to anonymously and covertly creating for him "a relative happiness that doesn't inhibit his production."

In the first application of this new procedure the team's psychological maneuvers produce in the laureate "a kind of moderate madness." This is not to be misunderstood as malicious, however, since the "madness" is a transitory stage in a comprehensive plan implemented by the team to establish the laureate's permanent well-being. The text then pivots on the phrase "Here is what resulted," taking a decided turn away from the unspecified third-person narrative and into an autobiographical allegory scripting Hernández himself (or Hernández the "character") in the role of the "poet" secretly awarded the Nobel Prize. As worded in a related passage from "The Flooded House," "My sadness was lazy, but in my imagination I lived with the pride of an unrecognized poet" (3:83).

The Nobel Prize letter is generated at the nexus where the frustration of unrecognized grandeur intersects with the fantasy of being secretly appreciated on a grand scale. The blow of rejection is softened under the guise of postponement ("Fifty years will pass before I'm recognized"). The laureate's artistic accomplishment has been awarded the highest honors (undisclosed grandiosity, the "golden larva"), but this secret is guarded even from the laureate himself, who is unstable and on the verge of madness (insecurity). The team of specialists—conforming to the model of the split mother imago, at once nourishing and devastating—manipulates and abuses the laureate for what is supposed to be his own good; this results in a "moderate madness" that progresses to become "a bit paranoiac and no longer moderate." Borrowing a few words from a separate context, the team "has found a way to make me feel other anxieties, productive ones" (3:176). The laureate consigns his fate to the greater wisdom of others and pays the price for creativity, as Hernández likewise habitually returned in subordination to the benevolent torment of his mother and masters. By surrounding his persona in the text with a team of specialists responsible for his well-being, Hernández represents the desire for a maternal protection "that would mitigate his terrible fear before the world."[76] The Nobel Prize fantasy further provides for the consistency and dependability of such protection (in contradistinction to the precarious mother imago, prone to mood swings and absences) by depicting the team's fulfillment of his needs as a formal, contractual obligation. Whereas the mother abandons him to his fate when called away to serve others (the father), the team of specialists is convened with the express and exclusive purpose of attending faithfully to his needs.

The Nobel Prize text then evidences a paranoia beyond those accounted for by its author when the specialists manipulating the laureate for his own good turn out to be idealized representations of Hernández's closest friends and loved ones. The fantasy developed by the text transforms this intimate inner circle into a paid team of benevolent impostors, "characters" representing themselves, specialists who enact a theater of intimacy to convince and stabilize the laureate but who are not authentic or genuine in their emotions. This cast of characters recalls the delusion of substitution characteristic of Capgras's syndrome, which entails the conviction that the persons around one are not their real selves but rather their own doubles, impostors who impersonate these real selves. Such a proliferation of substitutes is most helpful in understanding the extension of Hernández's psychology into his fiction, notably *The Hortensias*, but when the psychobiography itself is concerned a developmental perspective on the Nobel Prize fantasy reveals a mother who is not what she seems to be; a mother who abandons one, who is benevolent but absent; a mother whose benevolence, well-meaning though it may be, is painful; and a mother who acts on one unceasingly from behind the scenes, a mother from whom one cannot escape.

The delusional ideas of reference characteristic of paranoia are also patent in the text's depiction of this pseudocommunity of specialists that represents a kind of "secret society that meets someplace in my head" (3:203). To cite a parallel example, a hospitalized schizophrenic believed that the doctors and nurses on the ward (like the friends in Hernández's letter) were acting special parts, and she was further convinced "that her uncle, friends, and a former headmaster were influencing events in the ward with a special purpose relevant to herself."[77] In these perceptions as in the fantastic text, secret meanings ("mystery," *lo otro*) emerge and gradually estrange the reality around a projecting subject characterized by an "unusual degree of self-reference."[78] The strange life of objects is set in orbit around the self but nevertheless nothing can be trusted. Reina is Reina true, but behind the lover—doubling her—is the calculating "s~

who generates the perfect facsimile of emotions. In the Nobel Prize letter Hernández perceives the doting benevolence of the "impostors" as "a slight persecution with a positive tone": paranoia is aroused but alleviated since these friend/undercover agents pursue him relentlessly, but only for his own good. The ominous pursuit yields to the benevolent intentions; the mother, after all, is good.

The members of the team "prepare a plan to save the poet," which consists of planting an idealized woman, "the divinity" Reina Reyes ("a queen whose ancestors are Kings") whose "radiant beauty" humbles the laureate in reverence: "he kneels, raises his head with his eyes closed to see the blueness of the goddess's eyes." This divinity of awesome qualities is strategically introduced into the laureate's life to protect and nurture him with her maternal love. The idealization then yields to the narcissistic tendency toward exploitative relationships, toward subordinating the "deity" just created. As the text has it, the laureate is owed dutiful service because he is secretly meritorious of the highest honors, and the team members (close friends and the fiancé Reina) are therefore bound to the perpetual servitude of anticipating and catering to his needs, of insulating his fragile sensibility, and, generally, of providing the protection that facilitates his existence. The benevolence of the friends is thereby transformed into an unrenounceable obligation. The Hortensia dolls, the daughter in "The Usher," the tunnel girls of "Except Julia," the father in "The Balcony," and the protagonist of "The Flooded House" are all immediately recalled as the Nobel Prize letter reveals "a coercive enlistment of another person to perform a role in the projector's externalized unconscious fantasy."[79]

THE NARCISSIST BEFORE THE OTHER

The narcissist's "relationships with other people are clearly exploitative and sometimes parasitic," this "behind a surface which very often is charming and engaging."[80] Hernández's tendency toward interpersonally exploitative relationships—with the attendant charm conspicuous in some cases and absent in others—is well documented. One acquaintance recalls him feverishly "maintaining that a friend is nothing more than someone who is useful for something"; the friends for whom this argument was made were, needless to say, offended.[81] Giraldi Dei Cas makes similar but more general reference to actions that frequently "were not understood or accepted."[82] The narrator of "The New House," seated in a café with a friend, registers the tone of this depreciative, exploitative friendship: had he not excused himself to take some notes, he would have had to continue displaying "a smile, a gesture and some words that might [cor]respond to ideas that he [the friend] has formed of me," because it is beneficial to the narrator that the friend see him in this particular way (3:142). Exploitation of specifically material benefits is then suggested by Medeiros, who is reputed to have remarked to the other former lovers and widows at Hernández's wake that they held only one thing in common: having all supported him. Medeiros further observes in her *Felisberto y yo* that even Hernández's concept of "freedom" was predicated on personal gain, liberating him from the troublesome responsibilities of everyday life.[83]

If Hernández's interpersonal relations seem emotionally shallow, exploitative, fragile, menaced by the fear of deception, and susceptible to dramatic shifts in intensity, this is largely because to some degree "Others, including idealized others, are not in fact loved and valued in their own right, but simply as sources of narcissistic supplies."[84] A scene in one of the showcases of *The Hortensias* speaks to the acquisition of these supplies, but also to the developmental dynamics contributing to the need to exploit idealized others. A stairway in the scene has on each of its steps "a detached arm with its hand facing upward," and the legend accompanying the scene explains that a poor widow has arranged these hands as "traps" to assist her in begging (2:170). In one perspective the image represents the narcissist himself, fragmented, extending a needy hand indiscriminately toward anyone who might provide him with narcissistic supplies, and offering nothing in return. In another perspective, however, the image suggests a caricature of Hernández's widowed mother, constantly burdening his emotional and financial resources. Some of her Vishnu-like multiplicity of arms trap him in an inescapable embrace while the others pick his pockets and tap into his emotions through constant "begging." The multiple begging hands—particularly because they appear on a stairway that suggests hierarchy—further reveal a fragmentation of the mother imago and migration of the pieces into a view of all women as needy and demanding, using their respective octopus embraces to trap Hernández (in marriage, for instance) and then, like his mother, to drain him emotionally and financially. Indeed, when women give rather than take, as in the last showcase scene of *The Hortensias*, they are depicted as dead queens on whose behalf everyone prays (2:179).

While the narcissist is exploitative sometimes for material gain and always for reinforcement of his delicate self-image ("the partner is often treated as an object to be used to bolster the person's self-esteem"), he simultaneously experiences the "inability to genuinely depend upon others and trust them."[85] Narcissists, like Hernández, are frequently "considered to be dependent because they need so much tribute and adoration from others, but on a deeper level they are completely unable really to depend on anybody because of their deep distrust and depreciation of others."[86] The apparent overdependence on others and the deployment of charm seducing others' susceptibility to exploitation are often a drama enacting a depreciation in compensation for the narcissist's inability to genuinely establish a bond built on trust. The violation of maternal trust, aggravated by the extended residence with the sadistic Deolinda, certainly contributed to this inability in Hernández's case. "She was truly a very balanced person," says the narrator of *Clemente Colling* in reference to another great aunt, Petrona, but he then hastens to add under his breath: "(Though sometimes, under the greatest appearances of balance, we found the most surprising madnesses or the most inscrutable mysteries)" (1:35). The initial assertion implies trust, but the parenthetical qualifier undercuts it with recognition that the surface is deceptive and the ostensible stability untrustworthy. No risks can therefore be taken; the vulnerable self must be protected from affective damage; it enters interpersonal relations as an object, a mask, an impostor of itself, and it treats others in kind. Hernández's sister remarked that the women who married him "saw the artist and not the man," the "character."[87]

The wives eventually saw through the artist and into the man, however, and one of them would eventually observe that "Felisberto didn't have deep feelings that attached him to others, or he defended himself from feelings for fear of suffering; an affective anesthesia kept him withdrawn inside himself."[88] A compensatory, contrived affect takes center stage in the literary canon through the protagonist of "The Crocodile," who defends his false tears as "natural" and therefore as sincere as any others (3:99). His true emotion is represented by the false gesture that indexes it but that at once mocks and undermines it, because the crying delivers crocodile tears exploited for profit. In this sense Hernández resembles what is sometimes described as the "as-if" personality, a label particularly apropos in the present context, given the ambiguous "as-if" quality of Hernández's fiction. The as-if patient plays a role like an actor who is well trained technically but whose performance is nevertheless ultimately unconvincing because it lacks the quality of true life.[89]

The narcissist's lack of trust and inability to achieve true emotional substance in interpersonal relations often presents clinically as a lack of empathy. "He never concerned himself with other people's pain. He never stopped thinking of himself" (1:79), says the narrator of one of Hernández's earliest works. The emotional withdrawal into a fortified ego and the corresponding incapacity to empathize is perhaps most clearly documented in Hernández's life through a tragic episode concerning his daughter and granddaughter. Hernández's first daughter, María Isabel ("Mabel") Hernández

Guerra, had lost a child as the result of an accident that inflicted fatal burn wounds. When the child died after a week of hospital care, Hernández accompanied his daughter to the morgue, where he remained with her beside the corpse for more than an hour until the staff doctors led her away. Reina Reyes, Hernández's wife at the time, waited for him outside. When immediately following the ordeal she asked him what he had been thinking during the horrid episode, Hernández responded: "I was imagining a story to be titled, 'Other People's Pain'."[90]

The incapacity to empathize with the pain of others and the tendency to exploit while avoiding genuine mutual trust and interdependence all indicate a subject scarcely disposed to accommodate emotional needs not emanating from the almighty but beleaguered self. The result in intimate relationships was predictably grim, and no less so because Hernández's covetous mother "incapacitated him for the devotion [entrega] to love that he sought repeatedly."[91] Hernández's preoccupation with idealism further complicated this incapacity. He rehearsed with each new love an obsessive quest for an unattainable, imaginary love object; the result was "a pattern of unstable and intense interpersonal relationships characterized by alternating between extremes of over idealization and devaluation."[92] The pattern also includes vacillation between the threat of invasion by the other and the dread of definitive abandonment, resulting in a volatile and permanent contradiction that causes these subjects "to desire what they are scared of losing and to reject what is already in their possession but whose invasion they fear."[93] The fear of invasion by a lover, however, is itself ambiguous, revealing finally the infantile desire to wallow effortlessly in the absolute comfort of maternal protection: "If there is a struggle against the invading intrusion it is because there is a secret desire to be completely invaded by the object; not only to be united by it but also to be reduced to total passivity, like a baby in his mother's womb."[94]

Hernández's marriages and extended love affairs tended to conform to a pattern common to narcissism, with perception of the love object alternating between the poles of idealization and devaluation. The cycle begins with a passionate Hernández madly in love and invigorated by the challenge of conquest; at this stage a flurry of love letters idealizes the betrothed. The "honeymoon's over" marriage follows, plagued by Hernández's incapacity before quotidian responsibilities and by frustrations resulting from unacknowledged or unfulfilled needs of the spouse.[95] Deflation of the idealized image and rapid devaluation of the spouse seals the fate of the relation, though the couple's failure is often perceived by the narcissist as a violation of trust—she changed—and often measured in the diminishing gains of exploitative benefits, be they psychological or material, that had been provided by the spouse. Withdrawal from the relationship is the necessary conclusion, generally accompanied by Hernández's repair to living with his widowed mother, and always followed by repetition of "the cycle of alternating idealization and devaluation" with the next lover.[96] In Hernández's literary canon the cycle gains expression in two basic forms that interact dialectically and constantly renegotiate their interrelation: the "Pygmalion urge" to construct the ideal object of desire, and the "demolition enterprise" of fragmenting the love object into multiple, dehumanized clones.[97]

But the idealized romantic partner has her ultimate reference in the narcissist himself. "I'm very selfish," Hernández wrote in a letter from his later years, "it takes a lot for me to come out of myself" (3:218). All otherness must be imported and absorbed. The nuclear supposition of the narcissistic character reads, in effect, "I do not need to fear that I will be rejected for not living up to the idea of myself which alone makes it possible for me to be loved by the ideal person I imagine would love me. That ideal person and my ideal image of that person and my real self are all one and better than the ideal person whom I wanted to love me, so that I do not need anybody else any more."[98] The narcissist engages in "a surface-to-surface relationship, since mirror reflection is at work here": the self projects onto others, reconstructs them in his image, and retrieves them, but ultimately this gallery of objects—to use a trope appropriate to Hernández's canon—serves to insulate the self from actual otherness, to populate one's milieu with a pseudocommunity of mental constructs.[99] As Hernández's literature illustrates, "the situation is alienating in that neither the ego nor the other can locate each other because the image is constantly bouncing back and forth between the ego's internal mirror and the other's external mirror."[100]

Inside this mirrored showcase Hernández himself lived "in the melancholy celebration of idolized self and idealized object representations."[101] The love affair enacting its melancholy celebration provided the narcissistic supplies ("he looked in all women for a certain maternal protection" for example), while at the same time idealization brought the necessary depreciation of the partner's subjectivity, the domination of a love object rather than the recognition of the spouse as an independent subject worthy of one's love.[102] The Hortensia dolls again provide a paradigm manifestation of these dynamics, because "A person has to have special attributes as a thing-person to trigger off their [narcissists'] interest."[103] In the perspective of a narcissist, of someone himself earlier conceived by his mother as an "object of art" or a perfected doll, the idealization of the love object is an act of generous dedication analogous to artistic creation: just as "man sees woman and, as it were, makes her a present of everything excellent, so the sensuality of the artist puts into one object everything that he honors and esteems—in this way he *perfects* an object ('idealizes' it)."[104] But once the "object of art" is completed, is "perfected," it is also de-cathected and the artist or lover loses interest, turns away toward the next creation. Eroticized creation of the love partner is far more thrilling than attending to the every-day demands of maintaining a relationship in the long haul, just as, for Hernández, learning a new musical composition or beginning the reading or writing of a new book was far more desirable than the tedium of follow-ing through to the conclusion of an enterprise already begun.[105]

It is, ironically, the eroticized idealization of the love partner that ini-tiates the process of devaluation, for idealization necessarily objectifies the partner, denigrating or devoiding her subjectivity. When devaluation is more direct it evidences an inequitable distribution of attributes, with the posi-tive ones naturally gravitating toward the narcissist. As Kernberg noted, narcissism entails "the defensive construction of a pathological grandiose self consisting of a conglomeration of one-sidedly positive aspects of self and object and superego, with the negative aspects of self projected onto others," these others including the devalued lover.[106] Devaluation in the extreme—dehumanization—takes center stage in one of Hernández's most important works, *The Hortensias*, where the wife is displaced by a transi-tional object (a doll) that "reproduces" her. The insecure narcissist's self-image as subhuman—doll, art object, worm, and rabbit—is denied insofar as the subject himself is concerned and projected outward onto the partner: Ursula is a cow (3:18); Margarita of "The Flooded House" is associated with an elephant and a frog (3:69, 3:73), as well as with the house itself; the girls of "Except Julia" are entangled with objects; and many females throughout the canon are, like Hortensia, likened to plants. The woman as doll-thing, beast, or vegetable evidences dehumanization as "the ultimate strategy against the fears of human qualities—it protects against the vul-nerability of loving, against the possibility of human unpredictability, and against the sense of powerlessness and passivity in comparison to other humans."[107] Women, like the mother, are unpredictable, but in their ideal-ized form women are dolls that faithfully hold the posture in which they are positioned.

The "Felisbertization" of Reality

Heinz Hartmann referred to narcissism as the "libidinal investment of the self," by which one may understand—in Freudian terms—a constant negotiation between ego libido and object libido. In the *Introductory Lectures on Psycho-Analysis*, Freud described the flow of libido in a trope emphasizing the self's extensions (or "investments") and contractions. The "simplest of living organisms which consist of little-differentiated globule of protoplasmic substance" extend protrusions, known as pseudopodia, into which they then cause the substance of their body to flow. These organisms are capable, however, of withdrawing the protrusions and reconstituting themselves as globules. "We compare the putting-out of these protrusions, then, to the emission of libido on to objects while the main mass of libido can remain in the ego; and we suppose that in normal circumstances ego-libido can be transformed unhindered into object-libido and that this can once more be taken back into the ego."[108]

Extensions of the self probe out into and onto the world with a certain adhesiveness—the "viscosity" mentioned on occasion by Hernández—and then return with a libidinally enveloped object representation that is incorporated into the critical mass guarded in reserve. As evident in *The Hortensias*, in woman-water tropes central to "The Flooded House," and in the optic-retrieval system of eye light in "The Usher," the overflowing self often attempts an all-encompassing incorporation of the reality it surrounds, so that the objects penetrated and wrapped by libidinal investment forfeit their reality in-themselves and assume functions and identities assigned to them by the narcissist's "melancholy celebration." The narcissist—Horacio of *The Hortensias*, for example—occupies the center of his universe and around him a gallery of what Heinz Kohut terms "self-objects" ("objects which are not experienced as separate and independent from the self") extend his domain across a world that he nevertheless continues to perceive as independent.[109] His reality is thereby invested with self-referenced meaning; transitional objects populate an accommodating milieu that the projecting subject constructs and inhabits.

Several observers describing Hernández's personality have alluded to "his incapacity to get beyond a purely subjective attitude" and his resultant tendency to "felisbertize" the world around him.[110] "Felisberto gave preference to an imaginary world," "he isolated himself from realities," he was "always distracted, as though thinking about something else," and he was engaged in "a continuous play between the real and the unreal."[111] One of Hernández's closest friends, Esther de Cáceres, alluded to the same fictionalizing traits: Hernández's "world was an aesthetic world. Everything was transformed into material for Art." She added that in his youth "the real and the fantastic played a disconcerting game of chess: a game that is in all of Hernández's life and work."[112]

An egocentric reorganization, or the "tendency to change meanings of reality when facing a threat to self-esteem," is one of the central motifs of

Hernández's fiction, but perhaps the most apt illustration in this psychobiographical context is a passage from the hybrid Nobel Prize letter discussed earlier.[113] The text includes the following: "The poet [Hernández] has opportunities to get close to her [Reina Reyes], he admires her, but her radiant beauty and the proximity of the genius [Carlos Vaz Ferreira] for whom she is secretary produce in our poet a total inhibition, so he prepares to carry her off to his abstract world, absolutely separated from reality."[114] Fictionalization is patent here on two levels, the first entailing idealization of all players except the narrator. Everyone is so grand—awesome intelligence, radiant beauty—precisely because "the poet's" insecurity renders him so insignificant. Facing a threat to self-esteem in the shadow of such grandeur—a grandeur that his own insecurity has inflated out of proportion—the narrator then shifts the fictionalization into a higher register: his pseudopod, his projecting libidinal investment, locates, appropriates, and retrieves the idealized love object "to carry her off to his abstract world" and to access, possess, and transform her there, "absolutely separated from reality." Here, as in previous examples, reality is imported into fantasy; all sources of gratification (Reina) are internalized and therefore elaborated as internal constructs (Reina "perfected") emerging from the inexhaustible wellspring of autosatisfaction, while simultaneously the retreat from the world with a supply of confiscated provisions allows that narcissists "create their own protective shield against the dangers of the environment."[115]

Perhaps as a result of this "withdrawing into 'splendid isolation'," narcissists often experience the sensation of being separated from the world by an invisible but implacable barrier.[116] As the narrator of *The Lost Horse* describes it, "There was a very thick air between me and the world" (2:35). A clinical patient experiencing similar alienation "felt as if he lived in a plastic bubble"; others refer to life behind glass or surrounded by a membrane, where "Things seemed unreal, as though there was something shutting me off from reality," and where "Voices sound different and distant."[117] In Hernández's canon the paradigm of such enclosures or barriers delineating the borders between private and social realities are found in the glass showcases of *The Hortensias*. Here in "splendid isolation," in an "abstract world absolutely separated from reality," a self-object constructed of an idealized woman (doll) is libidinally invested and mobilized by projection (the gaze) in order to enact the "melancholy celebration," the "continuous play between the real and the unreal," that constitutes Horacio's private reality. At the same time the showcases more generally suggest the "world behind glass" sensation, a potential space of retreat in which one becomes imprisoned, and the impassable psychological distance that separates the narcissist from the elusive, hazy reality that he vaguely discerns on the horizon. Hernández's "fear of life" enforced such a distance, relegating him, like Horacio, to the position of an aloof spectator viewing the world as showcase or theater: "There was always a curtain between Felisberto and reality."[118] Even when drawn open, the curtain between Hernández and his reality, between Horacio and his showcases and mirrors, reveals a privately constructed milieu where the "inability adequately to separate self representations from object representations accounts for a continuing attempt to use objects as parts of missing self structure."[119]

As mentioned earlier, however, the doll theater of *The Hortensias* is not exactly static, because the dolls "add something of their own." An ultimate erasure of the distinction between what the dolls do on their own (which of course is nothing) and the "mobilization" of the dolls by projection contributes a sense of duality, of dialogue, to Horacio's autoerotic rituals. One simple but vivid example: Horacio hesitates to kiss Hortensia, fearing that the doll would taste like leather, that it would be like kissing a shoe. Moments later he notices that the doll assumed "an expression of cold haughtiness and seemed to take revenge for all he had thought about her skin" (2:144).[120] The "expression" indexes not the doll's emotions but rather those of Horacio. A doll's face does not change; Horacio's response to it changes when his guilt intersects with his desire. That change is then projected and external reality (the doll) is revised to conform to Horacio's evolving internal equilibrium. A monologue masquerades as a dialogue: Horacio's perception fixes on an object, animates it by projecting a desire (as does also, for example, the protagonist of "The Usher"), and then retrieves his own projection's content as though it emanated from that object itself, either because it originated there or because the object, as though "hypnotized," "carrying out unknown missions," transmitted it from some third source or composite of multiple sources.

The dolls of *The Hortensias* as recipients of these fantastic projections function much the same as the stimuli of standardized projective tests—the Rorschach, for example—in which subjects confronted with ambiguous data respond in such a way that their character traits and certain patterns of their behavioral and emotional organization can be read from what they have seen. Horacio's interpretations of glances that cloud around the dolls' faces, of reflections that layer a palimpsest in the depth of a mirror's surface, or of animistic objects' actions or intentions construct the reality in which he functions and, by doing so, index the psychological composition that makes him dependent upon that construct.

The fact that this manipulated reality is external to Horacio but not to the narrative that creates him returns us to Hernández, who in these fictions finds an ideal venue for expressing his more general tendency to "felisbertize" reality. The Hortensia dolls surface to represent "internalized object representations" that have acquired, like the devalued lovers discussed above, "the characteristics of real, but rather lifeless, shadowy people."[121] Those whom Hernández managed to love were ultimately encompassed in the "felisbertized" world as more objects in the showcases that "represent the narcissists themselves."[122] The risk in this narcissistic enterprise, as Horacio dramatizes, is an intermingling of subject and object, of fantasy and reality, of spectator and spectacle, to such a degree that the borders enforcing differentiation break down.

2
The Poetics of Reflection

NARCISSISTIC PROJECTION

He is enamored of himself for want of taking heede
And where he lykes another thing he lykes himselfe in deede
—Ovid, in reference to Narcissus
(Arthur Golding translation)

Like Narcissus, Horacio of *The Hortensias* rejects interpersonal love and instead directs his passion to a reified projection that he vivifies by investing it with his desire. This process of narcissistic projection, including the subsequent harvest of a new reality elaborated to suit the needs of the projecting subject, is championed more generally by protagonists throughout Hernández's canon. One, for example, "would not let any idea leave him without the condition of its taking a short trip and then returning to him" (*OC,* 3:12); emanations venture out on their mini-excursion away from the self but must quickly boomerang back to their source. Before the "idea" returns to the narcissist, however, it mobilizes transformative interactions with objects and splits off from the subject to declare its independence as a separate entity with inherent, animistic will. The procedure is inaugurated in the text through expression of a projective desire—"I want to see an idea move outside of me"—followed by a doubling technique that divorces the self from its projection: in order to see the externalized idea "move," the narrator "will have to represent it inside of myself," and consequently the external idea (external only because it has been projected) and its new internal representation will seem like "two simultaneous ideas" (1:184). Through this splitting the projected idea gains autonomy, is perceived by the subject as an objective phenomenon that he had nothing to do with it, and consequently is re-registered in the subject's mind as a second "idea" that records perception of the first "idea" masquerading now as an object.

The narrator wants nothing other than to instigate and witness a projection's "live movement that is accomplished outside of me and that continues living and moving on its own" (1:185). Since the independent movement of these emancipated objects is no more than a by-product of the self's unwitting perception of its own projections, the ultimate result—as Horacio experiences—is the collapse of fantasy and reality into a single palimpsest in which "the inside and the outside are one and the same" (1:184). If for Augustine "the visual sense is shaped by the object to which it is connected," for Hernández the object is shaped by the projective vision enveloping it.[1]

The consolidation of fantasy in reality and the process of splitting—this time of the projecting subject himself—is further suggested by the narrator of *Lands of Memory*, who establishes a thematic backdrop for the glass showcases of later texts (*The Hortensias* and "The Usher") by presenting dream images behind glass. The narrative splits the subject into the dreamer inside a glass enclosure and the vigilant self gazing through the glass into the dream and dreamer: "It was as though my curiosity as someone awake had remained outside of a glass house." When the dream world becomes inhospitable the vigilant self retrieves the dreamer: "The part of me that was waiting, awake, outside of the glass house called me in alarm; I went with him and left the realm of the dream" (3:59). This reunification of self-identities outside of the "glass house" reserves and exercises the privilege of migration back and forth between the omniscient position of the onlooker on one side of the glass and the populated dream space on the other side. The glass-encased dream space not only enacts a representation of one's fears and desires but also has the capacity—like the "idea" in motion—to continue doing so in the subject's absence. This autonomous, permeable, showcased dramatization leads rather directly to *The Hortensias*, where dreamy scenarios are likewise staged behind glass that is susceptible to the protagonist's permeations.

The showcases of *The Hortensias* are Hernández's perfected trope of narcissistic projection, of objectifying and dramatizing a representation of one's fantasies. Among the many readings accommodated by these over-determined showcases and their dolls is this one: the showcases epitomize the Hernández characters' inclination to flaunt their projected fantasies in the world *as though* these mobilized representations were independent realities. The *as though* merits emphasis since the rearranged reality so ceremoniously constructed as independent is ultimately restricted to represent nothing other than the projecting subject himself, disguised within a gallery of self-objects. What the projecting narcissist sees is not what-is-there, but rather a transformation of what-is-there into a mirror. Ovid recognizes much the same in reference to Narcissus's idealized reflection: "The thing is nothing of it selfe: with thee it doth abide, / With thee it would departe if thou withdrew thy self aside."[2] When the narcissist looks at the world, when Horacio looks at his showcase, he sees himself, but he does not see himself seeing. Borrowing a phrase from Christian Metz, Horacio is "acrobatically hooked up to himself by the invisible thread of sight."[3]

A similar "connection" is established in Wim Wenders's film *Paris, Texas*. In a sort of modified brothel featuring showcases that represent various locales—a motel room, a diner, a poolside—prostitutes who are accessible only visually engage in nontactile interaction with their clients. An alternating one-way mirror separates the showcase from the observation room: when the showcase is unlit before the girl arrives, the dark glass functions as a mirror and the client sees himself reflected. Once the showcase is lighted from inside upon arrival of the prostitute, the mirror/glass functions inversely so that the prostitute is seen (and sees herself reflected), while the client remains anonymous on the other side of the mirror/glass. The client's image, however, now ghostly, continues to reflect back to him with a certain translucence at the same time that he sees through it to perceive the prostitute, much the same as his vision would both penetrate and reflect off a lighted shopwindow at night.

When the protagonist Travis finds his lost wife working in the brothel, he visits the showcases for anonymous encounters with her. To assure himself of his anonymity he makes various investigations—hand gestures trying to attract her attention, observation of her eyes as he changes position, questions concerning his visibility—to determine whether his wife in the showcase can see through the mirror to identify him on the other side of the glass. She cannot. "You realize that I can't see you even though you can see me," the girl clarifies. When he leaves she continues talking to the mirror, unaware that he is no longer present.

The glass/mirror motif reaches its peak when Travis returns to the showcases for the encounter during which he reveals his identity to his wife. Just prior, after a bout of drinking, Travis explains how his father wanted his wife (Travis's mother) to be something more than she was. The father desired a "fancy woman," a woman from Paris rather than from Paris, Texas, a woman who conformed to the idea that he had imposed on her, his idea of what she should be. "He looked at her, but he didn't see her. He saw this idea." When Travis returns to the observation room to see his own wife in the showcase, the images again stress an interchange of seeing the girl and seeing his own reflection. At the climax, however, when the girl realizes that the anonymous voice is her husband's, she approaches the mirror trying to see through it, she crouches, she brings her face close to the glass.

The woman nevertheless sees only herself; Travis's back is turned, so he sees nothing. As Travis slowly turns his body around in the chair the interchange of reflections concretizes: we see his reflecting image on one side of the glass sweeping across the face of the woman on the other side, until at one moment his reflecting face is situated and lingers precisely in the space framed by her hair. Her face disappears and is replaced by his face's reflection superimposed on her body. Travis and his lost love are fused in an interchange of reflections. We no longer see her, but only "this idea." His next words—"If you turn the light off in there will you be able to see me"—serve as a transition on which the interplay of reflections pivots; the wife then sees Travis through her reflection.[4]

Horacio's showcase likewise functions as both glass and mirror, evidencing this human incapacity to "break through" and genuinely "see" another person, particularly another person who is loved. More specifically, however, it functions as a deforming mirror that warps out the grotesque inhospitality of reality and idealizes the remainder in service to Horacio's fantasies. The British painter Francis Bacon, himself a master of distortion, once expressed the desire for a room lined with distorting mirrors, occasionally interrupted by normal mirrors. In these few normal mirrors, Bacon calculated, "people would look so beautiful" because their appearance would be measured against the reflection of bodies disfigured by distortion.[5] For Horacio reality itself has this distorting-mirror quality of uncanny disfiguration. Framed images isolated from but simultaneously significant only in relation to their context are therefore contrived to fabricate an illusion of beauty: Bacon situates the normal mirror in a gallery of deformation, and Horatio exploits the showcase as a ritual confine that "normalizes" and idealizes reality by warping out the horror and replacing it with objectified projections. Both strategies are striving for "something that can only come into focus now by blurring the field of representation where our normal forms of self-recognition take place."[6] As evidenced by experiments of self-perception in an adjustable body-distorting mirror, a sustained encounter with grotesquely distorted reflections drives people to repair to the calming measure of cognitive consonance afforded by self-images reflecting from normal mirrors.[7] For Horacio, however, the mirror that "normalizes" is abnormal, a glass showcase asylum mobilizing fantasies that consolidate distortions of an idealized world and self. "I will project my entire soul toward that illuminated stage" (3:9), remarks one narrator who implicitly recognizes Hernández's showcases as displays for "an exhibition of psychic content."[8]

While they receive their most sustained development in *The Hortensias* and, to a lesser degree, "The Usher," glass and showcase poetics are thematically important throughout Hernandez's canon. Some images leave little room for doubt—people inside a lighted streetcar are "mannequins inside a shop window" (2:118). Elsewhere sheets of glass or other dividers emphasize a showcaselike separation of spectator and spectacle: Margarita's thick glasses transform her face into a shopwindow (3:68); a narrator enters "a gallery from where one could see a garden through a shop window" (2:47); and vision is filtered through "yellowed curtains" (2:80), a "blonde curtain" of hair (3:100), or "a very dirty red curtain" (3:112). In other instances the distance enforced by glass showcases is suggested by the unbridgeable space between a subject and the object of his desire: one protagonist spies on his cousin lover and her mother in church, "from some distance, protected by a confession booth" (2:189). In "Except Julia" the ritual distance is established by positioning girls at intervals along the dark tunnel's wall and is then reinforced as the girls are "genuflecting on kneelers [*reclinatorios*]" with "cloths on their heads" (3:73–74). In other instances the showcases are suggested by the muted lighting and stagelike settings of, for example, "No One Lit the Lamps," the opening of "The Crocodile," or the "windows painted white" in "Lucrecia" (2:105). In still other instances it is not necessarily the visual dimension of the showcase that is most insistent; these passages rather stress ritualized behavior, much of it gaze-related, that is reminiscent of Horacio and his dolls. The balcony of the story by the same title, for example, is looked out of rather than looked into, but with the same result that one encounters in *The Hortensias*: identities are constructed by intermingling the reality on one side of the glass with the fantasies on the other.[9] Margarita of "The Flooded House" employs "specialists" to stage her fantasy just as Horacio does to stage his (3:72), and water—including the reflective properties of water—plays a central role in both narratives. The showcase as a trope for the act of writing itself is also suggested, not only by Horacio's journal entries in their relation to the showcase scenes but also by descriptions of writing that emphasize "trapping a story and locking it up in a notebook" (2:125).

The "theater" or "cinema" of memories that dominates a great percentage of Hernández's work is also attributed showcase qualities. A description of looking at people in memories, for example, is almost indistinguishable from the experience of Horacio gazing at his dolls: "I felt that the inhabitants of those memories, despite the fact that they were directed by the person looking at them and that they followed his whims with such magical docility, at the same time kept hidden their own will full of pride" (2:31). Though their inherent passivity subordinates these characters to the service of the narrator's desires, the cast of these memories, like the dolls as Horacio sees them, "have a certain independence" and "carry out their mission within a suspicious silence." In the long view, however, those qualities of autonomy and independence are constructs of the spectator who "enlivens" the memories or the dolls with his perception, a selectively myopic perception intent on blurring the "quality of existence" that makes dealings with memories or dolls necessarily unilateral (2:31–32).

The poetics of the showcase as agency of disavowed self-perception are established in Hernández's canon partly through the association of glass (and the corresponding penetrating gaze) with mirrors (and the reflected gaze). When asked by the scene designers to comment on his passion for the showcases, Horacio explains that "seeing the dolls in showcases is very important because of the glass; it gives them a certain quality of memory." This "memory" quality deconcretizes the dolls, restoring their affinity to the image, the projected fantasy, that they represent, while at the same time the glass reinforces a ritual distance that mimes the temporal distance of memories with a spatial divide separating Horacio from his projection. Such is reinforced by Horacio's remark that he enjoyed seeing rooms reflected in mirrors (2:153). The quality of an "idea" or "memory" is again dominant: the concrete reality of the rooms is displaced by a representation, a framed reflection. Preference for these intangible reality surrogates is later explicitly stressed when "the room that appeared in it [the mirror] was more beautiful" than the actual room itself (2:164).[10] Here, as in the glass showcase, reality is idealized as it is displaced.

One highly nuanced example of the glass-as-mirror motif surfaces in the latter part of *The Hortensias*. The rituals once confined to the showcases have already been generalized and disseminated over Horacio's world at large, and Horacio now finds himself with the doll Herminia in the Las Acacias house that he has rented for amorous rendezvous with the dolls. The glass-as-mirror is established with this phrase: "One night when the two of them were seated before a painting, Horacio saw her eyes reflected in the glass." Since the glass is transparent as well as reflective, it intermingles—like the showcase, the *Paris, Texas* glass, and shopwindows— the image behind the glass with the image of the onlooker who is reflected in the glass.[11] In this case the image behind the glass is not Narcissus's silvery pond but rather an agitated, fragmenting reflector: the painting depicts a waterfall. The doll, cheek-to-cheek with Horacio as he looks into this confusion of reflectors and reflections, is wearing a mask for good measure, and in the glass-as-mirror her eyes "shined amidst the blackness of the mask and it seemed as though they had thoughts" (2:175). What presents here as a reflection is in fact a projection: the thoughts belong not to the doll—dolls have no thoughts—but to the subject, Horacio, who attributes thoughts to his transitional object. Horacio stages and retrieves his fantasies in the Las Acacias house just as he had done in his gallery of showcases. The doll's masquerade as an independent player is introduced into the space opened between the projection and the retrieval of ideations emerging from Horacio's narcissism. When Horacio believes that he discerns in the doll's reflecting eyes an expression of "humbled grandeur"—this by no coincidence the paradigmatic characteristic of clinical narcissism—then "he kissed her passionately" (2:176). His emblem in her eyes is the potent aphrodisiac that brings Horacio and his creation into contact. With this gesture of self-love detoured through layers of reflection, shifts of perspective, and masked dehumanization of identities, Horacio, like Narcissus, loses his image in disrupted waters—the waterfall, the stirred reflections, the waterlogged doll jostled. Unlike Narcissus, however, Horacio is stimulated by the loss and hastens to consummate the matrimony of the actual self with the idealized self and its objects. Intersecting tropes of reflection thereby superimpose Horacio's identity over that of the doll, much as the bride and bridegroom in modern India simultaneously look at themselves in a mirror to ritually strengthen their bond. The ancient Chinese custom of lovers breaking a mirror and each retaining half during temporary separations likewise pays homage to these poetics.[12]

The doll Herminia is not behind showcase glass like the dolls earlier in *The Hortensias* but is rather reflected in glass as though it were a mirror. The context for this inversion is established through mention of Carnival and is then sustained by the doll's Mardi Gras dress. Reflecting projections and inverting perspectives then entangle with confusions and fusions of identities: a doll stands in as idealization of an absent woman and of Horacio himself; the mask on the doll layers the disguises concealing these identities and simultaneously mystifies the absences that she makes present; the cheek-to-cheek posture intertwines the gaze of Horacio with the imaginary gaze of the doll; and the glass on the painting is sufficiently transparent to reveal the distorting mirror that it covers (the waterfall) but at the same time is sufficiently reflective to "distort" the doll's "identity" and to return the projection to Horacio as its source. And if that were not enough, the content of this reflecting projection—humbled grandeur—is assigned to the doll but is an attribute proper to Horacio and/or the narrator. The inspiration for passionate kisses cannot ultimately be assigned to the doll (because she and her glass eyes have nothing to do with it other than receiving whatever projections are cast onto them) but rather results from Horacio's autoerotic thrill derived through finding his insignia—humbled grandeur—in the reflected eyes of the other. Like the Lady of courtly love lyrics, the Hortensia doll is "a mirror in which everything else is seen," insofar as this "everything else" filters first through Horacio. To this degree Horacio, like the courtly man, "was wedded to the mirror."[13]

The glass/mirror relation and the corresponding themes of the penetrating gaze versus the reflecting gaze are similarly established in other Hernández narratives, notably "The Usher." In this text built around the concept of projection the protagonist remarks: "I tried to look at my face in unlit shop windows and preferred not to see the objects on the other side of the glass" (2:62). Once the usher has become conscious of his projecting eye light and its destructive potential, he changes course: "I was afraid of seeing myself reflected in the big mirrors or in the glass of the showcases" (2:65). This fear of the reflected gaze is counterbalanced by the delight that the usher now experiences with his penetrating gaze, which provides him voyeuristic access to the marvels of unknown worlds. Horacio likewise feared and covered actual mirrors, preferring mirror surrogates, like the showcases, that when properly illuminated reflected not his face but only the projected, rehearsed subjectivity displayed inside them.[14] When he fantasizes about the invention of "mirrors in which objects can be seen but people cannot," Horacio provides a precise definition of his showcases (2:164). Both Horacio and the usher obsessively pursue their reflections while they at once evade them, and both ultimately pass "through the looking glass" and are transformed on the other side into the dehumanized embodiment of their own projections. In the usher's words: "I was like a mannequin [*muñeco*] laid out in a shop window" (2:66).

In the world of the mirror, as Alice learned in *Through the Looking Glass*, "things go the other way." The inversion of perspectives resulting from mirror reflections and ricocheting projections is reinforced throughout Hernández's canon by several passages stressing changes of direction. In a dream in *The Hortensias*, for example, Horacio "saw a light that fell from a lampshade [*pantalla*] onto a table." A pun on the word *pantalla* initiates the competing perspectives: *pantalla* here signifies "lampshade," providing for the *projection* of light (like the usher's eyes and like Horacio's showcases as projections), while the *pantalla* thematically central to Hernández's canon—the movie-theater screen—is passive, inert, until "mobilized" by the projection that it receives.[15] Tropes of inversion are then generated from this double direction of projections: around the table with the *pantalla* are men, and one of them representing Horacio says, "It is necessary that the flow of blood change directions."[16] The reversal of blood flow in the dream is linked by the vigilant Horacio to his having heard that the flow of automobile traffic would be changing directions in his country. These two reversals—blood and traffic flow—reinforce the *pantalla* pun, which itself metonymizes the central motif: what appears to be projecting an image (showcase, *pantalla*) is at once the recipient of projected images. The reversed circulation of blood at the beginning of

The Hortensias is then echoed at the conclusion, when Horacio is already the victim of his own world beyond the looking glass and turns mechanically in circles, as though—borrowing the trope from an earlier text—his soul were installed in him backwards (1:176). This circular two-step combined with Horacio's infantile character further recall a passage from *Land of Memory*, where the narrator wants "to make the world spin backward with dizzying speed until arriving again at the days of adolescence" (3:40).

The sensation of being trapped between mirrors and caught in the crossfire of perspectives is also treated in the legend "The Woman of the Lake" that is related in *The Hortensias*. The store La Primavera is opening its exhibition of dolls, and in half of the featured showcase—designed by Horacio's staff and "divided in two sections by a mirror that reached the ceiling"—a scene depicts a young girl who lived alone beside a secluded lake in the forest. "Every morning she got out of her tent and went to comb her hair at the shore of the lake; but she took a mirror with her." The use of the hand mirror is never specified, although parenthetically we learn that "Some people said that she faced it toward the lake to see the back of her head." The narrative concludes with the silent girl walking around the lake to avoid social contact with some intruding society women (who repay her inhospitality by characterizing her "the madwoman of the lake"), and with a popular saying that links the concept of silence to the girl's circling of the lake (2:176).

Important in the present context are the competing perspectives generated by the mirrors and mirror surrogates: the girl is caught in the crossfire between the lake-as-mirror and the vanity mirror that she holds, this in turn multiplied by the floor-to-ceiling mirror flanking her in the exhibit. The gaze of Horacio and the other viewers follows suit, at once penetrating the glass and reflecting off it, while in the legend represented by the scene the girl in a chamber of mirror-multiplied reflections uses the lake as a prosthesis to spy the approach of the society women.[17] The circulation introduced earlier (the blood, the traffic, Horacio's movement) is then integrated into these reflection poetics by the girl's repeated circling of the lake. The layers of representation accumulate in tandem with the multiplied reflections indexing them: Horacio's projected fantasy, constructed for him by "specialists," is made manifest in a mirror-flanked scene that represents a legend that itself stands in for a popular saying that is offered as explanation for one's silence. The inversions likewise proliferate at the textual level insofar as the legend ("an old national legend") necessarily precedes the showcase scene designed to depict it, while, inversely, the production of *The Hortensias* works backwards from the scene to the legend, inventing the latter to imbue the former with its thematic charge. This double direction mimes the procedure rehearsed in the staging and then perceiving of the showcase scenes in Horacio's private gallery, where likewise Horacio's interpretation of a scene intersects with the "truth" of the legend against which interpretations are measured. This truth, however, is always itself an interpretation resulting from the scene producers' attempt to second-guess Horacio's fantasies. Horacio therefore again perceives only his own elaborately detoured fantasy, textualized now and asserting its canonical truth.

Following the lead of one of his patients, D. W. Winnicott made reference to Francis Bacon's use of glass over paintings and then quoted a critic concerning "the fortuitous play of reflections" that we have likewise seen in Hernández's treatment of glass. Bacon—according to the critic—noted that his dark paintings in particular "gain by enabling the spectator to see his own face in the glass."[18] The viewer sees himself and the painting simultaneously; as Oscar Wilde put it, "It is the spectator, and not life, that art really mirrors."[19] Bacon later backed away from the concept of glass-as-mirror ("I think it's just one of those misfortunes. I hope they'll make glass soon which doesn't reflect") and emphasized instead "the removal of the object as far as possible" via the interposition of glass as a psychological barrier between the artwork and the viewer. In Bacon's words, "It's the distance, this thing is shut away from the spectator."[20]

Insofar as Hernández's showcases and the narcissistic projection that they represent are concerned, both the reflective and ritual distancing properties of the glass are essential.[21] The characters' urge to "accommodate in reality what they had thought beforehand" (2:27) suggests the construction of a showcaselike reality directed from a distance and enforced by rehearsal. Ideas and feelings are elaborated in one's chambers and then projected for staging, already refined, before oneself-as-audience. Once the scene is reenacted—like the mobilized "idea" discussed earlier—the showcase enforces ritual distance with its glass, its curtained stage, its lighting, its aesthetic closure composed by specialist. Because these ritual boundaries are multiple and mutually reinforcing, because the scene is inviolable and sacrosanct, Horacio's pleasure is redoubled when he exercises his reserved privilege of access and reintroduces his living presence into the fantasy, which has taken on a life of its own. Like Narcissus, and like the voyeur-narrator of "The Usher," he "tries to break through the wall between himself and the 'external' object."[22] When he opens the glass door and enters the showcase Horacio penetrates the armor of a scene "shut away from the spectator," thereby releasing his staged, "delusional restitution of reality" from its confine and allowing it to spill across his world.[23]

Whether situated in their showcases or populating the textual world as a whole, the Hortensia dolls themselves are always overdetermined. The dolls represent Horacio's wife María, but also the perfection of María, the displacement of María by a reified idealization. Barely veiled behind this idealization is the mother imago, linked initially with María's mother but then generously overdetermined as the narrative progresses, revealing a salvaging operation through which projections attempt to construct and retrieve the ideal mother whom Horacio apparently (and Hernández certainly) never had. The idealization of the absent mother shapes the void in which future women are molded for display behind glass.[24] Dolls are prime candidates for overdetermination because their emptiness accommodates whatever is poured into them, and because they are "dead"-but-present and thereby immortal surrogates of the "dead"-but-absent women whose disguised identities dictate the doll's various forms and functions. Two of the three primary female social roles—mother and wife/lover—are thereby consolidated in the dolls, with the third, that of daughter, loaded on as Hortensia ambiguously fills this role for Horacio and María in the early part of the narrative. Hortensia as daughter echoes the doll's "duplication" of María and the mother, as well as suggesting the incest theme that intersects with most of the doll's feminine identities.[25] Death and the fear of death are also prominently represented by the dolls, as is apparent enough in the cool and corpselike nature of these inert, anthropomorphic bodies. "Our own death," Freud observed, "is indeed unimaginable and whenever we make the attempt to imagine it, we can perceive that we really survive as spectators."[26] The fear of death is among the spectacles in Horacio's showcase scenes, and like the mother imago, or entangled with it, it emerges from María. Hortensia is a front covering both a fear and a taboo: she softens Horacio's dread of María's death (ultimately of death itself), and she launders his unacknowledged desire for the forbidden woman par excellence, the mother.

María's imminent death is ostensibly what compels Horacio to have a doll surrogate fabricated in her image, but the speciousness of that argument—María is not ill, much less moribund—opens the field to the obsession never mentioned in *The Hortensias* but dramatized throughout it: Horacio's fear of his own death. Several surface indices set the tone— when Horacio scripts discourse for an imaginary other observing him, he comes up with, "Let's see how much longer he'll live" (2:170)—but the death dread is most forcefully represented by Horacio's descent into death's metaphoric surrogate, insanity. As Horacio takes refuge in his madness he is progressively reconstituted in the image of the dolls, which is to say—in this context—the image of a living corpse, a body that never dies because it is eternally and unalterably "dead." The narrative's two-way flow of relations links Horacio with the dolls coming and going: the dolls are brought into being and imbued with meanings by Horacio's projected fears and desires, and for this reason they have their ultimate reference in Horacio himself; while from the opposite direction, Horacio's madness recasts him in the image of his own creation, of the dolls that were supposed to monumentalize immortality but wind up "absorbing" him into their "death."

The overlapping identities of Horacio and Hortensia are established through projection and reflection, through the "confusion" that clouds the boundaries between players and keeps all identities in constantly shifting configurations, and through the many surface indices that individually are only suggestive but that collectively make an unmistakable contribution. The overlapping names themselves commence the proliferation of traces: Hor-acio, Hor-tensia. Horacio is then described as "a tall man" (2:137), with the dolls "a little taller than normal women" (2:138). An emblem of Horacio, the tuxedo, is worn on one occasion by Hortensia (2:141), and this suggested link is later reinforced by related blackness tropes when, for example, Horacio discovers the timid man's doll in a closet wearing "a black dress" (2:172). Horacio is the owner of the "black house," he wears a black mask (2:166), and his amorous escapades conclude with a doll representing a black woman. On another occasion the exchange of emblems linking Horacio with Hortensia migrates in the opposite direction, with the doll's essence as water receptacle assigned to Horacio (2:20). Horacio's "incarnation" in the dolls and his insemination of clones reproduced in his image is also suggested throughout *The Hortensias*, but it is perhaps best summarized with a phrase from another text: "I put something of myself inside her skin" (2:206).

María, meanwhile, cycles in and out of the Horacio-Hortensia schema as required to service the doll's fluctuating identity. With husband, wife, and doll together in bed, for example, we find María braided into a threesome, with Horacio delivering himself in resigned delight to a "confusion" of the six entangled legs and to indifference in discerning which of the legs are his (2:151). A page later, in a more sustained depiction of the Horacio-Hortensia link, María's role is decidedly written out. Horacio falls off of a tricycle and on top of the doll riding with him. This image, suggestive in itself, is then enhanced with a description of Horacio "with his feet in the air making movements like an insect" (2:152). The dehumanization of Horacio, stressed at the text's conclusion (2:179), suggests a general affinity with the nonhuman mistress, but this is then made more specific in the tricycle scene when Facundo, the maker of the Hortensias, compares Horacio's movements to those of "a wind-up toy" (2:152).[27] The doll-like, mechanized gestures become thematically central after Horacio's descent into madness, when he begins to "spin his body with tiny movements of his feet" (2:178). This circular two-step is reinforced with automaton attributes that definitively transform Horacio into the likeness of Hortensia; they include Horacio's "silence of a wooden man," "his fixed eyes, as if they were glass," and his "doll-like stillness" (2:178).[28]

The Narcissus myth survived in a number of versions in addition to Ovid's. One of them, by Pausanias, relates that Narcissus had a twin sister who resembled him exactly in appearance. Narcissus fell in love with this sister (the feminized representation of himself), and when she died he consoled himself by gazing into his water-mirror. What this Narcissus sees in the reflection is not himself—he dismisses that as quickly as Ovid's Narcissus does—but rather an image of the dead sister. He satisfies his love-lost longing by disavowing his own image and metamorphosing it, feminizing it, into an object representing an other who is, ultimately, himself.[29] That interchange of reflection and projection readily recalls Horacio, who likewise mingles himself with the absent object of his love, absent because it represents the "dead" María, the lost mother imago, the inaccessible idealized woman. Hortensia, like Narcissus's feminized reflection, stands in for the absence, and through her "immortality" she at once defends Horacio from the other feared absence, death. Both Pausanias's Narcissus and Hernández's Horacio find relief and refuge by gazing at an eroticized reflection of the self that they misinterpret as other and as feminine. The lover, as Plato put it, "looks into his beloved as into a mirror, without being aware that he is doing so."[30] Hegel expands on the idea by noting that the spirit—Horacio's for our purposes—"must be presented to itself as an object, but at the same time straightaway annul and transcend this objective form; it must be its own object in which it finds itself reflected."[31] If in normal cases "Being in love consists in a flowing-over of ego-libido on to the object," then here we have a hyperbolic distortion of the same: self-love is projected onto a prop (reflection, doll) and then retrieved in a roundabout celebration of autoeroticism.[32] Narcissists are "plainly seeking *themselves* as a love object," but always through the detour of an other.[33] "It is precisely because the mirror [or doll] has no image of its own that it can 'mirror' by showing something else."[34] The mirror deludes "a beholder who does not realize that the mirror [doll] is a mirror, that the reflected image is distinct from, or is ontologically dependent on, the object reflected."[35] Vivification of the image or doll fortifies the disavowal of such dependence and makes Horacio's game all the more exciting; even though the dolls present "a virgin surface passively receiving the other's messages," this virgin seems to have some experience.[36] Like Echo in Ovid's Narcissus myth, the dolls have no discursive capacity other than to reflect—in its etymological sense of "to turn or bend back"—the words and projections cast onto them. Reflection, however, implies inversion. This is expressed in the narratives in question as male becomes female, negations become affirmations, and subject becomes object. The speaking subject (here, Horacio) has his negated desire returned as an affirmation, as a request from a feminized reflection, and therefore acts not compelled by his own perversion but in fulfillment of the desire—even the demands—of the other. The mirror image always comes back to the subject with a "negative affirmation": Narcissus says *no*, Echo *yes*; Narcissus says *yes*, but his image on the water *no*; Pausanius's Narcissus and Horacio say *no* to their reflected selves but this comes back as a *yes* from a feminized other.[37] In a closed interpretive circuit Horacio sees the idealized female in her absence by looking at a representation of himself (Hortensia), and in her presence— which can only be a surrogate presence via Hortensia—he sees himself by looking at her. The common denominators are the omnipresence of the narcissistic self and the depiction of the female as an independent player while she is clearly a self-object in Horacio's service. The motif of the unattainable woman throughout Hernández's canon is grounded in these dynamics: she is unattainable because she is an idealized internal object "poured into" unworthy receptacles, but also because—à la Narcissus— she represents the reflected self and her image is stirred, "confused," when it is touched.

The feminine characteristics of Narcissus in all versions of the myth further contribute to constructing a context in which the narcissist— Horacio—is fused with the object of his love. In Ovid's version the trans- formation of Narcissus into a flower is one such gesture suggesting his femininity. The dead body vanishes because Narcissus "disappears" into the flower representing him. This exchange of identity is of central impor- tance in the present context, since "Hortensia" is, among other things, the name of a flower (Hydrangea), and its homonym is etymologically derived from the Latin *hortus*, meaning "garden." Hortensia-as-flower can be readily integrated into the plant conceit developed in Hernández's *ars poetica* "A False Explanation of My Stories," but most relevant in the present context is the replacement of Hor-acio by a flower (Hor-tensia), just as Narcissus was replaced by the flower that now bears his name.[38]

The narcissus flower developed its own tradition as an instrument of illusion and deceit. Its luster and fragrance—both of them narcotic, as the root of "Narcissus" provides—were used to fascinate Persephone so that Hades could abduct and hold her as the unwilling queen of the underworld.[39] The flower here functions like the water-mirror that mesmerizes and in a loose sense "imprisons" Narcissus, and like the mirror used by the Titans to fascinate and then dismember Dionysus. One is spellbound by the representation of an eroticized self-object and led as a result to destruction. In Hernández's canon Hortensia consolidates these poetics: she is both a flower (by virtue of her name) and a mirror (by virtue of the function she serves for Horacio), and Horacio's fascination with her results in his destruction à la Narcïssus (he turns into a flower/doll), à la Persephone (he is erotically "imprisoned" in an underworld epitomized by the showcase gallery), and à la Dionysus (he is fragmented, as we shall see).

Freud recognized in "On Narcissism: An Introduction" that under certain circumstances objects imbued with unconscious fantasies can displace actual interpersonal relationships. Such a displacement is readily apparent in *The Hortensias*, "Except Julia," "The Balcony," and "The Usher," among other texts by Hernández. Later, in "Mourning and Melancholia," Freud described the process by which a lost external object is replaced by an internal one that is modeled on it. A cleavage and consequent interplay between "the critical activity of the ego" and "the ego as altered by identification" with the lost object characterize these dynamics. Several other works by Freud (notably "Fetishism" and "Splitting of the Ego in the Process of Defence") further establish the defensive division of the ego. Object-relations theorists later described how each "subdivision of ego"—or what one Hernández narrator describes as "an unknown space in myself" (3:53)—is "capable of generating experience . . . in a mode modelled after one's sense of an object."[40] Wilfred Bion's discussion of "projective identification," or what I have been calling narcissistic projection, describes how this object is manipulated to play a role in the projecting subject's fantasy, much as Winnicott's transitional objects are recruited for subjective use. Other analysts in the tradition of Melanie Klein similarly argue that "Projective identification is the result of the projection of parts of the self into an object."[41] Bion envisioned "a defensive splitting of the mind into parts that include active suborganizations of the mind which then experience themselves as having become things."[42] Internal objects are "split-off aspects of the ego which have been 'projected into' mental representations of objects."[43] There is an object in the world (woman, doll, reflection), then the internal object which transforms it into a split-off extension of the projecting subject that "has become a thing."

Hernández's object-relations poetics belongs to a long tradition beginning with Ovid himself and coming forward through notable accomplishments such as Goethe's *Wilhelm Meister's Apprenticeship*, in which "the various women he [Wilhelm] encounters seem to be but fragmentary parts of himself."[44] The same phrase holds true for Horacio, with the exception that his "women" are inanimate surrogates and thereby highlight the objectification, the thingness, of "split-off aspects" of the psyche. If in "Except Julia" the tunnel owner himself is greatest object of the tunnel (2:79), then it may be said that Horacio is likewise the greatest object of his showcases. Amidst their galleries of transitional objects these characters become transitional objects to themselves.[45]

In perfecting himself as his own ideal object, the narcissist unloads his negative attributes by projecting them onto the objects that he otherwise, or at other moments, exalts; we saw these dynamics previously in Hernández's alternating idealization and devaluation of the love partner and in his ambivalent relation with his mother and the "masters." Horacio, menaced by the fear of death, "engages in an unconscious fantasy of ejecting an unwanted or endangered aspect of himself and of depositing that part of himself in another person in a controlling way."[46] The "other person" is here the doll, demetaphorized through Horacio's projective animation of it, while at the same time its status as inanimate, "dead" matter makes it the ideal recipient for the death-fear projected into it. A doll "contains"—as Bion put it—the projection; Horacio's investment of fantasy and private meanings is integrated into the doll's internal constitution.[47]

Hortensia as a "container" of projections assumes its fullest meaning when Horacio has the doll refabricated into a literal receptacle, a vessel. The element contained by the doll—water—then recycles back to the Narcissus and reflection themes insisted by the text around it. The water held by the Hortensia dolls functions not only as a warming agent that "enlivens" these "corpses" but also as an internalized reflector. The water-mirror in the doll, like the glass mirror on Horacio's wall, is covered, the latter with a curtain and the former with ersatz skin, with masks, overdetermined clothes, costumes, or disguises, and with projections that give these layers their meanings. The water inside the dolls, doubling as a mirror, reiterates the theme of Horacio's reflexive projections "contained" by the dolls that he has "penetrated." This fluid, internalized mirror capable of reproducing Horacio recalls the link between mirrors and sperm underscored by Borges: "mirrors and copulation are abominable, since they both multiply the numbers of man."[48] Copulation with the dolls, like narcissistic projection and like the pouring-in of the water-mirror, deposits the potential for reproducing Horacio inside the Hortensias. The progressive multiplication of dolls containing these internalized means of reproducing Horacio stands in for the multiplication of Horacio himself, a mass production of Horacios, which itself dramatizes the fragmentation of Horacio into split-off parts jettisoned as they "become things." Horacio's disintegrating psyche is objectified in the multiplication of self-objects with which the world around him is populated.

The Covered Mirror

The glass mirror common today dates from Roman times; metallic mirrors came into use much earlier, in the Bronze Age, and were themselves preceded by water reflectors. In many cultures mirror reflections, along with shadows, have been thought to represent a person's spiritual double or soul. Functioning something like a memory "continuously storing away its simulacra of people and things," mirrors are also frequently attributed the power to extract and to retain "the trace of every face they have ever reflected."[49] In Hernández's "The Flooded House," a natural mirror, water, is endowed with precisely this power. It retains presences of Margarita's dead husband and circulates them among additional otherworldly reflections that flow, ultimately, toward a mock wake for Margarita herself (3:76).[50] The poetics of the husband's presence mummified in these waters are similar to those of popular beliefs in northern India, where one avoided looking into mirrors in the houses of others because, after one's departure, one's soul held captive in these mirrors was susceptible to manipulation by the host.[51] Whether the departure is the simple leave-taking after a visit or the ultimate departure in death, something of the absent person is left behind and subject to exploitation. While Margarita enacts her ceremony with the residual remains of her husband for her own benefit, the narrator of "The Flooded House" has a separate agenda, believing that if he caters to and patronizes Margarita in her water rituals, then "she would confuse me with the memories of her husband, and I, afterwards, would be able to substitute for him" (3:83). The dearly departed, "retained" by the reflector and therefore vulnerable, is recruited into the service of distinct agendas.

Even more similar to retaining mirrors are the dolls of *The Hortensias*, endowed with the capacity to accumulate and then "transmit" the content of gazes. These properties of accumulation and transmission conform to Plutarch's belief that "quiet bodies of water [the dolls] and other mirrorlike surfaces [the dolls as mirrors] reflect the particles emitted from the evil eye in the act of vision." These particles can reflect back to the beholder and injure him, or can "lodge themselves in the flesh of [other] living creatures, influencing their thoughts and deforming their bodies."[52] The passage in Prov. 23:6 that warns, "Eat not thou the bread of him that hath an evil eye" also conforms to these poetics, as does the belief system of an Egyptian cook who would not purchase the sheep displayed in a butcher's shopwindow because "every beggar who passes by envies them; one might, therefore as well eat poison as such meat."[53] Common to all such examples is the gaze, particularly the envious or covetous gaze, empowered to penetrate and defile the objects that it strikes. In Hernández's canon, also in the context of a butcher shop, an ominous presence saturates "the faces of doors" from behind, and anyone who looks at the doors is harmed by a curse that stains "the depths of their eyes with an indelible poison" (3:60).

In *The Hortensias*, however, objects tend to receive and transmit the erotic rather than the destructive properties of the gaze. Projections penetrate the dolls until they are "full of omens" (2:145), and the dolls then function like a substation that emits what it has received in order to entangle unwitting players in a visual network. The displayed dolls receive "enormous quantities of greedy looks" that at some moments gather around their faces like clouds and at others "fly toward the faces of innocent women" and contaminate them. For this reason the dolls, like the character Irene discussed in the introduction, mediate mysterious relations between people and things, and like the manipulated mirror reflections are "hypnotized beings carrying out unknown missions and lending themselves to evil designs" (2:145).[54] A notebook fragment alludes to the same motif when disembodied thoughts in need of form borrow a face, any face that is handy, to express themselves, like a tired person who lies down wherever he finds room (3:201). A page later, "errant," "nomad," and "barefooted" thoughts that "must have hidden interests" position themselves before the narrator's eyes, so that when he sees an object he has the impression "that someone had been looking at it before" (3:202).[55]

The broken mirror as a portent of misfortune is understandable in the context of the mirror's capacity to retain reflections. One's soul, represented by one's image retained in the mirror, is fragmented when the mirror is broken, and, as the folk belief specifies, seven years are required to heal the soul (and to pay for the mirror).[56] The ancient Greeks' belief that a corpse has no shadow likewise subscribes to these poetics, since presumably the shadow is intrinsic to, identical with, or a dimension of the soul that departs. Anthropomorphic beings with no soul, such as Dracula, lack a reflection for the same reason, as do the protagonists of fantastic literature—Guy de Maupassant's "The Horla" or E. T. A. Hoffmann's "The Story of the Lost Reflection" are good examples—whose sold, abandoned, or otherwise lost shadows or reflections have taken on a life of their own. (If Horacio stood before a mirror and it did not reflect him, then "his body would not be of this world") (2:164). The reflection and the soul are similarly linked in the Melanesian belief that people who look into a certain pool die because an evil spirit abducts their reflections. The Basutos believe that a crocodile can kill people by dragging their reflections underwater, and the Zulus likewise have a terror of dark pools and the beasts within them who confiscate reflections.[57] These fears express variations—Horacio's among them—of self-gazing as detrimental or lethal: witness the ancient and unambiguous Indian *Laws of Manu*, "Let him not look at his own image in water." The ancient Greeks had a similar injunction, and Narcissus's tragic fate dramatizes the consequences of violating it.[58]

The Narcissus myth further attests that the danger of looking in the mirror is inextricably entangled with the erotic qualities of reflection. In antiquity "the backs of mirrors were decorated with scenes depicting social and erotic activities," and these mirrors were consulted, as ours are now, to make oneself desirable to others.[59] "Literary and iconographic evidence indicates that the mirror was an important attribute of Aphrodite, the goddess of love," and it was also associated with Venus through its use in adorning oneself.[60] Later Venus was depicted as a whore, and in related iconography Mary Magdalene counted the mirror among her attributes, John Mandeville associated the mirror with sinful allurement, and Luxuria was depicted holding a mirror.[61] The mirror is also associated with fertility in several cultures, among the Tibetans and Chinese is a symbol of the female sex organ, and for the Scythians was magically endowed with sexual powers.[62] Jews of the fifteenth century practiced rather specific mirror rituals to stimulate romantic love and sexual relations, while in Shakespeare the mirror represented the frailty of virginity.[63] Mirrors are used to enhance the eroticism of paintings, as they are likewise on the walls and ceilings of brothels and of certain no-tell motels available by the hour.

In Hernández's canon, particularly *The Hortensias*, the dolls as mirror surrogates are loaded with both the erotics of reflection and with the death, soul, and palimpsested-image properties commonly attributed to mirrors. The actual (rather than surrogate) mirrors of *The Hortensias*, however, tend toward the gloomy end of the spectrum as Horacio's enacts his morbid, ritualized, and quasi-comic fear of death. The very encounter with mirrors is itself frightening, so the mirrors of the "black house" must be covered with curtains to prevent Horacio from viewing his reflection.[64] On one occasion when the twin maids left the mirrors "naked" (2:160), "Horacio began to walk like a thief, hugging the wall; he reached the side of the wardrobe, pulled the curtain that should have been covering the mirror, and then did the same with the other wardrobe" (2:161). This practice of covering mirrors is not unique to Horacio (though his catoptricophobia is exemplary), but rather gains expression in several cultures in which it is customary to cover mirrors or to turn them to the wall upon the death of a member of the household. In an extension of the retentive-mirror poetics, various traditions hold that a person who sees himself in a mirror following the death of a loved one will himself die. "It is feared that the soul, projected out of the person in the shape of his reflection in the mirror, may be carried off by the ghost of the departed, which is commonly supposed to linger about the house till the burial."[65] If there is a sick person in the house, or if one is ill oneself, it is likewise advisable not to look into a mirror, lest one risk being sucked through the black hole of the looking glass to the ghostly hereafter on the other side. Mirrors are like foggy windows opening to an ominous beyond into which the soul can slip off or be abducted unawares. The fog dissipates in the spiritual world on the other side where we see "face to face," while "For now we see through a glass, darkly."[66] As George Herbert put it in the 1633 *The Temple*, "A man that looks on glass / On it may stay his eye / Or, if he pleaseth, through it pass, / And then the heaven espy." In less spiritual exercises mirrors also came to be associated with moribundity through their clinical use: a mirror placed in front of the mouth or beneath the nose was a common test to verify a patient's death.[67]

Horacio's mirror phobia subscribes to these poetics. He is not troubled when the mirror reflects objects, but "the dark color of his skin made him think about the wax figures [*muñecos*] he had seen in a museum on the afternoon that a salesman was killed" (2:161). The mirror's death-related qualities are suggested at least three times in the passage, first by the association of Horacio with the inanimate anthropomorphic figures that proliferate elsewhere in the text as dolls. While Horacio would like to stress the Hortensias as representative of immortality, these dolls' inert nature simultaneously emits a counterdiscourse signaling their affinity with death, with embalmed, "vivified" corpses. The death poetics are then echoed when the yellowish, postmortem, waxlike quality of the doll or the museum figure is extended to Horacio's face, and then again, on the next page, to his hands: "the skin on his hands also had the color of wax" (2:162).[68] And finally, the associative chain proceeding from the mirror to a deathish doll to a murdered salesman traces a path that leads back to Horacio, who was also a businessman in sales, and whose dolls and showcases are initially constructed on the prototype of mannequins in his shopwindow. The dead salesman associated with Horacio is then multiplied—as is Horacio's live body endlessly reproduced in "dead" Hortensias—by mention of other figures in the wax museum that also represent murder victims (2:162).[69]

As *The Hortensias* develops, Horacio becomes determined to combat his neurotic fear and to confront mirrors directly, but his reflective experiences nevertheless continue to be plagued by associations with death. He sees his face reflected through a mirror curtain made translucent by sunlight, and the rays make "his features glow like those of a ghost" (2:163).[70] Soon after, the "suspicious symptom" of encountering many mirrors in a single day puts Horacio back on guard: in the hotel where he takes refuge "he tried to climb the stairway without seeing himself in the mirrors" that flank it, partially because "the images got confused, he didn't know which way to go, and he even thought that there might be somebody hiding in the reflections" (2:163).[71] All of the hotel rooms have an abundance of mirrors—the one Horacio selects has three—and in the "confusion" of this labyrinth of reflection the eroticism is reintroduced as Horacio recalls that the hotel used to be a brothel. Horacio is therefore "not surprised" that there are so many mirrors (2:163), while the prostitutes' presence is implicitly retained in the depths of those "brittle emblems of corruption."[72] The overdetermined slot of "someone hiding" in the "confusion" of the reflections is thus filled once by the former prostitutes (not to mention their clients) whose faces and bodies burned into the mirrors now retaining them, and then again by María, who, coincidentally, is "hiding" in the same hotel where Horacio is lodged.

In the aftermath of another hotel episode, two of Horacio's reflectors—the actual mirror and the showcase as surrogate mirror—are consolidated. Horacio has mirrors installed in the showcase gallery in order to engender the multiplication of doll scenes in endless reflections, and now more than ever "No gaze is stable, or rather, in the neutral furrow of the gaze piercing at a right angle through the canvas [or the showcase], subject and object, the spectator and the model, reverse their roles to infinity."[73] The installation of "naked" mirrors, however, necessitates a compensatory reciprocal measure: Horacio wears the curtain over his face (2:166).[74] This new inversion—the face covered instead of the mirror—again associates Horacio with the dolls (since they are often masked or veiled, and always represent others "under cover") and with death (since the faces of the dead are covered). The borders are redrawn with this new placement of the curtain as Horacio's covered face calls into play the juxtaposition of the mirror and the mask—of seeing oneself versus disguising oneself. These two competing possibilities are reconciled finally as Horacio's intent is to see himself always but always disguised (in the showcases, the dolls, the "confusion").[75]

When the covered face becomes too troublesome, Horacio orders removal of the mirrors and has them positioned so that they continue to reflect at a downward angle but without threatening him with the possibility of reflection (2:166). Like the showcases, these mirrors now reflect only what Horacio permits them to reflect; they are humbled, tamed, subordinated: "the mirrors were servants that greeted him with their bodies bowed" (2:167).[76]

The fear of death associated with mirrors and the sight of one's reflection also interrelates *The Hortensias* with another of the central Narcissus themes, that of self-fascination. As understood in the perspective of evil-eye traditions, Narcissus perishes "through his own eyes." He is fascinated by them and then fatally wounded by destructive visual forces turning back on the subject emitting them. In the chapter of *Moralia* treating evil-eye beliefs, Plutarch describes the fascinator Eutelida's similar experience: "he casts the evil eye on himself, that baneful man, beholding self in river's eddy."[77] Plutarch further records the belief that young children could unwittingly fascinate themselves with the reflection of their own gaze.[78]

The fear of self-destruction through the reflected gaze is also prevalent in folk traditions. One case reports a "Sicilian with an evil eye so powerful that he bewitched himself on accidentally catching sight of himself in the mirror."[79] The eroticization of the evil eye in southern Italian traditions links it not only with the vision-sex-death cluster that will concern us in the next chapter but also again with Narcissus. Liriope, who bears Narcissus as a result of being raped, is told by the seer Tiresias that the boy will live to an old age provided he never comes to know (see) himself. Erotic attraction is then linked with death at every turn of the myth, beginning with Narcissus dying to know (in the biblical sense of the term) what he sees. Echo's love and Narcissus's death are then described in the same melting-wax trope, and both Echo and Narcissus are doomed to death-by-reflection as the penalty for erotically charged transgressions: Echo for defending Jove's adulterous orgy with the nymphs, and Narcissus for rejecting the amorous advances of various suitors.

The eroticized, destructive mirror is also amply expressed in the delusions of psychopathology. One patient was so terrified by sex that a mere glimpse of himself naked in the mirror would trigger a severe migraine.[80] Horacio is more careful, defending himself from the devastating fear of his eroticized reflection with curtains and "confusion," but the usher, unprotected like the patient, faints when his voyeuristic gaze reflects back to him (2:62). Another patient, this one psychotic, became obsessed by death at work on her face in the mirror. She scrutinized wrinkles, to be sure, but was mainly tortured by the delusion that large holes had been gouged beneath her eyes. This woman in one way and Horacio in quite another literalize Jean Cocteau's observation that "if you observe your whole life in a mirror you will see death at work."[81] Death at work is likewise evident in medieval Vanitas illustrations, which often feature a woman at her mirror accompanied by a death's-head or by Death personified.[82] The analyst of the woman with the gouged faced noted that "some inner force pushed her toward the mirror where although the picture was horrible she simply had to look." Attraction and dread, bliss and doom, compulsion toward the mirror and repulsion by its contents: Horacio holds these competing forces in common with the patient, but he negotiates his solution in mirror surrogates (showcases, dolls) that offer positive benefits and satisfy the compulsion while abating the negative fallout. "When she is not looking into the mirror [as Horacio does not, opting for surrogates] she sees throughout the day the mirror image of her changed face [Horacio's doll]." The world would therefore become her mirror, and "the vision would stand between her and another person," just as the objectified death fantasy—Hortensia—mediates all interpersonal relations in *The Hortensias*. The patient's death-image obsession was complemented by other delusions that are resonant in the context of *The Hortensias:* "she has the impression that she is in some way artificial" and that parts of her body are made of wood.[83] Her combined fear of death, dissociation, perception of self as artificial, and distortion of the reflected self into a grotesque other all recall the situation of Horacio, but with an important exception: until the conclusion of the story, when he himself becomes a kind of wind-up toy, a "toy-man" (1:82) "in some sense artificial," Horacio denies the depersonalized objectification of himself and postpones his ultimate fate by populating his world with the depersonalized objects (dolls) that represent him. In this regard Horacio's experiences are most closely related to another patient who saw others around him as "puppets in a marionette theatre." The other is objectified in a defensive strategy to save what is left of the self. This patient, like Horacio, and like the prototypical Hernández narrator groping from object to object with the poetics of naïveté, remarks: "I look upon the world the way an infant would look upon puppets whom he does not understand."[84]

THE MOTHER AND THE MIRROR

D. W. Winnicott's influential essay "Mirror-Role of Mother and Family in Child Development" explored the proposition that *"the precursor of the mirror is the mother's face."*[85] In the earliest stages of human development, when the infant "is unaware of its form" (3:73), "a vital part is played by the environment which is in fact not yet separated off from the infant." The mother is most important among these objects that are not yet differentiated as "environmental features." When the baby looks at the mother's face, "what the baby sees is himself or herself."[86] The breast-feeding infant sees him- or herself in the mother's eyes twice: first literally, as the infant gazes upward and appears in her eyes reflecting like mirrors, and then again figuratively, as the way in which the infant is seen (regarded) "in mother's eyes" will come to determines how the infant perceives him or herself.[87] It is this latter, figurative function of the mirror that Winnicott assigns to the mother's face. The mother is looking at the baby, and what she looks like in his or her perception *"is related to what she sees there."*[88] If the infant has what Winnicott calls the "good-enough mother," then the mirror of the mother's face "always assures the infant 'you are the fairest one of all,'" leaving his or her "blissful early world" and "state of joyful narcissistic self-experience" unchallenged.[89] Active mirroring begins, ironically, with the mother herself, who is disposed almost from the time of birth to imitate her infant, to reflect back "certain gestures which occur spontaneously within the baby's natural repertoire of activities."[90] By engaging in this dialogical mimesis the mother acts "as a psychobiological mirror, an active partner in the infant's developing capacity for social relations and the beginning of awareness of self-representation."[91] The infant's inaugural self-representation in the mirror of the mother's face is actually an other's reflected object representation; the child is malleable, formed by the mother's "impression."

When the mother is inadequate, many infants "have a long experience of not getting back what they are giving. They look and they do not see themselves." In compensation for the emptiness of the mother-mirror as an essential formative reflector—and here we intersect with the Hernández characters' narcissistic projection—these infants "look around for other ways of getting something of themselves back from the environment." Confused by their mother's violent mood shifts, they "grow up puzzled about mirrors and what the mirror has to offer." Winnicott's example is Francis Bacon, who owing to "some twist" in the dynamics of mirroring off his mother's face "goes on and on painting the human face distorted significantly."[92] The grotesque quality of Bacon's "twist" is generally alien to Hernández narrators, but though their aesthetics are less desperate these narrators also seem "puzzled about mirrors and what the mirror has to offer." In the early "Wrong Hands," for example, we read: "I looked in amazement at her face as though at a lake in which I had dropped an object, and I watched the waves that it produced without knowing what the object was" (1:175). The reflector's surface is, like Narcissus's, distorted by ripples caused by one's own "dropped" identity. Elsewhere the unreliability of what is supposed to be a high-fidelity, nonselective reflector makes a more general assault at the quest for self-identity: "the mirrors were blurred" (2:120).[93]

This out-of-focus, "blurred mirror" quality that confounds the boundaries between objects is also prevalent in Hernández's work, notably in *The Hortensias*. The body of a black cat, for example, "was confused with the color of the piano"; two blacknesses overlap and intermingle, and in homage to the central image of another text, "The Usher," the erased body leaves behind only the cat's glowing eyes (2:173). Another type of world-as-mirror distortion concerns a quasi-paranoid perception that engenders a "twist" reminiscent of Bacon. In one instance mirrors are leaning against chairs and "between the legs of the chairs they reflected the floor and gave the impression that it was twisted" (2:167). The twisted yields to the grotesque as the degrees of paranoia and estrangement become greater: when Horacio is near the river attempting an illicit tryst with someone else's doll, the physiognomy of a boy passing by features a "a huge head making horrible faces . . . only his mouth moved, a mouth as horrifying as a detached piece of intestine" (2:172).[94]

When Francis Bacon was asked if he preferred to have models present or to be alone while painting, he indicated an unequivocal preference to be "Totally alone. With their memory." The absence of the painting's subject facilitated Bacon's agenda to "distort the thing far beyond the appearance, but in the distortion to bring it back to a recording of the appearance."[95] The metafictional preoccupation with distortion of memories in Hernández's canon has an affinity with Bacon's dictum, "Totally alone. With their memory," but quite contrary to Bacon's conscious distortion of memories Hernández's narrators are troubled by the human incapacity to sift "events in themselves" from the distorting glosses cast over them by temporal distance and by the secondary revision of recollection. One narrator is "tortured" by a "secret anguish" precisely because the text and the memory that it ostensibly represents are not synchronized to his satisfaction. When he reflected on past events, "memories were deformed, and he loved the facts too much to allow them to be deformed; he tried to narrate them with total exactness, but he soon realized that it was impossible" (1:126). In the most interesting cases of such distortions, the word "reflection" overlays its mirroring qualities on its broader meaning as "thinking" or "pondering." Water, mirror, and memory are inseparably related in Hernández's canon because they are all subject—and one's self-identity with them—to an intrinsic and distorting fluidity. "When the water of memory moves," the images that it carries are "deformed" as though the "knots in the glass" of an ordinary mirror were set in motion (2:29). If one applies this trope to the texts developing it, Hernández's fiction itself evidences a retentive, choppy fluidity that reflects but also distorts this reflection to the measure and the rhythm of its movement swirling around "knots."

A confusion of an object with its representation and a complementary flattening effect in interpersonal relations are also consequences of an inadequately "reflective" mother and are both commonplace in Hernández. "If the mother's face is unresponsive, then a mirror is a thing to be looked at but not to be looked into."[96] The mirror becomes static, dead, nondialogical— a kind of framed, frigid portrait of the self-as-other, a blank gaze from the face of a doll. The adult needs for affection, caressing, and lovemaking "have their origins in the shared gaze, touch, holding and vocal 'conversations' of infant and mother."[97] Through symbolization these "conversations" with the mother's body are adapted to all object relations; their imprint is particularly legible in amorous relations or, those lacking, in autoeroticism.[98] A character like Horacio evidences a breakdown in this interactive, interpersonal origin of human affection because his relations with the world and his autoerotic rituals displacing true amorous relations are monological and unilateral, as epitomized by his "conversations" with the blank mirror-faces of the dolls that he uses to make love to himself. Horacio's covered mirrors, blurred mirrors, blank mirrors, and doll mirrors all attest to the impossibility of "seeing" oneself when the mirror of human interaction is lacking, pathologically distorted, or absent.

The infant's first perception of himself or herself as an introjection of an external interpretation is paralleled in the myth of Narcissus. When Narcissus's first true mirror, the pool, returns an enamored, admiring gaze, this reflector recalls in the depth of its surface the faces of Liriope (his mother, herself a water nymph) and of the suitors who were the reflector's precursors. There is a stable congruity between what Narcissus has seen of himself in the faces of others and what he sees in the pond. To look into the mirror is to look through the translucent mother imago and on to oneself behind it, but that self is always partially constituted by the mother's formative gaze, still misconstrued in the depths of the psyche as an authentic self-reflection. In the looking glass one confronts "the durable mark of the mirror which alienates man in his own reflection," thanks to "the subterranean persistence of the exclusive relation to the mother."[99] A female analysand overly concerned with "putting on her face" before the mirror therefore exaggerated "the task of getting the mirror to notice and approve. The woman had to be her own mother."[100] After surveying mirror imagery in a range of literature a critic comes to the same conclusion: "What a woman sees in such a mirror is, of course, her mother."[101]

In the case of male beholders, the mother is in the mirror of the lover's face, and the self is reflected from that mother-lover composite. Consider Horacio as an example: when he looks at Hortensia he looks through the layers of representation that constitute her identity—a mother layer, a María layer—but when his reflection returns from the doll he ultimately registers not the mother nor María, but himself. The same dynamics are more explicitly enacted by James Joyce's Stephen Dedalus, who after writing a love poem "went into his mother's bedroom and gazed at his face for a long time in the mirror of her dressingtable."[102] The mother, the lover, and the self coalesce in a reverie, a "confusion," that intermingles memorial reflections with current ones and with projections. When actual mirrors rather than doll-mirrors are concerned, Horacio is not so bold as Stephen Dedalus; rather than facing the mother-mirror with his reflective gaze—

rather than, in effect, facing her down to find his own face behind or within hers—Horacio opts for evasion. He veils the mother, drawing a curtain to foreclose her omnipresence and covering the mirror that in this perspective seems almost her framed portrait. If "it is an essential property of the mirror that it simultaneously reflects the child *and* mother," then Horacio's mirror aversion and his covering of mirrors can be understood not only as a simple expression of his fear of death but also as an avoidance of the mother's haunting image in the mirror, of "death by drowning," by absorption, into the mother-mirror.[103] This nexus of the mother image, the reflected or doubled self, and death is also curiously represented in a tale concerning the popular English belief that one standing on the church porch at midnight of Saint Mark's Eve can see all of those who will die within the year. One man on the right porch at the right time had the misfortune of seeing himself: "he could not be mistaken: the figure had turned and looked him full in the face, and he knew himself as surely as when he glanced into mother's looking-glass."[104]

When the mother's face as mirror is eventually replaced by the actual mirror, the infant—like Narcissus—initially presumes his reflection to be another person; he reaches out, he kisses, he woos.[105] A five- or six-month-old baby situated before a mirror with a parent recognizes the parent's image prior to recognizing his or her own. In an experiment described by Maurice Merleau-Ponty, "A child smiles in the mirror at the image of his father. At this moment his father speaks to him. The child appears surprised and turns toward the father." At first, the child "is surprised that the voice comes from another direction than that of the visible image in the mirror" and "gives the image and the model an existence relatively independent of each other"; he then negotiates a reunion, a consolidation, of the father in the mirror and the father belonging to the voice that speaks beside him.[106] With that feat accomplished the child later, at about eight months, overcomes the difficulties of self-identification and recognizes his or her own body reflected in the mirror.

> The child is dealing with two visual experiences of his father: the experience he has from looking at him and that which comes from the mirror. Of his own body, on the other hand, the mirror image is his only complete visual evidence. He can easily look at his feet and his hands but not at his body as a whole. Thus for him it is a problem first of understanding that the visual image of his body which he sees over there in the mirror is not himself, since he is not in the mirror but here, where he feels himself; and second, he must understand that, not being located there, in the mirror, but rather where he feels himself introceptively, he can nonetheless be seen by

an external witness *at the very place at which he feels himself to be* and with the same visual experience that he has from the mirror. In short, he must displace the mirror image, bringing it from the apparent or virtual place it occupies in the depth of the mirror back to himself, whom he occupies at a distance with his introceptive body.[107]

Mirror anxiety is experienced by some children as the result of this split between self and image, of being oneself and one's audience simultaneously. Exteriorization of the body image is disconcerting, because the child kinesthetically feels his or her gestures and claims them on the basis of the body's sensations, but simultaneously sees the gestures "othered," appearing to be those of the spectral double in the mirror. For the child as for Horacio, "The momentary lack of discrimination between reality and fantasy and between me and non-me produces the experience of the uncanny. . . . The reflected image poses to the child the problem of being *me* (since it moves in perfect synchrony with the kinesthetically perceived movements of the body) and *non-me* (because it is an external reality, outside the child's body boundaries)."[108] The real mirror horrifies Horacio because, among other reasons we have seen, it blatantly, crudely, intermingles subject and object; it must remained covered with a curtain to preempt this "split." Mirror surrogates like the dolls, on the other hand, can have their curtains drawn, their dresses opened, because they themselves mask the subject (Horacio) behind the objects (dolls) that represent him. They allow Horacio to simultaneously "see himself" and avoid himself, to see himself while looking at an other but not at himself-as-other, and to create with this masquerade of me and non-me the moderate "confusion" that he finds pleasing.

Merleau-Ponty's account of early mirroring experiences also stresses the child's realization that he or she can "be seen by an external witness *at the very place at which he feels himself to be* and with the same visual experience that he has from the mirror." In the act of recognizing the reflected self, the child registers the cognition that he or she can be seen by others; "I am certain that there are some eyes that are watching me live" (3:200). The mirror, already associated with the mother ("present next to the Mirror" as well as inside it), comes to seem omniscient, panoptic, like the magical mirrors of folklore.[109] The mirror *sees* and *knows*, the mirror surveils, "never ceasing to observe him" (2:167); the mirror—like customs agents, Santa Claus, and God—can discover the guilty party "simply by looking at the faces" (1:86). This capacity to see all and see through all is an attribute of the mother and her surrogates: Petrona, for example, "observed others and with great facility discovered, precisely, the slightest extravagance to which a person had succumbed" (1:35). Elsewhere the mother surrogate and the omniscient mirror are linked more explicitly: first we meet "an aunt who was like a wardrobe with mirrors," and we then learn that "there was nothing that didn't fall within her mirrors" (2:22). In "Ursula" the narrator relates that the eyes of a fixed stare "were as firm as a mirror and I had to turn my head" (3:119). Stared down by such menacing omniscience, the boy's opportunity to carry out, or even fantasize about, his adolescent sexual curiosities could be found only at siesta time, precisely because during that hour the adults "had their eyes closed" (3:50). The window of opportunity opens when the panoptic eye closes, but the boy is nevertheless always subject to later scrutiny by the penetrating gaze of the mother-mirror that can coerce his face into betraying him.

The panoptic properties assigned to mirrors has a long and multicultural history. Prester John, to cite one notable medieval legend, owed his power to a miraculous mirror that revealed all plots against him as well as all good deeds done in his service, and Merlin fabricated a similar mirror for King Arthur.[110] On this side of the Atlantic, the Aztecs associated obsidian reflectors with the god Tezcatlipoca, who through use of the mirror gained an omniscient panorama of his domain.[111] Panopticism is further suggested in the many magical powers assigned to mirrors in the most diverse literary and folk traditions: mirrors expose deceptive appearances, surveil rivals and monitor the fidelity of lovers, herald the approach of enemies, reveal the splendors of the world, and identify the location of hidden treasures.[112] Mirrors that foretell the future, answer questions, depict far-off places, and reveal the past similarly evidence panoptic qualities.[113]

In Hernández's canon the quasi-paranoid sense of being surveilled— particularly while committing some erotic transgression—commences with the mirror associated with parental authority and then extends to other objects. Glass-as-reflector is common among them: "The cross-eyed panes of the patio doors were looking at me" (2:104). In *The Lost Horse* the surveillance is generalized and distributed across the entire ambience in which the narrator's adolescent escapades are enacted, resulting again in the transparent (= reflected) self: "Celina and all those inhabitants of her living room [by which he means the furniture] looked at me from the side; and if they looked at me straight on their gazes passed through me as though I were not present" (2:38). The mirror-mother and her agents keep the boy under constant observation, reiterating their capacity to "see through" him and to thereby dissipate his subjectivity and reveal his disguised intentions. In the context of this prohibitive and intrusive maternal gaze, Horacio's covered mirrors register yet another determinant: the mother in the mirror is not merely veiled but rather her eyes are blindfolded so as to deprive her visual access to her naughty son's erotic rituals, and to therefore afford the private, open forum necessary for uninhibited celebration of Horacio's extravaganza. Even when her mirror is covered, however, mother is not so easily defeated, either because her X-ray vision penetrates the swathes that blind her or because she or her agents escape the rigor of their confinement. The ominous possibility of "an immense eye" in "a hole in the curtain" keeps the paranoid Hernández character policing himself under the surveillance of his own.fear and guilt (3:113).[114]

The panoptic maternal eye has also turned up in some other holes more loaded than the one in the curtain. While listening to Byron recite lines from "Christabel" about the lady's breasts, for example, Percy Bysshe Shelley sprang to his feet, screamed, and ran from the room: he had had a vision of a woman with eyes in place of her nipples. When pursued into the present context, Shelley's image suggests vision itself sucked out with the milk of a four-eyed mother, a woman who takes advantage of nursing her child or pleasing her lover in order to surveil, by the eye of her breast, what is going on inside. Even this image is modest, however, in comparison to those of Georges Bataille's *Story of the Eye*, in which eyes are insistently inserted into Simone's vagina and anus.[115] In Latin American literature a similar motif is central to Ernesto Sábato's "Report on the Blind," where a statue of a naked woman-monster features a shining "Phosphorescent Eye" in its naval. The eye mesmerizes the protagonist, summoning him fatally to penetrate it and to enter the tunnel—an archetypal rebirth-in-reverse canal—into which it opens once punctured.[116] In Sábato's next novel, *Abaddón: el exterminador*, the menacing maternal eye is sexually pierced and extinguished in a gesture reminiscent of Odysseus and the Cyclops. The protagonist S. "saw that instead of genitals Soledad had an enormous, greenish gray eye." This vaginal eye observing him is penetrated—"yielding its fragile elasticity until it burst"—and blinded by ritual fornication.[117] Not Oedipus but the mother herself is blinded by this "incest," and the mother will therefore no longer be able to see her son's "incest" symbolically repeated on the bodies of the lovers who replace her.

In Hernández's "unfinished" poetics solutions are never so drastic; the surveilling eye is not yet extinguished and only inadequately covered, and consequently the penetrating, panoptic gaze—the mother's or others'— gains access to the quasi-erotic forays that the protagonist is often eager to disguise. *Lands of Memory* offers a fine illustration when the boy alone in a bathroom (which of course counts a mirror among its standard fixtures) feels as though he is "surrounded by people" (3:29). The boy checks around to verify his solitude before pulling a pair of panties out of the hamper, but he nevertheless cannot rid himself of "the idea that I've already been seen"

(3:31).[118] On his "adulterous" adventure with someone else's doll Horacio similarly fears that he is being watched "despite the solitude of the place" (2:172), and in this same vein he imagines that his wife was spying on him when he crossed the glass/mirror barrier of a showcase and "entered the scene to look at the details" (2:140). On another occasion one of the dolls, Eulalia, is herself referred to as "the spy" (2:167). Later in Hernández's canon the narrator of the "Diary of Shamelessness" affirms that even his most essential self "must be under strict surveillance" (3:192). The "Diary" makes clear that, for Hernández, behind the mother in the mirror is a self subjected to the scrutiny of a reflexive panopticism, a self-reflection so determined and obsessive (and yet so self-deceiving) that it doubles the subject and then multiplies him in receding reflections.

In *The Lost Horse* the omniscience generally associated with the mother assumes another dimension—reminiscent of Merleau-Ponty's father-in-the-mirror example—when the paternal gaze is introduced. An oedipal pattern dominates here as a mother surrogate is the object seen and desired by a boy until his quasi-erotic designs are frustrated by the panoptic and pro-hibitive father. The boy casts his lustful gaze on the photographic portrait of a woman—"she was like a great dessert that was delicious no matter where one tasted it"—but the woman's husband is framed beside her, and the stern, patriarchal countenance of his portrait intercedes with its countergaze: "he always looked me straight between the eyes. Even when I walked from one place in the living room to another and bumped into a chair, his eyes followed the center of my pupils. And it was inevitably I who had to lower my gaze" (2:11). The father's eyes are inescapable, and the boy's lowered gaze is simultaneously a forfeiture of the object of his desire (he no longer lustfully looks at the mother) and a gesture conceding his subordination to the paternal power that humbles him.[119] In compensa-tion the boy scripts an imaginary line that recruits the mother-portrait as his ally: "Don't pay any attention to him, I understand you, my dear," the woman-portrait seems to tell him, thereby liberating the boy from the restric-tive paternal gaze and yielding herself lovingly to his designs (2:11). The boy is nevertheless overwhelmed by the father's greater power and he is consequently obliged to avert his gaze and to suffer "the anguish of humili-ation" (2:12).[120] The boy as seer, as subject of the gaze, is thereby trans-formed, as in the mirror, into the object seen. The boy's desire to "humiliate" the woman reflects back to him off of the face of the father and results in his own humiliation. And yet the discourse of this entire psychodrama is proper to no one other than the projecting boy at its source, since the mute and inanimate portraits—like Horacio's dolls—merely reflect whatever is projected onto them. Ultimately it is the boy's own eye that surveils him disguised as the eye of another. The self-spying Hernández narrator can never be for and in himself, "cannot surrender to the experience," and consequently "retains a split-off, dissociated manipulative ego-control of the situation," a spying eye that is integral to the self but that observes and monitors it, restricts and punishes it, from an exterior vantage point.[121] As Mikhail Bakhtin observed, "To be means to be for the other, and through him, for oneself. Man has no internal sovereign territory; he is all and always on the boundary; looking within himself, he looks *in the eyes of the other* or *through the eyes of the other*."[122]

A reaction formation protesting omniscient surveillance and appropriating the powerful eye responsible for it is evident in much of Hernández's work, most explicitly in the projecting eye light central to "The Usher." The early text that opens the *Book Without Covers* also pursues panopticism, but in a different direction, by exploring its relation to narcissism. A narcissist sentenced by the gods to hang from the ring around Saturn is given "a great power of vision and of intelligence so that he could see what was happening on Earth" (1:79). His vision will become progressively more powerful provided that he—like Narcissus—does not think about himself. Inverse commodities are bartered: introspection is stifled but then transformed, directed outward in the surveilling omniscience elsewhere associated with parents. In exchange for not reflecting (on) himself (not seeing himself in the mirror of himself), the protagonist is empowered to see others from the privileged vantage point of panopticism. Should he default on his end of the bargain, however, the heights of the position's privilege will measure the depths of his fall: "He made a superhuman effort not to think about himself," for if his vision were reflexive rather than projective, then "his hands would weaken and he would lose his hold on the ring." Self-reflection spells doom for this protagonist as much as for Narcissus, but—as in the cases of Horacio and the usher—that doom can be postponed by seeing others in the displaced locus of the self.

DISSOCIATION AND THE DOUBLE

> *I would to God I for a while might from my bodie part.*
> —Ovid's Narcissus,
> (Arthur Golding translation)

Whether the result of division, duplication, or—most frequently—the two combined, the double in literature is represented by reflections, shadows, substitutions, impersonations, twins, impostors, portraits, corporal clones, role exchanges, transferred souls, migrating identities, and split personalities, to mention only the most common manifestations. Hernández's treatment of the double is perhaps most readily understood when examples are classified and considered within the provisional categories of division and duplication. Generation of the double by division, which I shall first consider, is manifest primarily by dissociation and depersonalization. Duplication, as most evidently exemplified in *The Hortensias*, commences with an initial splitting that is then multiplied by a proliferation of doubles representing the progressive fragmentation of a subject, in this case Horacio.

Division

Having observed himself self-consciously during social calls, the historian Hippolyte Taine remarked: "I always feel as if I were a speaking automaton, or rather as if my ego were stationed outside, whilst a carefully dressed gentleman is making bows and polite speeches on my behalf."[123] A sensation of estrangement and alienation in social situations likewise plagued Hernández throughout his life, and his literature from its adolescent beginnings to its self-scrutinizing conclusion in the "Diary of Shamelessness" is predicated on the assumption that "The human being is his body and yet at the same time stands outside it, viewing the body as an object."[124] As a young pianist touring the Uruguayan provinces, Hernández—here in the grandiose swing of his narcissism—enjoyed the perception of himself as an exceptional talent. If he performed before uncultured audiences in the makeshift auditoriums of towns like Pico, Chivilcoy, Tres Arroyos, or any other "small town asleep with the dream of a brute," this in no way reflected negatively on his virtuosity. Rather, Hernández dismissed these demeaning piano tours as economic necessities, as the *via crucis* to which crude realities had doomed him. The carefully dressed gentleman making bows indeed doubled for the ego held in reserve, an ego tortured constantly because, as Hernández put it, "I am not living what is mine." Everything seemed to be "provisional and belonging to others" because a parenthesis opened in Hernández's life without its closure in sight, and consequently the realization of the grandeur—or even the normalcy—that he promised himself was constantly pushed out of range by forces that seemed to conspire against him.[125]

If one does not struggle constantly for its survival, the reserved self is gradually defeated and subsumed—or at least besieged—by the "other" that circumstances impose. "Because of despondency, solitude, incomprehension, and unselfishness I renounced what is mine and began to die in sensations that aren't my life, in a heavy and idiotic somnambulism that horrifies me, and you have no idea how desperately I try to wake myself up."[126] When after his concerts members of the audience would approach him and oblige him to endure their tedious harangues, Hernández would prop up the smiling gentleman in the tuxedo—"I left my face and took off [*Dejé la cara y me fui*]," as he put it—and would repair into his inner anguish.[127] Sometimes friends would similarly notice that Hernández had "gone" and "left his face," a face "without a doubt as inexpressive as the suit that we leave hanging on a chair while we sleep" (3:144). In *Lands of Memory* the narrator is doubly bothered by the face's vulnerability, noting that he "would have preferred death" to allowing someone "to discover my thoughts on my surrendered face," and then that the faced needed to be defended "as though it were a sleeping woman" (3:13). A later text meditating on the division between the face as a mask and a more authentic identity undisclosed behind it wonders "if my face belongs to my body or to my thoughts" (3:201). The disassociated face transcends the mask's inertia and is capable of acting of its own volition: "my face, on its own, began to cry" (3:102). A face is a front, a portrait that never manages to fully resemble its subject (3:43). It is shaped from without as much as from within because it is caught in the negotiations not only of mind-body dialectics but also of interactions between self and other.

Having dismissed his demeaning tours as insignificant, the great pianist, already doubled, already masked, eventually finds his fragile grandeur overwhelmed by insecurity as reality intrudes incessantly and reduces his lofty aspirations to mere dreams. During the early 1940s Hernández agonized over career choices in a series of letters addressed to his wife at the time, Amalia Nieto, but after entertaining the options he always returned, as his only viable option, to the provincial tours that he dreaded. As a pianist he felt himself lacking in resources and in, "simply, security," because the desire to "take on greater things" resulted in the premature abandonment of pieces already learned but not mastered. The gains were never consolidated "because the action of concretizing, of 'fixing,' was [more] an inferior function of the spirit than that of understanding or being or working in what is most lived by the imagination when it advances or progresses toward something in the making."[128] While the poetics of the "unfinished" combining with "the movement of an idea in formation" make for admirable fiction, they served as obstacles in the professional advancement of Hernández as a pianist (1:184).

A more accomplished piano career—entailing, as Hernández saw it, performing live or on radio in Buenos Aires—was dismissed because Hernández's limited repertoire left him feeling inadequate to the task. "I don't have sufficient works nor the facility to augment them rapidly and to deliver the diverse program demanded by radio and by the other opportunities that one must take advantage of in the big cities."[129] One must take advantage, and yet Hernández's "deficiency" handicapped him and foreclosed the possibility. He therefore made his peace with the reality that undermined his fantasy: "I try to adapt to this life whenever possible, so as not to become embittered." Hernández resigned himself to the provincial itinerary, arguing that he had no choice and insisting that he delivered himself with abnegation to a livelihood *that I have not chosen*, nor does it form part of any ideal—it would be ideal to tour to big cities, but not to these small towns that I know already all too well."[130] When aggravated by Nieto's insistence on tangible accomplishment and reasonable financial stability, Hernández's suffered from a profound sense of failure, frustration, and guilt, all of which further undermined his already beleaguered and debilitated illusion of self-worth. In his optimistic moments he perceived himself to be on the threshold of the success that would more than compensate for the brinksmanship of his protracted, formative agony: "While I had not completely ceased to be who I was and while I was not yet who I was called to be, I had time to suffer a very unique anguish" (2:29). Hernández's response to the "call," however, always seemed somehow inadequate, and the internal space of the ego held in reserve was gradually emptied as its dreams were depleted, leaving only the call's echo reverberating in its hollows. The armor of the carefully dressed gentleman ultimately had nothing left to protect; only an absence with a smiling facade remained, a "confusion" of identities, a face that came off with the mask.[131] The haunting interrogation *Who am I?* that runs through the letters to Amalia Nieto is, in Hernández's literary canon, transformed and corporally distributed into *Where am I?* As Fredric Jameson has observed, "Alienation of the subject is displaced by fragmentation of the subject," because the dissociated pieces begin to drift.[132]

The dissociated body and Hernández's piano career are linked in the literary canon right from the precocious beginning that is elaborated in "My First Concert." The narrator, already jittery on the eve of his debut performance, is thrown further off balance by "two big posters" that announce his name "in enormous letters." He remarks: "If the letters had been smaller, perhaps my obligation would not have been so great" (2:97). The boy repeatedly rehearsing his entrance onto the stage finds himself plagued by a self-consciousness so excessive that it disrupts the natural fluidity of his movements. On the night of the concert itself the pressure gets the better of him and reality begins to warp—the stage weirdly elongates, and to take even a few steps seems a task of insurmountable difficulty. The feared dissociation is first suggested—"thoughts surrounded me like hideous birds whose flight obstructed my way"—and is then concretized: he watches his steps "from above, from my eyes," but the perspective that dominates his experience, and his identity, is that of the audience perceiving his "way of walking" (2:101). In a similar scene elsewhere the narrator crossing the stage feels like "a wind-up toy" and refers to himself in the third person by expressing a "a certain curiosity to know what that man in the second-hand tuxedo will do" (2:203–4). The narrator observes himself as other, as performer, as object of the other's gaze, and marvels not at his incapacity to integrate his split components into a single identity but rather at his ability to spy on himself: "The most unexpected and strange part of all this was that I observed myself, that I observed that other character, and that I observed him more secretly than anyone" (2:208).

In *Lands of Memory* a very similar scene is enacted, but in this case the adolescent's dissociating self-consciousness is enhanced by the presence of girls. As they look at him, his body "Saw itself taking a few steps and sitting down at the piano" (3:33), and again, "I also looked at it [the body] as though I were another person who observed and tried to correct its movements" (3:33). An internal security system monitors and adjusts normally spontaneous acts as the narrator confronts not so much external pressures as internal representations of pressures perceived to be external. The mildly estranged persona negotiates what seems to him a threatening ambience by splitting the self so that one part can surveil and defend another. As it is worded in an early text, "I decided to observe myself: I did not lose sight of myself even for a moment" (1:155).

Doubling in this basic form grounded in social insecurity was an even more explicit characteristic of Hernández's later life and literature. Evident here is the existentialist's obsessive self-analysis, the ubiquitous spying on oneself, the contortions inherent to the struggle of viewing oneself objectively. Also evident, however, is Hernández's recognition of the futility and the self-defeating nature of that enterprise, since the compulsion toward authenticity via self-scrutiny is necessarily divisive, splitting the self into the one who acts and the one who watches, the one who is and the other who judges. As Hernández put it, "My self is like a fleeting premonition. In the instant that I think about it, it is as though I arrived at a place that it has just abandoned" (3:207). The *I* in itself and thoughts about the *I* can never be coterminous.

An authentic self defended (but also beleaguered) by a false self fabricated as insulation from abusive realities came into play as Hernández tried to cope with the piano tours, but even these tours were far more desirable and less denigrating than the menial clerical jobs that followed later, "those jobs that waste one's best energies and that accustom one to not striving very seriously in other matters and in justifying one's life."[133] The "confusion" of Hernández's fiction, like that of his life, arises when the fabricated self and the "true" self compete in a struggle for the hegemony that they both desire. The Hernández narrator's maintenance of the illusion of who he believes himself to be is always jeopardized by an inner insecurity and an inherent weakness, but also by the false self, the performer shaped by the audience and the performance, the front that diverts and depletes his resources. As the "Diary of Shamelessness" well evidences, Hernández's front while working at the National Printing Office took the compensatory form of showmanship, a kind of theatrics designed to evade others, to protect the wounded self held in reserve while feigning a jovial congeniality. Members of Hernández's family recall him leaving home early in order to meet someone at a café prior to beginning his workday at the printing office. When asked finally with whom he shared this mysterious, daily rendezvous, Hernández replied that in the café he met the person whom he turned himself into in order to cope with the job and with the brokers of petty power that he encountered there.[134] Much the same is argued in the "Diary of Shamelessness," but now accompanied by a condemning judgment: "The streets near the one of my office were cursed. I knew that upon entering them I was going to find a horrible, cowardly, artificial person who sickened me with anguish. That person was myself" (3:188). The true self evades, but the shameless false self, "cordial and full of jokes," headed insistently toward others, be they admired or detested, almost as though taking the offensive (3:188). The anguish that resulted is unambiguous in a fragment also from Hernández's later years: among the many detestable people at the National Printing Office "there is one who is the anguish of my life: he is cowardly and maladapted, he smiles and makes jokes to fill his time with others. . . . That person, who I am ashamed to live, is the one that is produced in me increasingly as I approach the door of that cursed place" (3:176–77).

Like many Hernández texts, the "Diary" is a hybrid fictional-autobiographical discourse narrated by an implied author with identifiable relations to Hernández himself. The act of balancing split identities during the years at the printing office is pushed, probed, elaborated, and to some degree purged as it is textualized in the "Diary." As is apparent in the following passage, which opens the "Diary," the text also serves as a forum for exploration of the dissociation that—if the canon read as a symptom can be trusted—plagued Hernández to varying degrees throughout his life. "One night the author of this work discovered that his body, which he will call 'shameless' [literally "shameless one"], does not belong to him" and "that his head, which he will call 'it,' has, in addition, a separate life: it is almost always filled with other people's thoughts" (3:185). The dissociated self, earlier doubled in mind-body or dual-identity splits, is now tripled in a collage comprising the self (here an author, which shall concern us momentarily), the "shameless" body, and the head. The mutinous head and body team up through "strange understandings and misunderstandings" to frustrate the narrator's search for the "true self," but in "fleeting moments," despite ambivalent relations with the body and head to which he is bound by dependence, the narrator gains sufficient glimpses of himself to verify his existence (3:195–96). In that endeavor he nevertheless finds himself in the unenviable "situation of wanting to grab hold of his soul with a hand that isn't his" (3:189). In better times "the author sought a certain united front" to combine forces of the three parts and thereby to achieve a posture before the world that might be more authentic than the one armored with joviality at the printing office (3:196). The effort failed and was abandoned, however, because the self was "solitary," an "unattainable ghost"; the head, despite "its astuteness and its immense power of alien thoughts" could not entrap this evasive self; and the body failed to make of it a legitimate "social 'I'" (3:196). The divided "author of this diary" is consequently an ensemble of parts, a human bricolage envious "of secure selves, with innocent shameless bodies and heads without huge problems." At the same time, however, this self wallowing in a fragmenting insecurity makes the realization that this condition is not particular to him but rather extends into a network of divided humanity, and that intra- and interpersonal relations are therefore managed by negotiating arrangements between the parts:

> This "I," this sick person, divided like a fief that has been ceding land to others, is not alone in its illness. He has looked at others, through his own condition, of course, and found that many are "divided" without knowing it. There are even some who have "shameless" bodies greater than his and whose heads make "deals" not only with their shameless bodies, but also even with the most profound, mysterious, and inaccessible "I's." And, in turn, with other "shameless bodies" and heads and "I's." (3:196)

A lack of integrity in all senses of the term thus serves as the basis for relations, in varying configurations, of the components that comprise disintegrated players.

As the word "shameless" implies, the negative attributes of Hernández's I/body/head schema gravitate toward the body as the incarnation of the false self. Pursuing a similar motif in romantic literature, Otto Rank recognized that guilt "forces the hero no longer to accept the responsibility for certain actions of his ego." The blame is cast instead onto a double—the body in the present case—that is dissociated from the self.[135] Someone or some *thing* vicariously takes the fall; a split-off part of the self is loaded with negative attributes and condemned in lieu of the whole. That process, evidenced in Hernández's work but certainly not central to it, was most prevalent in romantic and gothic literature, where the double projected out of the self was demonized, often through its ghoulish qualities, its depiction as a humanoid monstrosity, or its pacts with the devil and his surrogates.

In the more sedate dissociation of the "Diary," one is rather reminded of the so-called head/body split common among obese persons. Dissociation in these cases entails devaluation of and attempts to disown the body from the neck downward. The dissociated body, "accepting the responsibility" for certain actions of the ego, frequently bears the corresponding third-person denominations: for Hernández (obese in his later years, when the "Diary" was written) the body is "shameless," while for others it is referred to as "it," "this body," "that thing," "this stuff I am trucking around," and so on. I am one thing, this discourse reads, while the brute object in which I am housed—acting against my interest of its own volition—is quite another. The dissociation of the obese body is often represented in these subjects' self-portraits, which feature prominent facial and hair detailing while the disowned torso is barely sketched in and the limbs are either absent or incomplete.[136] Hernández's body takes the fall not so much for its obesity as for its more complex entanglement with "the horrible, cowardly, and artificial person" that the self endeavored but failed to overcome. The body was numb and clumsy and obstructing his way; searching for Dr. Jekyll he bumped into himself as Mr. Hyde. The blank page that he confronted—less accommodating than the blank page on which the denied body is barely sketched in—"is the most disagreeable judge before whom I have no choice but to confess."[137]

Failure in this search for a "true" self as thematized in Hernández's work owes something to the very means employed to accomplish it: writing. In the "Diary" generation of the text itself is posited as the means by which the true and false selves will be consolidated, by which "a self that I can look at without so much shame" will be retrieved, but this enterprise is doomed in advance because the "shameless" body writes "in name of an 'I'" that does not belong to it (3:189), with the whole affair further undermined by a head augmenting the dissonance with an uncontrollable discourse of its own. Embedded in the layers of divisiveness is the intrinsic split between self and author, between the one who is and the one who writes, which is treated most forcefully by Hernández in the "partner" concept that will concern us presently. The legends accompanying the showcase scenes in *The Hortensias* also suggest that same split, since they put at odds one's experience and one's text by proscribing a "correct" version against which perceptions of the scenes must be measured. The theme is further dramatized when Horacio accompanies his own actions with a spoken narration ("Now I will go to the study to look for the inkwell") or—stressing the doubling function of the self/author split—when he assumes an omniscient, third-person (and sardonic) voice to narrate what he himself is doing: "He's opening the drawer. Now this imbecile is taking the top off the inkwell" (2:170).

In *The Lost Horse* the doubling of the narrator is complemented by a symmetrical doubling of Celina, who reappears now in the guise of an ephemeral presence—"the memory of Celina"—that pays visits to the narrator and demonstrates its independence. When left alone, for example, this memory of Celina "did something in my house that I was unaware of," just as the narrator had done years earlier in her living room (2:24). During one of her visits the memory of Celina arrives and greets him, but looks beyond him, almost through the transparency of his body, to silently communicate with a "someone" in the back of the room (2:24). Other memories similarly pass through the narrator as though he were as ephemeral and intangible as the fictional, memorial beings that he evokes. The memory of Celina, like the imago of the mother, can see through him, and armed with that vision he can see through himself.

It is in this context that the narrator's double, the "partner," is properly introduced: "on a night when I woke up distressed I realized that I wasn't alone in my room" (2:25). The two spectral presences—Celina's and the narrator's—are united and engaged in a mutually self-producing activity as the partner generates the text ("he was the one who wrote the narrative") (2:25) based on memories (vivified in the "memory of Celina") that are recalled but also re-produced, re-presented.

The partner's collaboration—which is to say, the work of the author who doubles the man, the work of the narrative voice that, like the Hortensia dolls and Echo, adds something of its own—accounts for the discrepancy between the memories "in themselves" and the memories in a version insisted upon by text production. It may be the self's "theater of memory" (2:25), but "inside me an unannounced show opened. I don't know if the theatrical company made a mistake or if they simply took the theater by storm" (2:29). In either case one's discourse is invaded and displaced by another's, with the host who is staging the uninvited show struggling to recuperate his integrity and control:

I have had to keep guard around myself so that he, my partner, does not intrude at the moment of memories. I have already said that I want to be myself alone. Nevertheless, in order to avoid his coming I have to think about him always; with a piece of myself I have formed a sentinel that guards my memories and my thoughts; but at the same time I must keep watch on the sentinel so that he does not fall asleep, distracted by the relating of memories. (2:27)

A self-defeating circularity is thus established: In order to defend oneself from intrusions by the double, one has to split off a "piece" of oneself to stand guard.[138] One doubling is the solution for another, and the very tactics summoned to ward off the partner—"I have to think about him always"—make the partner ever more present. A conflictively interactive threesome comprising the self, the partner, and the sentinel represents the writing subject, just as in the "Diary" a threesome surfaces in the guise of self, body, and head. In the present configuration, the self is further burdened with the task of surveilling the sentinel, the "piece" it had created to surveil, for if the sentinel were to succumb to distraction in the narration of memories, which is to say in the production of the text, then the partner would have occasion to slip past his guard and to again distort the pure recollection treasured by the self.

When the partner does reappear, however, his intrusions and dominance begin to assume a certain benevolence. The narrator bemoans his own alienation—"I was in one place and the world in another" (2:35)—and recognizes that the partner is an extension (or "piece") of the narrator's own self consigned to this "other" place where the world is and the self is not. The partner is "the representative of the people that inhabit the world," but the partner who formerly invaded now assumes a positive, soothing, and protective quality (like that of the specialists in the Nobel Prize letter) as "a mother" who protects the self from the rude world's dangers. The ubiquitous mother in Hernández narratives thus surfaces not only as a ghost writer but also as a kind of guardian angel who reproaches the narrator for withdrawing from the world, for withdrawing into the story of his life, the fiction of his life, that she herself coauthors in the guise of the partner. The partner then slides from this maternal identity into that of a "friend" who "advised me to write my memories," much the same as the mother imago in Hernández's psychobiography established a pattern of "coauthorship" that was assumed later by friends—Vaz Ferreira, Supervielle—who brought the world to an isolated Hernández and thereby revised his life and his literature. The narrator most appreciates the partner when he resembles the "friends who I had loved," friends who through their wisdom and guidance "helped me to write" (2:35).[139] It is in this context, too, that the double assumes one of its most concrete expressions in Hernández's canon: "I had even felt, on occasion, that he put his hand on my shoulder" (2:35). The self dissipates into the text as though he were the object of his own memory, while in inverse relation the partner, the double, becomes progressively more tangible.

The alternation between loving the partner/mother/friend and wishing to be left in the peace of his splendid isolation further emphasizes the doubled subject's ambivalence. Withdrawal into memories—into "a forgotten feeling of childlike curiosity" that is compared to a house—requires his absolute solitude, "because my partner would enter that house making a lot of noise and would frighten off the silence that had settled on the objects" (2:36). The self longing for retreat into textualized memories "ran like a thief to the center of a forest to go through his memories alone," but the partner is "behind the trunks or hidden in the branches of some tree" (2:36). Renewed flight into solitude consequently ensues, and in an attempt to evade the partner's relentless pursuit the self engages in a kind of autodiminution, as though trying to become invisible: "I made myself smaller, I shrank and contracted until I was like a microbe pursued by a wise man" (2:37). The impossibility of the flight, of outrunning one's shadow, of detaching from the "obligatory cohabitation" (3:33) with one's mirror image, is the moral concluding this episode, because the partner in pursuit of the self "would also transform himself into another microscopic body and would orbit around me, attracted toward my center" (2:37).

Hernández's perception of himself as in some way "doubled" is preceded in the history of letters by many writers who thematize dissociation (Walt Whitman, for example, remarked, "I am always conscious of myself as two") and by others who report actual autoscopic experiences.[140] In this latter category Aristotle described how Antipheron, out taking a walk, saw his double advancing toward him. Following an emotional separation with a lover, Goethe saw his double galloping toward him on horseback.[141] Guy de Maupassant, upon returning to his empty house, frequently encountered his double sitting in an armchair, much the same as the Hernández narrator who remarks, "I saw myself sitting in a chair and wearing a light suit" (2:130–31).[142] Alfred de Musset saw his double after wandering through a cemetery with George Sands, and Percy Bysshe Shelley, strolling in his garden, was approached by his shadow, which indelicately inquired, "How long do you mean to be content?"[143]

Patients suffering from a range of psychopathologies also count profound dissociative and doubling sensations among their symptoms. We have already mentioned in passing those related directly to the doll themes of *The Hortensias*, including the experience of patients who believe that they are "mechanisms, automatons, puppets; that what they do seems not to be done by them but happens mechanically; . . . that they are as though dead."[144] It is "as if I didn't exist," one patient remarks, while another adds that

"Things just seem to go on, as though they are not happening to me. In fact, I don't seem to be here at all." A third patient concurs, "I felt empty and dead inside," while others again stress the doll theme: "I am quite mechanical," "I am like a marionette."[145]

When the double is envisioned rather than corporalized in sensations of the self as other, the experience "is not unlike looking at and being in a mirror at the same time."[146] One inimitable psychotic jumped off a balcony and simultaneously watched himself doing so; "The one who jumped was less real than the one who was looking on."[147] Common also are "disappearance" of body parts (a patient behaved "as though half of his body was non-existent") and Pinocchio-type distortions (another "perceives part of his body as abnormally large or abnormally small").[148] Another male patient "had the peculiar feeling that his sexual organs were somehow foreign to his body." His uncertainty regarding his dissociated, castratable genitals "was so strong that the patient would frequently grab himself by his sex organs to be certain that they were still there."[149] In another case of extreme dissociation yielding to fragmentation, a patient at times did not know where particular parts of his body were.[150] "His hands and feet felt detached, as though they did not belong to him and sometimes seemed to disappear altogether."[151] Consequently, "the patients look for their limbs in the bed."[152] In these patients, as in the tripartite Hernández of the self-body-head or self-partner-sentinel configurations, the fragmentation of the body corporalizes a psychic fragmentation and inaugurates a quest for a cohering principle: "I lack something to hold me together." A catalog of related complaints describes the experience unambiguously: "Everything is flying away from me. In the doorway I can gather together the pieces of my body"; "The skin is the only possible means of keeping the different pieces together"; "There is no connection between the different parts of my body"; "Sometimes the roof of my skull flies away."[153] For other psychotics it is the whole body, rather than a part, which is "missing." One woman—who also believed that "an invisible double, like a shadow" contained her mind—was prone to such sudden and intense attacks of depersonalization that she would abruptly stop a conversation to ask, "Am I really here?" The woman would then pinch her face in an attempt to tangibly verify her own presence.[154] Another psychotic similarly expressed this sensation of the lost self: "I feel as though I am not here at all, my mind appears to be here, but the rest of me seems to have gone. I have to touch things to make sure I am still here."[155] The double per se is more explicit in one woman's acute psychosis following surgery related to a miscarriage; she saw herself lying in a coffin and experienced a "solid and life-like" double "which faithfully copied all of her movements."[156] Elsewhere the synchronized movements of the specular image are othered, as when a schizophrenic looking in the mirror offers a counterexplanation for the mimesis: "That's not me. They put me inside people while I'm sitting on a chair."[157]

Sensations such as these, though devoid of the frankly bizarre quality of psychosis, are expressed throughout Hernández's canon. The frequent reference to invasion by "other people's thoughts" (3:191) and by memories, advertising, feelings, shadows (1:151), and alien discourses of all sorts reveal a thought process itself described as "a secret society that meets someplace in my head" (3:203).[158] But despite this overactive group effort the mind proves to be rather useless: "I had the need to be as still as if I didn't exist; I had a head like an apparatus that perceived everything but couldn't explain anything" (1:122). That cerebral uselessness is largely the result of the dissonant and competing voices, a kind of thought by committee, an uncooperative, internalized board of directors that bureaucratizes even one's most intimate feelings. Witness, for example, the circumstances in "The Flooded House," where Margarita speaks and the "hollow" narrator introjects her discourse "as though I were pronouncing her words" (3:77). The narrator is a bespoken mouthpiece here, as he is more chillingly when the death screech of a roasted cat winds up in his screaming mouth (3:60).

Dissociation and the double are also suggested in Hernández's "sleepwalking" (a vigilant but benumbed, semicomatose bumble through life, half absent to oneself and one's ambience) and in his corresponding preoccupation with "waking up." In the fiction, Horacio wanders dreamily but nevertheless directly to his target "like a sleepwalker" (2:165), while the grandparents in "The Flooded House" are "like sleepwalkers walking to different dreams" (3:83).[159] After describing how his body belongs more to his family than to himself, and how he is, in effect, an automaton without volition, a somnambulant narrator in *Lands of Memory*, like a wind-up toy, randomly changes direction when a family member blocks his passage (3:29). This trancelike state in which the body responds like an automaton is in *The Hortensias* then represented by the true dolls, constructed in the likeness of the dissociated self who is "quite mechanical" and "like a marionette." The repertoire of distorted and lost body parts that is seen in psychopathology also gains representation throughout the canon: the feet in one image are perceived to be a great distance away, while all parts of the body are experienced as "neighborhoods of a large city that was now asleep" (1:131). The "Diary" mentions a man who was shown his own hand and believed it to be someone else's, to which the narrator adds: "A few months ago I discovered that I've had that same illness for years" (3:185). Later in the "Diary" he documents that belief, explaining that one of his hands has been lost for many years, that it got confused with the night, that it grew up alone and survived by begging, "hidden in a black cloth" (3:190). Further reflection on the dissociated hand then leads him full circle to a more global depersonalization as he discovers that "His *entire* body belongs to someone else" (3:195). This belief is common not only to the narrator of the "Diary" and the psychotics cited earlier but also to Horacio, who had the impression "that he was living in the body of a stranger" (2:164).

Before self/body dissociation gained such extreme expression in the "Diary" and *The Hortensias,* it surfaced more moderately in the early *Lands of Memory.* The young narrator in the bathroom scene remarks characteristically, "I myself was another person who observed me while I filled the tub and got undressed" (3:29). The bathroom had been lent to "me and my body," so that "we could bathe ourselves—they lent the bathroom to me so that I could bathe him" (3:32). This happy arrangement of the self tending to its dissociated body yields in more sinister depictions to the uncontainable double wandering off like the wayward reflections and shadows of romantic literature: "I can't lock myself inside me" (3:169), and therefore "it didn't surprise me that my own shadow walked far from me (3:105), or that "the shadow has a body" (1:151). In a notebook fragment from the later years, the "incarnation" of the wandering double takes the final step toward romantic traditions through a "meeting with the body after it walks by itself" (3:198).

The unstable ego boundaries resulting in the psychotics' "confusion of destinies" (2:68) is also amply registered on the threshold where division yields to duplication. Such doubling sometimes assumes the form of slippage into others: "Beside me was a man dressed in blue and I felt a kind of terror that his suit was mine and that I would wind up being him" (3:108).[160] In other passages the self is othered by cloning—"from my own soul another new one was born" (3:81)—as if "a character with an absurd and fatal existence had been born inside me" (1:155).

Duplication

As described by Otto Rank in his pioneering study, the double "personifies narcissistic self-love" and at the same time represents "a wish-defense against a dreaded eternal destruction."[161] Rank arrived at this latter realization through analysis of the double—primarily shadows and reflections—as it relates to the concept of soul in religious traditions. The soul is generally understood in psychoanalysis as an expression of the denial of mortality, and its nature as a reproduction or representation of the self—a double—is registered by signifiers in various indigenous languages. The soul, for example, is "refined body," "image," "companion," "duplicate," "two," "reflection," and "the copy of the owner, his other self."[162] The double emerges as an agent brokering the denial of death; it is a replica of the (dead) self that defies moribundity and lives "on the other side" eternally.

Rank illustrated the narcissism that complements death denial through analysis of romantic literature and film, where the double's role as an "unequivocal rival in sexual love" is prevalent. In *The Student of Prague*, for example, "the eerie double must disturb only 'all hours of sweet company' of the couple, . . . his interventions become more terrifying in proportion as the demonstrations of their love become more fervent."[163] Since the double dedicated to separating the lovers is nothing other than an extension of the protagonist, Balduin's "own personified self," Rank interprets the interruptions as self-interruptions masquerading as intrusions by an outsider. These detours and self-imposed obstacles reveal that "the hero really turns out to be incapable of love."[164] In a discussion of impotence Freud came to much the same conclusion, describing an analysand's "counter-will which successfully interferes with his conscious intention" of making love.[165]

When the death component of the double recycles back into the narcissistic component, Rank's intruding other is definitively revealed as a denied and projected dimension of the self. In *The Student of Prague* such is first suggested through surface indices (the double intrudes on the lovers meeting at a cemetery) and is then finalized unmistakably at the tale's conclusion. Balduin, on the verge of committing suicide, shoots the double instead and rejoices in his salvation from the ghost that plagued him, but only briefly. He notices in a mirror—in which he appears now after a long absence, since his wayward double (reflection) has now been "fixed"— that in shooting the double he has shot himself.[166] The entanglement of love and death in his lamentable conclusion reveals an indirect suicide via murder of the self as other: Balduin attempts to kill the double that represents his narcissism, the dissociated part of him that intrudes between himself and his love of another, but he winds up killing himself instead because the narcissism represented by the double is essential to and ultimately inseparable from his own being.

Rank's prototype of the romantic double is a useful backdrop for understanding the double as duplication in Hernández's work, notably in *The Hortensias*, where narcissistic self-love, the reflective confusion of self and other, and self-destruction rerouted through doubles are all thematically central. There is, however, a fundamental difference between the double in *The Hortensias* and in narratives such as *The Student of Prague*. Whereas the romantics' double emerged from the protagonist and then came back to haunt him, frustrating his amorous desire by denying him the object of his love, in *The Hortensias* Horacio is doubled *as* the love object. While they foreclose the possibility of any genuine relation with a woman, and while they do indeed ultimately deliver Horacio to his doom, the Hortensia dolls as Horacio's doubles do not prohibit his amorous encounters but quite the contrary make them possible by dehumanizing the love object and reforming it in the shape most conducive to his exotic eroticism. "In love, the other is one's double," and when that love is pathological and the other is a doll, the double is "a pathological attempt to replace the image of the other with that of the self."[167] The replacement of women by passive inanimate surrogates makes the double more readily manipulable by Horacio's fantasies (the double "stared at me with a helpless expression as if he needed something from me," as one patient put it), thereby making a direct link with themes of perverse sexuality.[168] "The double functions as a figure onto which are externalized inadmissible and tabooed desires."[169] With such desires projected and attributed to another, the self can more readily bypass prohibition, guilt, and decorum to indulge in lustful extravaganzas. All perversions, including Horacio's, "entail a fundamental alienation from self" and an attempt "to find personalization through the elaborate machinery of sexual experiences." The effort is as damaging as it is healing, however, since "so long as the pervert seeks to make the reparation to his own idolized self, either through masturbatory practices or through projective identification with another who represents his idolized internal self, there is no possibility of true relating or mutuality."[170] The supplement of serial women surrogates crowds out the possibility of genuine love, and even when a true woman (rather than a doll) is concerned—as for example in "The Flooded House"—she is duplicated as though the protagonist were seeing double: "I was very confused with my two Margaritas and I vacillated between them as though I weren't sure which, of two sisters, I should prefer or betray; nor could I fuse them together, so as to love them both at once" (3:83).

In the original case study by Capgras of the syndrome that now bears his name, the patient believed not only that those around her had been replaced by doubles (Hortensia as María) but also that there existed doubles of herself as well (Hortensia as Horacio). This astute patient referred to her own illness as *l'illusion des sosies*, the last word, meaning "resemblance," reminiscent of Hernández's double as a *socio* (partner). *Sosies* is etymologically linked to Socia, a servant of Amphitryon.[171] As the tale is related in its most popular classical version—namely, that of Plautus—Amphitryon and his servant Socia are away at war. Jupiter desires the favors of Amphitryon's wife, Alcmena, and taking advantage of the absence he assumes "the shape of her own husband" and has his servant, Mercury, take the form of Socia. The impostors move in, and Jupiter standing in as husband impregnates Alcmena. The adulterous wife, duped by duplication, is innocent, but the fruit of her womb redoubles the theme in a separate register: Alcmena had been impregnated by her husband prior to his departure, and then again by Jupiter, so she accordingly gives birth to twins.[172]

The simple symmetry in Plautus's *Amphitryon*—two ejaculations, two children—is somewhat more complicated in Hernández's canon. Consider for example the use of twin maids in *The Hortensias*. The two here, as is frequently the case, are made into a threesome: one of the twins bears the name of Horacio's wife, María, and to support that link the twins wear María's clothes, appear in her mirror, and (like the dolls) are mistaken by Horacio for the wife whom they "replace" and duplicate. Horacio's underused capacity to "see through" the replacement is suggested in another scene, where windows "were twins, like those of María" (2:164). The duplication (and "confusion") occasioned by the overlapping names of María-the-twin and María-the-wife appears in an earlier text when Juan and Juana communicate through the intermediary of the latter's sister, also named María. Juan and Juana resemble Hor-acio and Hor-tensia not only in their triangular relation with a María but also in their doll-like, mechanized nature: "neither character shows exuberance in gestures or in movement" (1:105). Dolly and Muñeca (= doll) of "The Dark Dining Room" are similarly linked by their names and then by the strange love triangles overlapping in the "black house" that they inhabit.

In another text the narrator arrives with his father at a small town, where a restaurant's advertising billboard boasts the son's name, along with the slogan, *Minutas a toda hora* (3:164). The temporal pun is resonant when imported into the context of *The Hortensias*, since in one branch of its popular etymology the name "Horacio" comes from *hora* (hour). Horacio's name also echoes the fear-of-death motif apparent throughout *The Hortensias,* since *hora* deified delivers the Greek goddess by the same name who—like the *Hor*tensias—is the goddess of youth.[173] The young and eternal Hortensias are objectifications of the denial of death, while Horacio is the keeper of hours, the one with *minutos a toda hora,* the one whose clock is ticking and ticking in tune with his author's.

As the fragment in which the billboard appears continues, the father and son eat in the restaurant, the father relates to the restaurant owner the coincidence of names, and the two men share a good laugh. The son, however, is troubled by sharing his name with another, because "I could be that man or who knows who" (3:164). The boy's identity is called into question by the like-named double, and to protect himself from equation with this other he calculates some countermeasures—sending a photo with a letter rather than signing it and looking into a mirror when he thinks of himself—to firmly establish his identity on visual rather than nominal grounds. The results, however, mock his intentions: "I recalled all of the 'I's' that I had seen in mirrors the day before and saw them now sticking out their tongues" (3:164–65). The double with a different appearance but the same name is then inverted to deliver the fear of a physically identical impostor who— "although he might have a different name"—could replace the boy (as Jupiter had done) at home in his absence (3:165). This brief passage thus catalogs the means by which the self is vulnerable to duplication through name, appearance, reflection, and displacement by impostors.

Imaginary companions—the Hortensia dolls, for example—are also in some sense "impostors," standing in for another (María) and at the same time for a projected extension of the self. One patient with delusions that populated his solitude had the impression that a companion accompanied him on nightly expeditions to gather salable trash. He had never seen the companion—though he had a glimpse "as if through bad glasses"—but he felt the companion's presence on his right side. The man talked with the companion, shared his bed with him, left food for him. "I would find some fruit in a basket and I'd give him a half [sic], but he wouldn't eat it because he wasn't there, so I would eat it myself." He associated the companion with "the ghost of my father," with his brother-in-law, and with a friend.

This companion, like the Hortensias, is doubly an impostor, once standing in for the father, the brother-in-law, or the friend, but then ultimately constituting "a projection of the patient's body-image or a mirror image of himself."[174] In Hernández's "The Balcony" a private world is similarly populated by the overdetermined offspring of duplications as unwitting real people become rivals in the love triangles of an imaginary cast of characters (2:53). When seen by the daughter through the glass of her balcony, passersby—or, more accurately, composite characters assembled from parts of various pedestrians viewed from her windows—are transformed into a pseudocommunity that populates the girl's private fictions (2:55). The people around her—her father, the narrator, the balcony perceived as her lover— become entangled in this part-object collage by which the girl, not unlike Horacio, constructs a world-behind-glass in which her dissociated self enjoys its own company.

THE FRAGMENTED BODY

> *The subject is no one.*
>
> —Jacques Lacan

Representations of corporal fragmentation have been prevalent in Western civilization at least since the fifth century before Christ, when Empedocles proposed a theory of evolution featuring body parts floating in space and joining randomly in a series of collisions. "Many heads sprang up without necks, / arms wandered for lack of shoulders, / and eyes strayed alone in want of foreheads." The formation of bodies by random union resulted in many monstrosities—two-headed beasts and "men with the heads of oxen," for example—but through trial and error these collisions also generated human and animal forms adequate for adaptation and survival.[175] While the monstrosities produced by colliding body parts could not endure, preoccupation with the fragmented body continues to deliver a proliferation of images quite similar to those found in Empedocles' theory. Consider Frankenstein's monster, comprised of dismembered body parts gathered from various sources to assemble a new humanoid being. In Hernández's *The Hortensias* one finds psychological part objects rather than corporal fragments utilized to construct the dolls, but nevertheless the Empedocles-like drift of body parts is explicit at the narrative's conclusion when one of the showcase scenes—this one without the customary legend—features a softly lit pool with loose arms and legs floating in it among plants. As the body parts circulate and collide, various configurations are presented; "Horacio was distracted for a while looking at all of the combinations that the loose members produced, until the toes on a foot and the fingers on a hand joined together and came before him" (2:179).

The persistence of fragmented-body representations is partially explicable in the psychoanalytic terms proposed by Jacques Lacan's concept of the "mirror stage." Among the consequences of the child's cognition—or, as we have seen, miscognition *(méconnaissance)*—of the reflected other perceived to be the self is a retroactive awareness of the fragmentary quality of infantile experience and, consequently, of the possibility of actual corporal fragmentation. The mirror reflection affords the child a first glimpse of him or herself as a totality, an "orthopedic" whole. With these gains, however, comes the price: "What the child has to relinquish here is a state of undifferentiation."[176] In the infantile bliss of undifferentiation the concepts of whole and part are incomprehensible. The mother's breast and child's mouth are not yet deciphered as belonging to separate beings, and similarly the infant's hand drifting across his or her field of vision is perceived only gradually, only after repeated rehearsals, as belonging to the same self who simultaneously perceives it kinesthetically and visually. Differentiation is definitively instituted as a capacity of the developing psyche when, thanks to the "external" or quasi-objective view afforded by the mirror, borders are drawn to delineate one body from another and one part from another within the same corporal whole.

The child unifies the body through recognition of a coherent image of the self, but this perception of unification makes comprehensible differentiation and, consequently, the possibility of separation or disintegration. For Lacan and his interpreters, "The body is not experienced as fragmented . . . until there is a coherent image against which to measure the fragmentation. Thus the individual looks forward to the ideal coherence and backward to the anguish of dismemberment, each perspective depending on the other."[177] The mirror stage—"a drama whose internal thrust is precipitated from insufficiency to anticipation"—thus "projects the formation of the individual into history." It "manufactures" for the subject "the succession of phantasies that extends from a fragmented body-image to a form of its totality," and it carries the ominous reminder that what is whole today could be as fragmented tomorrow as it seems to have been in the past.[178] These temporal nuances and the double direction of fragmentation are suggested by a Hernández narrator who complains that the parts of his own body "wanted to live an independent life" and then refers to a past when "my parts were not divided up" and "together we were one thing" (2:88). Traces of mirror-stage themes are also evident in Hernández's perception of human totalities as composites of their "independent" parts: "Suddenly I saw my friend as though he were a mathematical addition that for the first time was totalled up" (1:117).

If the fragmented body is imbedded in the depths of the mirror, also reflected is a kind of "armour of an alienating identity, which will make with its rigid structure the subject's entire mental development."[179] The identity is alienating because, like Narcissus, one misconstrues oneself to be the other in the reflector, one's grasp of oneself is a displacement, and one's capture of the self through mirror reflection is "inseparable from a *misrecognition* of the gap between the fragmented subject and its unified image of itself."[180] "We have only to understand the mirror stage as an *identification*," the last term denoting the "transformation that takes place in the subject" when it assumes an imago, when it is founded on an image external to it.[181] Even the early Hernández was troubled by the idea of a self founded on the basis of reflections that "cast a spell" (1:43), and as his work matured Hernández would progressively and more daringly probe the Lacanian self "located from the beginning within a damaging *imaginary* space, inserted into a radical split between an illusory sense of selfhood and something profoundly other."[182]

Horacio with his mirrors and showcases is of course a champion of this imaginary space, a tragicomic antihero dramatizing Lacan's contention that the subject is transformed by an introjected exterior imago, that he is "sucked in by the image" that fragments him at the same moment that it unifies him.[183] Horacio's experience as "disconnected, discordant, in pieces" is repaired through the "alienated unity" he constructs through his rituals with the Hortensia dolls doubling as mirrors. His ritual, like any, is efficacious only insofar as it disguises its symbols; the misrecognition must be protected, the mirror must be "covered," the migrating identities must hover on the blurry borders between self and other so that Horacio's reconstitution in a roundabout autoerotic ritual is never revealed for what it is. "The body in pieces finds its unity in the image of the other, which is its own anticipated image—a dual situation in which a polar, but not symmetrical relation, is sketched out"[184] The psychotic who complains that "they cut me up every day, I have no brain, legs or hands" takes mirror-stage fragmentation literally while at the same time she preserves enough of its figurative nature (she is not, after all, dismembered) to corporally represent her psychic fragmentation. This woman, like Horacio, then extends her fragmentation via the "not symmetrical relation" characteristic of projection, sending her body parts out into the world, attaching them to members of a pseudocommunity (mirror images, dolls) and then retrieving them back to her own "othered" self: "That lady (pointing to the lady physician) tore my eyes out, she has my eyes. I once was larger, now I'm small and everyone has my legs and hands attached to them. They take away my legs and hands and pin them to themselves. They cut them away from me, take them for themselves and then sew them back to me."[185] The patient is "broken up" and "falling to pieces," but she defensively reassembles herself like a rag doll quilted together from scraps of herself that she peels off the world as mirror.

When Lacan argues for the image of one's body as a prototype, as "the principle of every unity he perceives in objects," he likewise speaks to the experience dramatized by Horacio. Horacio "only perceives the unity of this specific image from the outside, and in an anticipated manner." He establishes a paradigm—the "double relation which he has with himself"—and consequently "all the objects of his world are always structured around the wandering shadow of his own ego." As the dolls of *The Hortensias* well exemplify, these objects assume a fundamentally anthropomorphic and even "egomorphic" character. The perceived object—the showcase, the doll—is rarely definitive and final in its own right; it is rather a segment of a puzzle of which pieces are lost, a contribution to the elusive "ideal unity" that "is never attained as such" and that "is evoked at every moment in this perception." It appears in the trope of the world behind glass, "in the guise of an object from which man is irremediably separated." Although his pursuit of himself in the dolls becomes increasing more desperate, Horacio will never "recapture" the object, he "will never truly be able to find reconciliation," he will never achieve "perfect complementarity on the level of desire" through this divided and divisive object "which by essence destroys him." Lacan thus concludes that "It is the nature of desire to be radically torn. The very image of man brings in here a mediation which is always imaginary, always problematic, and which is therefore never completely fulfilled. It is maintained by a succession of momentary experiences, and this experience either alienates man from himself, or else ends in a destruction, a negation of the object."[186]

The progression from transformative identification with the dolls through fragmentation and on to the ultimate destruction of Horacio is developed in *The Hortensias* by quotas. Multiplication and then fragmentation of the dolls dramatizes what Lacan refers to as the "imaginary plurality of the subject," the "Freudian crowd" that challenges each human's pseudo-singularity.[187] In the hyperbolic expression that self-multiplication gains in the discourse of psychosis, patients experience themselves as Noah's ark, as a baggage car, as a Trojan horse filled with people.[188] These patients share an "I'm multiple" (3:189) sensation with Hernández characters, a sensation made manifest in the text sometimes by a self-image infinitely reproduced between mirrors (3:164) and sometimes by multiplication of the fragmented subject in self-objects, often lovers, who are narcissistically invested and "replaced one by the other with relentless regularity."[189] Both are patent in *The Hortensias*, where the physical multiplication and fragmentation of dolls counts among its highly overdetermined meanings the psychic fragmentation of Horacio himself. The reader is drawn into a text structured like a mirrored room with no exits where Horacio reproduces himself and the narrator celebrates "This disarray, this fragmentedness, this fundamental discordance, this essential lack of adaptation, this anarchy" that "is characteristic of the instinctual life of man."[190] Horacio's perpetual balance along the rift of insanity caricatures and makes legible the mirror-stage fracture and the rituals of convalescence that in normal psychology are dramatized more subtly.

The progressive disintegration of Horacio is perhaps most efficiently elucidated by tracing the evolution of the doll that represents both his pathology and his attempt at self-cure. Hortensia's identity commences in an

unchallenged prototype and terminates in a devalued object of mass production as Horacio "substitutes one image for another and remains in the
dangerous condition of a man who takes tropes literally."[191] At the narrative's
opening the signifier "Hortensia" is a proper noun specifying a single doll
specially manufactured to resemble Horacio's wife, a privileged doll treated
as though she were human. Hortensia is presented from the start in the
company of other dolls used for the showcase scenes, but these are generic,
unnamed players, mere mannequins devoid of "human" properties, objects
propped up for the gaze. When they are not being used in one of the showcase scenes, they are warehoused, like so many goods, in an adjacent showcase. The contrast between Hortensia and the dolls that contextualize and
contribute to her identity thus initiates the play of multiplications that will
accumulate exponentially as the narrative progresses. Hortensia, herself
the double of María and of Horacio, is multiply doubled by the proliferation of unnamed dolls around her. She and these clones are—borrowing an
image from elsewhere in the canon—the same portrait in different frames
(3:131).

Multiplication rises to a higher register when Horacio returns Hortensia
to her maker, Facundo, so that the latter can devise a manner to endow the
doll with "human warmth." In these pages the narrative commingles the
identities of Hortensia and María and includes several other moves to "humanize" the doll (including implicit reference to her soul), until at the conclusion of section two an image of entangled legs interlocks the identities
(and one might say the fate) of María, Horacio, and the humanized Hortensia
(2:147–51). The doll that began in the semblance of an image in the mirror,
an inanimate and passively reflective other, is now enlivened as the retrieved mirror image is consolidated in an "alienating unity" with the reflected subjects.

No sooner is Hortensia given life, however, than she is "murdered."
This crime inaugurating the corporal fragmentation that progressively gains
currency occurs at Hortensia's second birthday party, and the identity of
her mysterious assailant is revealed when Horacio confesses to Facundo
that he stabbed the doll as a pretext to necessitate her return, again, to her
maker. The purpose of the refabrication this second time is more sinister:
to equip the doll for amorous relations, to remedy a lack with a hollows. A
hole will provide Horacio the means to make himself whole, but if María
were to discover his intentions the effect on her would be fragmenting: "all
of the places on her face would be destroyed" (2:156). Horacio continues
to visit the showcases, surrounding himself with the gallery and the clones
that he penetrates with his gaze, but his desire is clearly bound now to the
exotica made possible by his newly replumbed Hortensia. When María

does indeed discover and is "shattered" by Horacio's perversion, the fragmentation itself begins to migrate: María parcels it out by wielding the knife against the bloated Hortensia—cut up again—before packing her bags and leaving her "adulterous" husband. Everything is falling to pieces, while in the margins fragmentation images begin to assume a supporting role and later in the text will take the lead. A fine example at this juncture is offered by one of the twin maids, who "saw Hortensia's mutilated body in the mirror" (2:160), and another, shortly after, by a dream that reveals "a dark place through which a white arm was flying" (2:164). When the mutilated Hortensia herself resurfaces, she is inside the piano that "was a large coffin" (2:165), as though María's "murder" of the doll could restore it to its pre-plumbed innocence as "dead."

It is over Hortensia's dead body that true multiplication commences in the narrative. Before the second "murder" of the doll Horacio managed to more or less confine his projections to the showcase gallery (with some overflow into the "black house"), but now the fantasy world defies all measures of control and spills across the narrative milieu as a whole. This dissemination of private fiction over social reality counts among its consequences a multiplication of self- and love-objects (dolls) as Horacio is overtaken by his frenzied Don Juanism. The serial monogamy begins with an "affair" that Horacio has with a blonde doll. Horacio ponders a clandestine rendez-vous in an apartment rented for this purpose, but he then schemes to satisfy his passion domestically: "he would bring her home and put her in the showcase of dolls waiting to be placed [in a scene]. After everyone went to bed he would carry her to his bedroom" (2:161). The blonde doll, a double that displaces the double (Hortensia) that displaced the wife, is thereby situated among other dolls—multiple doubles—from which she is distinguishable only by Horacio's trained eye. The blonde would seem to be one of the others; she *is* one of the previously less significant others, but the one (Hortensia) makes its transition to the many as Horacio breaks down the barriers of differentiation (represented by the showcase glass) and privileges a succession of dolls, one becoming the other as each is ritually exhausted and serves finally only as catalyst for flight into the next. This rush from one variation of self-object to the next is reminiscent of the psychotic who, when he encountered his double, "changed his facial expressions so rapidly that the alter ego could not keep pace with the transformation."[192] But Horacio's pace, at this point, is still moderate; the narrative pauses to unambiguously establish the blonde doll, now named Eulalia, in the privileged position once held by Hortensia. In a new round of showcase scenes Eulalia sits besides Horacio "and he hugged her while he looked at the other dolls" (2:169). Eulalia is the doll who escapes the showcase, the humanized doll sharing Horacio's viewpoint as seer rather than seen, but she differs from Hortensia in that she is a replica of a doll prototype that preceded her but never a prototype in herself.

At the same time that the dolls begin their proliferation in the private world of the "black house," the multiplication of doubles expands exponentially in other quarters as Facundo acquires plans and prototypes for mass production of Hortensias. Facundo explains: "Their generic name is *Hortensia*; but then each owner gives his doll the name that she intimately inspires in him" (2:160–61). The original name "Hortensia" thus assumes expanded signification providing the model for massive multiplication at a higher level: whereas earlier "Hortensia" *was* the "intimately inspired" personal name of a namesake doll singled out and humanized (2:141), it here becomes the generic name, the trade name of a prototype under mass production. In this progressing genealogy "Hortensia" thus functions something like a surname, already in place at birth, while the parents or, in this case, doll owner, add to it another name of their choice.

On the threshold of the ensuing dissemination of multiple clones, true corporal fragmentation also becomes insistent. As J. Hillis Miller pointed out, prosopopoeia (the trope that "ascribes a face, a name, or a voice to the absent, the inanimate or the dead") always entails "dismemberment," "mutilation," and "fragmentation," naming "bits and pieces of the human body here and there throughout the world." "Prosopopoeia projects not the wholeness of a self, body and soul together, but fragments that stand for the whole, as the face stands for the person who presents that face to the world."[193] As that face changes to the tune of Horacio's frenzy, a predilection for dismembered limbs becomes more prevalent. Having remembered seeing loose arms and legs in Facundo's study, Horacio puts in his request: "When you have extra arms or legs that you don't need, send them to me" (2:162). Actual multiplication of dismembered body parts is then immediately reinforced and redoubled by imagistic reproduction: Horacio, himself reduced by a mirror to "nothing more than the knot of his tie," would like to incorporate self-multiplying fragments into his showcase scenes, "an arm on top of a mirror," for example (2:162). After extended passages exploring Horacio's complex relation with mirrors and reflections, the same reduplication is generalized as Horacio "had large mirrors delivered and placed them in the gallery in such a way that they multiplied the doll scenes" (2:166).

The ad infinitum multiplication and fragmentation of dolls by mirror reflections is short-lived, but mass production steps up and carries the theme forward as Facundo and the store La Primavera join forces for a public exhibition of dolls. Fragmentation proper is simultaneously sustained by arrival at the "black house" of the body parts that Horacio had ordered. The box full of arms and legs is gleefully received, but Horacio, progressively losing his own head, "was afraid of finding some loose head" among the pieces (1:170). When the body parts are designed into a showcase scene, the motifs of fragmentation and multiplication are strategically combined: a mourning woman is seated on a stairway and "from under her skirt came an amazing number of legs: there were some ten or twelve, and on each step there was a loose arm with its hand facing upward" (2:170).

The loose arms with their solicitous palms are significant in context of one's being both the subject and object of begging (as discussed earlier) and again in context of Celina's "dismembered," fetishized arm (as discussed later). They also intersect with the fear of an alien hand touching one's own hand hanging out from under the bedcovers (3:190), this a fear made even more resonant in Hernández's case when compared to a patient's deluded conviction that her mother's hand was under her pillow.[194] In *The Hortensias* Horacio's madness is finally triggered when his hand is touched by that of his wife disguised as a doll representing a nun. As discussed earlier, Hernández narrators are generally distrustful of "being in the hands" of others, particularly the hands of mother and her surrogates.

The excess of limbs in the showcase scene is echoed by Horacio's hypnagogic vision—"he saw the widow walking with all of her legs as though she were a spider" (2:171)—and then again when the body as a collage of fragmented parts is complemented by the multiple-part objects that are pieced together to construct the dolls' identities. In the instance precipitating Horacio's madness, for example, the "Freudian crowd" constituting the doll's identity includes contributions from the nun, Horacio, the mother imago, María, the fear of fragmentation and death, and the original Hortensia. These are then compounded by a countersubstitution that functions like a wayward mirror image when the doll in the showcase is displaced by María pretending to be a doll, and that consequently incorporates a second generation into the "crowd": María represents the doll that represents María, but that also stands in for Horacio, the mother imago, other dolls, the fear of fragmentation and death, and so on, until the prototype and the mass-produced replica all have polysemous, self-generative, reversible identities so confused that "Everything appeared with an uncontainable multiplicity" (3:104).

The almost comic outrage that the multilegged widow scene inspires in Horacio—"What idiots . . . the idea isn't to use every arm and leg in the house" (1:170)—yields finally to Horacio's exhausted despair and disillusionment with the scene designers, with the dolls, and even with his cherished Eulalia. Yet the "pressure of an intention" exerted over his bewildered desire "reflects the 'images' by which the subject has conceived himself in relation to the world around him"; Horacio bounces back.[195] If the fragmentation of those images ultimately fails to satisfy him, Horacio may still exercise the option of receding into that dimension of reflection where the one becomes many, where the object of his desire is multiplied and he, beside and inside it, is reconceived and made immortal by infinite duplication of a part standing in for the whole.

The "pressure" sustaining multiplication thus accelerates Horacio's Don Juanism, which trades off division (the fragmented body) for duplication (multiple dolls). The lineage of substitutions is again compounded as this time Horacio opts for a surreptitious adventure—not with his wife, not with Hortensia, and not with the doll displacing Hortensia, but rather with someone else's doll, the forbidden doll, the doll to which he has no right other than an implied, dubious one by restitution of the doll's trade name, "Hortensia," which connects it to the prototype that Horacio once owned. The covetous affair is, in any case, a failure, and Horacio again despairs: "he thought about going away to another country and never looking at a doll again" (2:172). He has Eulalia removed, he makes peace with his wife, he terminates the showcase viewings, "and contrary to his custom he left the dolls in the dark—only the noise of the machines accompanied them" (2:173). That noise, a refrain throughout the entire text, is associated on the next page with "memories of the dolls as the remains of a shipwreck," an image recalling not only the doll's "death" but also the body parts floating in the pool. In this transitory backslide into fragmentation María, too, provides an image of her own—"You made me undo Hortensia and now you want me to kill the cat" (2:174)—but soon the mode of multiplication resumes as Horacio delivers himself "to thoughts of a relapse into his vice as though into a voluptuous fate" (2:175).

As Horacio gears up for a new bout with his private passion in a house rented for that purpose, multiplication of the dolls is gaining parallel treatment through developments in the dolls' mass production. Earlier in the narrative the one prototype doll, Hortensia, was situated among replicas that were visually similar to her but distinct in that they lacked her privileged position and, later, also lacked her "plumbing." In the La Primavera exhibit of mass-produced dolls the same structure is repeated: one Hortensia (or sexually "plumbed") doll, here a product of mass production, is in the exhibit (as in Horacio's showcase) situated among non-Hortensia dolls, and the similarity between the plumbed and the unplumbed is such that Horacio himself must consult with Facundo to determine which doll in a certain scene is the one properly equipped (2:177). Horacio has this doll, Herminia, delivered to the rented house, thereby expanding the serial succession of love objects to now encompass María, Hortensia, Eulalia, doll-of-the-other, and Herminia. Shortly after, Horacio returns to La Primavera for the grand exhibition in which the mass-produced dolls have their debut, and the public, like Horacio before them, wants "to know which among the dolls were Hortensias" (2:176). The dolls that earlier seemed impostors (mass-produced Hortensias) are now themselves in some sense genuine and "impostored" by the non-Hortensia dolls indistinguishable from them, save the plumbing. These multiple duplications are then exponentially expanded and fragmented by floor-to-ceiling mirrors incorporated into the exhibition, as was the case earlier in Horacio's gallery.

With his "pressure" now exerting itself in a desire not only for more dolls but for more exotic dolls, Horacio fancies a black Hortensia—"semi-naked" with skin paintings "like a cannibal"—and has her extracted from her selvatic scene and installed in the bed of his rented house. The lineage that began with María and passed through a series of dolls finally comes full circle when Horacio, climbing into bed for his tryst with the black doll, encounters his wife there instead. The displacement of the woman by the doll is thus again reenacted in reverse, but the flip side of the arrangement finds Horacio, flipped, at the end of his line and slipping irretrievably into the depersonalization that he had to this point detoured through the dolls. Horacio's descent into a catatonic dollishness is suggested by the last doll's blackness in relation to the black house owned and occupied by Horacio, and it is then confirmed when Horacio's breakdown is expressed in images that transform him into the likeness of his Hortensias. Stunned upon encountering María's screaming body where he presumed a doll to be awaiting in the splendor of her mute beauty, Horacio succumbs to "a strange tranquility," with "fixed eyes, as though they were glass," and with the "stillness of a doll" (2:178).

This last failed fling dramatizing Horacio's self-multiplication ushers in the final round of fragmentation with which *The Hortensias* concludes. Hesitating on the threshold of his insanity Horacio returns "to the relatively innocent pastime of the showcases," a pastime presumed to be calming and therapeutic.[196] But the first showcase scene, the one with the body parts floating in a pool, swirls before him as a kind of warping mirror magnifying his grotesque fragmentation, while a "surprise" in the second—María has taken the place of one of the nun dolls—confuses the world inside the showcase and the world at large to such a degree that Horacio definitively loses his equilibrium. Horacio has entered the showcase, and when María's hand touches him he falls into an agitated, automatized psychosis not merely because the "live" doll was too much for his fragile sensibilities but also because the hand and its touch are associated with a series of macabre images—the hand that touches the sleeper's unprotected hand, the hand that locks fingers with the toes of a foot, the hand on a white arm drifting through a black room, the dismembered hand palm-up on a stairway, and the hand that does not belong to the man who writes with it. Trapped inside the showcase, Horacio the spectator becomes part of the spectacle, locked in his own fiction, an agitated doll pounding its fists against the glass between itself and the world.

In this plight of sealed enclosure within his own externalized image, Horacio shares the fate of a "beautiful, unfaithful sweetheart"—as she was described in a 1913 London news article—who was imprisoned inside a room of reflective glass. The punishment intended to oblige the girl to confront her reflection no matter where she turned, "so that she might contemplate it, and vow to improve her ways in the sight of herself." The results, however, turned out otherwise: the lady "felt such horror of the ever recurrent image of her own face that her reason began to be confused," and like Horacio trapped in his showcase she was soon "striking the reflecting walls with both fists." For the young lady and Horacio alike, an erotic transgression ends in a mirror-world transformed into a gallery of ubiquitous selfrepresentation, followed in short order by fragmentation: "fragments were flying around and into her face, but she paid no heed to them; she kept on smashing, with the only purpose of no longer seeing the image of which she had conceived such a horror."[197] The girl's face and fate, like Narcissus's, and like Horacio's, supports Jean Cocteau's contention that "The mirror would do well to reflect a little more before returning our image to us."[198]

Showcases as much as mirrors can "magnify and diminish, they can eliminate and multiply, they can open up vistas of infinite regression and they can close in on an object." The baroque era's mania for mirrors is particularly illustrative of these transformational properties of reflection, as is epitomized by Athanasius Kircher's *Ars magna lucis et umbrae*, published in Rome in 1646. With a great thematic affinity to the Hernández of *The Hortensias*, "Kircher sketches out a series of metamorphic rooms in which the spectator can see himself change from the self into a variety of others—other sexes, other people." Whereas Horacio's metamorphoses are psychologically generated, in Kircher's case

The gimmick that makes the room work is a box that hides an octagonal drum that rotates on its side. On each face of the drum is depicted the image of a desired transformation, and this image has a direct and open sightline, through a concealed slit in the box, to a mirror hanging above it, but angled in such a way (like the mirror in a periscope) that the spectator standing in front of the drum-hiding box can look up and see, not the humdrum, expected image of the self, but the hotly desired appropriation to the self of an alien other. With careful lighting, drapes, a hidden amanuensis to rotate the drum, and other adjuncts of baroque showmanship, the illusion of actual transformation can be effected.[199]

Specular and theatrical pyrotechnics delivering a "hotly desired appropriation to the self of an alien other" describes Horacio's showcases precisely, and the commercial purpose of Kircher's metaphoric rooms further reveals an agenda, like that of Facundo and La Primavera in *The Hortensias*, to turn a profit on the common human desire to be someone other than oneself or to exchange one love object for another better suited to the shape of fantasy. The affinity with the showcases of *The Hortensias* is also unmistakable when Jurgis Baltrusaitis lists the names of "the various museums and catoptric 'cabinets' found in Rome, Milan, and as far north as Copenhagen" and then refers to "Multiplications, substitutions, reversals, magnifications, reductions, dilations, formal compressions," and an "entire operation" bending the laws of reflection into the spectator's service.[200]

The fragmentation absent in Baltrusaitis's catalog of mirror properties is present and prominent in Hernández's fiction as well as in legends associated with Hernández himself. In this last regard, an unsubstantiated but widely circulated anecdote relates that Hernández had a girlfriend who, as the result of an automobile accident (or, in an alternate version, of a bombing during World War II) had lost an arm, a leg, and an eye. When friends asked Hernández how he could be attracted to such a woman, his response was unambiguous: "I love taking her apart." The difficulty apparently arose the morning after, however, when he was recruited to put her back together. The attribution of this physical disassembly to Hernández—be it legendary or not—is perhaps the result of his more general tendency to "take the world apart and put it back together" in his thinking and his writing, to reject all blindly accepted givens so as to reconstrue and reconfigure reality in accord with his own vision.[201]

When the body is disassembled and reassembled, as Empedocles understood, some odd combinations and spare parts result. Likewise in psychopathology the composite body image "is liable to undergo partial or complete schism with separation (by projection) of the sequestered portion," and these projected parts can appear anywhere.[202] Just as a psychotic holds the literal belief that "There's an ear, cut off from a Jewish gravedigger, bouncing all over the room, also amputated legs and hands," Hernández's canon offers in a figurative register "a piece of a naked man" (3:16), chopped-up people mixed with pork in a European deli's cold cuts (3:59), a room "with arms and legs whitened and enlarged by casts" (2:84), "a lion broken to pieces" (2:74), a madman prepared to kill his mother with a hatchet (1:26), "decapitated" laughter (1:33), and facts "like legs and wings of insects in a swamp" (1:59).[203]

Elsewhere, in a corner with two mirrors forming a right angle, fragmentation as "projection of the altered elements of the body image" takes the form of reflective deformation: "I saw half of my head plus an ear from the other half" (1:123).[204] "The Usher" is punctuated with the refrain of "noises of sawed bones, chopped with a hatchet" (2:59, 2:62), while its protagonist sees his face "divided into pieces that no one could put together nor understand" (2:62) and at the conclusion of the narrative deploys this same destructive gaze to fragment a girl's body (2:70). In "The Balcony" the dining room is just below street level, "and through small, barred windows one saw the feet and the legs of those who passed by on the sidewalk" (2:49). Other fragmentations resulting from tight framing similarly deliver a "sequestered" body part—"an open hand in the middle of a sheet," for example (2:80)—that is "unattached" and often acts of its own volition. At the table, "hands and arms enter the whiteness of the tablecloth" (3:43), as though passing through the space reflected by a mirror, and these hands "seemed to be natural inhabitants of the table" (2:49). In another passage pairs of hands appear "on top of the bannister's velvet" (2:100), while elsewhere fingers that seem to be dispersed in the darkness are gathered together as they reunite on a girl's face (2:78). In some cases—"The Balcony" is a good example—images of body parts chopped off by cropping are integral to greater thematic developments: the narrator's vision restricted by the basement windows fragments the pedestrians, just as the daughter's vision, seeing these pedestrians unobstructed from the balcony but "cropped" by the restriction of her delusions, fragments people and confiscates the parts to construct the players in her imaginary dramas. Whereas Frankenstein collaged real corporal fragments to construct a humanoid monster, the Hernández character assembles the fragments of (often delusional) perceptions, reflections, and projections to populate a pseudocommunity around the self.[205]

The image of people as composites, as unifications of otherwise disconnected parts, evidences not so much the tendency to construct others by projecting parts of oneself (as in *The Hortensias*), but rather the intervention of one's self-image as fragmented into the perception of others. Parts of a girl's face, for example, "didn't seem to have come together spontaneously," but were rather assembled as though by "a person that calmly buys the best things from different stores and then brings them together and tastefully arranges them without forgetting anything." The girl had "everything necessary for a face" but the whole somehow never materialized from the sum of the parts (3:47). Earlier in *Lands of Memory* the parts of another face are "little beings," and the narrator looks at them "as if waiting for them to give me an idea that would bring together everything that I had known about that man and that I might be able to accommodate in a single word" (3:42). Later he adds that he had no choice but to "recognize the happy gathering of all parts of his face" (3:44). In another text a body rather than a face is concerned, and Ursula's corporal mass as an embodied lack of order is compared to the sprawling growth of a town (3:118).

The body as a composite of parts is further evidenced in Colling, who is "His cigarette, his cough, his hands, his fingernails, the brown stains under his nose," and so on (1:44). In "The Dark Dining Room" a light turns on and the illuminated "whiteness of the jacket, the shirt, and the teeth of Arañita" contrasts with the blackness of "the tie, the eyebrows, the eyes, and the hair" (2:111).[206] Elsewhere the fragmentation is by negation. Emphasis is not on what is seen, but on the absence that a "partial" object evokes: Marisa's white dress seemed like "Marisa without a head, nor arms, nor legs" (1:93). In "The Metaphysical Beard" the composite image is assembled, or disassembled, in the opposite manner: the parts are fragmented due to the "invisibility" of the being whose erased presence presumably would unite them. "There was something that attracted one's attention," but as in the previous examples of Colling and Arañita this was not a whole man but rather "there was a beard, a pipe, a wide-brimmed hat, a walking stick, and a pair of yellow shoes" (1:103). By the end of the section the free-floating fragments are reunited—"All of these things and he formed one single thing" (1:103)—but later the narrator is overtaken by the urge to disassemble, "to know what he would be like without his beard" (1:104).

A body part can also become fetishized through a metonymic condensation, as is the case in *The Lost Horse*. The boy taking advantage of distractions to gaze at Celina's bare arm remarks that "all of her was in that arm" (2:28).[207] "When the boy's eyes take a part of things, he supposes that they are whole" and consequently "proceeds as though they were" (2:28). Just as a broken mirror can deliver an unfragmented, complete image, the voyeuristic eye is skilled in demanding that the part "reflect" the complete body: "the broken pieces were as though whole" (2:131).[208] "Ursula" provides another example of the same when the entirety of the eponymous girl is concentrated into her eyes (3:118).

Fragmentation is also evident in Hernández's thematic evocation of and allusion to film. As Lisa Block de Behar has observed in this context, the screen presents *"fragmentary visions* of a totality that remains excluded." According to Béla Balázs, the response of a cleaning woman's first glimpse of the silver screen was horror: "I have seen people broken into pieces: the head here, the feet over there, the hands somewhere else."[209] Hernández's plays on reflection and projection, on mirror and cinema, suggest that the fragmented body of the mirror stage "is undoubtedly reactivated by the play of that *other mirror*, the cinema screen, in this respect a veritable psychic substitute, a prosthesis for our primally dislocated limbs."[210] But if certainly "film is like the mirror" (according to Eco, "A photographic plate is in fact a freezing mirror," and in film "the frozen image *moves*"), it differs from the mirror precisely where projection parts company with reflection. In the mirror the spectator appears among objects and the reflection "is present in the presence of *a referent which cannot be absent*," whereas in film the objects appear but the spectator's body is absent on the screen.[211] The intelligible progression of the film is made possible despite that absence because the spectator has already experienced the true mirror "and is thus able to constitute a world of objects without having first to recognize himself within it."[212]

Misrecognition of oneself in the mirror results, for Lacan, in alienation and fragmentation, and nonrecognition of oneself in the mirror-object results, for Christian Metz, in the possibility and comprehensibility of a world of illusory objects. Horacio is the subject interposed between these positions: his alienation and fragmentation gain expression through his complicated relation with mirrors, while he is simultaneously entangled with self-objects in an illusory world of projections. Narcissistic projection intersects with fragmentation precisely in the cinema images constituting the nuanced substructure of *The Hortensias*. The constant generation of images by a "projector" (reinforced by the emanating eye light of "The Usher," whose protagonist works in a movie theater); the "black house" as an implied darkened theater; the frequent appearance and play on the word *pantalla* (screen) in this and related texts; the lighted, curtained, screenlike showcases; the "machine noises" that accommodate projector sounds among their many meanings; and the pianist Walter, with his back turned like the accompanist of silent film—all contribute to the text's cinematic qualities.[213]

The mirror, film, and fragmentation are consolidated in an exemplary manner during scenes depicting the estranged Horacio's retreat to the hotel. The "machine noises" and the "black house" are first provided in their absence by negation—Horacio misses them ambivalently—and are then replaced by the noise of footsteps in the adjoining room and by the "dark place" crossed by the white arm that we have already seen (2:164). The mirror as cinema is then introduced as light from an opposite building "fell on the mirror that Horacio had beside him," as though a projected image were illuminating a screen. This silver-screen image then generates mirror-stage type reflections as Horacio "thought about his youth, had memories of other mirrors, and fell asleep" (2:164). A few lines later the mirror-film is repeated when the lighted windows of a house across the street cast their illumination onto the mirrors in Horacio's room. The program then abruptly changes, however, and with this change the definitive link between film and the mirror is established: Horacio "saw flames in his mirror" and "looked at them as though on the screen of a movie theater" (2:164).

Horacio's use of dolls as mirrors—internalized mirrors covered with "skin"—is also suggestive in this context, since "the whole cinematic institution is as it were *covered* by a thin and omnipresent garment, partially because the celluloid strip is a *pellicule* or 'little skin.'"[214] The narcissist wants to break through the membrane between himself and the world: Horacio crosses the glass barrier between social reality and the staged fantasy of the showcases, and, like the film viewer, penetrates the "skin" of his illusion (doll) by disavowing it as an illusion, by suspending reality tests so that the ritual (or film) preserves its meaning through to the conclusion. Should Horacio see himself rather than the other in this mirror, the show would be abruptly foreclosed: "Narcissus is in danger when he sees the image but not, because of that, lost. He is lost when he recognizes himself in the image."[215] The urge is therefore to find something beyond the image, to embark on the impossible quest of seeing oneself without recognizing oneself, of breaking through the mirror without fragmenting—as Narcissus did—the image that it returns. One narcissist obsessed with this quest to penetrate the illusion, to break through to the depths beyond the mirror's "skin," referred to his conquest of women as "unwrapping," getting beyond the surface to the withheld treasure of "a person 'underneath' the skin of women."[216] The "underneath" of Horacio's hollow women is no more than another reflecting surface, another self-as-other illusion in a series of sloshing images locked in a mirror without exits. "The adult child's flight is hopeless, for what it is feeling accompanies it everywhere it goes as its own mental projection."[217] Once Horacio "goes to pieces" at the conclusion of *The Hortensias*, he has nowhere to turn except toward the "machine noises" that crank out his mass-produced fragmentation and his projection of—and now into—an illusory, cinematic world.

3

The Tactility of Sight

The eye is the lamp of the body.

—Matt. 6:22

VOYEURISTIC THEFT

Each day has a body of its own, Plato reckoned in the *Timaeus,* made of sunlight that diffuses in the air until its withdrawal at nightfall defines a corporal closure. Because human bodies find themselves situated within that greater body of light, endowed with vision guiding their movement through it, Plato sought to understand sight as the mechanism by which the one body (human) interacts with and finds its orientation within the other (day). He came up with this:

> Whenever there is daylight round about the visual current, this latter flows forth, like to like, and coalesces with it and forms into a single homogenous body in direct line with the eyes, wheresoever the current issuing from within collides with some external object.[1]

In his physics of vision Plato thus imagined light rays projecting from (rather than entering) the eyes, interweaving the "pure fire within us" with the "proper body of each day," like to like, with daylight serving as intermediary between the object seen and the eye light making contact through projective vision. The theory of vision by eye emanations, known as extromission, had substantial currency prior to Plato (Theophrastus, for example, believed that "the eye obviously has fire within, for when one is struck [this fire] flashes out"), and was later reinforced variously by Galen, Euclid, al-Kindi, Roger Bacon, and John Pecham, among others, before falling out of favor under the sway of more sophisticated science in early modern Europe.[2]

If in *The Hortensias* and other texts the subject and the object of his desire are interrelated through the poetics of reflection, in "The Usher" gaze themes take a decided turn toward the fantastic as Hernández pursues what William Butler Yeats described as "the mirror turned lamp." The eye as one mirror bound to another escapes its Narcissus-like imprisonment inside a series of receding self-reflections when the protagonist of "The Usher" demetaphorizes the trope of projection, his eyes actually emitting a libidinous stream of light.[3] In a hyperpsychological discourse Hernández here utilizes fantastic vision that projects, that touches, to explore a complex of entangled themes: voyeurism as a means of "violating" forbidden or inaccessible women; the projective construction of others as players in one's fantasy, including the "retrieval" and ritualized use of fetishized objects or images representing these players; and the penetrating lucidity of a narrator celebrating his narcissistic grandiosity, notably in his ability to "see through" others.[4] The Hernández characters' "great necessity to see" (*OC,* 2:67) deploys sight as an instrument of the erotic urge to intermingle physically and psychologically with others, just as eye light intermingles with daylight in Plato's rendition, the two creating "a single homogenous body."

The sexual properties of the eye have a long history apparent enough in the Narcissus themes discussed in previous chapters, as well as in the more general coalescing of sexual transgression, vision, and punishment in Greek mythology. Freud's understanding of Oedipus's self-blinding as a symbolic castration in punishment for his unwitting incest with Jocasta is one notable case among many. Tiresias was blinded by Hera for judging that women experience greater erotic pleasure than men; Gyges found himself in a fatal double bind for having gazed upon the naked wife of King Candaules; and both Psyche and Orpheus lose their love objects (Cupid and Euridice, respectively) in punishment for forbidden peeps or glances. In the Old Testament the eye stands in for the phallus as the seeing of nakedness is metaphorically equated to physical sexual union.[5] In dream imagery, too, eyes are conspicuous representatives of the phallus, and colloquial language likewise addresses the power of vision to access in fantasy what is denied in reality through phrases such as "undressing with the eyes."[6] The popular belief that masturbation is punished with blindness also conforms inversely to these same poetics, suggesting, among other things, that sight will be deprived to those who opt not to use it erotically in pursuit of love objects beyond the self.

The commonplace function of the eye as an organ of erotic pleasure and as an instrument of incorporation is most legible in its pathological extremity, voyeurism. The protagonist of "The Usher" follows the narcissistic patterns we have identified in Hernández's psychobiography and in the tragicomic romantic escapades of *The Hortensias,* but he laces them with paranoia and extends them into decidedly voyeuristic behavior. The usher attests to Otto Kernberg's recognition that "sexual promiscuity of narcissistic personalities is linked with the sexual excitement for a body that 'withholds itself' or for a person considered attractive or valuable by other people."[7] Another clinician more generally observes that men in Western societies are "unceasingly informed, openly and subliminally, from childhood on, that they may not look, but that if they could the vision would be astonishing."[8] Narrators throughout Hernández's canon, intrigued by this "mystification of the anatomy, functions, and pleasures of sexuality," never miss an opportunity to steal a peep: "I realized that I could look at her with impunity so I got as close as I could" (3:47); "I took the opportunity to look at her legs" (3:100); "It suited me that she talked continuously, to conceal the fact that I couldn't take my eyes off of her" (3:147). In some cases the eyes wander back to their target despite the narrator's efforts to control them: "while I was distracted, my eyes had touched the mannequin's bust" (3:61). The gaze is averted, however, when its thrill is undermined by an object's accessibility: "A girl was doing exercises so that I would look at her. I realized that and continued looking at the white floor." When the same gaze—recharged now and glowing with voyeurism—finds its way back to the girl it has a menacing quality that frightens off its prey: "she took off running" (3:156).

The Hegelian sense of desire as mimetic, as entangled with the desire of others, drives the Hernández protagonist into the voluptuous quest of conquering women who are forbidden.[9] Horacio's escapades in *The Hortensias* are driven precisely by the thrill of accessing the forbidden woman represented by a succession of dolls, and the vicarious, symbolic, and onanistic nature of his rituals evidences the rather common tendency—both within and outside of the canon—to carry out in fantasy the romances that are denied one in fact. In *The Hortensias*, in passing moments throughout Hernández's canon, and notably in "The Usher," voyeurism serves as a primary instrument of such fantasies.

Just as the forbidden woman behind the doll in *The Hortensias* is symbolically violated but never actually touched, voyeurism maintains a distance between the subject and the untouchable, ominous (and almost numinous) female who is conquered only by vision. Like the autoerotic rituals of *The Hortensias*, "Except Julia," or "The Usher," clinical voyeurism and the masturbation that frequently accompanies it are "a way of being close and keeping distance at the same time."[10] Horacio with his showcase glass, the tunnel man with his obfuscated part-objects and covered faces, and the usher with his projecting gaze "touching" from a distance are all not-so-distant relatives of the voyeur who "is very careful to maintain a gulf, an empty space, between the object and the eye."[11] Such "erotic distancing" fixes the woman at the threshold where the protagonist's desire for her yields to his fear of her; she is situated at the range where "His sex is all in his eyes."[12] As in vision by extromission, a projection is "emitted from the eye to capture the object seen," but the voyeur ceremoniously maintains a distance that protects him from his own prey.[13]

From the safety of his vantage point but aroused by his transgression, the voyeur recharges his powers by visually absorbing the luxuries inaccessible to his touch: "my eyes had been empty and she began to refill them" (3:57). The woman who is seen must be forbidden, because "Perversion is made of two parts: danger and gratification."[14] "It's not just the nude body," as one voyeur put it, "but the sneaking out and seeing what you're not supposed to."[15] Most voyeurs consequently show no interest in strip shows, pornography, or sexual looking at the women to whom they have access. The mania in *The Hortensias* or "The Usher" for progressively more illicit trysts conforms to the voyeur's belief that the "forbidden fruit is sweeter," insofar as the harvesting of this fruit accomplishes in fantasy what is absent in reality and at the same time is *confined to fantasy* (in a showcase, in a tunnel, in a ritual) to insulate the subject from the genuine contact that he ultimately dreads.[16] One adolescent noted his predilection for peeping at coeds who "dated the football players," girls who he "considered too good for him" and "placed on a pedestal." These girls made him feel insignificant when he had legitimate social contact with them, but having violated and conquered them in the onanistic fantasy accompanying his voyeurism the roles were reversed and the voyeur was empowered by bravado: "I could laugh up my sleeve at them afterwards when I passed them on the street."[17] As a Hernández narrator expresses the same emotion, "I felt an evil pleasure in having deceived them" (3:101).

The groundwork for the voyeur's projecting spotlight as developed in "The Usher" is established earlier, in *Lands of Memory*, by a description of thoughts that reside throughout the human body, "although not all of them go to the head and get dressed in words" (3:30). The two meanings of "reflection"—thinking and mirroring—intersect when the eyes are vacated because the mind is preoccupied with some internal proceedings: "I reflecte, as the sonne beames do."[18] The wordless thoughts, or desires in the present context, rise through the body like Plato's "pure fire" to fill the vacancy in the "reflecting" eyes emptied by the intellect's momentary withdrawal.[19] The desires take advantage of the fortuitous distraction; they take position and "look for an object on which to fix their gaze" (3:30). Like light rising from what Plato would call the soul, these pre-articulate thoughts shoot out of the eyes to establish quasi-tactile contact with the world, pinning down an image, as Hernández put it elsewhere, like a butterfly into an album (2:28). "The ideas of a man are the continuation of the man," (1:103), on some occasions emanating "barefooted" or "undressed" to target a specific object and on others distributed more broadly in a circular process of "felisbertization": "it seemed as though my entire body had slipped out of my eyes and had returned to me like a very light air that lay on top of everything" (1:121).[20]

Development of an erotic visual/tactile synesthesia begins in "The Usher" when the narrator wakes one night to discover that light is projecting from his eyes, that he can see in the dark, that he can "touch" objects (which he hangs about his room specifically for this purpose) with his emanating illumination. Synesthetic images, particularly those consolidating the senses of touch and sight, are not uncommon in Hernández's canon. In an early text a woman covers her knee with her hand because she senses the narrator's gaze falling upon it (1:191). Elsewhere eyes that touch are paralleled by a nose that hears and sees (1:132); by a perception that is registered "as if the ears saw" (1:42); and by eyes that "ran from one place to another like dogs that smell everything" (2:204). A cross-sensual phenomenon receives more extended treatment in "Except Julia": if in "The Usher" one touches by seeing, in the tunnel rituals of "Except Julia" one sees by touching.

The usher's eye-light projections interrelate with cinema tropes (supported by his employment in a movie theater) and are accordingly voyeuristic from the start. Even before the usher discovers his gift he is happy, for example, "seeing ladies in diverse dresses" passing through the semidarkness of the movie theater, this quiet erotic pleasure gradually yielding to the more ambitious desire to "see something more through partially opened doors" (2:59).[21] For the usher as for the clinical voyeur, the eroticism is most exquisite when all of one's resources are challenged, one rises to the occasion, and the gaze manages to penetrate private enclosures where the objects of its focus are unsuspecting. Once secretly possessed they are as inalterably fixed as the past but simultaneously as manipulable as a memory. "I feel a strange sensualism," Hernández explained to a lover, not only because he is violating something but also because "the violated thing doesn't know that it's being violated."[22] The usher dramatizes a clinician's observation that, for the voyeur, "A fleeting fourth-inch peep under a window shade is infinitely more exciting than any form of legitimate or quasilegitimate erotic stimulation."[23] The obstacle is the essence of the quest and the catalyst of desire; "fantasy love does not seek out satisfaction but feeds on obstacles that are challenged by the eye."[24] The terra incognita of the contiguous room beyond view, of the enclosures made vulnerable by the partially opened door, and of the elusive daughter who enters the field of perception but cannot be "fixed" are all "indispensable ingredients" of the usher's recipe for erotic excitement.[25]

The nonerotic objects first drawn into the usher's projecting gaze—bottles and hanging pieces of glass—are promptly displaced by the more evocative secrets guarded behind the partially opened door that leads into a room of showcases. If "the paraphilic person is a survivor of catastrophe who repeatedly goes on camera or stage, so to speak," then the Hernández protagonist is one who inverts that urge by making a spectacle—in a showcase, "on a pedestal," framed by a window or mirror—of the love object created by his fantasies.[26] This spectacle is a "focusing lens" and "a place of clarification" where a ritual externalizes and activates fantasies, but it nevertheless must be veiled, must always retain the pressure of the forbidden.[27] The showcases and partially opened doors in Hernández's work satisfy these opposing demands of staging and hiding, of "seeing without being seen" (1:27), and they join with a cluster of related tropes—the tunnel, the balcony, the adjoining room, the dimly lit parlor and dining room—in representing an eroticized desire, like that of the clinical voyeur's, to make a ritualized spectacle of privacy, to cross prohibited borders and to "steal" the secrets jealously guarded there. The fact that the texts depicting these thefts tend to be uncanny is perhaps predicated by the etymology of *heimlich*: "From the idea of 'homelike', 'belonging to the house', the further idea is developed of something withdrawn from the eyes of strangers, something concealed, secret." The image "fixed" by the voyeur or held in the usher's penetrating eye light takes on an uncanny quality because *unheimlich* "is the name for everything that ought to have remained . . . secret and hidden but has come to light."[28]

Hernández narrators repeatedly confess their "need to be in unknown houses" (2:103), and their actions are often governed or interpreted in light of this desire to penetrate: "the dramas in other people's houses attracted me, and one of the hopes that my concert aroused was to make new acquaintances that would gain me entrance into unknown houses" (2:113).[29] These narrators are always favorably disposed to "violate some secret" and experience "the pleasure of violating something serious" (2:10): "there were many things that aroused my desire to search for secrets. Being alone in an unknown place was in itself one of them" (2:13). The haunt of "indiscreet curiosities" (2:12) compels Hernández narrators to make direct visual contact with the objects of their desire ("I couldn't stop passing my eyes across her naked arms") (3:19) or to indirectly access a person or persons via "relations" with fetishized surrogates, as in the bathroom scene of *Lands of Memory* where the boy enjoys "some objects that belonged to the intimacy of people I had just recently met" (3:30).[30] There is no sacrosanct place that escapes the gaze: "He is capable of opening the eyes of a dead man in order to register their content" (2:28). Overtaken by "an uncontainable vice" (2:198), "his eyes delivered themselves, with gluttony" (2:170). The "voracious looking" and "'oral' use of the eye" suggest an appetite that these narrators find difficult to satisfy, while simultaneously—particularly in "The Usher"—the "gluttony" reintegrates voyeurism into the ritual meals that often serve as its counterpoint.[31]

Among the objects of the showcases bedazzled by the usher's eye light are "fans that seemed like ballerinas opening their wide skirts," but the sexuality of his violating gaze becomes more explicitly insistent as his desire detaches from inanimate objects and fixes on an objectified subject, the phantasmal daughter of his dinner host. Here "the lust of seeing" properly speaking emerges: the narrator's visual projection of "the pure fire within us" makes tactile contact with and acts erotically upon the daughter as the seeing becomes doing, becomes a sexual gesture in itself.[32] The ritualistic, unilateral pseudorelationship between the narrator and the daughter dramatizes the projecting eye light's function as the agency of an extending self's envelopment and introjection of the objects he desires. The usher's perceptions, always negotiating a balance between his narcissism and his paranoia, are "conclusions of unconscious inductive inferences."[33] When she is enveloped and possessed by the usher's gaze the daughter becomes "the screen and the projection, all in one."[34]

"Stealing with the eyes" is a strategy that the usher shares in one way with the voyeur (who warehouses the "stolen" image in fantasy) and in another with the photographer (who "fixes" the "stolen" image in an artifact).[35] In clinical cases the figurative stealing characteristic of voyeurism is sometimes demetaphorized, with the voyeuristic theft of images alternating with actual crimes of burglary. One convicted voyeur-burglar remarked quite explicitly that "Somehow my Peeping Tom tendencies were converted into the urge to steal." Other cases are similarly characterized by "the interchangeability of voyeurism and burglary," with the spoils of the theft migrating between tangible commodities and the intangible but reified spoils of "stealing with the eyes."[36]

The retention of a "stolen" visual image is represented early on in Hernández's canon, notably in "The Poisoned Girl," where the corpse draws a crowd whose members are only ready to leave when they "knew by heart the details of the matter and of the poisoned girl's body" (1:128). In *The Lost Horse* the narrator arrives at Celina's living room with "his eyes full of everything that they had gathered on the street." When these same eyes rapaciously survey the objects now before him in the living room, "it seemed as though everything that the eyes brought with them would be extinguished" (2:9). The "absorbed" street images are being displaced by the living-room images, but when the boy momentarily rests his gaze he discovers that "things from the street returned to my eyes," taking advantage of the emptiness before gradually "accommodating themselves in oblivion" (2:10).

In "The Usher," where the retention and appropriation of quasi-tangible images is most fully developed, the narrator has spied the showcases behind the partially opened door and demands that the butler provide him access. The usher assures the butler that he will not steal anything, and then—as good as his word is literal—he "steals" everything in sight with his eyes: "I could look at a thing and make it mine," merely by enveloping it in his emanating eye light (2:65). In the most significant instance of his voyeuristic theft the usher, "like a bandit," casts his gaze on the daughter and appropriates a part-object: "My light not only illuminated that woman but also took something of her" (2:69). This "something" is a composite that counts attributes of the daughter among its components, but that elaborates what it has confiscated from the daughter, coalesces these attributes with the projection that floods them, and retrieves the composite into fantasy. The voyeuristic theft appropriates not the seen thing itself (the daughter) nor an objective image of her per se, but rather the "single homogenous body" of a projected desire fused with its object and then reincorporated into the seeing subject. The phantasmal nature of the daughter, as though she were a film image that sleepwalked off the screen, owes precisely to this appropriation and reconstitution of her within the spotlight of the usher's fantasy. The girl is untouchable, but her image is susceptible to the visual fondling that sees through her to the desire mobilized by her body.

This motion picture of the daughter flickering in a cone of light is one image among many underscoring the centrality of cinema tropes in "The Usher." The motif is reinforced elsewhere in Hernández's canon by, for example, the "black house" of The Hortensias (trading on its many allusions to movie theaters as salles obscures) or, in the quasi-biographical narratives, by memories that are compared to silent film and that are textualized with something of the graininess, choppiness, and Chaplinesque tone of the cinema's early history.[37] In "The Usher," cinema motifs are evoked not for a nostalgic replay of the past but rather to explore voyeurism, to borrow cinema's essence as an authorized version of unauthorized peeping into private lives, a collective voyeurism based on "the legalisation and generalisation of the prohibited practice."[38] The cinema in this perspective "represents a kind of enclosure or 'reserve' which escapes the fully social aspect of life although it is accepted and prescribed by it."[39]

It is in such a reserve of voyeurism that the usher's eye light is recharged and enhanced, but the conclusion of the narrative demonstrates how penetration of the confine can bring a permanent end to the rituals rehearsed there. In this case the butler bursts into the showcase room and—turning up the house lights—neutralizes the usher's projecting gaze that falls across the daughter's body. The interruption of an enclosed fantasy world by an intruding external reality is similarly represented in "Except Julia," where the owner explains that he cannot talk about the tunnel in which his obsession is played out darkly because the bright light of day damages his idea of it. Daylight bleaching out the tunnel owner's memories is like "the light that enters photographers' cameras when the images aren't yet fixed" (2:75).[40] In "The Usher" a variation of the trope obtains: the entrance of the butler and then the father disrupt the confine, the darkroom, in which the visual/tactile ritual's fixedness "takes," or—in the cinema metaphor—in which the screen (daughter), darkness, and projection (usher) collaborate as the necessary components for production of the show. Shortly after this intrusion the usher's emanating eye light is extinguished, partially because the source that had replenished it was "washed out" by the light of others. "The clarity was as inopportune as if at the cinema, in the middle of a movie, someone had turned on the lights" (2:21).

Christian Metz has further stressed the voyeuristic quality of cinema by observing that "it is always the other who is on the screen; as for me, I am there to look at him. . . . I am *all-perceiving*. All-perceiving as one says all-powerful."[41] This other on the screen, like the daughter recreated in the usher's fantasy and ritual, is absent as a true subject and is therefore completely vulnerable to interpretive manipulations by the viewer who gloats in the safety of omniscience. In the cinema "the actor was present when the spectator was not (= shooting), and the spectator is present when the actor is no longer (= projection): a failure to meet of the voyeur and the exhibitionist whose approaches no longer coincide (they have 'missed' one other)."[42] Metz stresses again that "During the projection this camera is absent, but it has a representative consisting of another apparatus, called precisely a 'projector'."[43] Like the usher with his projecting eye light, Metz continues, "I am 'casting' my eyes on things," and these, "thus illuminated, come to be deposited within me." A metaphoric negotiation between extromission and intromission completes the process, elucidating, for our purposes, the projective identification and voyeuristic theft that are dramatized in "The Usher": "A sort of stream called the look . . . must be sent out over the world, so that objects can come back up this stream in the opposite direction (but using it to find their way), arriving at last at our perception, which is now soft wax and no longer an emitting source." A series of absences and replacements are consolidated in the perception of the spectator who, again like the usher, "is the searchlight I have described, duplicating the projector, which itself duplicates the camera, and he is also the sensitive surface duplicating the screen, which itself duplicates the filmstrip."[44]

Reveling in the "confusion" of these multiple layers of duplication, the usher, like Horacio of *The Hortensias*, and like the voyeur, exploits an absent subject (absent because it has been objectified) as a screen that lends its blankness to a projected fantasy. With his all-perceiving capacity translating, à la Metz, to a sense of omnipotence, the usher assumes a privileged position among the objects of his gaze and masters the world as his creation. He projects his light to penetrate, to appropriate, to transform, to eroticize a milieu with him, his vision, and his secret power emanating at its center. This godlike posture—Christ's eyes, too, were "like a flame of fire"—attests to his narcissistic grandiosity, but egocentric reorganization of reality (though less hyperbolic) is similarly legible in the pragmatics of all perception.[45] Each seeing subject differentiates circumambient space in accordance with the schema of his or her own body. The objective space around one is constantly reorganized into new front-back, left-right configurations with the body (and its ego) always granted the privileged, central position in reference to which all other points are defined.[46] The body-centered universe constantly redefined from its roaming locus then yields readily to an egomorphic recreation because "men look at everything through their condition" (1:91). Characters like Horacio or the usher may try to "penetrate the mysteries toward which my imagination was projected" (3:33), but the mystery, always more formidable than the desire to demystify it, resists penetration, accepting the gaze as would a screen or mirror. The "imagination," the projection, precedes the mystery rather than arriving a posteriori to pursue it; the mystery is mysterious precisely because it is egomorphic and denied as such.

The emanating eye light of "The Usher" is a hybrid trope consolidating cinematic projection; narcissistic projection (encompassing body- and ego-centered perception and the tendency to "see through one's condition"); voyeurism, or the "seeing through" translucent others to the object of one's desire; "thoughts of the body" (desires) in search of screens for expression; and pseudo-omniscience as power. When this overdetermined, empowered vision is—as we shall see—exploited by the subject to narcissistically disavow his mediocrity, to congratulate himself for exclusive superiority, and to presume license to engage in the autoerotic extravaganzas afforded by his tactile, penetrating gaze, then "The Usher" offers a comprehensive understanding of Hernández's "lust of seeing," by which a projection of light, desire, and egocentrism not only touches its object but also secretly confiscates it as a reified image, eroticizes it, and exploits its fetishistic potential.

The process is clear enough in the following passage from *The Hortensias*. Horacio explains that when he looks at one of his showcase scenes, he extracts

> a memory that a woman has had in an important moment of her life . . . as if I opened up a crevice in her head. I then keep that memory as if I robbed from her an undergarment with which I imagine and deduce many things, and I could even say that going over it I have the impression of violating something sacred. (2:153)[47]

The visual violation of the sacred, of the forbidden, is a theft that yields an intangible commodity (the "memory," though *recuerdo* in the original here suggests "souvenir") that is *in*duced and then readily transformed into a concrete fetish (the underwear). For voyeurs, as for pilots in another Hernández text, "the knowledge that they call into play *what is not theirs* increases their emotion" (1:192). The passage from *The Hortensias* again recalls the *Lands of Memory* bathroom scene in which the narrator, naked prior to bathing, opens a hamper, takes out a woman's undergarment, and meditates on the intimate relation between it and his nakedness (3:31–32). In the bathroom scene, however, the narrative offers a concrete fetish from the start; the woman is absent but the boy's fetishistic urge demands that her sexuality be present in the garment that represents her. The passage from *The Hortensias*, in contrast, entails an "undergarment," a fetish three times abstracted: first, because it is a memory from the head of an imaginary woman-construct represented by dolls; second, because the memory is metaphorically concretized and eroticized as an undergarment; and third, because it is not a memory at all but rather a projection cast onto the dolls and then retrieved with its original source (Horacio) disavowed. The doll is "a virgin surface passively receiving the other's messages."[48] The lust of seeing ultimately provides, here as in "The Usher," that an object of erotic desire be displaced not by a concrete representation associated with it, but rather by an elaborated *image* (in a mind, in a mirror, on a screen, in a text) that can be exploited fetishistically. The daughter engaged in the rituals of "The Usher" is, as a subject, ultimately incidental to the process; she shrinks away as the narrator expands and projects. When his focus fixes on her he sees his desire enveloping its object. His image of her replaces her. The object of desire must be absent to be loved.[49]

A Penetrating Lucidity

The usher is a failure in life, unable to keep even a menial job, bewildered by a large city that dwarfs and demeans him. The single task that he performs satisfactorily—polishing the buttons on his usher uniform—is a metaphorical gesture of indulgence for his glowing eyes (2:61).[50] Solipsism is his burden but also his pride. He belongs to no community; most significant others in the narrative are cast in relation to his alienation. His single friend and the other dinner guests are all explicitly "foreigners," as is—first by suggestion (as a refugee from death) and again when she resurfaces as "German"—the daughter whom he desires. The men wearing caps, emblems in the text of all otherness troublesome to the usher, are "beings who could be found everywhere but who had nothing to do with me" (2:69).[51]

The usher is distanced from mankind by his existential woes, but in compensation for them and at once summoned forth by them he is endowed with his projecting eye light. He is another of many Hernández narrators vacillating between the poles of insecurity and grandiosity, with their grim self-perceptions ("I consider myself, with profound sincerity, worse [than others]) (1:185), alternating with their grandiose elations ("I will feel superior to everyone even if they and I myself prove that such is pure stupidity") (1:157).[52] The eye light will be the quality that distinguishes the usher, that sets him above all others rather than merely apart from them. This emanating "power" appropriates his alienation (in the same way that it appropriates the object of his gaze), names him as its source rather than as its victim, and brings it into his domain and his arsenal. "Instead of continuing to receive impressions from everything," remarks another Hernández narrator, projecting from his solitary confinement, "I will make an impression that will be received by others" (1:101). Indeed, the humble usher's inflated, Dostoyevskian pride emanates precisely from his visual power—"Who, in the world, has seen with his own eyes in the dark? (2:62, reaffirmed on 2:63)—and from the *secret* privilege that it affords him: "I felt proud to be an usher, to be in the poorest tavern, and to know—only I knew, even she [the daughter] didn't know—that with my light I had penetrated into a world closed to everyone else" (2:69).[53] The usher's vision thus enacts a metamorphosis not only of the object seen but also of the voyeuristic subject who appeases his fragile self-esteem and his paranoid sense of mediocrity by appeal to his secret powers, including his intellectual brilliance and his unimaginable sexual prowess, both characterized by their exceptional ability to penetrate. Like the adolescent voyeur mentioned earlier, he can "laugh up his sleeve," and like the Hernández of the Nobel Prize letter he can regulate his paranoia and restore his self-esteem by recalling that his penetrating lucidity is held reserved, quietly guarded from the perception of commoners. The secret nature of his eye-light emanations fortifies their potency; the narcissistic pleasure is redoubled because others "did not suspect how superior I was" (2:59).[54]

An interplay of perspectives characteristic of Hernández's work is thus generated: the voyeur gains visual access to the private delights otherwise inaccessible to him, while his guarding of this secret behavior keeps the defining aspect of his own character (voyeurism) private and inaccessible to others. The exhibitionist tendencies of the usher—consider, for example, the demonstration of his eye light for the butler—nevertheless stress a counterurge that betrays his ostensible endeavor to keep his power secret, thereby providing a "partially opened door" that opens into the spectacle's semisecret forum. Clinical voyeurs likewise often evidence this reversal of roles, revealing themselves by attracting the attention of their victims and then, in some cases, exposing their genitals or masturbating.[55] One voyeur realized "that he was knocking over things and making various noises outside the windows, as if he wanted to be noticed."[56] The seer thereby becomes the seen, or—perhaps more accurately—the scene.

The usher dramatizes voyeurism's expression of an inverted but pronounced desire to be seen. By "seen" I wish to imply recognized more than surveilled, although the panoptic, parental eye that many Hernández characters flee from does indeed contribute, by way of another counterformation, to the entire canon's obsession with escaping repressive supervision in order to "look without being seen" (1:27). In the clinical literature some patients indeed evidence a transformation from being the object of parental surveillance to becoming a voyeuristic subject. One patient's history begins with recollections of unfulfilled urges to shout at his mother, "Stop watching me." The man grew to become a professional photographer (an authorized voyeur), and during sexual relations he had fantasies about poking out and eating his girlfriends' (which is to say his mother's) eyes. The surveillance was thus symbolically neutralized through the blinding carried out in fantasy, while the voyeur, "aware of a feeling of hiding behind the camera," transformed himself from the object to the subject of the gaze by incorporating his mother's eyes through "eating" and by dedicating himself to a career in which he could "look without being seen."[57]

Hernández characters are likewise perpetually haunted by the mother's omniscient gaze, but in "The Usher" it is a paternal presence that surveils and interdicts. When the usher is caught in the act by the girl's father, one is reminded of the similar circumstances in *The Lost Horse*, where an eroticized transgression is halted (at least temporarily) by the ominous gaze of the husband-portrait (= father). The boy's voyeuristic gaze (like the usher's) intends to "undress with the eyes," but instead the boy is seen and seen through, his ritual foreclosed by surveillance.[58] Likewise the entire oedipal fantasy "Mamma's Tree" pivots on voyeuristic, peek-a-boo rituals that are terminated abruptly by the father's presence. The protagonist has spied his cousin's "naked legs" and awaits the opportunity to "touch" them with his gaze, but the opportunity is lost at the moment that it presents itself because "the door suddenly opened and her father appeared" (2:187).

While parental surveillance and interdiction are prominently represented in Hernández's work generally and in "The Usher" specifically, the usher's voyeurism as a projected desire to be seen expresses not so much a reaction to surveillance as a longing to be seen—in the sense of to be recognized—*as a subject*. His excessive, voyeuristic looking is a symptom of his desire to be acknowledged, to be more than an absence in the darkness, to himself fall under the spotlight of someone else's amorous gaze. As D. W. Winnicott put it in reference to the contorted portraits of Francis Bacon, "In looking at faces he seems to me to be painfully striving toward being seen, which is at the basis of all creative looking." Playing off of the Cartesian formula, Winnicott further suggests the reversals noted above in the interpersonal construction of identity: "When I look I am seen, so I exist."[59]

The emanating eye light may make a success of a failure, but it is precisely the aspect of himself that the usher cannot bear to witness. While his gaze projected upon objects and objectified others empowers him and brings him great joy, its reflection turning back on him is painful and destructive. A glimpse in the mirror of his glowing, Peter Lorre eyes ("a greenish yellow color that shined like the triumph of an unknown illness") along with the accompanying image of his face "divided into pieces" overwhelms him to the point of losing consciousness (2:62). He is calmed from the trauma only by an alien fragmentation, by the recurring sounds of a butcher's saw and hatchet hacking at bones. The usher evades the lethal mirror more effectively than Narcissus and Horacio only because he has mastered his power and learned to project his destructive gaze outward.

Entangled in competing demands, however, and ultimately most faithful to his onanistic agenda, the usher decides to confine his eye light to private rituals that carefully process out whatever otherness manages to infiltrate them. He is able to enforce the privacy of his showcase gazing— beaming among a constellation of objects—until the somnambulant daughter wanders in uninvited. The autoerotic ceremony is initially protected from her intrusion by the projective construction of the daughter as quasi-real and quasi-human; she may enter the ritual space but only as an object or image among others enveloped by his gaze, only with the translucence of a projection. She drifts in with the phantasmal distance of a sleepwalker enacting her own dream within the dream of another, of a drowned girl returned from the dead. The dreaminess of the daughter as a present absence is then reinforced by its complement in the narrator's own ambiguous state of mind: "I had the sensation of having slept a little" (2:66). The text's characteristic ambiguity, its hovering in the *seems* that never concretizes into an *is*, here functions precisely where the Greek term *opsis* intersects its meaning as "sight" with its meaning as "dream."[60] Either the projecting vision of the usher *sees* the daughter, or else he *has a vision* in fantasy or dream. The dynamics of those competing interpretations then generate a third: he sees her with his projections (represented by the eye light), which transform her into a vision of his fantasy. Since that fantasy demands that she not be there, that she not be there *as a subject*, the narrator compounds her phantasmal nature by describing her more as a spot-lit work of art (not unlike the sculpture associated with Celina in *The Lost Horse*) than as a human: "she seemed to have been made by hands after having been sketched on paper" (2:66).[61]

Be that as it may, the daughter as a subject manages to infiltrate the usher's ritual space and her presence immediately dominates the focus of his gaze. The girl is yet more threatening because she arrives with "another light that was not mine" that "wraps" and insulates her, resisting penetration after having itself penetrated the sacrosanct domain constructed by the usher's emanations (2:65). The daughter's (candle) light is strange, indirect, mysterious, feminine: the antithesis of the usher's phallic gaze.[62] This competing woman-light, contained by the light of the usher that wraps but cannot penetrate it, has the same effect on the narrator that his light has on others. As the daughter approaches, her light first makes his body burst into spasms and then objectifies *him*: "I was like a mannequin [*muñeco*] laid out in a shop window" (2:66). The roles reverse, with the voyeur now cast as the object of the gaze, the inanimate human object displayed under light. The resonance of this reversal into the showcase poetics central to *The Hortensias* underscores the shifting positions between the spectator and the spectacle that will bind the usher's fate to the daughter's in the same manner that Horacio's fate was bound to Hortensia's.

Once the daughter has entered the ritual space and has dominated the usher's focus, the act of looking in itself is no longer intrinsically gratifying. The usher must now *see her*. He cannot take his eyes off her, and this new demand conditioning his ritual ultimately undermines it, because for voyeurs "it is the experience of looking and not the seeing that is important."[63] Once the daughter has intruded, the usher loses interest in his eye light; he is prepared to forfeit his light, and with this forfeiture his claim to superiority and distinction, in order to sharpen his image of the daughter in her light. "I had forgotten my own light; I would have traded it all for a more precise memory of how the light of her candelabra enveloped her" (2:67). The usher—in words borrowed from elsewhere in Hernández's canon—has fallen in love with one of his victims (2:33). His imagination, compared to a lantern, shines on elusive "pieces of the past" that now absorb all of his emanations (2:26).

The stage had been set for this pending loss of eye light earlier, during the central ritual of the narrative, when the light's synesthetic tactile properties were compounded by olfactory sensations. The daughter, walking on his body, "passed across my face the entire train of her perfumed negligee" (2:66), and this sensory extravaganza (another "opening of wide skirts") is sufficient to overwhelm the eye light and effect a blackout: "I passed out" (2:66). Both in the ritual itself and in its recollection, the usher loses his light to a sensation or image of the daughter in her light. His desperate vulnerability, ratified by obsession, resurfaces because his claim to distinction has been bartered away and his last light has been squandered on a fantasy.

The walk-on-the-body ritual central to "The Usher" takes place in the showcase room, but it is alien to and interrupts the usher's original purpose there. He had in mind the casting of his eye light on the objects in the showcases, but this obsession is displaced by a far more intense one inaugurated when the daughter trails her negligee across his face. The perspective afforded by his prone position in relation to her upright and striding posture recalls a number of other scenes thematically central to Hernández's canon. In *The Lost Horse* the ambiguity of the word *pollera* (= skirt and furniture cover) is exploited as the narrator recalls his efforts to "violate" the secrets of Celina's living room by lifting and looking under the *polleras* on chairs. The white coverings are repeatedly associated with Celina (she once appears in "a white housecoat made of light and starched cloth") (2:14), and the lifting and peeking gesture correspondingly shifts from the furniture to Celina as the true object of the narrator's curiosity.[64] When described as "small, inoffensive ghosts" (2:15), these feminized white coverings further suggest a phantasmal female presence like that of the daughter in "The Usher," who moves the translucence of her glowing negligee through the narrator's hypnagogic field of vision. Elsewhere, in "The Crocodile," the lucky narrator is the passive player as a *pollera* is lifted to reveal a representation of his head carried under it: "She smiled and lifted the left side of her skirt to show me the top of her stocking where she had stuck a small portrait of me cut out of a program" (3:101).

The child's upward perspective in relation to the forbidden world defended by skirts and dresses gains more direct treatment in another

Hernández text, "My First Teacher." As the title announces, the woman in this case, like Celina, and like Hernández's first wife, is a teacher. The pun on the word *pollera* continues: the "skirt" meaning remains constant, but the *pollera* as furniture cover is complemented by the word's additional meaning as chicken coop (*pollo* = chicken). That wordplay is reinforced by another on the word *paraíso*, literally "paradise" but also figuratively signifying a theater balcony or, by extension, an overhang.

> Under a *paraíso* a hen was lying down; it began to cluck and from beneath its body—a gray color like that of the teacher's skirt—yellow chicks appeared. They must have been just as warm as my fingers in the teacher's hand. (3:151)

The relation between the hen and the teacher is definitively clarified a moment later, when the narrator adds: "That night, when I was alone in my bed, I remembered the hen and her chicks and I began to imagine that I lived beneath the teacher's skirt" (3:151).

The narrator's expression of his desire has intensified, progressing from a longing for a peek under symbolically laden dustcovers to a more permanent arrangement in the "paradise" under the teacher's skirt. As worded in a manuscript fragment, "I have often felt as though [I were] in Paradise—sinning a lot—and often as though in Purgatory—suffering a lot" (2:207). In the posthumous *Lands of Memory*—from which Hernández extracted "My First Teacher" for publication in a moderated version—the urge for the forbidden is yet more intensive and is finally followed through with action. The mood is set by yet another pun anticipating the *pollera* plays to follow: the boy's imaginary intrusions under the skirts begin when he lived "*en* [= in or on] the *falda* [= skirt and hillside] of a hill" (3:50). He daydreams that a crawl under the teacher's dress "would seem very natural to her" and that "while I was under her skirt she would look in another direction and if I touched her leg she would remain as still and as calm as the hen with the chicks" (3:50). After having assessed various possibilities and rehearsed "by every possible means" the way to carry out his desire, the boy slipped under a tablecloth—already a bold entry beneath a metaphoric *pollera*—as naturally "as an explorer who lives in his tent" and then "looking upward I stuck my head inside her skirt," taking care not to touch her legs with his head (3:50-51). Like Freud's "Rat Man," who at the age of four or five crept under the skirt of Fräulein Peter and fingered her genitals, the Hernández narrator derives from this inaugural experience "a burning and tormenting curiosity to see the female body."[65]

Echoes from the scene in "My First Teacher" disseminate in a different direction when one pursues *pollera* in its meaning as a chicken coop. In "No One Lit the Lamps," for example, the narrator is referred to as a "fox" by an old woman who intuits his ambiguous erotic intentions concerning the girl with whom he converses, herself compared to a hen. The trope is simple enough: the fox wants to penetrate the boundaries of the forbidden *pollera* (chicken coop, skirt), and then incorporate—with the (phallic) eye or with the mouth, as the case may be—the delicacies protected there. The theme returns full circle to "The Usher" and to the gaze when the predatory attribute is localized in the narrator's "eyes like a fox" (2:45).

The word "paradise," too, links into a more sustained series of quasi-erotic associations. In *Lands of Memory* the narrator recalls his having attended, at the age of fourteen, his first concert offered by a famous pianist. Having climbed up the many stairs "until reaching the *paraíso* of the theater," the boy remarks: "I thought about the 'effort' that it took to climb the stairs and what I would find when I 'reached' the top," and he considers the word "heights" in its relation to *"paraíso."* He then adds: "this was because the piano teachers, the students' mothers, and the journalists who praised the famous pianists used no cliché other than 'the effort to reach the heights of art'" (2:9). The upward perspective, the climb and the rising, the reference to the teacher (Celina) and the mother, and the suggestive word *cumbre* (summit, heights, peak) in its relation to the equally suggestive "paradise" all echo the erotics of climbing under the teachers' skirts, particularly when one recalls Freud's observation that, in dreams, "Steps, ladders or staircases, or, as the case may be, walking up or down them, are representations of the sexual act."[66]

These associations most effectively inform the over-the-face ritual of "The Usher" in light of a trope from *Clemente Colling*, where a grand stairway "opened like the train of a wedding dress" (1:24). Much the same is repeated in *The Hortensias*, where the stairway is María's "marble dress" (2:137). In "Except Julia," too, a *cola* (tail, train of garment, end) surfaces in proximity to a stairway, in this case because the *"cola* of the tunnel" is located at "the stairway in the back" (2:74). The tunnel central to the narrative itself carries obvious sexual implications, and these are fortified by the tunnel's camouflage, by its eroticized rituals, and by the *cola* poetics trailing behind them.[67] A passage in "The Crocodile" works the eroticized escalation trope in reverse, revealing a pair of legs followed by a green *pollera* as a woman descends the rungs of a ladder (3:93). When a narrator himself rests his foot on a step, he says, "It is incredible what pleasure this gives my body" (3:179).

The desire to slip underneath the skirts of the teachers is a specific paradigm manifesting—and perhaps engendering—the more general urge of Hernández's characters to cross any forbidden boundary and to invade any "abyss of promises" that withholds its eroticized pleasures (1:52). "There is an obvious similarity between the voyeur's sexual search in the realm of the forbidden and the child's sexual curiosity which is met with silence, evasion, and frank rebuttal, thereby encloaking sex with an enticing aura of forbiddenness."[68] Once the child's curiosity is awakened by anatomical differences of male and female bodies, "the desire to look becomes intense, insatiable, and permanent to the extent that the body parts are forbidden and at the same time considered desirable by the parents; in their forbidding, parents let their child know there is dangerous pleasure possible."[69]

The specific ritual of the negligee trailing over the face—supported by the various *pollera* episodes from the biographical fictions—is particularly suggestive when compared to an incident related by Hernández in a 1936 letter. The Hernández family's situation of desperate poverty in 1929, at the time of Hernández's first concert in a Montevideo theater, necessitated the selling of the household's furniture. After the concert, the young pianist returned home "to sleep on a mattress on the floor."[70] The coincidence of the mattress on the floor here and in "The Usher" is in itself only suggestive, but it gains resonance in light of the associative continuum that in dream imagery links phantasmal images with nightgowns and mothers; in light of the daughter's negligee linked to "the sheets of my childhood" (2:67); and in light of the short distance (which we will bridge in the next chapter) between the mother imago and the "teachers" whose dresses are directly and indirectly penetrated by the boy protagonists. The maternal qualities of the nightgowned daughter of "The Usher" are further enhanced when we recall that the daughter was saved from drowning; if Freud is to be trusted, "A man rescuing a woman from the water in a dream means that he makes her a mother."[71] What the Hernández text perhaps expresses through allusions and feints is made explicit by Stendhal's character Henry Brulard. An oedipal admission opens the episode—"I want to cover my mother with kisses, and for her to have no clothes on"—and is followed by a negligee-train scene reminiscent of "The Usher": "One evening, when by some chance I had been put to sleep on the floor of her room, on a mattress, this woman [mother], as light and agile as a deer, bounded over my mattress to reach her bed more quickly."[72]

If the daughter's entrance into the usher's world of rituals was traumatic, her exit will be even more so. When the usher believes that he sees the daughter on the street—a belief that the narrative confirms only insofar as "The paranoid projects and regards his projection as a reality"—she is accompanied by a man "dressed in black and wearing a cap like a crook's" (2:67-68).[73] An agitated, almost delighted jealousy overtakes him as his desire is enhanced by competition with his rival: "I had never experienced such excitement" (2:68). The usher's pursuit and his fantasized conquest of the inaccessible stimulates him beyond measure, and his excitement is further enhanced, now masochistically, by the abuse implied by the girl's "infidelity" and by her "violation" of the pact to which—as far as the usher is concerned—she is bound by virtue of their secret ceremony. Earlier the usher had an ambiguous response to the demeaning treatment of being walked on during the negligee-over-the-face ritual: first he rejoiced as he delivered himself in ecstasy to the erotic sensuality of the experience, but later secondary revision elaborated the episode to restore his wounded dignity. In these retrospective fantasies the aberrant "caress" of being walked on is displaced by an endearing and revering gesture: the daughter kneels down and kisses him (2:67). In his dream she walks down the wedding aisle as solipsistic as he is, with no groom and with her one hand holding the other; the usher as such, as subject, is apparently excluded. But on the train of her wedding gown, like the train of the negligee that passed over his face and "erased dirty memories," she drags a dog with which the usher identifies (2:67).[74] Instead of walking over his face the bride now drags him in tow. Just as she entered his ritual as an object, he enters her love (also his fantasy) as a dog. The dream then salvages his dignity from the insult by splitting his identity between the dragged beast and a man standing apart, as the usher stands, witnessing the ceremony, casting his gaze upon it. This man transmits an idea to the dog: "Let yourself be carried along; but think about something else" (2:67). Understood as the usher's discourse scripted for the dog, the lines of the dream read: "It is tolerable (and mildly ironic) that I'm treated like a dog, that I'm walked on, that I'm a worthless usher in a run-down movie theater, because I learned to 'bow my head with respect and contempt' [2:59], because I 'think about something else,' reserving my knowledge of the attribute that enlightens and distinguishes me and holding my powers in reserve."

Soon, however, the bravado of the dream and the "discreet pride" (3:67) are pierced by the unforgivability of the daughter's capital crime, her "infidelity." The daughter not only defiles the sacrosanct ritual into which she sleepwalked uninvited, but she is also "seeing" a foreigner while failing to recognize (see) the usher. The "cuckold"[75] thus changes his tune to sing the woes of betrayal:

> I thought that the world in which she and I had met was inviolable; she cannot abandon it after having passed the train of her negligee over my face so many times; that was a ritual in which the fulfillment of an order was announced. (2:69)

The daughter's intrusion into the ritual and then her indifferent violation of its solemnity breaches the usher's secret pact and silent oath. His idealization of the girl consequently swings into its antithetical counterpart, devaluation, then beyond it into the extreme desire to literally destroy her. "I have to do something," the usher concludes, because his madonna has become a whore, his work of art has taken on a life of its own and has sleepwalked out of his dream (2:69).

THE EVIL EYE

> *What has been created that is worse than the eye?*
> —The Wisdom of Sirach

If in the extromission theory of visual perception rays emanate outward from the eyes to strike objects in the world, in the evil-eye beliefs prevalent in Western culture these emanations are endowed with the malevolent power to injure or destroy whatever they "touch."[76] As defined by Alan Dundes, the evil eye "is a fairly consistent and uniform folk belief complex based upon the idea than an individual, male or female, has the power, voluntarily or involuntarily, to cause harm to another individual or his property merely by looking at or praising that person or property."[77] Whether in the first-known reference to the evil eye—a seventh century B.C. Chaldean manuscript—or in contemporary Mediterranean, American, North African, and Near Eastern folk beliefs, both sexual and destructive attributes consolidate in the eye's power. The destructive forces emerge from the evil eye's close association with envy; if endowed with the evil eye, one person envious of another's looks, loves, possessions, or luck could injure or destroy these with an emanating gaze. "The word *envy* is etymologically derived from the Latin *invidia*, which in turn comes from *in videre*, thus ultimately from 'to see' or 'seeing'."[78] It is for this reason that protection against the envy-motivated evil eye often takes the form of symbolic degradations, of demeaning an object so as to de-emphasize the positive attributes that might arouse envious or covetous emotions. One washes one's infant in the pigs' trough or in a tub with hog's excrement, for example, as a precautionary gesture to ward off the evil eye. One avoids praise because, as Hieronymus Fracastorius remarked in 1550, "praise creates a peculiar pleasure and pleasure in turn opens the heart, the face and especially the eyes so that the closed doors are opened to receive the poison."[79]

The "poison's" potency, as reported by Gaius Julius Solinus, is lethal: certain women in Scythia "kill people by sight if they happen to look at them when angry." Similarly in fourteenth-century England it was generally accepted that the Black Death was transmitted by the gaze of contaminated individuals. In earlier Egyptian mythology, the deities themselves emerged from the eyes of Ptah, and the supreme sun god Ra floated with his eyes closed in the primordial ocean until, arising, he opened them to create the universe. When plotters conspired against him, it was the eye of Ra that took vengeance and destroyed them.[80]

The destructive eye also has considerable currency among the delusions of psychotics. One hospitalized patient repeatedly remarked, "I'm evil because me eyes can hurt you," while a clinician more generally observed that "The 'spirit-infested' eye of a psychotic person becomes a terrifying, aggressive organ that can change the course of events, maim and kill others, and force one to look at tempting or forbidden persons or things."[81]

These premodern, mythological, and psychopathological representations of the eye's power obtain more moderately in contemporary folk beliefs, summoning forth a barrage of preventatives—veils (notably for brides), amulets, gestures—to protect one's self, one's family, and one's property from the evil gaze readily disposed to harm them. The evil eye can kill one's goat, break down one's truck, ruin one's business, because eyes and the gaze are piercing, penetrating, keen, deadly, and sharp. Popular expressions register the figurative capacity of the eye to "burn holes" when one is stared at from behind, while looks can kill, penetrate, shoot daggers.[82] The "shooting" of a film or light "shooting" out of the usher's eyes likewise suggests visual violence, particularly in the context of Etiennes-Jules Marey's 1882 experiments with motion photography. "'Shoot' quite literally applies to Marey's experiment, for his camera looked like a shotgun."[83]

In Italian traditions, notably in Naples, the evil eye is personified in men known as *jettatore* (from the verb *jettare*, "to cast off," "to throw out"). The gaze of the *jettatore* is harmful by virtue of erotic rather than aggressive projections.[84] One of the oldest extant texts concerning the evil eye, a Sumerian incantation from the "House of Light," includes among the evil eye's preferred targets the female body "undressed with the eyes": "Unto the maiden it approached and seized away her robes."[85] Plutarch also treats the motif through allusion to the erotic eye's burning and piercing capacities, noting that the eyes of lovers shoot fiery rays while the eyes of the envious are like poisoned arrows that pierce the objects of their gaze.

In studying traditions representing the erotics of visual destruction, Géza Róheim has observed that the phallus is predominant in countermagic deployed as protection from evil-eye emanations. "In Latin *fascinum* means both the evil eye and the penis as averter of the evil eye." Other etymological examples carrying over into modern Italian are cited, but most convincing are the many apotropaic amulets and gestures that evidence clearly phallic elements. In the *mano fica* gesture used to ward off the evil eye, for example, the thumb stuck between the index and middle fingers carries strong suggestion of sexual union, particularly since the "fig" in Greek and Latin traditions is closely associated with the vulva.[86] The manual gesture also condenses and reasserts the relation between the erotic gaze and the sexual touch that it represents.

Punitive actions to disempower carriers of the evil eye are in many cases also overtly sexual. In Greece, for example, one hears: "If it is a woman who has cast the eye, then destroy her breasts. If it is a man who has cast the eye, then crush his genitals."[87] The latter case contributes to the psychoanalytic recognition of the substitutive relation between the eye and the phallus as represented in fantasy, dream imagery, mythology, and artistic expressions. The association between the eye and the genitalia also further contributes to the folk belief that excessive masturbation causes blindness.

If the punishment for masturbation implies the deprivation of sight to those who fail to use it in search of a love object, it also reflects the consequences of excessively draining one's vital fluids.[88] Once the sexualization of vision or the "unconscious 'genitalization' of the eye" are introduced, one can understand the "blinding" in "The Usher"—implied by the protagonist's loss of eye light—as a squandering of the light-fluids and drying up of their source as a consequence of the autoerotic ritual that fails.[89] As Dundes has pointed out, "The most common effect of the evil eye is a *drying up* process." Cows' udders go barren, trees whither, "it is the blood, the sap or vitality of youth, the maternal milk, or masculine semen that is coveted" and, from the other perspective, that is expended and depleted.[90] One schizophrenic accordingly believed that a powerful eye surveilling her had the capacity to suck vital fluids from her body.[91] This delusion conforms to a common function of the schizophrenic's "influencing machine," which more broadly entails "the transmission or 'draining off' of thoughts and feelings by one or several persecutors."[92] The progressive depletion of eye light as the usher expends himself on his fantasy lover can in this context be understood as "the draining off, into the outer world, through projection, of much affect and ideation which belongs to his self."[93]

The nexus of the eye, the phallus, and vital fluid has also generated substantial traditions relating eye emanations themselves (including the eye light of "The Usher") to ejaculation. For the Egyptians the magical fluid *Sa* that flowed through the veins of the pharaoh was the gold of the sun's rays. The verb *sotpou* was used to describe the emission of *Sa*, but also denoted the shooting forth of water, flames, and arrows, as well as the ejaculation of semen. According to Ernest Jones, the sun's rays are often regarded as "a symbol of the phallus as well as of semen." At the same time, in several Egyptian tombs each ray of light stretching out to the sun's adorers terminates in an open hand, making the tactility of these emanations clearly legible.[94] In 1625 Francis Bacon also sounded the theme by noting that envy provokes an "ejaculation" from the eye, and a variation is registered in northern Rhodesia, where the possessor of the evil eye is referred to as "hard-eyed."[95] The terms *jettatore* and *ejaculation* are derived from the same Latin root, and in evil-eye preventatives among modern Greeks and Greek Americans the phrases used to defend oneself from the evil eye are likewise "ejaculated."[96]

The eye light of "The Usher" relates directly to these poetics of the evil eye: a projection of erotic desire (glossed with malignant and envious properties and recast as "aggressive looking" or "envenomed exhalations")[97] brings harm to those upon whom it falls, particularly upon the daughter who occupies the focus of the usher's voyeuristic gaze. The projecting light as "the triumph of an unknown illness" (2:62) sends its disease outward and, when it reflects back from a mirror, is sufficiently powerful to fascinate and level even the subject who has cast it. The narrative's loading of the gaze with destructive attributes is then significantly advanced when the usher stages a demonstration of his eye light for the butler. This spectacle takes place in the hat room, a site previously associated with death (the dead dinner guest was carried there), and the danger of the eye is duly registered by the butler's terror.[98] Prior to the hat-room spectacle the butler protects his eyes from the usher's damaging gaze, and after it he runs from the room, exclaiming, "Get out of here, sir," while "he had his hand over his eyes and was trembling" (2:63). The associations that modulate forward (via the link hat-cap) into the "death" by eye light (via the link cap-light) will concern us presently. At the narrative's conclusion the evil-eye themes are made even more explicit when the butler unambiguously exclaims that the usher "has a hellish light in his eyes" (2:70).

When the usher returns to the showcase room for the final ritual he is excited by envy, burning with desire, and determined to fulfill his mission. His demeanor is well described in the big-game tropes used by a clinical voyeur: he is on a "safari" in search of "prey."[99] The usher arrives armed not only with his emanating light loaded with evil-eye properties, but also with a cap, established earlier in the text as the insignia of others "who have nothing to do" with him. Standing out in this amorphous, anonymous mass of otherness is the usher's rival for the daughter's favors, a man who wears a cap like a crook's and who is "seeing" the daughter and "stealing" the delights that the usher's voyeuristic theft intends to recover.

By confronting the daughter with, precisely, a cap, the usher has appropriated the insignia of otherness and stamped it with his own insignia: light. From the resulting composite of the self consolidating the other, the cap is styled "a black lantern," fusing the cap and the blackness proper to the rival ("dressed in black") with the light proper to the usher.[100] The faltering eye light is thus temporarily salvaged by resort to its antithesis (blackness/rival) as the usher co-opts the other. The usher's penetrating and absorbing eyes extract attributes from the daughter and from the rival, and the usher consequently experiences, like Dracula, a sense of rejuvenation, a replenishing of his lucid fluids, "like I had taken something powerful from them."[101]

The "auxiliary power" generated by the lust of seeing is not derived directly from the object itself but rather from the deposit of eye light into the object and then the withdrawal of this investment to retrieve the "stolen," self-object image that the usher reincorporates into the self. The process reads more like a recharging than an empowerment. In the same way that erotic desire is enhanced through gradual, striptease revelation of an inaccessible body, the objects eroticized by the narrator's gaze return back up the cone of vision to reciprocally reload the same desire that at once "touched" and distanced them. Alternating currents are channeled through subject and object in a circular process of autorejuvenation. Ultimately the recharge ritual is self-defeating, however, for the same lustful seeing that excites and enhances the eye light at once drains off the reservoir that feeds it, leaving the usher, like the compulsive masturbator, repeating his ritual at progressively more frequent intervals to appease the frustrated satisfaction that at once propels and depletes him.

The ritualization of such autoerotic tendencies are represented with great currency throughout Hernández's fiction, particularly in *The Hortensias*, "Except Julia," "The Balcony," and "The Usher." Strange and rigid systems regulate what one is permitted or not permitted to see (3:75); what one is permitted to know or when one is permitted to inquire (2:137; 2:153; 3:76); what one should do or not do (3:84; 3:129); and where certain actions are appropriate or inappropriate (2:81). Also common are ritual postponements, or the required awaiting of the proper moment for realization of some action imbued with private, mysterious meaning (2:48; 2:77; 3:77).

The primary purpose of ritualization in "The Usher" is to preserve and recharge power, an endeavor that this fiction has in common with an analogous (if more severe) case from the clinical literature. One evening, while sitting in his kitchen watching television, a psychotic man "looked up and saw a man's face at the glass kitchen door and heard a voice say 'do the habits and things will go right.'" Before going to bed that night he performed his first ritual by rolling the television cord into a tight coil. The delusional system reorganized the patient's life in pursuit of "a 'Power' that could bring him luck, provided he could retain it within his possession through ritualizing," and within a few months rituals had virtually taken control of him. Auditory hallucinations with the quality of real voices ordered him to repeat certain actions—"do that again" or "go back and touch that door"—and his "connections" with reality were (like those of the usher and, figuratively, Horacio) mediated by emanations or projections from his own body. "He frequently saw a 'Black Dot,' about the size of a fist, leave his body and enter some object in his environment. When he experienced the loss of the 'black dot', he felt compelled to ritualize to regain the 'Power' that he believed was contained in it."[102] Be it a black dot, an emanating eye light, a cap of black light, or a narcissistic projection that exerts an invisible control over others, the rituals of this patient and his literary counterparts in the work of Hernández all entail projection and retrieval within a closed circuit of alternating currents.

When the daughter approaches the usher during the final ritual in the showcase room, he throws the cap at her, hitting her breasts.[103] By throwing the hat he casts onto the girl not only his (faltering) eye light but also its emblem, his "great black seal," an objectification of his gaze othered, his gaze blackened, his gaze blacking out (2:69). The usher's subjectivity is thus objectified and extended by gesture rather than by vision: the tactility of the gaze is further concretized as a projectile displaces the projection. The gesture reads: "I adopt the insignia of the other, who has contact with you, in order to make contact with you. Instead of projecting my light, which is luminous (but extinguishing), I extend my touch by throwing this black light at your breasts. I knock you down so I can 'see' you."[104] The assault that physically immobilizes the daughter and predisposes her to the usher's lustful, injurious gaze is reminiscent of that of a voyeur who, atypically, filled a sock with pebbles, entered the home of his victim, and "hit her over the head, intending to knock her unconscious so that he could look at and feel her breasts."[105] The voyeur is armed with a sock and the usher with a cap, but both "fix" their victim's disposition for an aggressive, erotic ritual during which tactility migrates between the eye and the hand.

When she is hit by the cap the daughter faints; her lights go out.[106] She cannot hold a candle to the usher. With her protective wrapping of light extinguished and her body collapsed and vulnerable on the floor, the daughter now assumes the role of shopwindow mannequin that her light had previously assigned to the usher. She has, like the Hortensia dolls elsewhere, "fallen" to become the eroticized object that the usher's projective gaze endeavored to make of her. Again like the Hortensias, and like the woman knocked unconscious by the sock, she can be "touched" at will, dominated by his tactile light taking inventory ("like a bandit searching her body with a lantern") (2:69); "stealing" ("My light . . . took something of her") (2:69); and metamorphosing (her body "was no longer the same") (2:70). In this scene like no other in Hernández's canon, the ubiquitous desire to "violate some secret" reaches a climax as the phallic properties of the eye bring *violar* to its most sexual meaning as rape, here symbolic rape, the long-distance rape of the voyeur.

In the iconography of Annunciation paintings the Virgin's divine impregnation is often represented by light passing through a window.[107] The image is suggestive in the context of *The Hortensias* showcases—where Horacio's gaze passes through glass to "penetrate" the dolls—but it is most resonant when the usher, like a voyeur outside a window, makes love from a distance, projecting a light that stands in for the phallus and penetrates the translucence of the daughter's body. If in Annunciation paintings the unbroken window serves as a symbol of the Virgin's virtuous hymen and of the bodilessness of her impregnation, in other traditions the window is equated with the eye itself. Ambrose is explicit—"Your eye is the window" (of your body)—and the eye-with-window motif of Albrecht Dürer portraits also makes the connection unambiguously.[108] Rather than being the active, projecting lamp of the body, the eye in these cases is like the Annunciation window, passive and receptive, an anatomical orifice disposed to penetration by sexually symbolic light emanating from other sources. In contrast to the male characters who avoid light because it challenges their own emanations, the dolls of *The Hortensias* have eyes with a certain prostitutional quality, readily (if passively) disposed to "annunciation": "The sunlight did not bother the doll: it penetrated into the depths of her eyes."[109] Women in Hernández's canon tend to be penetrated by light, to have light shined onto them, to appear in the voyeuristic spotlight, or, like the Virgin, to be accessed through glass by the light that works on their bodies. Male characters, in contrast, tend to emanate light as a trope of erotic and narcissistic projections, and when glass is involved (portrait glass, eyeglasses, shopwindows, showcase glass) it lends itself in varying configurations to penetration that accesses an eroticized object or to reflection that attests to these characters' impenetrability and their use of the world as a mirror. The usher with his emanating eye light is of course the paradigm of the male projector, but even the blind Clemente Colling "projected some beam of crude light" (1:48), and in his dentist mode the mild-mannered Scout leader in *Lands of Memory* features eyeglasses that shine like headlights (3:45).

Once the daughter of "The Usher" is knocked unconscious, both the destructive and the erotic properties of the evil eye operate simultaneously in effecting her metamorphosis. "Born of Desire," as Kojève put it, "action tends to satisfy it, and can do so only by the 'negation,' the destruction, or at least the transformation, of the desired object: to satisfy hunger, for example, the food must be destroyed or, in any case, transformed."[110] This tendency to transform the desired object makes a decided turn toward erotic destruction in perversion as defined by Robert J. Stoller, who understands it as "habitual sexual fantasy or acts at whose root lies hostility."[111] In men, according to Stoller, perversion entails a "triad of hostility," the components of which are extremely suggestive in light of Hernández's psychobiography and literary canon: "*rage* at giving up one's earliest bliss and identification with mother, *fear* of not succeeding in escaping out of her orbit, and a need for *revenge* that she put one in this predicament."[112] When these components, notably the last one, gain expression in voyeurism, "a man must believe he is acting forcefully, sadistically, upon an unwilling woman: he is doing what, so the fantasy goes, she decidedly does not want. If he can do so he defeats her; he gets revenge."[113] Expressing this "act of cruelty and triumph over trauma of an early parental humiliation," one voyeur felt that his erotic looking "punished women who were careless with their nudity," in the same way that the usher's vengeful gaze punishes the daughter for her careless "infidelity."[114]

In a more general discussion of object relations, Winnicott argued that after "subject relates to object" comes "subject destroys object" (as it becomes external) and then "*object survives* destruction by the subject." The subject's (usher's) implied discourse addressed to the object (daughter) thus reads, "While I am loving you I am all the time destroying you in (unconscious) *fantasy*."[115] In pathological instances, such as those of the voyeurism that concerns us, the closed circuit of erotic cruelty is strategically exploited: the object survives so that the process of destruction can be rehearsed repeatedly. In cases of voyeurism such as the one dramatized at the conclusion of "The Usher," the sadistic phallic properties of the eye reveal a subject who "wants to see something in order to destroy it." Fenichel further observes that often "looking itself is unconsciously thought of as a substitute for destroying ('I did not destroy it; I merely looked at it')."[116] The eye is used to dominate, injure or destroy, but these are symbolic gestures that may ultimately constitute "a defense against aggression in that it is safer to look and destroy unconsciously than to act and destroy literally."[117] Like the through-the-window impregnation and the long-distance caress, this destruction, this "revenge," is carried out only symbolically. The fantasy is enacted but only by the eye or, in Hernández's case, the eye in the text. Rather than a woman clobbered over the head with a sock full of stones, the daughter of "The Usher"—twice a fiction, once of the author and again of the usher—falls under the blow of a textualized fantasy paying reluctant homage to an elusive, "unfaithful," and transparent body adapted from the author's "film of memories."

The sadistic and evil-eye qualities of the gaze that are patent at the conclusion of "The Usher" are expressed more moderately earlier in the narrative through use of the eye to dominate. The pattern commences as the usher appropriates and mimes the parental use of the eye to surveil. Such is apparent, for example, in the usher's spying on the daughter and her "boyfriend," and this in itself is an extension, an externalization onto self-objects, of the Hernández narrators' incessant self-spying. Surveillance then yields to more determined expressions of domination through a voyeurism that recruits all others into the usher's autoerotic drama, scripting supporting roles for those who fall under the usher's spotlight. The daughter, the butler, the men in caps, the rival, and the dinner guests are all "being manipulated so as to be playing a part, no matter how difficult to recognize, in somebody else's fantasy."[118] In *The Hortensias*, "The Flooded House," and the Nobel Prize letter, the participation of others in a protagonist's fantasy is even more explicitly present as specialists—technicians—are contracted to enhance the fantasy and, on occasion, are themselves emotionally engaged by it. Margarita attracts the narrator of "The Flooded House," for example, "with a force that she seemed to exercise from a great distance, as though I were a satellite" (3:82). In other texts passive players are similarly drawn into the orbit of one character's dominating fantasy, be it expressed in the tunnel owner's ritual in "Except Julia" or in the pseudocommunity constructed by the daughter in "The Balcony."

In "The Usher," the projecting eye light serves as the trope representing the "coercive enlistment of another person to perform a role in the projector's externalized unconscious fantasy."[119] The "secret" guarded by the usher and projected by the eye light thus encompasses "the idea of seizing something, with the sense of possibly dominating it" (3:18). Manipulative control of an overpowered object entails not only the usher's final episode with the daughter but also his relation to the coerced butler, who trembles when the usher's eyes "touch" him (2:64). The same dynamics are central throughout *The Hortensias* (Horacio "felt the desire to dominate her," for example) (2:175), as they are again in "Except Julia," where the girls and, to some degree, the narrator are coerced and controlled by the tunnel owner. While less explicit in the earlier work, the urge to dominate is discernible in, for example, *The Lost Horse*, where it intermingles with the desire for role reversal and "revenge": "How is it that Celina struck me and dominated me, when it was I who had made myself the secret promise to dominate her?" (2:19). In this as in all the cited cases, "Imagination not only acts on one's own body but [also] on the body of others."[120]

Coercive recruitment of others into one's externalized erotic fantasy takes a decidedly more drastic turn in Hernández's work when the desire to dominate the love object progresses into the obsession to destroy it. The destructive urge is a close correlate of Hernández's tendency to dehumanize the lover (into a doll in *The Hortensias* or a cow in "Ursula," for example) and of the handicapping or disabling of the lover (into the ideal mute woman, for example), both of which are discussed in previous chapters. Its most frequent representation, however, is found in the seemingly incidental but thematically insistent presence of the dead or potentially dead females who populate Hernández's narratives. One of the earliest texts, "The Poisoned Girl," concerns a writer in search of subject matter who breaks through the block by utilizing the dead girl as his muse. This narrator can write because the girl killed herself, while at the metafictional level her death is not the catalyst but rather the product of the text that "kills" her in order to constitute itself. In "No One Lit the Lamps" the narrator exudes "enthusiasm" upon reciting the story of a woman who repeatedly attempts to commit suicide by throwing herself off a bridge, and then—casting the characteristic erotic haze over the episode—relates how on one occasion yet another attempt is frustrated when a stranger makes the woman a proposition (2:42). Elsewhere, the morose daughter of "The Balcony" is for no apparent reason condemned to death in the narrator's imagination (2:46), and then at the conclusion of the story the love-sick girl almost herself takes the jump where her "lover," the balcony, had plunged to its "death" before her (2:58). In *The Hortensias* the entire conception and then multiplication of the dolls is inextricably bound to Horacio's ungrounded fear of his wife's imminent death (beginning 2:143), with the doll then herself "murdered" twice (2:155 and 2:159) even though she is "dead" to begin with. When in the same narrative Horacio sees the first doll of the inaugural showcase scene, it is uncertain "if she was dead or if she was dreaming." The scene's legend clarifies that the doll, dressed as a bride, poisoned herself shortly before the wedding ceremony in order to evade marrying a man whom she did not love. Horacio's response is significant: "'She was truly a divine bride.' And a few moments later he felt pleasure in realizing that he was alive and she was not" (2:140). In "The Dark Dining Room" yet another girl commits suicide by poisoning (2:112), and mention is made in the same story of an additional suicide (2:107) and of a third girl who presumably died of natural causes (2:104). Back in "The Usher," finally, the free dinners are a kind of ritual of gratitude celebrated by the father "because his daughter was saved from the river's waters" (2:60). That same girl, however, "dies" in the narrator's imagination—"I insisted upon supposing that the daughter had drowned" (2:60)—and then again in his ritual at the narrative's conclusion when the girl is metaphorically murdered.

This "murder" at the conclusion of "The Usher" is the most explicit instance of erotic cruelty in Hernández's canon. The usher has been wounded by what he perceives to be the girl's infidelity to him and her breach of their sacred ritual bond, and he is consequently intent on exacting revenge through conquest, through an imposed love so intense, a passion so ardent, that it consumes its object. Once the daughter has fallen and her protective light has been extinguished, the usher's projecting eye light becomes a death-glow that spreads across her body. The greenish-yellow color of this light (2:70) is suggestive in its relation to the coloration of corpses (particularly the corpses of those who have drowned) as it progresses "toward a yellowish brown and then to green."[121] The first sign of postmortem putrefaction is a "green stain" that—as in the scene in question—appears in one place and then spreads across the entire body.

As destruction progresses under the usher's X-ray gaze, the daughter's body forfeits its integrity as a corporal whole and succumbs to an ensuing fragmentation. She melts away, reduced to skeletal remains, to abused bones recalling the butcher's sawing and chopping that echoes as a refrain throughout the narrative. This "visual absorption" of the daughter occasioned by her "total submission to the lover's gaze" is played out inversely in a more distant Echo: "Having caught the fleeting and toxic glance of Narcissus, Echo catches love's illness and turns to stone."[122] In their respective ways Echo and the daughter of "The Usher" are metamorphosed into nonhuman hardness: Echo is reduced to bone/stone dominated by the image and voice of the other, and the daughter is reduced to bone dominated by the light of the other. The toxic quality of the gaze as "love's illness" underscores the daughter's relation not only to Echo but also to the many poisoned girls in Hernández's canon, all of them subject to a contagion as the protagonists project "the triumph of an unknown illness." Reduction of the daughter to skeletal remains further recalls the evil-eye's "dehydration" capacities: the daughter's vital body fluids are dried by the ardor of eye light as "the lover soaks up the loved one through his gaze."[123]

The daughter that the usher "wished to destroy with his penetrating, sadistic, X-ray gaze" thus undergoes her Echo-like metamorphosis while the usher struggles to reconcile his competing erotic and destructive urges.[124] His searchlight penetrates her body as though he wanted to see what was inside it, to find her life at its source, to find the madonna kernel wrapped in the dirty light of the unfaithful whore, but in the process the usher discovers that he must take her life in order to find it, in order to "fix" it, in order to save it, and that by doing so, by loving her to death, he fetishizes her corpse.[125] The usher struggles to close his eyes, to turn off the projection that destroys the daughter, but his eyes overpower him "like two worms that move on their own in my sockets," two worms devouring the corpse, as Baudelaire would have it, "with kisses" (2:70).[126] The worm-eaten daughter's remains recall the "skeletons of thoughts" from an earlier text, thoughts that lost their substance because "words had eaten their tenderness." The passage then slides from *ternura* (tenderness) to *ternera* (calf/veal), from an emotive state to its incarnation and disincarnation, with another dead girl thrown into the bargain. Many calves are going to the slaughterhouse, and "Among the calves was a girl who was also carried off to the slaughter" (2:34). The premise that "your eye shall have no pity" is sounded again in *The Lost Horse* when its narrator articulates what the usher expresses only in gesture: "My eyes are now insistent, cruel" (2:27).[127]

The daughter's skull is hairless now like the head of a doll, and as it glows with the usher's light it seems distant and cold, a "star seen through a telescope" (2:70). The usher is no longer the "the center of a constellation" that he fancied himself to be among the objects organized around him earlier (2:65). His light is out of control. The ritual destruction of the daughter brings an abrupt end to his tenure of illuminated superiority. But in implicit homage to Winnicott's formula of "object survives destruction by the subject," the "dead" daughter (not unlike the "dead" Hortensia) recomposes her corporal integrity. She rises from the dead as she rose from the river. When the butler bursts in—"he turned on all the lights" (2:70)—the fire of eye light is paled; the show is shut down; the usher's libido is withdrawn ("I no longer wanted to look at her") (2:70); and the erotic-destructive light detaches from its object because the surveilling paternal light intervenes first through its surrogate (the butler) and then through the presence of the father himself. The father carries the daughter away in his arms as though out of the river that nearly drowned her, out of this river of light that instead of bloating her had absorbed all of her fluids.

As was the case with Horacio in relation to his dolls, the usher is too intricately entangled with his love object/victim to not share in something of her fate. In her eerie, trailing negligee and later in her "white bonelike form" the daughter resembles the old European White Goddess of Death, which entered modern traditions as the White Lady, foreboder of death, and is notably represented in the New World by the wandering La Llorona.[128] The usher attached himself to the daughter and to this tradition of death trailing behind her by forfeiting his light in exchange for her illuminated image, and by compromising his light with otherness when he adopted the insignia of his rival (cap = black lantern) in order to gain access to her. He then destroyed the composite of his projective identification—the daughter—in which all of his desire, all of his light, was invested, and he did so with the same projections by which he had constructed her.[129] Among the most apparent signs of any human death is the emptiness of the eyes, "like two lamps that are extinguished."[130] In "The Usher" the daughter "dies," but the extinguished eyes migrate to the protagonist. The usher's lamps go out just as the daughter's candles had previously. If Echo's metamorphosis into stone is reenacted when Narcissus subsequently "transforms himself with a glance into a statue," then the denouement of "The Usher" can script no fate for its protagonist other than to "extinguish" him in turn.[131] When the usher throws his light he throws it away. The illness of his solipsism— once triumphant, now defeated—returns at the narrative's conclusion to fill the void emptied by his dimming projections. "Your eye is the lamp of your body; . . . sound, your whole body is full of light; . . . not sound, your body is full of darkness."[132]

4

The Maternal Body

Among the distinguishing characteristics of Hernández's fiction is the migration of attributes between human beings, subhuman life forms, and inanimate objects. The seemingly dialogical interchange that emerges in this animistic milieu—be it through humans interacting with things or things interacting among themselves—is of course a "doubled" monologue, but in Hernández's fiction, as much as in myth, folk beliefs, and psychopathology, the mobilization of the inanimate world is often perceived as the autonomous self-expression of objects. If humans gain a glimpse of things acting of their own volition or if humans manage to engage in mysterious dialogues with furniture, water, or dolls, this is thanks to fortuitous circumstances, to refinements of our sensibilities, or to learning and playing by the rules that govern this underworld.

One simple entry into Hernández's animistic milieu is provided by the narrator of *The Lost Horse*, who remarks that after having seen magnolias, "a certain idea of magnolias" remained hidden behind his eyes. The use of "hidden" bestows a measure of volition on the magnolias; the flower images are not imprisoned in the eyes by the narrator's lingering perception but rather are, in effect, stowaways that have chosen these eyes as their carrier. The magnolia "idea" transported behind the eyes is then projected by extromission: the narrator looks at black-and-white furniture, but his perception is now tinted by the "idea" that envelops the colorless furniture "with a certain radiance of magnolias" (*OC,* 2:10). The image of one thing (magnolia) casts its gloss over the image of another (furniture) by riding the intermediary waves of human perception. The resultant mutation is registered by the same "doubled" sensory capacity—vision—that had bedazzled the black-and-white furniture with the projected hue of an "idea."

Elsewhere a similar extromission is replayed but now evidences a more general deployment of vision as the agency for transmittal of "ideas": "many strange thoughts that wandered through the air got into me through my head and exited through my eyes" (2:132).

On other occasions—these more prevalent—an object serves an intermediary role between distant human beings who, by choice or by chance, are brought into contact. In previous chapters we have seen a few examples, notably the mirror that archives reflections and then makes these retained images available for use or abuse by others. In "The Flooded House," where the transmittal of images, thoughts, emotions, and memories gains perhaps its most sustained treatment in Hernández's canon, it is not a glass reflector but water that exercises the capacity to archive and then release the human traces that it has gathered. Water pumped into and circulating through Margarita's house makes mysterious communications possible because it "carried inside it something that it had collected somewhere else," including thoughts "that are not mine" but "that are for me" (2:88-89). Similarly, in *The Hortensias* the displayed dolls (also associated with water) absorb lustful and covetous gazes throughout the day, and then, like relay towers transmitting what they have received, seem "hypnotized beings carrying out unknown missions or lending themselves to evil designs" (2:145). Clearly implicit in these phenomena is Hernández's gnawing awareness that language itself (as discussed in the introduction) is the paradigm "transmitter," first because it facilitates human communication but also because it speaks for itself as the vehicle of "certain memories" that "want to enter the story" uninvited (1:23). The inherent intertextuality of language glosses one's discourse with an "immense force of other people's thoughts" (3:54). Alien words come out of one's mouth just as the "radiance of magnolias" comes out of the eyes.

In some instances images of animism seem to have no purpose other than to enhance the normalized fantastic quality that makes Hernández narratives so haunting. The silence listens to music (2:46); the bed is asleep (3:187); the wallpaper and the sink understand poems (2:167); the glasses collected on a tray clink into one another and seem "happy to meet again" (2:139); the flame tries desperately to detach from its candle (3:109); and ideas move as though they were drunk (3:20).[1] On other occasions, and these more frequent, the animistic images stress the permeability of boundaries between animate and inanimate matter. A bent-over woman is a table that began to walk (2:92), and exclamations from the throats of humans and from the necks of bottles become confused (2:152). Musicians are identified with their instruments—one boy is "the Mandolin," another "the Violin"—

necessitating a play of clarifications: "the Mandolin (man) took the 'mandolin' (instrument) out of its case and began to play" (3:11-12). In the same context hands "seemed like gloves," but gloves "made of human skin" (3:13). The examples could be multiplied, but all of those in this category maintain that at some moments "objects are more alive than we are" (2:18), that animals and people are merely "things that move" (3:133), and that the borders between the animate and inanimate are blurred and ultimately indefensible.[2]

The animistic images that make the greatest thematic contribution to Hernández's canon are those revealing the inanimate world "mobilized" by fears and desires. While projected desire provides a constant undertone and a frequent manifestation—Horacio, for example, "realized that Hortensia was looking toward the road by which he always came home" (2:154)—projected fear is most typical of Hernández's protagonists, whose narcissism tends to be laced with paranoia. Ideas of reference are the rule, with an attending, escalating derogatory tone measuring the intensity of paranoia. The process is exemplified through the blurred recollection of a painful past in "Except Julia": a woman's "mocking smile" graduates to a "mocking laugh" before it is finally denied altogether (2:84-85). In another typical case paranoia combines with suggestions of animism as the voyeuristic gaze—an emblem of the Hernández protagonist—returns "othered" as surveillance: clothes piled on a chair seem like "the head of an Arab who watched me with a sort of triangular eye" (3:160). Elsewhere it seems "that the door laughed at one" (2:110), with this ideation of ridicule by objects anticipating a central motif of *The Hortensias*, where Horacio believes that the dolls are conspiring against him, belittling him, tricking him, mocking him, or otherwise establishing themselves in adverse relation. In *Lands of Memory*, similarly, a mannequin inspires "a certain feeling of distrust" (3:57-59). The same paranoia also turns up in Celina's living room when the objects there conspiratorially exchange signals and engage in "mysterious acts" that mock the narrator (2:13).

Paranoia is intensified significantly when the love object itself is concerned. In "The Usher" the narrator imagines discourse to fill the daughter's silence and in doing so reveals the fear compounding his desire: "My dear, I lied to you" (2:67). The lover betrays (projected fear), but ultimately she returns, succumbs, and confesses (projected desire). The two intermingling emotions intensify the usher's fantasy. In this case the coldheartedness of the imagined deception is assuaged via the imagined confession by which the usher regains what he has lost, but in *The Hortensias* the doll skin that quickly loses its human warmth connotes an emotional coldness that gets only worse. The dolls are entities with no emotions other than those poured into them by a paranoid narcissist; their expressions are limited, like Echo's, to a mimetic distortion. Having thought that kissing Hortensia's skin would be like kissing a shoe, Horacio senses on the doll's face "an expression of cold haughtiness" because she was "taking revenge for everything he had thought about her skin" (2:144). This aloof coolness and vengeful posture yields at other moments to outright mocking; one of the dolls is indeed named Eulalia, recalling Rubén Darío's celebrated poem in which the "beautiful and evil" Eulalia "laughs, laughs, laughs" "upon hearing the complaints of her gentlemen."[3] When Horacio is fearing death and working through the angst of his loneliness, the dolls can only respond with a frigidly logical, anti-animistic comment that mocks him merely by underscoring their limitations: "We're just dolls; you go work it out however you can" (2:170). As animism breaks down in proportional relation to its author's breakdown, Horacio experiences ridicule not by virtue of what the dolls do but rather as the result of their incapacity to do anything, their very constitution as inanimate: "he did not dare to look her in the face because he thought that he would find the unshakable mockery of an object" (2:172).

A range of other animistic images are generated when mild but chronic paranoia coalesces with reactions to specific situations. A character hiding under the bed of his cousin-lover fears that a servant's feet can "see" him (2:191); a window gets frightened upon seeing what happened to another window (2:165); the machine noises are trying to insinuate something to Horacio (2:139, 2:141); objects exchange rejecting glances (3:74); a closed door changes its expression according to who is behind it (3:16); the walls of a hotel room prefer that the narrator occupy it forever, rather than accommodating other travelers (3:163); and "the most severe judgment was that of silence" (2:198).[4]

More extended passages treating animism often complicate the role of objects as intermediaries between people by compounding this function with the opposite: one person serves as intermediary, as medium, to afford another person access to objects and sensations that would otherwise remain inaccessible. This variation of the animistic motif—central to "The Balcony" and "Except Julia," among other texts—often further entails the revivification of memories, the "awakening" of a memorial past monumentalized in objects, such as those of Celina's living room. "From one object in a room to another," writes Gaston Bachelard, "housewifely care weaves the ties that unite a very ancient past to the new epoch. The housewife awakens furniture that was asleep."[5] While there is little housewifely about the women in Hernández's canon, Bachelard's point nevertheless

THE LUST OF SEEING 170

obtains: when it falls upon certain objects the human touch unites the "dead" past with the living present and thereby awakens not only the inanimate object but also the intangible presences that it is thought to embody. That touch is a special one, often feminine, and its intermediary role unites not only past with present but also—notably in "Irene's House"—a cast of disparate players who are mysteriously connected through an inanimate medium. Referring to Irene, the narrator relates the following:

> When she takes an object into her hands she does it with such spontaneity that it seems as though the objects have an understanding with her, that she has an understanding with us, but that we could not have an understanding directly with the objects. (1:99)

In order to arrive at an understanding with objects, one must pass through Irene. On the following page this general rule of order is expanded—but also returned full-circle to the original use of an object as medium—through specific application to the piano. First an animistic reciprocity is established: "she gets along [*se entendía*] better than anyone with her piano, and it seems the same for the piano with her" (1:100).[6] The narrator then builds the channel for a back-and-forth free flow of attributes by describing the girl and the piano as "united by continuity" (1:100). When the narrator plays Irene's piano after she has played it, the compositions have "a different emotion and even a different rhythm" (1:100). Something of Irene remained behind in the object associated with her, much the same as the "idea" of magnolias lingered behind the eyes in a previous example. As a result the narrator realizes that Irene is in some way present in her piano, that something of her has intermingled with it, that *tocar* (to play) the piano means also *tocar* (to play/to touch) Irene.[7] Whereas earlier Irene was posed between the narrator and objects, now the detour is rerouted in reverse: an object, the piano, is posed between the narrator and Irene.

This brief example from "Irene's House" is useful in understanding the eroticism—often a frustrated sexual desire—that gains encoded expression through the intermingling or fusion of women and objects. The code of this woman-object consolidation is legible enough in the animistic dolls of *The Hortensias*, in the tunnel objects of "Except Julia," or in any number of more or less explicit passing instances, such as one in which a bed is benevolent because it "let me get on top of it; it stayed still, retained something of my warmth and gave a little warmth of its own" (3:58). In other cases, however, notably in the memorial texts epitomized by *The Lost Horse*, the objects mediating relations between humans are sexualized only by nuance, by an erotic haze as dissipating as it is insistent. As in "Irene's House," the union with a female—now Celina—is detoured through a general fascination with objects relating or belonging to her. We recall from the previous chapter that at the opening of *The Lost Horse* the boy is waiting, alone, in his piano teacher's living room. Celina's black furniture is covered with white dustcovers [*polleras*] that tempt the boy who has "enough time to enter into intimate relations with everything in the living room" (2:9). The consolidation of woman and objects advances as Celina appears here not in her customary clinging black dress but rather in a garb that links her visually to the "violated" furniture: "she had put on a house-coat of light, starched cloth" (2:14). In a manuscript draft of the same scene, the description linking Celina with her furniture is even more patent: "she came in a completely black dress and put on top of it a completely white dust coat [*guardapolvo*]" (2:205).[8] Celina protects her sleek black body with a white dustcover, while the black furniture is protected with white "skirts" [*polleras*].

The coolness and colorlessness of the black-and-white, curvaceous Celina is also calculated to link her specifically with the piano. Consider-able attention is dedicated to smoothing out the wrinkles, to polishing Celina's corsetted curves until the black dress assume something of the high-definition, enamel-like (and mirrorlike) finish of pianos (2:14). Where the black dress ends at the neck, a keyboard alternation of black-and-white begins with "her very white face, her very black eyes, her very white fore-head and her very black hair" (2:14).

The migration of attributes between women and objects not only vivi-fies Celina's furnishings but, in one passage, also classifies them in accor-dance with human personality traits. First people are transformed into "pieces of furniture that change position," and then: "I loved the pieces of furniture that were still and demanded nothing of me; but the pieces that moved not only demanded that I love them and give them a kiss but also made worse demands, and they suddenly opened their doors and threw everything out on top of one" (2:22).[9] Some women-things make demands and dump on one, while others—like the bust, the Hortensia doll, or the dress that accepts a penetrating head in the *pollera* fantasies—remain still, demand nothing, and readily accommodate one's "caprices." In Celina's living room, as in Irene's, animism brings objects to life in order to telescope the distance between desire and its inaccessible or inhospitable object; ani-mism provides sublimated symbolic fulfillment. Because Celina—in an extremely suggestive trope—"had all of her drawers locked with a key" (2:22), because she is "so severe and held her secrets so tightly," the boy is predisposed to a compensatory "strange emotion, the desire to discover or violate secrets" (2:13). While the gaze and the touch only gravitate toward charged inanimate objects, these objects are surrogates for "the insinuating undulations of the curves of women" (2:13).

If in *The Lost Horse* women are metaphorically equated with home furnishings, elsewhere in the canon the desire for female passivity is expressed by entangling women and plants. Considered through the erotic haze of animism in Hernández's fiction, the female-plant suggests a passive, cultivatable lover available at one's pleasure for defloration. The naming after flowers of Hortensia (hydrangea) and of Margarita (daisy) from "The Flooded House" certainly contributes to these poetics, as does the wandering gaze that links plants and a teacher's arm (3:18) or the "quiet and blind plants" (3:15) that recall our earlier discussion of the ideal woman (Echo, for example) as mute, incapacitated, handicapped, or even dead. Hortensia, herself a plant-thing, on one occasion appears as "the dead woman in a tree" (2:154).

The selvatic poetics of female sexuality are also evoked, as girls are "happy plants in a clearing of the jungle" (3:28) and reference is made to "thoughts from some jungle that have come out of deep caves and moved forward with strange powers" (3:201). In a letter Hernandez describes one of his lovers as "a virgin jungle," and in "Except Julia" the vaginal suggestions of the tunnel combine with the concept of defloration.[10] In the eroticized confine in which his symbolic rituals are enacted, the tunnel owner remarks, "I like knowing that among this darkness there is a yellow flower" (2:82). It is no coincidence that the flower was smuggled into the tunnel and is held by the Lolita-like girl whom he loves, Julia. Another narrator pursues the theme by allusion with "I like solitude among plants" (2:49). In *The Hortensias* the flower-doll poetics of the Hortensias is paralleled by the vegetal qualities of Horacio's wife. María has plants in the green of her eyes and is implicitly transformed into an anthropomorphic plant (which is to say, Hortensia) through plays on the greenish color of her complexion, which according to Horacio she achieves by rubbing her skin with olives (2:138). Hortensia grows out of María's death like one plant from another, because "a tree is a friend that never leaves" (2:43).[11]

The poetics of the woman-plant further extend into the oedipal themes that will concern us presently, particularly when the mother imago is considered in the broad, archetypal view as mother earth and giver of life.[12] To cite one noteworthy example among the tropes of vegetation, those close to Hernández recognize the stout, fat legs of his mother, Calita, in passages such as the following: "When she walked—her hips and legs were very heavy—she made one think of a plant walking with its flowerpot" (2:183).[13]

The title of the text in which this potted plant walks off—"Mamma's Tree"—is in itself more than sufficient to link the mother with the woman-plants, but the text generously offers more. Confusions in the narrative entangle the identities of mother and daughter as a lover surreptitiously accessing a second-story window almost climbs the "wrong tree." The oedipal bells are rung as the daughter—who herself has chunky legs and a fat knee stretched like a bald head—becomes involved in illicit erotic rituals with the tree-climbing lover, to whom she is related. The mother is also evoked more implicitly if her "piano legs" are considered in the context of women as furniture and, more specifically, of Celina as piano.

As it is worded in Ezek. 19:10, "Thy mother is like a vine in thy blood, planted by the waters: she was fruitful and full of branches by reason of many waters." This prolific mother inseminated by "waters" and climbing like a vine through one's blood provides apt imagery for introduction of the final layer that Hernández imbeds into the plant-woman-mother palimpsest, namely the plant as text. In his *ars poetica* statement "False Explanation of My Stories," Hernández compares the writing of his texts to the growth of vegetation, but he does so with images that at once suggest impregnation and gestation.[14] First the planted seed germinates: "In a given moment I think that in some corner of me a plant is being born." The plant-text, inseminated "by many waters," is cared for but left to gestate and grow on its own, to be what "it itself is destined to be" (3:6).

Both the woman and the text are plants; both are inseminated; both are ostensibly left to grow on their own but are actually carefully monitored creations, revised and remade and destroyed if deemed unfaithful to their seed. And both always return for their ultimate reference to the mother in the blood of their author. What one analyst said of Freud might as well be applied to the oedipal Hernández; his writing enables him "to explore the Unconscious—the Mother's body—and to send a flood of light into its dark depths, without lurching himself into the abyss."[15] Hernández's texts are drenched and illuminated by this plant-generating composite that consolidates his greatest emblems: water and light. The author's role is seminal: his approach to this forbidden maternal abyss is entangled in the vegetation of texts and women. He experiences "the madness of a man who runs lost in a jungle and is excited by brushing against unknown plants" (3:191). Hernández's fictions are women and his women are fictions; the symmetrical balance calms him; the garden grows. Association of (maternal) woman with the text eroticizes his writing (much the same as piano playing is eroticized within it), and the erotic haze settles like dew over each deflowered plant that tells his story.[16]

ANIMISM AND THE FETISH

Strangely fruitful intercourse this, between one body and another mind.

—Thomas Mann

The "confusion" of women and dolls that receives sustained treatment in *The Hortensias* is amply reinforced throughout Hernández's canon. In *Clemente Colling*, for example, a woman moves like a "wind-up toy" (1:29), and Celina in *The Lost Horse* is similarly described as "a clumsy wind-up doll" (2:28). A page after the mentioned *Clemente Colling* passage, one discovers a doll characterized by its human height, associated with death, bilaterally bound to mother and daughter figures, and accessible to the gaze but not to the touch, all qualities that later reappear in the Hortensias (2:30). A separate passage in *Clemente Colling* also anticipates the Hortensia dolls—in their later, "plumbed" versions—through description of bed-warming rituals orchestrated by Petrona. The presence in bed of a hot-water bottle (*porrón*) is in itself an antecedent of the Hortensia dolls full of water (on 2:147 Hortensia is compared to a *porrón*), but the text goes further by "doubling" the representation.[17] In addition to receiving her own bed warmer during the tuck-in ritual, the narrator's sister's also receives an ink bottle filled with water to warm the toes of her doll (1:34). In yet another passage reminiscent of *The Hortensias*, Colling displays dolls—among them a bride and bridegroom—in a showcase that makes them seem very far away, as though "in his youth" (1:61).

The famous bust of Celina's living room also stands out as a pre-Hortensia woman surrogate. The fragmented woman-thing has "known" aspects (it resembles a human woman, it is made of marble) and "unknown" aspects, above all its qualities "that had to do with Celina" (2:10). Some aspects of the bust, like Hortensia before Horacio has her modified, "were bothersome." When the boy's caress heads for the breasts "the bust ended and the cube began on which the entire figure was supported." That clunkish, unsatisfying form yields in turn to a still more troublesome sculpted flower, whose edges are sufficiently sharp to turn the caress into a wound (2:10–11). In a Platonic ruse the boy is unimpressed by the sculpting of an imitation flower, since there are plenty of real ones within easy reach from any sidewalk (2:11). Like Horacio, however, he makes no complaint about the ersatz women, perhaps because the gardens of real women are less easily accessed.

Or because the boundary between the real woman and her inanimate surrogate is sufficiently blurred to make such a distinction irrelevant. A girl in "A Woman Who Resembles Me" carries "a large doll" and announces that she is having it baptized (2:92). In "No One Lit the Lamps" the narrator's eyes alternate between voyeuristically surveying a girl and repairing to the statue where his gaze "deposits" her image (2:142). The tunnel owner of "Except Julia," in a related expression of the same dynamics, prefers the face of a girl as a ritual object to that girl as wife (2:85). In "The Usher" the real daughter is displaced by a phantasmal apparition that—as in *The Hortensias*—is associated with showcased objects. When the usher first sees her she is all whiteness in candlelight, stepping like a mannequin out of "the wide avenue bordered by showcases" (2:65). An inanimate, surrogate woman is also the common denominator of a quasi-comic play on names in "The Dark Dining Room." The señora's name is "Muñeca" (= doll) and her maid follows suit with "Dolly." Muñeca (not unlike the dollish María) is what remains of a woman devastated by an unfaithful lover, while Dolly carries Hortensia themes in the aquatic direction, as her name was borrowed from "a luckless woman who had thrown herself into the sea in a film from those times" (2:107). The integration of the film with the water, with the love triangles, and with the piano music that provides the emotional cueing for the drama all likewise steer toward *The Hortensias*, as does the retrieval from oblivion of a discarded name. A relation with "The Usher" is also signaled in the drowned Dolly's return to life.

"It may be madness," says an Horacio enamored with dolls, "but I know of sculptors who have fallen in love with their statues" (2:155). Pygmalion, the prototype of such sculptors, chose to live alone, without a wife, because the "many faults which nature has implanted in the female sex" made futile his search for a woman who could meet his standards. As in *The Hortensias*, his turn away from real women was counterbalanced by the creative construction of an idealized surrogate. Pygmalion "gazed in wonder" at his creation, and "in his heart there rose a passionate love" for his woman-thing contoured and polished to the specifications of his desire, made in his image, mute. Again like Horacio, "Often he ran his hands over the work, feeling it to see whether it was flesh or ivory, and would not yet admit that ivory was all it was." This refusal to accept the fantasy lover's inanimate thingness indexes a series of related moves that give Pygmalion's monologue an echo he can interpret as conversation. Pygmalion "kissed the statue, and imagined that it kissed him back, spoke to it and embraced it, and thought he felt his fingers sink into the limbs he touched." He dresses the statue, he adorns it with jewels, he gives it gifts, and finally—still paralleling Horacio—he takes it to bed, his autoerotic ceremony now populated not merely with female company but with a partner "lovelier than any woman."

She is, nevertheless, a statue. Pygmalion's strategically indirect supplication to Venus seeks to remedy the situation: "'If you gods can give all things, may I have as my wife, I pray—' he did not dare to say: 'the ivory maiden,' but finished: 'one like the ivory maid.'" Venus understood the prayer: when Pygmalion returned home "he made straight for the statue of the girl he loved, leaned over the couch, and kissed her. She seemed warm: he laid his lips on hers again, and touched her breast with his hands—at his touch the ivory lost its hardness, and grew soft." The statue grows soft and Pygmalion hard: Galatea is born motherless of the father she will marry. "Timidly raising her eyes, she saw her lover and the light of day together."[18]

The affinity between Hernández's Horacio and Ovid's Pygmalion is remarkable, perhaps first because the two characters hold in common a passion for idealized constructs. Like Dürer, who "believed that the ideal nude ought to be constructed by taking the face of one body, the breasts of another, the legs of a third, the shoulders of a fourth, the hands of a fifth—and so on," these protagonists craft idealized feminine forms tailored to the measure of their passion.[19] At the same time, however, there is a fundamental difference that distinguishes the respective agendas of Pygmalion and Horacio. Like Orpheus, Pygmalion brings a "dead" lover to life; he legitimates his perversion by vivifying the statue and making it—her—his wife. Horacio hastens in the opposite direction. He has a wife at the outset, but she is "killed" and replaced by the "dead" doll, and then the serial replication of dolls, on which he rehearses his increasingly illegitimate ceremony. In this perspective, Hortensia as a sexual object and as a recipient of identities and projections is useful to Horacio only insofar as she is "dead." Hortensia suits Horacio because she is mute, passive, malleable, unwifelike, disposable. Bringing her into life, into subjectivity, is out of the question, for that would negate her perfected objectivity, which is, precisely, what is loved.

In Horacio's perspective, however, much of the original parallelism with Pygmalion is restored. For Horacio as projecting narcissist, María is dead. His fear of her death is indistinguishable from the death itself, and, like Pygmalion, he therefore begins his quest with dead matter and with the desire to vivify it, to love it, to perfect it, to experience "the miraculous fulfillment of impossible love."[20] In Horacio's case the life-giving urge takes the form of replacing María with a nonmoribund surrogate; like Galatea, Hortensia brings the inanimate (which is to say, impossible) love object to life, in this case life eternal because she is "dead." Human warmth is poured in by both Horacio and Pygmalion; the insemination and the "birth" are one.[21]

The many versions of the Icelandic *Tristrams saga*, most popular during the fourteenth and fifteenth centuries, also hold much in common with Hernández's "Pygmalion" themes. Having lost the love of his life in *The Saga of Tristram and Isönd*, Tristram hires craftsmen to mount a piece of compensatory theater in the vaulted edifice where his obsession will be staged. A statue replicates the lost love "as though she herself were standing there," providing an ersatz Queen Isönd adequate for the erotic ritual that Tristram privately celebrates on her body. The showcase aspect is rounded out by a supporting cast of statues accompanying the queen—a dwarf, the attendant Bringvet, the dog—all staged to replay (and in some sense to undo) the scene during which the sad fate of Tristram and Isönd was sealed. Tristram's attention to detail outdoes even that of Horacio when a fragrance is made to issue from the surrogate Isönd by means of "a contrivance that Tristram had devised: under the nipple near the heart he bored a hole into the breast and placed therein a small herb container." Two tubes led out of the container: "One of these tubelets gave forth fragrance from the hairline of the neck, and the other one in a similar manner led to the mouth." The inanimate surrogates are made—by Tristram's means or by Horacio's—to "activate" the roles assigned to them and to metamorphose their thingness into the designated idealized identity. Tristram, like Horacio, has a wife (Isodd) whose name overlaps with that of the inanimate lover (and of the lost queen), "but he had no desire to have conjugal relations with his wife." Instead he repairs to his statue as the monument of his memorial love; "he kissed it and took it in his arms and embraced it as if it were alive," revisiting with it the trauma that might be gradually eroded away through rehearsal of a caress suspended in the "as if." Again like Horacio, Tristram recruits into his psychodrama the erotic participation of other statues (Bringvet) and of third-party outsiders (Kardín) who, in the manner of the Hortensia purchasers and the narrator of "Except Julia," want a piece of the exotic action: "Make me a partaker of your joys." The reproduction of a love object, the staging of the replica in a theatrical narrative scene, the rejection of a wife in favor of an idealized representation, the metaphor of the inaccessible woman as queen, the participation of others in one's private fantasy, the hiring of craftsman to construct a subjective reality, and the use of a subterranean chamber as a ritual confine all interconnect the *Tristrams saga* with central themes in Hernández's canon.[22]

Horacio's doll and the statues of Pygmalion and Tristram may be provisionally understood as transitional objects, for their thingness-in-itself, their nature and function as objects, has been sequestered and placed in service of their respective owner's fantasies. But unlike the simple transitional object—the teddy bear, for example—these idealized representations of women are "intrinsically connected to the devaluation of women and defenses instituted to counter that devaluation." The devaluation: displacing a woman with a thing; the countermeasure: vivifying the thing so that it resembles and perfects the woman. Because Hortensia, Galatea, and (to some extent) Isönd are sexually exploited as objects representing absences, however, they are perhaps more accurately understood as fetishistic formations. In Horacio's case, in particular, "the manipulation of the representation is often excessively sadistic in its inflexibility."[23] The sadism is not necessarily violent; in *The Hortensias* it rather assumes the form of rigid adherence to a delusion that "destroys" reality, totalitarian domination of the love object, and the literal injuring and figurative "killing" of María. Something of sadism is registered, too, in exploitation of the fetish as a necessary condition of one's sexual satisfaction and even of one's identity. The analysand who remarks that without his props he is nothing speaks as well for Horacio. And like Horacio this patient was obsessed with dolls because "they don't get sick or grow old or die." But whereas Horacio externalized the doll (a doll, we recall, ultimately representing himself), this patient "took refuge in an idealized representation of himself as a cute, exhibitionist doll playing continually to a doting audience." One constructs the doll in the world of objects and the other on the body, but both share the absolute sovereignty over the potential space in which their private theaters are enacted. As the analyst said of her patient, by "controlling the play, he controlled the world."[24]

If the fetish indeed "symbolizes the triumph over an early humiliation, usually a parental figure," then the extratextual case of Hernández as author recalls the complications resulting from abuse by the mother-surrogate Deolinda. The process of fetishization entails that "the individual who has originally traumatized the patient will be harmed in fantasy by the repetitive fetishistic act." Hernández's complex mother imago here fills the slot of those who inflicted the trauma, and to enact the symbolic sadism that repays mother in kind, "the originally offending individual is stripped of his [or, in this case, her] humanity and transformed into a part object."[25]

In another perspective, the thing that becomes a fetish, that "accepts" the eroticization, does so because it is associated with an absent—and usually inaccessible—love object. In Hernández's case this trail endlessly detoured through replications also ultimately leads back to the mother. The fetish, however, may function as such only insofar as it enters the erotic space of one's ritual; like a transitional object, it exists in the world as one thing—a shoe, a pair of panties, a piece of rubber—but is transformed into another when enveloped in fantasies. The thing may belong to the person who owns or owned it, but the fetish belongs to the person who transforms that thing during the course of a sexual ritual. As Hernández put it in a early text, we highly value the mystery with which things are imbued because we ourselves have created the mystery (1:106). In "The Metaphysical Beard" the unilateral nature of that creation is stressed: the beard has "an unconscious force that he [the bearded man] had not foreseen and that had nothing to do with him. It had more to do with us" (2:103–4). The beard is not a fetish in this text, but the process of the fetishistic formation is nevertheless registered. The subject disappears behind the beard; the owner of the beard (or fetish) is taken unawares by the power that the dissociated part-object assumes in the perception of others.

The fetish may be detachable, but its power is contingent upon maintaining a relation with the absence that empowers and eroticizes it: "objects acquire soul to the degree that they enter into relations with people" (2:50). These people's absence is required for the formation of the fetish, because once they are gone one can glean through their ruins for objects or "traces" overlooked or misplaced in the confusion of their departure. The object eligible for fetishization must have been used, must monumentalize something private, must embody an act or an aspect of its owner that is inaccessible even to the voyeuristic eye. Once the object is located, the fetishism is derived (as in *The Hortensias*) by "enlivening" the object through its association with the person or persons now gone. Objects "had entered the lives of these people" and "had begun to carry out some mission or to mean something for those who used them." With that channel to secret lives, missions, and uses opened, the narrator would take advantage of the moments when the objects were unattended in order to discover their owners' secrets or else "traces of their secrets." These objects thus become "intermediaries," which is to say fetishes (2:12–13). Just as in popular medieval veneration a relic did not represent a saint but *was* the saint, likewise the fetishized object exploits the magic of metonymy to make an abstract whole present within a concrete part.[26]

The "presence" occupying the fetishized object in Hernández's fiction is, of course, generally female. The narrator of "Lucrecia" characteristically hopes that some coins will retain traces of the girl who held them and that by touching them he will "find some secret," "something more of Lucrecia" (3:116). Another narrator is cheered up because the shirt that a girl gave him still held something of her (3:169). When he is feeling guilty Horacio avoids looking at María's things, because she is somehow "in" them, just as she is "in" Hortensia (2:162). In the bathroom scene in *Lands of Memory*, the naked narrator about to bathe cannot believe his luck at having access to objects that seem "to offer themselves" and that belong "to the intimacy of people who I had just met." He fixes his gaze on the hamper containing clothes "that I didn't know" and "like a magician pulling out of a top hat some connected objects that earlier were separate" he begins his rummage through the contents. An "encounter between two very intimate things: my nakedness and her clothes" results, and with a "rather large" pair of blue panties in his hand the boy associates immediately to the girl he admires: they must be hers. This direct link from the underwear to the girl underscores the "presence" of the inaccessible lover in the object representing (or, often, displacing) her, but the fact that the underwear could not be hers—she does not live in the house, either—stresses his desire for that specific presence against the facts, his channeling of *her* into the intimate object that he fondles. An encounter between his nakedness and *her* panties would have been fortuitous, but when he realizes that the underwear belongs to an undesirable fat woman he loses interest and closes the hamper (3:31–32). If one is going to exploit a thing to represent a woman, as Pygmalion and Horacio demonstrate, then it might as well be the woman of one's dreams, a masterpiece, a woman "lovelier than any woman." With a kind of voodoo spookiness, the fetishist is adept at demanding that the object represent, that the fetish *be*, the victim of his desire, even if the panties belong to someone else. And even if the victim is herself a fantasy, a collage of parts.

Complex fetishes collaging or palimpsesting multiple representations are evident in *The Hortensias*. Once Horacio has devised his plan for María's life-after-death in the form of Hortensia, he buys María "many dresses made of strong cloth," because "these memories [or souvenirs] of María must last a long time" (2:146). The traces left by María on her clothes serve to vivify and humanize the doll standing in as her postmortem surrogate. The doll, itself a fetish, wears fetishized clothes—almost tomb shrouds—loaded with memories representing the "dead" wife, while the "strong cloth," migrating in the opposite direction, consigns to María the thick skin of the dolls and at the same time echoes the "very heavy" cloth that is used to "dress" fetishized objects in *The Lost Horse*—specifically, the furniture in Celina's living room (2:205). One of the showcase scenes provides a separate elaboration of the same type of layering: sponges are fetishized and represent the dolls, which—again—are themselves fetishes (2:158).

In "Except Julia," similarly, the objects that are handled in the tunnel—enveloped in an erotic haze, integral to the quasi-sexual ritual rehearsed by the tunnel owner, and capable of arousing "memories" and "confusion"—are overdetermined fetishes. In one passage they are referred to as "pieces," this word serving as the nexus of eroticized objects through the fusion of a piece of music and a piece of clothing, all of a piece (2:77). The layering continues as the tunnel objects then represent distorted part-objects associated with the girls positioned along the tunnel wall. But not the girls exactly: it is more their faces that are represented, faces that are themselves fetishized as part-objects detachable from the girls who wear them as though they were masks. The objects on the table represent the girls' faces, which represent not so much the girls themselves as the tunnel owner's manipulation of their subjectivity, his molding of them into the masklike faces, piles of flour, empty birdcages, and pairs of shoes that whisper their secret messages into his perverse desire. The girls behind the masks of their faces, like the man behind the beard discussed above, disappear as the fetish absorbs them.

It is partly for this reason that women in Hernández's canon—the daughter in "The Usher" is the best example—are often little more than phantasmal presences. Like all transitional objects, they are partly themselves (the part that tends to disappear) and partly what narcissistic projection has made them. The brilliant pun in "The Crocodile" captures this celebration of fetishized part-objects: *¿Quién no acaricia, hoy, una media Ilusión?* (3:90). "Illusion" is the brand name of stockings (*medias*) sold by the narrator, and accordingly the passage first offers a marketing slogan suggesting the quasi-fetishistic fondling of hosiery: "Who, today, doesn't caress an Illusion stocking?" The word *media*, however, also means "half," yielding a second translation that overlaps the first and returns the fetish to the part-me/part-other composite of transitional objects: "Who, today, doesn't caress half an Illusion?" The love object is what one makes of it, half herself and half the screen of narcissistic projections. Superimposing the one rendition of the slogan onto the other, the caressed stocking itself is "half an Illusion," half of a pair. The stocking is there but the woman is absent, so the fetishist gets up his half and fantasy rounds out the whole.

In the final analysis, fetishes are concrete manifestations of the general tendency in Hernández's canon to displace social reality with the reified ideations of a projecting subject. In the extreme cases, like that of *The Hortensias*, the projections are so insistent that the entire milieu is dominated and transformed by their ubiquity. Any attempt to test reality is ludicrous, for reality has been sealed out of a world governed by fantasy and delusion instituted as matters of fact. The legends accompanying most of *The Hortensias'* showcases are resonant in this context, for they provide a quasi-definitive account of the objective "meaning" or "truth" of the scenes staged for Horacio. When Horacio views a given scene he forms an interpretive opinion and then measures this assessment against the "true" meaning written in the legend. This gesture mimes the testing of reality—the verification of one's perception in objective sources—but Horacio's feint is unconvincing, first because "reality" was checked at the door of the confine in which his ritual takes place, and then more specifically because the scenes and their accompanying legends were designed by specialists paid not to trouble Horacio with intrusions from external "reality" but rather to create a reality that caters to and reinforces his fantasies. When Horacio compares his interpretation with the "facticity" of the legend, he merely measures the success of others in externalizing, in institutionalizing, his fantasy. When his control of the world-as-showcase, the world as extension of himself, is jeopardized—as it is when María disrupts his totalitarian order by introducing her surprises—then Horacio himself becomes the writer of legends, immediately picking up his pen to appropriate these independent acts of María by recording them in his register (2:145–46). The chronicling of her behavior and the signing of his name in "large letters loaded with ink" transforms her acts, her facts, into his interpretations. Horacio labels María's surprises—her scenes—with legends so that they makes his sense; he has the final, definitive word on their meaning (2:141). In "The Crocodile" the same dynamics are engaged when a girl asks the pianist to autograph her stocking, her "half an illusion." Since the pen will not write on the stocking, since the illusion cannot be inscribed, he suggests signing a label and sticking it to the stocking, as though to attach himself, to append himself to the transparency that takes the form of her leg, to label it with his trademark, but to still preserve his autonomy and detachability (3:100).

THE FREUDIAN CROWD

As mentioned in chapter 3, the original case study of Capgras Syndrome analyzed the delusions of a psychotic woman who believed not only that the people around her had been replaced by dolls but also that she herself had been multiply doubled.[27] In *The Hortensias* the situation is similar but somewhat more complicated, because the same doubles, the same dolls populating a pseudocommunity around Horacio, simultaneously represent Horacio himself and a series of female constructs emerging from a mother imago. Hortensia-as-Horacio makes the transition to Hortensia-as-mother partly because the idealized imago that the dolls represent "is the projection of one's own original perfection onto the parent with an accompanying fantasy of idealizing another."[28] Approaching this same line of reasoning from the opposite direction, in *The Hortensias* a "special type of early relationship from childhood" is being reenacted, and this unconscious phenomenon is essentially "a repetition of the mother's idolization of the infant-child as her created-object, which the child had internalized and hidden."[29] The dolls' representation of idealized or idolized women evidence Horacio's rehearsal

183 4 / The Maternal Body

of this creative maternal function that "perfects" the self along with the object born of it.

Because Horacio's relation to his objects is pathological, his amorous adventures display the corresponding traits of fetishism, overvaluation (alternating with devaluation), and exploitation of the lover as a mirror that perfects. As summarized by Masud Khan, "the object is treated as a sacred fetish," "some aspect of the object is invested with an exaggerated intensity of virtue," and "the object is used to mirror the self in a defensive attempt to hide feelings of inferiority and unworthiness in the self."[30] The patients displaying these patterns in object relations all recalled mothers who were—like Hernández's mother—"cold or wooden or impersonal and interfering."[31] This inanimate mother-thing not only provides a prototype for the cold, "dead" dolls replicated in her image but also produces in Horacio a compulsion to endlessly repeat the ceremony by which he attempts to recover her and himself in one defensive gesture. This Pygmalion-like urge suggests "that in essence all desire is ultimately a desire for a body, one that may substitute for *the* body, the mother's, the lost object of infantile bliss—the body that the child grown up always seeks to recreate."[32] Horacio places his kiss on the dead lips of the doll as though she were Snow White: he is the Prince who will awaken what André Green calls "the dead mother," not one physically dead but "a distant figure, toneless, practically inanimate" who is, "so to speak, psychically dead" in the eyes of her child.[33]

Giving birth to one's mother in the form of an anthropomorphic or humanoid surrogate is not uncommon in the literature of the double. Consider once again the grizzly case of Frankenstein, who "creates the monster to fill a gap—the absence caused by the death of his mother—and it is the quest for the lost mother which informs the whole text. By becoming an unnatural mother, 'giving birth' to another, who is a reflection of himself, Frankenstein is able to *be* the mother he lacks, to supply to himself his own need for a mother."[34] The predoomed, tragic enterprise of a character like Horacio or an individual like Hernández is to resuscitate the idealized mother—the loving mother one never had—in the bodies of women regarded, ultimately, as unfit to contain her. That double bind where the need meets the lack results in ex utero, singly paternal procreation of "perfected" humanoid surrogates, designed as masterpieces worthy of mother but made manifest in a range of beings spanning the gamut from Galatea to Frankenstein's monster. Among such beings the golem of Jewish traditions is particularly suggestive when literary fictions are concerned, because in creating the golem dust or clay is brought to life precisely by the power of language. In one technique the golem is vivified by inscribing the Hebrew word *emet* (truth) on its forehead, and is destroyed by erasing the first letter to leave the word *met* (he is dead).[35] If one were to erase the *tensia* from Hortensia's name, she would be reduced to the prefix that she shares with Horacio, *Hor*, recording her reabsorption—her dying *into*—the man whose projection created her, the man whose polysemous name also means "spectator."[36]

The "mothering" function that engenders a part-object monster collage like that of Frankenstein is implicit too in the discussions of chapter 3, where we considered the process of narcissistic projection through which Horacio multiply recreated himself in dolls. A long history of metamorphoses map out such a male-to-female generative progression: Eve is born of Adam's rib; Galatea is born of Pygmalion's craftsmanship and desire, brought to life by his erotic caresses; Echo's subjectivity is sequestered and bespoken by the discourse of Narcissus, to whom she is bound by a partial mimesis. In each of these cases and many others like them a part-object or a projective investment extends the identity of a male protagonist into a female counterpart who is created or recreated in his image. Hortensia is likewise a feminized extension of Horacio, "vivified" by both his body and his projections.

The essential generative relation between Horacio and Hortensia is, however, brokered through a series of intermediaries that afford Horacio a handsome return on his autoerotic investment. Hortensia, "the doll that resembles his wife" (2:140), is of course first and most apparently a surrogate for María. The text is unambiguous in its frequent overlapping of the identities of María and the doll, be it by virtue of their physical resemblance, by the investment and idealization of María's qualities in Hortensia (and vice versa, as the two "mutually adorn" one another) (2:150), or by plays on "confusion," exchanges, and mistaken identities (Horacio "bumped into Hortensia only to fall on María," for example) (2:148). Once the doll has been introduced into his matrimony, Horacio "could not accept the idea of María without Hortensia" (2:148). "Whenever he thought about María, he remembered her beside Hortensia." The doll does not merely complement María but is "her most enchanting feature." Hortensia is the perfection of María, and as Horacio measures his humanly flawed wife against his magnum opus he must ask himself "how he was able to love María when she did not have Hortensia" (2:148).

María is enlisted to participate in a fantasy of which she is only partially cognizant, and as a consequence she often unwittingly contributes to the dreaded "adultery" in which Horacio indulges. Her most desperate attempts to retrieve her drifting husband are counterproductive, resulting in her "disappearance" into the very dolls that she emulates. To better compete with her inanimate rivals for Horacio's love, for example, María remakes herself in the image of the dolls that, ostensibly, had been modeled after her (2:140–41, for example). The circularity of such mimetic rivalry is particularly evident in María's "surprises," which entail masquerading as a doll and showing up dressed for the part in a showcase or in a bed. María forfeits her subjectivity and her privileged position as human, as wife, and as prototype in order to compete with her mass-produced surrogates at the level where Horacio's game is played. She literalizes a comment made by her aunt—"he controls you like one of his dolls" (2:168)—perhaps to enact her recognition that doll-like subordination is a prerequisite of Horacio's love. One of Hernández's ex-wives expressed the same phenomenon, and the marriage fell apart precisely when she "stopped being for him the 'doll' that he had created with his imagination."[37]

Even when María asserts her subjectivity rather than forfeiting it, she sometimes unwittingly contributes to Horacio's escapades. On one occasion Horacio becomes jittery during one of Hortensia's extended absences. María, still insulated in her cloud of naïveté, believed that the doll had been returned to Facundo for repair after the first stab wounds, but Horacio—the secret author of that "murder"—had wielded the knife only as a pretext. The "murder" was a cover for a more dubious "repair": the reborn—and replumbed—Hortensia would return from Facundo sexually equipped to more satisfactorily serve the plans that Horacio held in store for her. Unaware of these intentions, and believing that Horacio would lose his mind in morose longing for the couple's absent "daughter," María telephones Facundo to expedite the doll's return. When she apprises Horacio of this conversation he immediately recognizes the demented irony of her unwitting collusion, of her contribution to "a pleasure of mine that will be my betrayal and her madness" (2:157). Once María comes to realize that Horacio "not only did not have a father's love for Hortensia but also wanted to make her his lover," and that she has foolishly misread the situation and participated as a pawn in "organizing his betrayal," then the results would be devastating: "all the places on her face would be destroyed" and "the horror would drive her out of her mind" (2:156).

It was Horacio's fear of death, rerouted as fear of María's death, that first engendered the scheme to have an inanimate and therefore "immortal" surrogate fabricated. Although María was not ill (and although even the doll that replaces her seems ill) (2:145), Horacio was obsessed with the "fear of being left without her" and "It was then that it occurred to him to have a doll made exactly like María" (2:143). In one significant episode Horacio falls asleep thinking about María's "illness" only to awaken the following morning beside the feared "corpse": "he touched her arm and it felt cold." Horacio screams, the bedroom door swings open, María appears, and Horacio realizes "that he had touched Hortensia and that it had been María who, while he was sleeping, put her beside him" (2:146). It is after this "surprise"—María forfeiting her exclusive privilege by displacing herself in the matrimonial bed with her as-yet-undisclosed rival—that Horacio decides to ask Facundo to equip the dolls for "human warmth" (2:146–47). The "dead" object that replaces the "dead" María must be refabricated to exude the semblance of life.[38]

As this episode suggests, when María's surprises are subjected to Horacio's interpretations they are elaborated in such a way as to reinforce and advance his perverse agenda. Other "omens" that spell María's death are similarly exploited to endorse Horacio's flight into the plumbed dolls. In one of Maria's "surprises" Hortensia falls into Horacio's arms, and the doll's silence serves as the tabula rasa for Horacio's scripting of the doll's imaginary discourse: "Hug me, because María will die" (2:143). Horacio further calculates that María herself had planned this secret announcement to him unawares, "as innocent as if she were revealing an illness that she herself had not yet discovered" (2:143). Horacio further associates Hortensia's fall into his arms with the fall of another doll—from the lighthouse scene—that he had inadvertently tumbled with a kiss. The two falling dolls, together with a collection of sonic omens and the piano depicted again in coffinlike imagery, leave little room for doubt: the bells toll for "the death of María" (2:143), fulfilling Horacio's prophesy and authorizing his "fall" into the dolls, themselves fallen women, that monumentalize María for all eternity.

The sentencing of María to death by means of this imaginary illness is then figuratively and vicariously executed when Horacio "murders" Hortensia. By stabbing Hortensia, Horacio symbolically "murders" María and María's presence in the doll, first because awareness of the perversion that was enhanced by the "murder" destroys María, and then because the replumbing for which the "murder" served as pretext feminizes Hortensia (as the "warmth" of the first plumbing humanized her) into the "woman" who replaces María. Hortensia dies as doll—María symbolically dying beside and within her—so that Hortensia can be reborn as wife. María and Hortensia are metaphorically united in this death as life fluids drain out of both of them: water pours from the stabbed Hortensia, and "a crisis of tears" explodes from María (2:154).[39] This confluence of waters is repeated later when Hortensia is "murdered" for the second time, now by María, who has discovered the doll's "femininity" and Horacio's use of it. The streams of water squirting from Hortensia's multiple stab wounds "crossed one another like those in the garden's fountain." María joins in the water-loss by again crying along, accompanied—via a tactile image associated with keyhole voyeurism—by one of the twin maids who serve as another of María's doubles throughout the text (2:159).[40] Later, when María passes through the "black house" to retrieve her clothes, the "dead" Hortensia representing her is finished off by a burial in the "coffin" of the piano. In the same image the doll's hair, "entangled with the instrument's cords," braids one eroticized object (doll) with another (piano) and the *tocar* themes again begin to resonate.

On occasion the link between Hortensia and María takes the form of a relation between sisters. In one case the trope is employed simply to rein-force the visual semblance and the hierarchical relation between María and the doll. Horacio returns home and sees the two seated with a book in front of them, and "he had the impression that María was teaching a sister to read" (2:144). Elsewhere Hortensia's identity as María's sister beats a straight path back to the death themes. The neighbors of the black house have created a legend (which thematically interconnects with the show-case-scene legends and with the annotated surprises in Horacio's register) relating that Horacio and María allowed the latter's sister to die in order to inherit her money. The couple, according to the legend, now expiates its sin by living with "a doll that, being exactly like the dead woman, reminds them constantly or their crime" (2:145). In this configuration Hortensia stands as a monument to death and guilt, a kind of anthropomorphic, omni-present object of penance in retribution for the spoils (money, sex) derived from one's transgression. But once placed in the broader narrative context, the sister of the neighbors' legend readily accepts a reading as María her-self, who Horacio "allowed to die" in order to harvest the gains of her attributes inherited by Hortensia. At the same time, the concept of penance incorporated by the neighbors into the doll's essence provides the unbeat-able opportunity for sinning and atoning in one and the same erotic cer-emony. The layers of sister, wife, penance, and death can alternate on the surface as the need of the moment warrants. "A garden enclosed [and with a fountain] is my sister, my spouse"; a flower (Hortensia) among other women-plants readily accepts defloration under the guise of circulating identities.[41]

Hortensia's role as daughter, also of considerable currency, is always most significant when considered in its relation to María. At the simplest level the daughter identity is introduced and insisted upon in a balancing operation by María, who attempts to moderate her husband and to recover the wholesomeness of the "family" during the earlier doll days. The more Hortensia becomes Horacio's lover, the more María insists on Hortensia as daughter. Indeed, the various roles and conflicting uses of Hortensia leave María tongue-tied in search of a word to describe her: "our . . ." (2:169). María's mother-father-daughter configuration cannot endure, but before it disappears entirely it is superimposed onto Horacio's more sinister threesome, the "adulterous" love triangle. The loaded occasion is a party commemorating Hortensia's "birth." Horacio is giving Hortensia a ride on a tricycle when one wheel—representing María—falls off and, as a result, "Horacio fell on top of Hortensia" (2:152). The efficiency of the image provides that with the same "fall" María is out of the triangle and Horacio is on top of her replacement, making leg gestures as though he himself were a wind-up doll. The number two that is introduced by the wheels remaining on the tricycle—Horacio and Hortensia as a couple, with the third player-wheel, María, excluded—is then echoed by the occasion being celebrated: Hortensia's second birthday.[42] The birthday party itself carries the theme in both directions, one emphasizing Hortensia as the daughter of dedicated parents and the other reinforcing the doll's rebirth as a "woman," as Horacio's lover.

Whenever Hortensia is stressed "as our daughter" (2:156) the text necessarily registers the corresponding stress of María as mother and Horacio as father. The latter makes explicit a father-daughter incest reminiscent of the similar—if hazier—situation of the tunnel owner in "Except Julia," surrounded as he is by a harem of "four girls who approached him as they would a father" (2:72). The father-daughter configuration further provides an inverted complement for the less explicit but thematically more important relation of mother and son. María-as-mother contributes significantly to these oedipal implications because her childless motherhood suggests not true parenting but rather her relation, as mother-wife, with Horacio, who throughout the text covets the role of His Majesty the Baby. In one passage María's speech mouthpieces the discourse that one images for a mother like Calita, a mother distraught because her son has "abandoned" her in order to take a wife or lover, and a mother who exploits her pathetic condition—deploying stockpiled reserves of guilt—to make the wayward son return to her bosom: "I am a woman who has been abandoned because of a doll; but if he saw me now, he would come back to me" (2:167).

In *The Hortensias* María is a pivotal figure in the constant intermingling of mother and lover, but elsewhere in the canon the layering, interchange, and migration of maternal identities tends more toward the older women who are the targets of quasi-erotic adolescent indiscretions. As worded in *Clemente Colling*, "I always found myself predisposed to fall in love with whatever teacher I had and whatever friend that mamma brought home" (1:28). Having introduced the neologism *abedules* ("*abe* would be the bulky part of the white arm and the *dules* would be the fingers that caressed it"), the narrator of *Lands of Memory* recalls having written "I want to do *abedules* to my teacher" (3:19).[43] Elsewhere, as we have seen, the boy protagonist wishes to fondle not the flapping arm flab of a school-teacher writing on a blackboard but rather the correlate body part—thighs—that are hidden away, darkly forbidden, and therefore all the more enticing. This desire to crawl underneath the dresses of teachers is as much a mani-festation of sexual curiosity as it is an innocent adolescent urge for the maternal warmth and protection that the mother herself could never ad-equately provide.

Another teacher, Celina, is less accessible than her predecessors and is frigidly stiff, but she too carries the double attributes of mother and lover. Celina is thirty years older than her ten-year-old suitor. She makes demands of him, scolds him, and punishes him like a mother, but in the final analysis her maternal attributes are subordinated by the boy to the amorous desires that she inspires in him. The intense attraction that libidinizes Celina's en-tire living room delineates the adolescent's early interest in women and his choice of love objects who are not mother, but who at the same time are closely associated with mother. By displacement and chain reaction this genealogy progresses from the mother to Celina to objects associated with Celina (Celina's piano, Celina's furniture, Celina's "bust"). A dedication that Hernández wrote to his own mother in *The Lost Horse*—a text that treats this (failed) "love affair" with Celina—further suggests the link of teacher and mother: "To my mother, because in this book [of adolescent love for Celina] I feel so close to her."[44] When Hernández's brother Ismael was asked during an unpublished interview if Hernández had fallen in love with any girl or woman during his early adolescence, Ismael responded, "No one knows, he was very reserved," but then added, "The first case could have been Celina, his piano teacher."[45]

Celina's is a particularly apt representative of the mother imago devel-oped in Hernández's work, for she is desirable but inaccessible, kind but emotionally frozen, compassionate but capable of cruelty. In one passage from *Clemente Colling* the attributes of this dual maternal nature are split and distributed: the actual mother is depicted as loving and benevolent, while Aunt Petrona—another surrogate on the model of the sadistic Deolinda—is pure malevolence. In one notable episode of her cruelty the narrator relates that Petrona "came to my bed and I saw her lifting the covers quickly; suddenly I felt on my feet the cold and viscous belly of a frog" (1:34). As in the under-the-skirt episodes, oedipal suggestions emerge together with the need for maternal protection when the boy, terrified by imagined frogs in his bed as a result of Petrona's practical joke, is consoled by the loving mother: "My mother carried me to her bed and my father came to mine" (1:34). Actions of the evil mother (Petrona) thus provide ultimately that the father is displaced from the matrimonial bed so that the good, loving mother is free to comfort and pamper her son.

The short text "The Ball" is based upon one of Hernández's experiences with Deolinda herself, the paradigm representative of the dark side of the mother. The narrator begs Deolinda to buy him a ball at a local store, but she refuses his repeated requests, threatens to punish him for the insistence, and finally makes a rag ball to appease him. The substitute ball—described as ugly, flat, and in the end not a ball at all—is of particular interest because it is given to the boy by a substitute mother, whom it comes to represent. The beauty and maternal roundness of the ball in the store (inaccessible, seen through glass) contrasts sharply with the tired, fuscous, rag-tag improvisation offered by Deolinda. The boy invents a game in which the hated object is punished and destroyed as he plays with it. The rag ball sustains the most furious kicks and the boy expresses his pleasure in beating it (3:149–50). He soon tires of his game, however, and of others that follow it—putting it on his head like a hat, rolling it on its side like a wheel, and planning to throw it at whoever is unlucky enough to first pass by. The frustrated boy finally returns to the grandmother to protest that the rag-thing is not a ball and that he will die of sadness if she does not get him the ball in the store. She laughs, her huge stomach quakes, and the text concludes by associating the ball with the pregnant womb and with the comfort of maternal protection. Having no ball (mother) and nowhere to turn for consolation other than to the very woman who deprives him, the boy succumbs to defeat and drifts into a lull suggesting interuterine peace: "I put my head on her abdomen and without moving it from there I sat down in a chair that my grandmother pulled up for me. Her belly was like a great, warm ball that rose and fell with her breathing. And I lost myself in sleep" (3:150).

In other scenes the mother imago gains expression not in the disguise of an aunt or a teacher but rather as the mother of someone else. In Horacio's musings he works through the mysteries of Hortensia's identity by wondering if his mother-in-law's soul has inhabited the doll. In search of a clue, Horacio questions María about her (dead) mother and is pleased to learn of mother-in-law's inanimate, doll-like qualities: "she had an astonishing tranquility; she was capable of spending hours in a chair without moving and with her eyes in a void" (2:151). The doll that serves Horacio as sexual object is thus linked with María's mother. As it is worded elsewhere, "one portrait [was] so well hidden behind another that her mother was mine" (2:131).

In the instance from which this hidden-portrait image was borrowed, a narrator's dream depicts his amorous "triumph" with a daughter, but this is suddenly interrupted when her mother enters through the doorway of a contiguous room. The narrator tries to lie his way out of the predicament by telling the mother that he is in love not with the daughter but with a friend of the daughter, and that he has come to the daughter's room with the exclusive and innocent purpose of discussing the girl he loves. This comment results in a bout of disconsolate crying, but the cloudy referent of a pronoun makes it unclear whether the one crying is the mother or the daughter. The context indicates the daughter, but the ambiguity opens an alternate reading. If one pursues that alternate through the dream interpretation that follows in the text, the phrase "she cried because I loved someone else" (2:131) again reveals in encoded convolutions the discourse of a mother who mourns the loss of her son's exclusive love. The mother bursts in on the lovers, in effect, to put an end to the son's "infidelities" and to reclaim her maternal monopoly. Oedipal suggestions are equally prevalent when one approaches the passage from the other direction, with the daughter as the crying subject. In this reading the daughter cries because the narrator loves not her but one like her, her "friend," which is to say her mother-under-cover (as with María's mother in Hortensia). To close the gap between the girl's mother and the narrator's, the interpretation accompanying the dream in the text explicitly clarifies, twice, that the girl's mother "was my own mother" (2:131).

Another interesting instance of one character's mother represented by another's and then retrieved symbolically is found in "Mamma's Tree." The manuscript of this curious piece survived in two versions, one shorter and presumably earlier, and the other more developed and apparently in a final or semifinal draft. In the shorter version, which is narrated in the first person, the sexual suggestiveness is minimal, no relation is established between the cousin-lover and the mother imago, and the fat legs thematically central to the later version are absent. In the later version, narrated atypically in the third person, the erotic haze thickens considerably as the quasi-incestuous relation between the violinist and his cousin offers an ambiguous but unmistakable dramatization of oedipal themes. Rewriting of "Mamma's Tree" in the third person seems to have afforded Hernández the emotional distance necessary to give the disturbing subject matter more sustained treatment. Such also seems to hold true for The Hortensias, likewise laden with oedipal themes and among the few texts written in the third person.

"Mamma's Tree" offers fat legs rather than dolls as the charged part-objects standing in for mother. Obesity in Hernández's work is generally eroticized and often associated with the "big and fat" teachers as maternal figures, and the legs in particular—"thick, plump"—are in many instances the body part held in focus (3:50, 1:199). Perhaps the most compelling of these fat-leg images is the one that brings the narrative lens under the skirt to have a look at the thundering, fat-swirled thighs that one imagines there. These legs in "My First Teacher" take yet a more insistent maternal turn later in the text when they are associated with a mother surrogate closer to home: "the legs were fat like my grandmother's" (3:151). When texts like "My First Teacher" or "Mamma's Tree" are given biographical readings, the fat legs are clearly recognizable not only as those of Deolinda but also as those of the woman noted for them, Hernández's mother herself.[46]

The "difficult steps of those heavy legs" in "Mamma's Tree" thus carry the burden of the pudgy cousin compounded by the mother imago loaded onto her (2:189). Mother is obviously present in the title of the narrative, and then again in the tree-trunk legs that the Hernández protagonist is dying to climb. The peek-a-boo of the knee poking out of the kimono, the downward-up perspective of the violinist hiding under the bed, and the fetishistic sexual contact with the legs all link "Mamma's Tree" to the *pollera* fantasies in Celina's living room, to the mysterious underworld beneath the teacher's skirts, and to the negligee ritual of "The Usher."[47] Such fat legs also reappear in the quasi-erotic water rituals of "The Flooded House," the maternal qualities of which will concern us in the final section.

While the image of fat legs thus runs its course down a series of seemingly endless and self-generating associations, the fatness as a trope in its own right disengages from the legs and pursues a parallel course that likewise leads back to mother. In *The Hortensias* a mother figure—"a cousin of her mother"—shelters María in her time of need, and this woman has an "immense body." When she walks "she makes the floors creak," while her pet parrot wisecracks a refrain—concerning milk—that evokes both "Ursula" and maternal lactation (2:168). The aunt's name is Pradera—"Pasture," and echoing the name of Aunt Petrona—and her Ursula-like qualities further include a hyperbolic representation of maternity, "immense breasts" (2:169). Such female fatness can inspire a patronizing empathy and endearment because it is "so ignorant of its clumsy disproportions that it tempts us to love and protect it more," but one nevertheless experiences the contrary desire to "betray that defenseless innocence" (1:199).

Ursula herself is exemplary in this context of maternal rotundity. In one passage her massive body is seen from the frequent bottom-up perspective as she approaches the narrator's bed. He is an adult, but her looming and enormous presence suggests the bigger-than-life world that children experience owing to their relative smallness. A child's relation to overwhelming physical volume is further suggested when the narrator remarks, "I wanted to put my arm around her waist but my arm wasn't long enough" (3:126). Maternal suggestions accumulating around Ursula's fatness are then reinforced through the insistence on her cowlike nature and, as part of it, her association with a primary emblem of maternity: milk. When asked whether he wants coffee or tea, to cite a simple example, the narrator looks at Ursula and responds, "I love milk" (3:121). Ursula smells like milk, and her fullness, her swelling with milk, resembles a pregnancy as the narrator contemplates "her big belly, waiting" (3:126). The short distance from mother to oedipal mother is then bridged by repeated reference to the protective father, who guards and monopolizes Ursula's favors as though she were his wife (3:126–27).

Against the backdrop sketched in by such traces, the concept of mother-as-lover is brought to the foreground if we return to "Mamma's Tree." The violinist must climb a tree to enter the room of his cousin-lover, and he mistakenly almost climbs the wrong tree, "mamma's tree" (2:184). He is warned beforehand not to climb mother's tree (2:190), and he is twice punished for merely having touched it. Leaving aside the vaginal suggestions of the "tree," this touching is resonant in the content of *tocar* poetics (the eroticized piano as woman), and then again in the context of touching the tree-trunk legs in the under-the-dress episodes.

The touching of the mother's tree also seems almost a gesture of "touching base" with the mother before climbing into the "tree" of the lover. The cousin-lover is, in effect, overshadowed by her mother's extending foliage: the violinist "couldn't see her well," his vision obstructed by "the great volume of her mother" (2:189). As previously one had to pass through Irene to arrive at objects, here one must pass through the mother to arrive at the lover. And yet the metaphorical structure of the text manifests that detour in reverse, as it did likewise in "Irene's House": the mother is figuratively touched by the protagonist because her imago is "behind" the cousin-lover who serves as her front. To arrive at the mother he touches the lover who represents her. This lining up of bodies and themes one behind the other is typical of Hernández, and in one passing image it gains graphic expression as a boy "grabs his sister's skirt [*pollera*] and for a moment they remained in a line, the mannequin, the girl, and the boy" (3:92). In the boy's perspective, as in Horacio's, we see a mannequin just behind the mother-girl.

The infantile qualities attributed to the lovers in "Mamma's Tree" also carry oedipal implications, particularly in light of a remark made by Hernández's second daughter: "My father let me know by signs that he was younger than I and that Calita was also like a child."[48] The mother and her son are as immature here as the cousin-lover and violinist are in "Mamma's Tree." In the text the cousin is reduced to an infancy that conjures up images from Botero: "she turned her back to him, put the bottle [*mamadera*] on the pillow and began to suck it, slowly, with her eyes half closed" (2:186). In lieu of the customary downward-up perspective of the male belittled by looming females, we have in this instance a carnivalesque reversal: the woman (mother) is brought down to the level of the man-baby who desires her. Later, however, the *pollera*-style hierarchy is restored and the child identity redirected toward the protagonist when his fat cousin "kissed him on the mouth, pinching his cheeks with her fingers, as one does to children" (2:188).

Depiction of the adult male lover as a misdirected boy searching for his mother is as ubiquitous in Hernández's literary canon as it is in the author's life outside of it. Because Hernández, according to Paulina Medeiros, was "immature" and unequal to the struggle of everyday life, "he searched for a certain maternal protection in all women." In her love letters Medeiros demonstrates her own participation in Hernández's need for a mother-lover, referring to Hernández as "my fearful little boy" and endearing herself by reference to his special need: "You are still a boy, and you don't know it." Hernández responds in kind with comments like, "See how your baby tells you he was a little sick?" Even in the passing details of everyday life one notes an eerie maternal tone, as for example when Medeiros writes to Hernández, "And if you come in the morning, I'll leave the milk and the bath ready for you," or elsewhere: "I give you peace, my little boy who came to me wounded: sleep."[49] Such adolescent dependence on a maternal woman is also alluded to by many others close to Hernández. The essence of such observations is perhaps most succinctly captured by his sister, Deolinda Hernández, who remarked that her brother searched for wives "who resembled our mother."[50]

While Medeiros suggests that Hernández himself was unaware of his childishness, the literary canon seems to indicate quite the contrary. In *Lands of Memory*, for example, childishness is initially projected outward onto another boy—"he had an attitude of still belonging to his mother" (3:20), but a few pages later the narrator retrieves it: other boys would become adults, but "I would remain a child my whole life" (3:25). The awareness of this boyishness then makes the decided turn toward oedipal themes (and toward successful deception of Medeiros) when it is strategically deployed as an instrument of seduction. When a man yields the assertive position in a relationship, or at least feigns such a forfeiture, some daring women are attracted by his timidity and thus "help him." "Maybe they feel a little above him"—this expression recalling the downward-up perspective of the *pollera* and related scenes—"or experience him as a boy, or are stimulated by a maternal instinct" (1:195). The same argument is expanded by another passage in which the narrator splits himself into the boy who seduces women and the man in whom this boy resides. We learn that it was the boy "who first attracted and deceived them. Then the man deceived them taking advantage of the boy. The man learned to deceive the way children deceive; and he had a lot to learn and to imitate" (2:32). Childish helplessness is thereby converted into an asset, and the need for a mother deployed as an instrument to seduce and manipulate.

The early Hernández's confessions are even more telling when they move from the quasi-autobiographical texts into the more developed fictions. In *The Hortensias*, Horacio is a "bad-mannered little boy" (2:146) because he does tricks for a girl at the dinner table, but he is more profoundly a child—and a confused one at that—because as an adult he still plays with dolls. Once Horacio has abandoned both María and the doll who represents her (Hortensia), he experiences a kind of gleeful freedom that rejuvenates him and launches him into his Don Juanesque journey from doll to doll. His youthfulness is stressed as he is overtaken by good luck "that he had not had since his adolescence," and consequently "he could dominate the events with the impulse of a young man" (2:161). The adolescent conquest of love objects itself sounds an oedipal note, first because the dolls are mass-produced replicas of a prototype (the mother), and then because the perpetual availability of the dolls and their "doting," subservient demeanors expresses the "unconscious wish to be the preferred child of an enslaved mother."[51]

Implications of a mother-son relation acted out symbolically are also apparent in the insistent urge to access, or "violate," forbidden realms. One patent manifestation of this was discussed in the previous chapter, where vision as a prosthesis was used to overcome barriers and to "touch" women inaccessible to the subject's tactile caress. The maternal dimension of lustful seeing has been identified by many clinicians, who argue that "Voyeurism begins in the home with mother or mother surrogate as the sexual object and thence spreads to other unattainable women."[52] In folk tales as much as in psychopathology, the forbidden object of desire often takes the mother-surrogate form of "a queen or fairy or some other elevated female." This construct is followed by "a prohibition against looking at her, an irresistible curiosity, and finally a punishment which often seems disproportionately severe."[53] One voyeur used the term "placed on a pedestal" to "elevate" both the mother and the unattainable girls whom he conquered through voyeurism.[54] The trope, reminiscent of Galatea, again registers the downward-up perspective conducive to a peep. In *The Hortensias*—where Horacio,

THE LUST OF SEEING 196

like any narcissist, expects to be "treated like a prince"—the conquest of dolls leaves María, standing in for the mother, as "an unfortunate queen" (2:159).[55] A variation on the same theme comes at the conclusion of the narrative, when Horacio's passion has run its confused course and madness is imminent: a doll cast earlier in the role of "the lusty queen" is recast as a dead queen in the final showcase (2:179).[56] In all instances the display of dolls in showcases affords them an on-a-pedestal quality as well as a semblance to the women seen behind windows by voyeurs. As Balzac tied these themes together in a separate context, "With his eyes, Sarrasine devoured Pygmalion's statue, come down from its pedestal."[57]

The desire to conquer the forbidden (maternal) love object is even more explicit in the chapters that Hernández deleted from *The Hortensias*. Despite the fact that he has a monopoly on Hortensia (not to mention his wife) as well as easy access to any number of other dolls, Horacio concocts a desperate scheme to "violate" a doll that is forbidden. The doll belongs to a countess ("a queen or fairy or some other elevated female") who Horacio has romantically "adored" since his childhood as though she were a "goddess." Horacio's obsession for this one forbidden doll, accompanied by dismissal of all legitimate options, suggests that the most exquisite, voluptuous extravaganza is with the single doll always out of range, the doll standing in for the primary, inimitable love of childhood and the maternal body beyond the barrier of incest.[58]

An episode in the published version of *The Hortensias* similarly documents Horacio's passion for the forbidden. A man referred to as the Timido (timid one) has a doll that is a "sister" of Horacio's doll, and the Timido's doll is therefore—as Facundo jokes—Horacio's "sister-in-law." The status as sister recalls the doll named Herminia (*hermana* = sister) as well as the depiction of Hortensia as María's sister, and the concept of in-law is suggestive as an echo of the mother-in-law who "occupies" Hortensia. The mother is then folded into the scheme of these almost-relations as the Timido keeps his doll hidden and only comes to it at night because "he is afraid that his mother will find out." These oedipal suggestions are enhanced by a move to which we are now accustomed: the man who desires the mother-doll's forbidden delights is alluded to as a boy. After Horacio arranged his entry into the Timido's house to abduct the doll, "he again felt the excitement of adolescence." His boyishness is coupled with dream-book sexual penetration imagery, reminding us that mother, like Celina, protects her secrets under lock and key. The door granting access to the forbidden doll is "dirty like a indolent old lady," so Horacio "turned the key in the lock with disgust" (2:171). The disgust accommodates multiple readings: fear he experiences upon "entering"; the disgust with himself for the compulsion; guilt for the transgression; and the adolescent discovery that the fruit under the *pollera* and up "mother's tree" is perhaps not as sweet as one had imagined.

The forbidden woman guarded under lock and key is closely related in Hernández's canon to the concept of the contiguous room. Like the child who wonders exactly what goes on beyond mommy and daddy's closed bedroom door, the protagonists' eyes and desire always wander from the room they are in to that other, mysterious, erotically charged space just beyond it. A patient reported by Karl Abraham reenacted his unconscious childhood desires so literally that the oedipal drama is barely disguised. In sexual relations he could "obtain gratification only under the condition that a man and a woman have intercourse in an adjacent room. The patient would begin to cry; then the woman would have to leave her partner and rush to the patient."[59] While in Hernández's canon the oedipal qualities of the contiguous room lack this tragicomic explicitness, the same themes are treated with a more subtle hand. In "The Usher" the father's entrance from the contiguous room into the dining hall is in itself sufficient to arouse the usher's desire ("I felt the desire to put my eyes in there") and to inspire the scheming that will ultimately gain him access to the unknown ("I began to plan a way to enter that room") (2:62). It is in this forbidden, contiguous room that the usher indulges in his showcase gazing and the negligee-over-the-face ritual, entrapping the daughter in his fantasy and tapping her oedipal qualities. The daughter assumes a maternal aura first because she is forbidden and accessed through the mystery of a contiguous room through which she, like the father, moves freely. She is characterized by a billowing negligee, which in dream imagery is associated with the mother. She is seen from the bottom-up perspective introduced by the *pollera* and under-the-dress episodes in which maternal surrogates are "violated." And like the Hortensia dolls who give the mother life everlasting, she is associated with water and the survival of death.

The eroticized room is often contiguous with or associated with a dining room. In some cases it seems as though the laws of table etiquette governing lengthy, ceremonious meals represent the protagonist's confinement to a quasi-fulfilling but burdensome reality, and that the half-opened door provides an escape from that repressive ambience by revealing a glimpse of the possibilities on the other side. A more haunting appetite always beckons once one's hunger is satisfied in the dining room, and the erotica just beyond the divide are perhaps yet more exquisite if ritual aspects of the meal wander with one. The link between the one appetite and the other is suggested most directly in "The Flooded House," where Margarita's dining room and bedroom are adjoining, but it is also evident in the showcase-dining room link of *The Hortensias* and "The Usher," or in the eating rituals alternating with tunnel rituals in "Except Julia."[60] In all of these cases a revolving door turns between explicit gluttony and muted lust. As Hernández told one of his daughters, he loved food "with a romantic passion."[61] Conversely, as demonstrated in his fiction, the love object tends to be "devoured."

A variation on the theme of the contiguous room is developed in "The Balcony." Whereas in the other mentioned cases a male protagonist penetrates the erotic confines of the contiguous room, here, in reverse, the girl exits her bedroom in order to enter the adjacent "body" of her lover, the balcony. The oedipal suggestions are likewise developed inversely as the balcony and the girl's father are linked through nuances concerning the father's overhanging lower lip that resembles the railing of a theater box; its excessive size is later compared to a house "too big for the two of us" (3:46-47).

The balcony, in addition, assumes special status as a transitional space, an intermediate area between interior and exterior. Like the transitional object, this transitional or potential space is inherently paradoxical: the balcony is both inside and outside, a kind of "green room" between the player and the performance, "a cord between the indiscretion and the secret, the lookout from which one looks and is looked at, from which the street becomes a spectacle and toward which one's curiosity converges."[62] On the balcony, as in the showcase gallery or before the partially opened door, transitional space grants access to mysteries on the "other side." The balcony goes further, however, for the access it grants is physical rather than visual. One may not be permitted to cross the threshold into forbidden realms, but the balcony eliminates the need because it clouds the boundaries and brings the "other side" into one's house. The showcases of *The Hortensias* are designed specifically for this purpose of internalizing and normalizing the forbidden, authorizing spying, and appropriating fragments from the privacy of others. In their own way the passages that Horacio inscribes in his record accomplish the same mission, and it is no coincidence that the study where this recording takes place is contiguous with the showcase gallery. In the context of *The Hortensias* and "The Usher" there is perhaps no illustration of transitional space more apt than a ticket girl in a glass booth positioned between a movie theater and the street. In this intermediary area—not quite theater, not quite street—she appears lighted in a showcase, vulnerable to covetous gazes, but more than a spectacle in herself she is a medium like Irene, a doorkeeper, a ticket to the more moving illusion that she screens.

MEMORIAL SEARCH AND MATRILINEAL SUCCESSION

The adult lover depicted as a desirous adolescent boy, the erotic pursuit of symbolic mothers, the urge to "violate" the forbidden, and the poetics of the eroticized contiguous room together establish the context in Hernández's canon for the dissemination of the mother imago through a "mass-produced" series of women and women surrogates. Horacio's compulsive and relentless pursuit of an ideal doll-woman reveals "an endless memorial search for something in the future that resides in the past."[63] The quest to rescue the mother from the irretrievable and largely imaginary past provides an implicit substructure for Hernández's memory-based fictions, while in *The Hortensias* the memorial search more dramatically launches Horacio through a series of mother representations that register his progressive desperation. The mother imago manifest in María is soon displaced by the doll, Hortensia, herself constructed on the maternal prototype but then established as a prototype in her own right. The showcase dolls introduced concurrently with Hortensia echo her maternal relation but a bit more distantly, in a configuration reminiscent of the in-law status discussed earlier.

As the memorial search progresses after María is discarded, Hortensia herself is metamorphosed into an other (when she is remade to hold water for "human warmth") and then again into a third when she is "murdered" and reborn replumbed as a functional sexual object. Plumbed though his sweetheart may be, however, Horacio's compulsive search presses onward, and Hortensia is consequently displaced in turn by a succession of dolls bearing her name. The mass production and socialization of the Hortensia dolls index the endlessness of the process, as does further multiplication through ersatz Hortensias, Brand X clones that seem indistinguishable from Hortensias but that lack the special feature that makes the authentic dolls most like the mother.

In the case of both Hernández and his protagonists it seems as though the full transition from mother to lover, from primary love object to postoedipal objects, was never satisfactorily accomplished. As Freud put it, "The libido has remained attached to the mother for so long, even after the onset of puberty, that the maternal characteristics remained stamped on the love-objects that are chosen later, and all these turn into easily recognizable mother-surrogates."[64] The distorted Don Juanesque adventures, the "craving for stimulation" that delivers "an endless series of substitutive objects," evidence the author and the protagonist's relentless quest to recover an ideal, the omniperfect woman that defensive fantasy made of the deficient mother.[65] The protagonists, like Hernández himself, are ultimately unable to remain in love because no woman adequately impersonates the all-satisfying fantasy mother. "The trait of overvaluing the loved one, and regarding her as unique and irreplaceable, can be seen to fall just as naturally into the context of the child's experience, for no one possesses more than one mother, and the relation to her is based on an event that is not open to any doubt and cannot be repeated." Considering the multiplicity of lovers and wives in cases like those that concern us, Freud remarked: "If we understand the love-objects chosen by our type as being above all mother-surrogates, then the formation of a series of them, which seems so flatly to contradict the condition of being faithful to one, can now also be understood." When something is irreplaceable but active in the unconscious, it "frequently appears as broken up into an endless series: endless for the reason that every surrogate nevertheless fails to provide the desired satisfaction."[66] If one of Horacio's dolls is hardly distinguishable from the next, if each of Hernández's wives is poured into the same mold, it is because "passionate attachments of this sort are repeated with the same peculiarities—each an exact replica of the others," and all replicas are manufactured from one and the same prototype.[67] The "perverse refinement of quality" yields to "the vulgarity of quantity" (1:43) when a Horacio or a Hernández succumbs to the "search, ever to be disappointed, for the adequately nurturant mother."[68]

In later psychoanalysis, Melanie Klein described how the infant negotiating a complex and ambivalent relationship with the mother treats "the relationship as if it were many relationships."[69] The splitting of the mother imago preserves the inviolable excellence and sacrosanct purity of a maternal part-object while it projects the negative qualities elsewhere, allowing Horacio, like the infant, "to create a psychological sanctuary," a showcase world or, as Winnicott calls it, a potential space.[70] In a related formulation by Heinz Kohut a child whose primary narcissism is disturbed by inadequacies of parental care responds by creating a grandiose self (as discussed in chapters 2 and 3 above) and by reestablishing the lost perfection in "self-objects" (Hortensia dolls) constructed of "the idealized parental imago."[71] The Freudian crowd populating this maternal imago is the product of an intense ambiguity that another analyst describes as syncretic. Owing to "a lack of discrimination," the boundary between mother and other becomes blurry. The analyst could be as well referring to Horacio when he remarks that "for us two different people are concerned, but for him it is the same person."[72]

Representations of an endless series of surrogates proliferating from a prototype reappear with considerable currency throughout Hernández's canon. In passing instances the text merely registers the capacity of a person or object to reproduce itself; it refers, for instance, to a fat person having many souls or to people who "multiply themselves in deeds and memories" (2:32). On other occasions the multiplication of specimens from a specifically maternal prototype is more thoroughly developed. The paradigm of such cases is the ingenious discussion of names in *The Hortensias*. Horacio's wife "is named María Hortensia; but she liked to be called María." When the doll resembling María is made "they decided to take the name Hortensia—as one would take a discarded object—for the doll" (2:141).[73] The name "María" that is not passed to the doll reappears in the dedication of *The Hortensias* to Hernández's third wife, *María* Luisa Las Heras, suggesting a link between the wife function inside and outside of the text. But in Hernández's biography the name "María" can hardly be evoked without recalling the lost love from which Hernández never quite recovered, that of *María* Isabel Guerra, his first wife. "María" thus runs a succession from the wife displaced by a mother-doll inside the text to representatives from a series of women—one of which, the first, is idealized in the distant past—who likewise are replaced in succession and tend to be maternal in their relations with Hernández.

The name-play becomes most pertinent, however, when one pursues the transfer of the name "Hortensia" from María to the doll, and then dolls, who become known by that name. In her early youth Hernández's mother's name was Juana *Hortensia* Silva.[74] When the girl was adopted by Deolinda Arocha de Martínez her name was adjusted accordingly to Juana Martínez, and the surname "Silva" was consequently discarded. That pattern of discarded names then applies both to the "Juana" and the "Hortensia," the latter falling out of usage—as it does in the text—and the former replaced by the nickname "Calita." When Hernández retrieves the name "Hortensia" from oblivion he decidedly consolidates his own mother with the textual wife (María) by having the latter carry the mother's name and then, again like the mother, discard it. It is further noteworthy that with his selection of the name "Hortensia" Hernández seems to retrieve the pre-Deolinda mother. This mother summoned forth from *her* earliest years may be a representation of the idealized mother that the memorial search strives to recuperate from *his* earliest years, *his* pre-Deolinda years during which the mother smothered him exclusively in her affection and before which the sadistic side of the mother surrogate had shown its face. In any case, the matrilineal migration of the name "Hortensia" provides that mother and wife hold something very essential in common (Hortensia), but that the wife veils mother's presence with attributes of her own (María).

The wife, however, is not the end of the line for the name "Hortensia," but quite the contrary is its point of departure in the "Don Juan-like fragmentation or multiplication of objects."[75] The name first passes from María to the privileged doll, Hortensia, grounding her identity as wife-mother. "Hortensia" is then extended from this one prototype doll to the mass-produced assortment of others, each of which carries the mother-wife name and many of which are called upon to perform the corresponding services. The name "Hortensia" is further used to distinguished the "authentic" dolls (those like the mother) from the imitations. These authentic Hortensias follow María's suit by taking the mother's name and then—in service to the accumulating identities—"covering" it with another. Each of the dolls carries "Hortensia" as a brand name in homage to its source, but then the man who purchases a doll "gives it the name that she intimately inspires in him." The name "Hortensia" thereby once again falls out of usage as a facade of independent subjectivity is constructed for the dolls. These poetics depict the love objects—be they dolls or women—as volatile reproductions of the mother that are faithful in essence to their prototype but capable of "adding something of their own." The concept of syncretism mentioned earlier describes the process precisely: the mother makes a contribution as prototype, attributes are added by the woman who evokes the mother in the eyes of the beholder and who perhaps emulates the mother, and the composite of this mother-wife is further elaborated by the projections of a Hernández or Horacio. What is loved is not the woman-in-herself but the absence evoked by this syncretic composite, an absence shaped by the hollow doll. In the end desire "has no object, at any rate no real object; through real objects which are all substitutes (and all the more numerous and interchangeable for that), it pursues an imaginary object (a 'lost object') which is its truest object, an object that has always been lost and is always desired as such."[76]

Prior to *The Hortensias*, serial production from a maternal prototype gained more innocent expression in an early Hernández text. "Cradle Rocking" depicts an earth facing imminent destruction and men of one country constructing "six little planets" upon which life can continue. These "planets," actually enclosures constructed of cement, are reminiscent of the showcases in their ironic deployment of reality-replacing fictions. The landscapes perfectly painted on concrete tempt the inhabitants to enter them, but "to enter that beauty and to bang oneself against the wall were one and the same thing" (1:86). Pounding oneself into a fiction is characteristic of Horacio in more than one way, the most literal being his constant banging into the invisible wall (glass) that separates his fantasy (showcase) from the social reality beyond it.

"Cradle Rocking" is more suggestive in the maternal context when the poetics of its title are echoed at its conclusion through a cradling function assigned to the earth. With the fear of mother-earth's imminent destruction (one recall's María's "illness"), men "could think of nothing other than indulging in pleasures" (Horacio's desperate, Don Juanesque flight into the dolls) and they were unconcerned that these pleasures "were at the expense of the pain of others" (1:85). Some few, however, recognize that the moribund mother-earth must be replaced, multiply replaced to negate her oblivion, to "perfect" her memory in monuments, to "cradle" the men so much in need of her. The six replicas are thus constructed in her image; life survives inside the replica "mothers" in which the mother, too, figuratively survives her own death.

But the earth, it turns out, is spared: "The world did not end" (1:87). The mother lives beyond the doom date assigned to her, thereby eliminating the necessity of the replica planets, which, obsolete, come to *their* end. This variation contrasts with *The Hortensias*, where the mother imago— lost, dead, or jeopardized—is never sufficiently retrieved from her true or symbolic moribundity to render her human and inanimate surrogates obsolete. She does not come back to life and thereby eliminate the need for replicas, but rather lives on eternally in the "dead" dolls that ritually protect Horacio from her ultimate and absolute absence, as well as from her menacing presence.

Another example of reproduction from a prototype was suggested in a discussion that was conducted during the 1976 University of Poitiers seminar dedicated to Hernández's work.[77] A pun concerning a "piece of music" in its relation to "piece of clothing" initiates the theme in *Lands of Memory*. A few pages later the erotic haze thickens as the piece of music rejoins with the woman via a separate metaphoric configuration. The narrator makes reference to a "piece" that a touring pianist made known, affording the narrator, also a pianist, "the privilege of taking it home and shutting myself away with it," as though he had abducted "a foreign woman" (3:37). This idea of bringing a fetishized object home as the centerpiece for one's private rehearsals is familiar to readers of "The Usher" or "Except Julia," and it is also treated in passing in "The Flooded House"—where the narrator seizes an image "to then take it to my solitude and caress it" (3:77)—and in "The Crocodile": "first I robbed with my eyes any unattended thing on the street or inside the houses and then I took it to my solitude" (3:90).[78] In the *Lands of Memory* example an extremely suggestive description of keyboard digitation combines with the running pun on the verb *tocar* (to touch/ to play an instrument) in establishing the technique of "playing" woman-compositions.[79] The narrator feels an "anguished voracity" to have not one but all of them "between my fingers," and he imagines "the muscular pleasure of holding their bodies made of sound in my hands and of dominating their movements." The muted sadism introducing itself through the desire for domination becomes more insistent as he "would make their melodic voices suffer" in what seems almost their groans of ecstasy (3:36). By the time he reaches home after having purchased one of these women-compositions he has already memorized the way "she" smells. When he has had the opportunity to play/touch her, "she revealed herself slowly, lying down in a slowly spreading tempo, as though in a bed that she herself had prepared for eternity" (3:37).[80]

Although there may be many sheet-music copies of a given composition in the music stores, the narrator regards his copy (or prototype) as though it were the only one; "to see several was like a defect of vision" (3:37).[81] An exclusive preference for one's own object (everyone, after all, has a mother) psychologically annihilates all "reproductions." Others, the narrator concedes, had heard his prized "piece" performed in the concert and therefore had as much right to it as he did, but "I thought that the others had forgotten it and that now it would be exclusively mine." He therefore goes in search of the woman-composition as though "searching for a sleeping woman someplace in a forest" who would passively grant him the "privilege" "to initiate all kinds of affection" (3:36).

All copies of the sheet music reduce to a single copy, his, the one that he plays/touches as though—in his own trope—he were blindfolded, as though the defective vision he projects to others could reorganize reality to conform to the paradigm that gives his secret ceremony its most exclusive, voluptuous meaning. To play/touch the composition-as-woman on a piano itself metaphorically charged with feminine attributes is again to create, to compose, a woman based upon something inscribed (the sheet music, the mother prototype) but then elaborated by one's arrangement and phrasing of the notes found there. The sheet music thus stands in here for a master plan, a guiding paradigm against which specimens are measured, but with sufficient freedom of interpretation to allow the piano and pianist to "add something of their own." Considered against the more explicit case of *The Hortensias*, one can argue that the attributes of María consolidating with the attributes of the mother imago define but do not constitute what the Hortensia dolls are in their essence, in the same way that the sheet music defines but does not constitute the multiple versions of the composition interpreted by various performers. The most important aspect, as Mahler put it, is not in the sheet music, and yet the sheet music, the prototype, provides the basis for the improvisations that ultimately return to it for structure and meaning.[82]

In *The Hortensias* the multiplication of specimens forgoes the figurative detours of earlier texts and dramatizes the memorial search through a trope on the threshold of literal expression: anthropomorphic clones, women-things, proliferating in a matrilineal line of succession. If one pardons the overlap of an occasional clumsy transition, Horacio is serially monoga-mous, moving, like Hernández himself, through a cycle that alternately overvalues and devalues the love object. The woman-doll's identity is monitored and manipulated by an imposed maternal paradigm, and each object is sometimes loved for its malleable accommodation of poured-in identity and sometimes hated for it.[83] Among the by-products of these com-plicated dynamics is the loss of interest in and the abandonment of the love object once it has run the course of its cycle. In the simpler cases the libido flees almost immediately upon "conquest": no sooner does one narrator have the opportunity to kiss a girl than he discovers that his desire for her is dissipating (2:130). It is in *The Hortensias*, however, that women are most explicitly depicted as disposable. Once Horacio perceives a doll to be some-how defective, he prefers "to throw it out" like the "horse full of holes that he had as a child," or like the psychologically charged rag ball discarded in "The Ball" (2:160). One surrogate is dumped to pursue another because the hunt is more libidinized than the prey. Something of those dynamics, along with the "memorial" nature of the search and the migration of desire from object to object, is underscored in an uncollected text from the early years. A prologue sets the mood: "Maybe I take pleasure in loving like a complicated fraud"; and then: "Sometimes when I have a new love I am so happy in that joy that I promise myself to leave her and to be faithful to my old love. But I well know that it is the new love who gives me the joy, and that before long I will deliver myself with even greater delight to my be-trayal" (1:193). When love is experienced the urge of the memorial search is retroactive, but it nevertheless propels the protagonist into the future.

As we have seen, then, Horacio's invested and then withdrawn desire hastens his journey through the gauntlet of substitutive objects that can never adequately satisfy him. A speedy summary of his progression from one object to the next—recalling and adapting the discussion of multipli-cation from chapter 3—will be useful in the present context to illustrate our previous observations and to preface analysis of why dolls in particular surface as the trope for replication of the mother imago.

No sooner has Horacio abandoned María than "he thought that he would also betray Hortensia" and consequently schemes an assault on "a divine blonde" (2:160). These early indices of multiplying love objects are re-played in the margins of the narrative by the twin maids, one of whom is

named María and both of whom wear María's clothes and reproduce themselves in mirrors. Hortensia is palimpsested onto that schema of reduplication as she, too, wears these same clothes.

As Horacio's compulsion for serial surrogates becomes more desperate, the multiplication of objects increases exponentially and spills over
the textual field as a whole. Mass production commences as Facundo announces
that "the first experiments have been successful" using doll-fabrication plans
acquired from a manufacturer "in a country to the north" (2:160). The commercial proliferation of dolls on the market is complemented in Horacio's
private rituals by scenes now populated with "more *characters* than usual"
(2:169). Multiplication of this cast of extras is then carried to the extreme
when reflections provide for an endlessly self-generating succession of dolls
occasioned by the huge mirrors that Horacio has installed in the showcases
(2:166). This infinite reduplication of now imagistic surrogates is reinforced
later in the narrative when the mass-produced dolls are likewise multiplied
by wall-size mirrors installed for the grand exhibition at La Primavera
(2:176–77).

The land of plenty is nevertheless insufficient to satisfy Horacio's craving for the absence that these surrogates represent. Horacio soon experiences a "great disillusion" with the showcase scenes, the dolls displayed in
them, and even his new "divine blonde," Eulalia (2:171). The fire can be
rekindled, as we have seen, only when the object of his quest is forbidden:
he is newly—if temporarily—aroused when the Timido's doll is brought to
his attention (2:171). A page later, however, the disillusionment returns in
the wake of failure with the Timido's doll, and "Horacio thought about
going to another country and never again looking at a doll" (2:172). That
drastic fugue manifests rather as a retreat: Horacio has Eulalia shipped off
and returns to María, confessing "his disillusion with the dolls and how
awful life has been without her" (2:173). The hopeful wife "believed in
Horacio's definitive disillusion" with the dolls and acquired a black cat as
a substitute for the women-things that are themselves substitutes, while
Horacio suspended the showcase viewings "and contrary to his custom
had left the dolls in the dark—only the machine noises accompanied them"
(2:173).

The honeymoon beyond the renewal of vows is, however, short-lived;
Horacio's "craving for stimulation" gets the best of him. First a quarrel
with María and then strong "remorse" combine with fear-of-death musings
to deliver Horacio once again to his perversion. He lands on the idea that
"he could rent one of those little houses in the park" for his rendezvous
with the dolls and thus he succumbs again to a fall into perversion "as
though into a voluptuous fate" (2:175). Horacio goes shopping for a new

love object, inquiring as to which of the dolls in La Primavera are authentic Hortensias. There is only one, and the Renaissance costume worn by this single Hortensia perhaps pays homage to the rebirth of Horacio's vice. Within a few days the doll—Herminia—is installed in the rented Las Acacias house, which is tended to, like the showcase scenes, by employees: one fills the doll with water before Horacio's arrival, another sees to the housekeeping.

But the "affair" with Herminia that inaugurates Horacio's new wave of "adultery" is also short-lived. Horacio's roaming desire gravitates now toward an object that is as exotic as his search for an adequate surrogate is desperate. Surveying the showcases of La Primavera, Horacio falls for a selvatically situated black doll that "only had her breasts painted: two little negro heads with little mouths polished in red" (2:177). Horacio verifies that this many-in-one specimen of exotica is an authentic Hortensia and requests the doll's delivery to the Las Acacias house. What he finds there when he pulls down the covers, however, is not his savage African queen but rather his screaming wife, who has been informed of his game and staged this "surprise" to bring an end to his "adultery." The narrative thus runs full circle as the multiple doll surrogates are finally displaced by the woman surrogate (wife) upon whom their appearance was originally modeled.

Why the desire to enshrine and revere the mother imago takes the form of a perverse attraction to anatomically correct dolls is a paradox that remains to be unraveled. In the clinical literature many analysands enslaved by the memorial search described earlier ("an unconscious search for the ideal mother") tend to dissociate love from sexuality.[84] Romantic intimacy or lovemaking as an expression of genuine noncorporal sentiments becomes impossible as sexuality is exclusively (and almost vindictively) enacted as lust, as expending oneself in a disposable body. "Love," conversely, is directed toward those few de-eroticized women whose bodies have been reserved from defilement. As Freud put it, "Where they love they do not desire and where they desire they cannot love. They seek objects which they do not need to love, in order to keep their sensuality away from the objects they love."[85] This phenomenon, a result for Freud of "the interposition of the barrier against incest," manifests in patriarchal societies as a polarization of women into a madonna-whore dichotomy, which defends a rigid symbolic distinction between women regarded as sexual objects and women eligible as wives.

In Latin America such a dichotomy is quite legible in the complementary traditions of *machismo* and *marianismo*, which dictate that women eligible for marriage champion the pure qualities so nobly exemplified by Christ's mother. The madonnas of *marianismo* are virgins before marriage and afterwards are matronly, asexual, abnegate mother-wives dedicated to their husbands, the kitchen, the nursery, and the church. These wives engage in intercourse with their husbands as a necessity for fulfillment of their procreative responsibilities; they pay "the debt," but they do so nonerotically, without pleasure. Their insemination resembles more a replay of the Annunciation than an act of actual lovemaking. The *machos* married to these neutered women doomed to emulating the mother-in-law and the Virgin Mary have, however, their own non-negated sexual desire and a social responsibility to demonstrate their virility. Outside of their marriages they therefore seek those other women posed antithetically to the madonna whom they have wed, women who are ineligible for their love but skilled in satisfying the *machos*' sexual desire. While the wives tend to the children and the dusting and the tamales, the husbands satisfy the demands and reap the benefits of *machismo* by squandering their passion on women beyond the pale, women whose lovemaking disqualifies them for love.

In *The Hortensias* Horacio's wife is more or less obligated and limited by the *marianismo* that she carries in her very name, although she is subtly devalued and eroticized by showing up at the hotel where Horacio, too, is lodged, an establishment that was once a whorehouse. Horacio rejects María in the matrimonial bed at home, but in this haven of whores he longs for María's company: "If María were lying beside him, he would be completely happy." The text enhances this nuanced implication of María desirable as a prostitute but undesirable as a wife by adding, "As soon as she returned home he would propose spending a night in this hotel" (2:164).

The doll more readily accepts the multiple roles that Horacio's conflicting needs demand of it. Horacio's ritualized sexuality requires that one and the same doll fill the mutually exclusive rolls represented in the madonna-whore dichotomy. The motherly madonna role can be contained by the dolls because they are receptacles that hold whatever symbolic constructs one wishes to pour into them, while simultaneously the maternal presence with which they have been imbued can be de-emphasized or veiled—permitting sexual defilement—by resort to a desymbolized, literal reading: the dolls are, after all, only things. While María-as-madonna could never adequately serve this dual purpose, a fetish, a doll as a psychologically loaded sex toy, can be violated and at the same time reserve in purity the mother imago that it represents. Horacio's fetishized sexuality distances "the wicked and degenerate ecstasy of the sinful act" from the mother by clouding symbolic incest in the volatile "confusion" of identities. The ritualized sexual extravaganzas with the dolls thereby afford the double benefit of satisfying Horacio's perversion and at once redeeming the madonna-mother from defilement.[86] Horacio thus steers a course around Freud's "barrier of incest," reveling in the tabooed union but retrieving himself from the consequences by alternately stressing one part or the other of the doll's split madonna-whore identity.

At the same time, however, the "immortal" quality of the doll as inanimate mother surrogate "fixes" the perfected love object, making that monumentalized perfection eternally available for a kind of vengeful defilement that punishes the mother for falling short of her idealization in fantasy. "One determinant of the fetishistic representation was the unconscious devaluation of the mother's body and an attempt to preserve a perfect body not subject to such devaluation."[87] In Horacio's case the mother's body and the fetish are one and the same; the mother is preserved in the immortal body of the doll that is repeatedly "killed" and resurrected for ever more refined erotic use.

THE MOTHER'S DEAD BODY

Mother thus becomes mummy, embalmed in the memorial perfection represented by the dolls. Horacio penetrates her memory as though "violating something sacred"; her memory is like an "undergarment," a memory that "has remained in a dead person" and that Horacio must extract "from a cadaver" (2:153). Loving the dolls is Horacio's way of getting to know, even in the biblical sense, his mummy. The eroticization of the sacred memory provisionally closes the abyss between madonna and whore, it rehearses the oedipal capitulation that "the difference between his mother and a whore is not after all so very great, since basically they do the same thing."[88] Like the photographs of a dead husband that an analysand strategically placed throughout her house so that "she felt herself to be seen by him at all time," the dolls make an absence present. In always seeing the dolls, Horacio is always seen by his mother. His voyeurism is dialogical. He and his mummy gaze deep into each other's eyes until the guilt of his transgression overwhelms him, is projected outward, and returns as the mother's threatening surveillance. The woman who surrounded herself with photographs believed that "her husband's features changed according to his moods which, in turn, reflected his responses to her daily activities." She would, like Horacio with his mummy-dolls, embrace the photographs, kiss the glass, and apologize for her transgressions. Though aware all along that the changing photographs represented nothing more "than a projection of her own thoughts and moods," this woman, again like Horacio, was unreceptive to realities that intruded rudely into the enactment of the fiction that sustained her.[89] Though it may be "difficult to do something living with the dead," Horacio and his counterparts are dedicated to the "energetic denial of the power of death," deflecting that power back into a life constructed of disinterred pieces.[90]

If there is a lover "beyond the limits, privileges, and protection of being saintly and undefilable," then that lover par excellence is not the prostitute but rather the corpse brought back through the permeable borders of death and "enlivened" by fantasy.[91] "The ultimate extreme of erotic eligibility distancing is in necrophilia: the partner must be dead."[92] Hortensia is "objectivized and infinitized by death"; she is "the untouchable absolute that serves as halo for the forbidden mother" who, even when touched, remains eternally pure because the "dead" doll absorbs her defilement.[93]

The most common motives for necrophilia are the urge to possess an unresisting and unrejecting partner (the doll) and to reunite with an absent romantic partner (the doll as the "dead" María veiling the mother imago).[94] Among the five primary defense mechanisms contributing to necrophilia are three directly pertinent in the present context: "identification with a parental figure"; "introjection of a parental image"; and a "counterphobic reaction against a fear of the dead."[95] In *The Hortensias* identification and introjection of the mother imago are well established, but Horacio's counterphobic reaction seems to respond more to the fear of death than it does to fear of the dead. Horacio's fear of his own death, masked by fear of María's, also has a referent in the mother's absence, in her mock-living presence represented by the "dead" dolls, and in her imminent death (like María's) occasioned because Horacio cannot keep pace with the dissemination—or insemination—of the surrogates in which her death must be repeatedly reborn. As Freud recognized in *Mourning and Melancholia*, in identification one not only remembers a lost external object ("death" of María/absence of the mother) but also replaces it with an aspect of oneself (doll as an extension of Horacio through narcissistic projection) that has been modeled on the lost external object. Horacio and his dead object must coincide in the syncretic "replacement" known as Hortensia.

The advantages of the dead lover thus begin with the detoured autoeroticism discussed in earlier chapters: as he loves the "dead" doll, Horacio loves himself. The devaluation, dehumanization, and destruction of women that is characteristic of actual or symbolic necrophilia are likewise satisfied in the text by "dead" Hortensias as representatives of passive, conquered, and enslaved objects. One of the dominant traits of narcissistic personalities—"the pathological devaluation of women (in the final analysis, devaluation of mother as a primary object of dependency)"—gains its most resounding expression in the dolls as tropes of women devalued to the extreme of representing dead, totally vulnerable sexual objects.[96] If earlier the mute, handicapped woman seemed attractive, here the "dead" Hortensia is ideal. She is readily postured and catatonic: "the dolls had the air of sublime madwomen who thought of nothing but the pose that they maintained and did not care if they were dressed or undressed" (2:177). She is consistent and incapable of María-type "surprises." She accepts projections, "holds" them, and lovingly returns them upon demand. She is discreet about indiscretions. She responds as faithfully as a mirror. And she loves and makes love inexhaustibly.[97]

The dead lover also affords emotional distancing benefits that uphold the dissociation of madonna and whore. If the madonna becomes visible through the disguise of the doll-as-whore, then the whore must be killed to save the mother from defilement. Dolls are happy to die for so noble a cause. The "murdered" and resurrected (but still "dead") Hortensia speaks to that necessary death (though in her resurrected form she more resembles a whore), as do María's "death" and the death in abandonment that is assigned to each love object as Horacio pursues the next. In a parallel clinical case, the sadistic masturbation fantasies that a man experienced during childhood found another way to separate a revered madonna from the company of whores. He envisioned himself tearing up and torturing women, then freeing one of them "who seemed innocent, gentle, good, loving, and forgiving—an ideal, ever-giving, ever-forgiving, beautiful, and inexhaustible mother surrogate." In his discussion of the fantasy, Kernberg identified a split in internal relations with women similar to that which we have recognized in Hernández's case: on the one hand idealization and dependency on an "absolutely good mother," and on the other devaluation and "retaliatory destruction of all other bad mothers."[98]

Another clinical case remarkably similar to Hernández's childhood scenario is grounded in the extended absence of a mother ("a cold woman," like the cold doll) and father, with their son left "in the hands of a very cruel nanny." A borderline between the mother's life and death—which is to say her survival in the child's psyche—is delineated by the child's capacity to understand and tolerate her absence: "Before the limit is reached the mother is still alive; after this limit has been overstepped she is dead."[99] The cruel nanny who keeps the mother alive in death is of course reminiscent of Hernández's Deolinda, and for the analysand in question "every woman is a replica of nanny, whom he hated and whom he wanted to kill." This analysand's complicated lovemaking therefore became "nothing but an act of murder," a symbolic ritual of hateful sexuality, loving the object who is present in order to "kill" the absent object (bad mother) that she represents. The devaluation of women in *The Hortensias* to sexually exploited, disposable, "dead" things perhaps owes something to the vengeful erotic destruction of the "bad mother" (Deolinda) who survived the "death" of the "good mother" (Calita).

The dynamics are ultimately more complicated, however, because Horacio lovingly reveres the doll-mother with the same sexual ritual by which he murders her. If the doll's nature as "dead" matter, as an inanimate surrogate displacing real women, as a punching bag for "retaliatory destruction" of the bad mother, and as an object of perversion ("the erotic form of hatred") are all exploited, the doll nevertheless simultaneously offers Horacio rewards as the innocent, good, loving, forgiving, and beautiful mother.[100] Kernberg's patient, again like Hernández, feared that his lover would become dependent upon him as the relationship grew beyond sexual satisfaction, and this "evoked fear that she would want to rob him of what he had to give." The fear of robbery suggests that the voyeuristic theft discussed in the previous chapter may be, in part, a reaction formation: one stockpiles what he has "stolen" from others so that his warehouse is full when a woman comes—as did Hernández's mother—to burden his reserves. In *The Hortensias* a similar counterformation is revealed: Horacio fears absorption, and yet his fetish is a body of water.

The general fear of being swindled expresses a more profound lack of trust that incapacitates these subjects for genuine love, and it launches Kernberg's patient as much as Horacio into a "desperate search for gratification of erotic longings to replace his need for love." Kernberg also speaks to Horacio's case when he observes that his patient longed to break through the facade that he himself had created in order to reach a "relation with a person 'underneath' the skin of women."[101] The protagonist of "Mamma's Tree" also dramatizes this psychology, searching for the "filling" beneath the layers of obesity that envelop his cousin. The girl implicitly mocks that endeavor by halting his attempted caress with an uncouth comment that signals her internal sloshing with a murky but maternal substance: "I have *café con leche* in my stomach" (2:189–90). Horacio's dolls are also receptacles, but underneath their skin is the more crystalline water of the mother imago floating in a mirror.[102] The hollows of the bloated dolls speak to Hernández's often expressed quest to access, to uncover, authentic human beings underneath the masks of their faces (his own included), not to mention underneath their clothes. But the flight from doll to doll—a kind of glide along the surface—indexes the failure of that quest and a compensatory, "desperate search for gratification of erotic longings to replace his need for love."

Calita may be lovingly remembered in the idealization of childhood, but the profundity of Hernández's oedipal complications implicates her for a share of the "bad mother" attributes that gravitate more readily toward

Deolinda. What is certain is that the devalued and dehumanized depiction of women in Hernández's fiction evidences "the perverse defense against fears of passivity when confronted with maternal malevolence." Among the unconscious, intermingling fantasies identified by Arnold M. Cooper as integral to this defense is the supposition that the mother "is really non-existent; that is, she is dead or mechanical, and I am in complete control." The passage speaks, for itself, to *The Hortensias*, and it becomes yet more suggestive when combined with the third fantasy described by Cooper: "I triumph and am in total control because no matter what cruelty my squashing, castrating, gigantic monster mother-creature visits upon me, I can extract pleasure from it, and therefore she (it) is doing my bidding." The horror of cruelty is reversed and transformed into a vehicle of pleasure; the mother, as the dolls well illustrate, has been brought under control.

The price, however, is high. The intermediary fantasy connecting the first and the third mentioned here anticipates the conclusion of *The Hortensias*, where the dehumanization projected outward to a harem of love objects returns home finally to Horacio as its source. "I am beyond being controlled by my malicious mother because I myself am nonhuman—that is, dead and unable to feel pain." Horacio's "triumph" and "total control" collapse finally into his own "death," which is to say his doll-like madness.[103] If the focus is broadened from Horacio to his author we can suggest, as Julia Kristeva put it in another context, that "those dead women" may be a "manner of idealizing the loved one as she loses her characteristic of being an other—an other sex—and unites with the lover's desired power." The woman-mother "has been abolished, yet to be reborn again in that maximal crystallization constituted by postmortuary love where the writer projects the almightiness of his desire to possess her, to possess himself beyond her."[104]

WOMB WATER

In a study of the "Great Mother" archetype Erich Neumann posits the vessel as the "central symbol" of the feminine.[105] "Woman as body-vessel," Neumann observes, is the natural expression of the human experience of woman bearing the child 'within' her and of man entering 'into' her in the sexual act."[106] Neumann documents his observation with a vast catalog of examples from world cultures, many of them perhaps epitomized by the water jug in Egyptian hieroglyphics, which serves as the symbol of femininity, the female genitalia, woman, and the feminine principle.[107] In Judeo-Christian traditions a woman is similarly "a spring shut up, a fountain sealed," a whore is "a deep ditch," and the body more generally is the receptacle of liquids or "humors."[108] Medievals were inclined to view female bodies as "containing excess fluid that had to be purged," while at the same time they stylized virginity as a "precious liquid" contained in a "delicate vessel, balm in a brittle glass."[109] As one author warns, "this precious balsam in a fragile glass is virginity and cleanness," which one might lose "like some miserable wretches in the world who clash together, break their vessels, and shed their purity." The Bawd in Shakespeare's *Pericles* provides an alternate take more apropos of Horacio breaking the seal of his virginal doll: "use her at thy pleasure: crack the glass of her virginity, and make the rest malleable."[110]

Liquid-holding tropes concerning intercourse and the impregnated womb are elsewhere complemented by a related series of images depicting the breasts as vessels. One recalls Hernández texts such as "Ursula" when "The breast motif involves the symbolism of milk and cow. The Goddess as cow, ruling over the food-giving herd, is one of the earliest historical objects of worship," and "the cow as a mother-symbol" appears in "innumerable forms and variations."[111] The milk-bloated breast and the life force associated with maternal nourishment are deified and then reincorporated into daily life, as "Goddess vases frequently have breasts that can have holes in the centers as spouts."[112] In some Native American cultures pitchers were also made in the shape of the breast itself. Zuñi women responsible for this seemingly sacred craft left the nipple open until the ritual's end, when the sealing of the breast vessel was "performed with the solemnity of a religious rite, and with averted eyes."[113]

In Hernández's work the paradigm of the woman as vessel is of course the Hortensia doll, and the very name of the dolls makes a significant contribution to the poetics establishing them as receptacles. "Hortensia" is the Spanish signifier for the flower *Hydrangea macophylla* or, as it is known in English, simply "Hydrangea." Etymologically "hydrangea" is composed of the Greek *hydro*, meaning water, and *angion*, meaning bowl or tub. Denominating the dolls "Hortensias"—water bearers—thus stresses their essential nature as containers of the warm water that is poured into them, and, further, as maternal- or womb-water vessels through their link to the "discarded" name of Hernández's mother, Juana Hortensia Silva. As worded by Hernández in a separate context, "Her name is like her body" (3:76). "Hortensia" (which is also used in English as an alternate name for the hydrangea) further suggests something of the amorous use of the water-bearing dolls, because the plant was named "Hortensia" after the sweetheart of the scientist who introduced the flower into botanical literature.

While women-as-vessel themes are treated throughout *The Hortensias*, one showcase scene is particularly noteworthy for its development of these floral poetics. A doll situated in a garden is surrounded by "big sponges"—water holders—but "her attitude is one of being among flowers." The legend indicates that the girl is crazy, and that "no one has been able to find out why she loves sponges." Horacio is unsatisfied with that interpretation ("I pay them to find out") and offers his own: "These sponges must symbolize the necessity to wash away many sins" (2:157–58). But if the sponges are flowers that hold water, then they also "must symbolize" the text's central water bearers, the Hortensia dolls. An alternate interpretation of this showcase scene—reminiscent of "Cradle Rocking's" mother-planet divided into minireplicas—thus surfaces: the Hortensia doll as mother-vessel is surrounded by sponges that share the doll's essential attribute (water bearing), and that therefore again represent a prototype disseminated through multiple clones. Rather than a flower (Hortensia) among flowers (garden), the showcase scene offers a sponge among sponges, all of which absorb the liquids of Horacio's "sin."

Many of the variations on the woman-as-vessel archetype further inform Hernández's development of the Hortensia dolls. The ideal of a silent and non-threatening lover represented by the dolls is, for example, paralleled by primitive "women jars" characterized by the conspicuous absence of a mouth, and this absence was "already typical for the Primordial Goddess."[114] While the mouth ("as rending, devouring symbol of aggression" and as locus of discourse) is absent, the breasts ("which typify women as giver of nourishment") are accentuated.[115] The doubling and serial multiplication of the Hortensia dolls is also resonant in the context of certain ceramic figures in which "the woman represented as a jar carries a second jar," or of the many-breasted mother figures, such as the Mexican "goddess with the four hundred breasts."[116] One Peruvian jar carries the theme yet further: "The woman is represented as a vessel, but also as carrying a vessel and holding her breasts."[117] The mother figure who—like Hernández's mother—cannot let go is also integral to the archetype, since what Neumann calls the Great Container "tends to hold fast to everything that springs from it and to surround it like an eternal substance. Everything born of it belongs to it and remains subject to it; and even if the individual becomes independent, the Archetypal Feminine relativizes this independence into a nonessential variant of her own perpetual being."[118]

In many clinical cases these Great Container qualities of the mother reappear among the symptoms of offspring who to one degree or another remain "nonessential variants of her own perpetual being." A male patient with whom we are already familiar lived "primarily inside a myth he shared with mother" and seemed to "empty himself compulsively of his true self needs in order to create an empty internal space to receive mother's dream thoughts." The same figure gains expression in *Lands of Memory*, where the narrator experiences himself as "an empty room, not even I was inside it," because a girl "had tried to change my ideas and rearrange my room in her way" (3:52-53). A defensive strategy resisting this "rearrangement" emerges in the ritual organization of the showcases in *The Hortensias* or of the tunnel in "Except Julia," and it is likewise legible in the behavior of a patient who created "a kind of shell of observable objects around her."[119] One's space and one's self are defended by structures constructed around the inner emptiness: witness the armor of a patient who conceived of his body like that of "some bugs that have a shell but not a skeleton." The externalization in another case is made manifest by the empty double of a patient who felt "that her body was always a little ahead of her and she could never get herself inside it."[120] When the hollow, vessel-like quality of the depersonalized body is itself stressed, patients tend to employ graphic imagery that depicts a total depletion. "I'm a vacuum," one says, another similarly remarking, "I felt like a bag of skins with a vacuum inside," and a third, "My brain seemed scooped out."[121]

Horacio's "emptiness" (or, one might argue, Hernández's) results less in direct self-referential expressions than in the proliferation of a gallery of empty objects around him. The population of his world with vessel-dolls protects him like the ectoskeleton or "shell of observable objects" in the clinical cases; a plenitude of empty objects externalizes Horacio's condition and at once creates the illusion of his fullness, of his prolific and virile capacity to provide. The vessel-dolls that result, however, also externalize the desire that his emptiness be filled, and the dolls consequently seem to have a "vacuum inside" or to absorb him with the thirst of gigantic sponges that suck away his dwindling reserves. Hernández himself felt his relationships with all women—beginning with his mother—to be plagued precisely by this sensation of draining. Calita made unreasonable demands on his resources, his autonomy, and his affection, and the empty man struggling within the sphere of this Great Container had little left to offer when reasonable demands were made by his wives.

Filling of the dolls with water thus accommodates among its many meanings Horacio's (or Hernández's) desire to himself be filled, to be replenished rather than drained. An analysand who sees an empty ashtray and remarks "It makes you want to fill it," is indirectly referring to herself, because "she is as empty as the ashtray and is expressing her desire to be filled with content and meaning: with herself."[122] The same analyst observes that "The emptiness and the consequent search for objects can lead to sexual promiscuity." This contention is borne out by Horacio attempting to fill himself with himself in *The Hortensias*. During his sexual relations with the dolls Horacio "uses his genitals to fill the emptiness that one can never finish filling, and the promiscuity becomes compulsive (like masturbation)."[123] Horacio's promiscuity and autoeroticism are enacted in one and the same doll copulation as a ritual reunion with himself. But although he penetrates and taps into the maternal "belly-vessel that bears all things," Horacio exits his dolls more vacuous than he entered, more drained, and he hastens back to the compulsive search for replenishment that his promiscuity somehow never satisfies.[124]

Earlier in Hernández's canon, in *The Lost Horse*, something of the groundwork for these themes was established. Mother, water, and the double are introduced together as the "partner"—who protects "almost to the point of being a mother"—accompanies the narrator to the shores of a river running with "the water of memory" (2:35). Here the mother is internalized as part of the self and then projected outward as a component of the double or "partner." The agenda at hand is to contain the flowing "water of memory" so as to recuperate the lost boyhood love of Celina, who, as we have already recognized, herself doubles the mother. When the narrator draws water (= memories) out of the river, the partner (= mother-self) helps him "invent receptacles in which to contain it" (2:37). As in *The Hortensias*, memories associated with both mother and lover are here represented by water and poured into a receptacle that is "invented" through a collaborative effort of the self and the internalized (but then re-externalized) mother. Should we be surprised that Hernández's mother herself had an inauthentic personality "poured into" a facade, "as though she had invented a character and then put herself inside it"?[125]

Water vessels associated with the mother include not only the likes of Hortensia but also women as plants, "naked widows" compared to bottles (3:46), women as rooms or buildings (notably Margarita in relation to her flooded house, which is "like a human being") (3:69), and the many fat women who, like spongy receptacles, are bloated with milk or water. Ursula is a prime candidate in this last category, but one also recalls the many rotund mother surrogates, the tubby cousin-plant in "Mamma's Tree," the reciting girl in *Lands of Memory* who is "three times more corpulent than me" (3:52), and the "immense body" of Margarita, which is compared to "an immense vase" (3:68, 3:74).[126] (Margarita's link to mother—and Hortensia—is also suggested when her eyes-behind-glass "seem to say: 'What's the matter, my son?'") (3:69). In *The Hortensias* the concept of women as vessels takes a more suggestive spin when Facundo and Horacio, discussing the sexual refabrication of Hortensia, talk "as though they were taking turns drinking from the same jug" (2:155).[127]

In "The Flooded House" Margarita's oceanic body extends not merely to the water container with which she is compared but also to the very house flooded around her. If her central ritual seems a wake (but must not be called such), it also resembles a birth: in this dual function Margarita's flood is "the regular symbol of the beginning and the end of a cycle."[128] Something of the "sin water" soaked up by the sponges in the showcase scene is also suggested, since in many myths flood is a form of punishment.[129] The womblike structure of the flooded house with its floating sanctuaries and its uterotubal contraptions more convincingly suggests Margarita as a huge baby—like her chubby counterpart in "Mamma's Tree"—rehearsing in the waters of memory some prenatal fantasy that haunts her. Margarita's obsession with water includes preoccupations with drinking it, as well as expelling it—like María—through complicated bouts of crying. She "contains" many Hernández themes by indicating a preference for water stilled at night "so that silence spreads slowly over it and everything fills with dreams and entangled plants." Margarita then links herself to another water-bearing flower, Hortensia, when she remarks that this spooky, occupied water most "resembles the water that I carry inside me" (3:80).

Margarita's dedication to her aquatic rituals contrasts conspicuously with the situation of another "flooded house" described in the quasi-autobiographical fragment "My First Concert in Montevideo." In this case the narrator's house "was like a sea of greenish waters"; "We navigated through them like poor pirates not particularly motivated to battle for any treasure" (2:201). Such an aimless float through greenish waters is alien to Margarita, who as a vessel of plant-bearing water is so intricately entangled with her flooded house that when it is drained for cleaning she sends the narrator away because "I don't want you to see me without the water" (3:82). It is not so much that the feminine "treasure" under her metaphoric "skirt [*pollera*] of water" would be revealed by nakedness resulting from the draining, but rather that the water itself constitutes her most treasured attribute, that without the water, like Hortensia, she would be relegated to a dead emptiness (3:79).

When he is present at the flooded house, the narrator rhythmically rows Margarita through the waters of this maternal body, at once evoking interuterine existence (he seems to be "born" from the house) (3:88) and, more insistently, the parting of female waters in copulation. Freud is unambiguous in reference to images such as those central to "The Flooded House": "Rooms in dreams are usually women," and the interpretation of "various ways in and out of them" is "scarcely open to doubt."[130] Whether the woman is "a cathedral" (3:14), "a clean bathroom with white tiles up to the ceiling" (3:161), or, as she is by extension in "Except Julia," a subterranean tunnel, "the feminine vessel character, originally of the cave, later of the house (the sense of being inside, of being sheltered, protected, and warmed in the house), has always borne a relation to the original containment in the womb."[131] As one poet has it, "I say Mother. And my thoughts are of you, oh House."[132] Neumann further observes that the sheltering cave is the natural form later developed in "such cultural symbols as temple and *temenos*, hut and house, village and city, lattice, fence, and wall, signifying what protects and closes off. (Here gate and door are the entrance to the womb of the maternal vessel.)"[133] Jung had earlier established the groundwork for such observations by cataloging multicultural illustrations of his belief that "The city is a maternal symbol, a woman who harbours the inhabitants in herself like children."[134] The entrance to the womb-vessel is also represented in the clay models of temples, the oldest dating circa 6000 B.C., that take the form of various goddesses. One, particularly relevant for its aquatic component, "depicts the goddess's sphere as the watery realm symbolized by meanders, to which an entrance (at the bottom) has been provided."[135]

When water is poured, always by women, into the vessel-dolls of *The Hortensias*, it represents the "dead" past flowing in memories toward the present; it represents the vital substance—elsewhere breath, soul, incantations, potions, inscriptions—that gives warmth to inanimate matter brought to life; it represents femininity, with a decided bias toward maternal qualities replicated in the love object; it represents the sperm with which the dolls are filled by Horacio; it represents the internalized mirror reflecting Horacio's narcissistic projections back to him; it represents dissolution into one's transgressions and compulsions, a drowning in maternal waters, an absorption in oceanic plentitude; and, more generally, it represents the death of the love object and the attempt to resuscitate its polysemous "corpse." Storms, tears, clouds, floods, spills, oceans, rivers, lakes, fountains, pumping contraptions, and other similar images and motifs are ubiquitous reminders that the central thematic functions of water gloss Hernández's canon from one end to the other. Memories flow, gather on the surface of bodies of water, slosh inside the womb water of dolls. Words at one moment are "tiny pebbles dropped into the pond of reveries" and at another are equated with water itself, as though each narrative—as in "False Explanation of My Stories"—were a growing plant absorbing the flow of words and memories. But women are plants too, women fictions that grow when watered, that come alive, that entangle their textual and corporal vines with the author who has planted his seed. When one customer purchases a Hortensia he signs his check with a fountain pen compared to a submarine, a projectile that enters the meanders of Hortensia's dark waters from below, that writes her life with the "waters of memory" drawn from a personal account nearly depleted. Horacio drinks constantly, hears the piano music and sounds of the machines as though he were underwater, dreams of blood flowing backwards through the body, and abducts a doll to make love beside a river. And the showcases, finally, seem almost aquariums and boast scenes depicting water-related themes—the woman surrounded by sponges, the pregnant woman living in a lighthouse, the madwoman of the lake.

At one moment in *The Hortensias* Horacio compares the spirit that occupies Hortensia to an "inhabitant that didn't have much to do with her room," and he then suggests that this poorly accommodated spirit is responsible for provoking María to "murder" Hortensia (2:163). When the doll is stabbed, however, the postmortem body releases not a spirit or soul but rather water that squirts from the wounds as though the corpse were a sardonic fountain of youth. If its tragicomic quality is set aside, the image readily aligns with Frye's assertion that "The world of water is the water of death, often identified with spilled blood."[136] The "water of death" also appears in "The Usher," where the nearly drowned daughter seems almost a ghost; in the pseudowake and accompanying death-water themes in "The Flooded House" (3:85, for example); and in other resonant passages from the same text, such as one in which Margarita gazes at the water "like a girl that had lost a doll" (3:87) or others in which water images lead to associations of a girl pulled under to her death (3:79, 3:85). In "The Poisoned Girl" death water is doubly suggestive, first through the poison used in the suicide and then through the arroyo that divides the living from the dead. The arroyo associated with death turns up again in "The Crocodile" (3:93), while poison as an internalized death water receives metaphoric mention in "Lucrecia," where "all of my organs wrung out their shamed faces and cried the most poisoned tears inside me" (3:104).[137] An image in *The Lost Horse* further contributes to this complex by depicting angst as a drowning in one's fluids: "the tide of anguish had risen almost to the point of drowning me" (2:34). Among the many aquatic "deaths" in *The Hortensias* is Horacio's progressive dissolution into madness, externalized in the "dead" water-laden dolls and in the showcase scenes displaying insane doll characters. The "madwoman of the lake" of the La Primavera exhibit comes immediately to mind, though shortly after in the text all of the vitrina dolls are described as "sublime madwomen" (2:176–77).

Once filled with the projections poured into it, the dead world of objects leaves moribundity behind and comes to life with "its own will full of pride" (2:31). A caress must be accepted; "a receptacle is needed: the analyst's body or the mother's, which allows itself to be more or less passively penetrated by the projected parts."[138] The dolls as empty maternal containers are bound to absolute inertia and servitude, but the warm waters of projection transform them into transitional objects that are endowed with a life and will of their own. That process is expressed succinctly in regard to the (transitional) objects of Celina's living room: "although they had no choice but to be under my orders, they carried out their mission amidst a suspicious silence" (2:31). Such are likewise the rules of the game in *The Hortensias*: the dolls are subjects of Horacio's absolute monarchy, but a fault in the logic of perceiving them introduces the possibility—one might say the necessity—of their autonomous volition and, beyond it, their feisty insubordination to His Majesty.

This mobilization of the dolls closely conforms to the process of projective identification as described by Wilfred Bion. The projector (that signifier also recalling "The Usher") engages in the fantasy of "ejecting an unwanted or endangered aspect of himself and of depositing that part of himself in another person in a controlling way." The intent is to coerce the "recipient" into "experiencing himself and behaving in a way that is congruent with the unconscious projective fantasy."[139] The vessel imagery compounded by the "depositing" provides sufficient reminder that among the liquids poured into the dolls is one, sperm, that to no small degree has a controlling effect upon another person's body. Many ancient beliefs intermingle water and sperm as the source of life, and "the words 'water,' 'semen,' and 'saliva' stem from the same root in Egyptian, as do 'water,'' 'sperm,' 'conception,' and 'procreation' in Sumerian."[140] In this light Hernández's ongoing concern with the water that carries memories may have a one-word response: semen. For Apollo in Aeschylus's *Eumenides*, the mother, like the Hortensia dolls controlled by a "deposit," has no active roll in what happens to her body. "The mother is no parent of that which is called / her child, but only the nurse of the new-planted seed / that grows. The parent is he who mounts." The same holds true, for example, among the strongly patrilineal Kaliai in Melanesia, who hold "that the fetus is composed exclusively of the father's semen," with the mother providing no more than her vessel, "a place of protective growth."[141] Luce Irigaray has arrived at the same conclusion from a different approach, noting how in patriarchal lines of reasoning procreation is limited to male "activity," to the seminal "pro-ject," while the female "is nothing but the receptacle that passively receives his *product.*" The seed is entrusted to the womb, to the woman "held in receivership as a certified means of (re)production," so that the seed "may germinate, produce, grow fruitful, without woman being able to lay claim to either capital or interest," since she has only submitted "passively" to reproduction.[142]

In another perspective the liquid filling the Hortensia dolls is not unilaterally masculine but quite the contrary is insistently deployed to represent the feminization of Hortensia, the pouring-in of female attributes and identities. The twin maids (doubles of María) first pour in the water that gives Hortensia the semblance of life, and then María's presence in the doll is enhanced as she herself—immediately prior to Horacio's inaugural "adultery"—pours in the water (2:154, 2:158). Earlier in the narrative María is invested in the doll as she wraps it with her identity and fills it with her most private discourse: Hortensia "was more mine than yours," María says to Horacio. "I dressed her and told her things that I couldn't tell to anyone" (2:147). In other passages María's presence in the doll develops in tandem with vessel images: "María put the hot water in Hortensia, she dressed her in a silk nightgown, and she put her to bed with them as though she were a hot water bottle" (2:151). Even the "surgery" in Facundo's workshop to remake Hortensia as a water-holding vessel is left to the expertise of women who "had invented a procedure." Horacio experiences "a very hidden pleasure" when he thinks of these women "who put something of themselves in Hortensia" (2:150). As a counterpoint to this feminine filling of the vessel-doll, Horacio, with "contained emotion," replenishes his own hollows by pouring down copious quantities of wine, "stocking up on happiness like camels that eat and drink enough for many days on the desert" (2:158, 2:206).

It comes as no surprise that the water poured into and contained by the dolls fills them not only with femininity but also with specifically maternal associations. "The maternal significance of water is one of the clearest interpretations of symbols in the whole field of mythology," Jung notes, adding that "Water, and particularly deep water, usually has a maternal significance, roughly corresponding to 'womb.'"[143] In the Vedas, water is referred to as "the most maternal," and the French homonyms *mer* (sea) and *mère* (mother) register a similar equation. For Homer, the "generation of all" is the body of water Okeanos that envelops the earth and is associated with "mother Tethys."[144] Water as the maternal, life-giving, and life-sustaining fluid is contained but also contains, and "This containing water is the primordial womb of life, from which in innumerable myths life is born."[145] Evolution commences when some prehistoric life form squirms ashore from an ocean that, like the Hortensia dolls, is itself a quasi-living container, "an immense skin" whose ripples reveal the movement of muscles beneath the surface (3:85).[146] One of the showcase scenes features this oceanic maternal body being surveyed by the roaming eye of a lighthouse (not unlike the conclusion of "The Usher"), but with a Möbius-like twist: a pregnant woman (mother) lives in this lighthouse beside the sea (mother). She has retreated from the world because her love affair with a sailor was criticized, and she thinks: "I want my son to be solitary and to only listen to the sea." In response to the scene Horacio thinks: "This doll has found her true story," but the true story that she has expressed is his (2:142). Horacio assumes the roles of the sailor, whose bow parts the oceanic body and whose love affairs inspire criticism; of the woman in the lighthouse, first because he projects a phallic gaze, then because he tends to repair to a mother surrogate (in this case the sea), and again because he retreats from the world, as in the scene, to avoid ridicule for his unacceptable love; and finally of the solitary son who lives without loving anyone but his sea-mother and who hears her inside of his own body as though he were an empty shell.

There is something ominous about the ocean, a plentitude with little to offer, a "desert of water" (3:173), a dry, frigid mother undercover in a wet, warm doll. The sea moves its massive body slowly, a ship's passengers ride this "flank of a monster" with impunity, navigating "dangers that never materialize" (3:172). The water can be mounted but the experience is uncanny. There is something ominous about the mother. A coldness covered with a compensatory warmth, a transitory warmth, a transparent cover, an improvised warmth that fades as the doll's water cools (2:147). We should not get on the ocean, "knowing that beneath us there is something," a body, "not proper to us naturally" (3:172). The parting of maternal waters is yet more insolent because over the ocean we carry "another water distinct from the ocean's." We privilege this purified water that we take inside of ourselves, but we "submerge in the very water of the ocean, we domesticate it and put it in a bathtub" (3:174). The domesticated bathwater, processed and contained like doll water to serve one's needs, is itself a woman, a "bride" who accepts and caresses one's floating flesh moving to the rhythm of her swells (3:32). Water "insists like a girl who can't explain herself" (3:79). There is something ominous about the mother, "as though her body sank in the water and dragged me down with it" (3:81).

Horacio's obsession to get inside of the mother-doll is partially a reaction formation inversely manifesting his desire to purge the mother *inside of him*. In the clinical literature this attempt at ejecting (one is tempted to say ejaculating) the introjected mother takes a variety of forms. One man who corporalized the imago rather than projecting it onto an external object took his own tropes quite literally: "he wanted to tear his mother out of his stomach," where he had pains that he believed to be caused by her. In desperation "He purchased a gun to shoot himself in the stomach and get rid of the mother and her pain once and for all," not unlike the romantic characters who shoot their doubles and themselves all in one.[147] Another patient, this one female, "scribbled on a piece of paper and blackened it with great vigour. Then she tore it up and threw the scraps into a glass of water which she put to her mouth as if to drink from it. At that moment she stopped and said under her breath: 'Dead woman.'"[148] This patient dramatizes in one way what Horacio does in another: there is only so much of the mother that one can absorb. The excess, in Horacio's case, gets poured into dolls.

The mother and water are also related in the Narcissus myth (as discussed in chapters 2 and 3), when the river nymph Liriope is impregnated with Narcissus as the result of being raped by the river-god Cephisus. "Narcissus by identification with Cephisus was predestined also to seek the love object in water," and as a result the fascination exerted on him by the image reflecting from the pool is a palimpsested love object comprising mother as much as self.[149] Water poetics are then extended into the love triangle between Narcissus, his image, and Echo. Both Narcissus and Echo dry up when the acquisition of their love becomes impossible. In Narcissus's case this dehydration can be read as a trope for purging the internalized mother represented by and reflecting from the water, a kind of forfeiture of the mother-mirror that requires the simultaneous forfeiture of oneself. The gentleman who pointed the shotgun at the mother in his stomach is a case in point, as are the many girls shriveling to death in the battle of wills expressed as anorexia nervosa. The professional crying in "The Crocodile" also evidences a "wringing out" of the protagonist, a tendency that he holds in common with—or perhaps adopted from—his former lover (3:93-94). When he has completed a staged demonstration of his crying he feels like "an empty bottle," a depleted vessel (3:97). A caricature depicting him as a crocodile has one hand soaking up his professional tears with a stocking ("half an illusion") while the other hand plays his mouth stylized as a piano keyboard (3:101). He hides behind "a mask of tears," his face is tired, he wants to be alone in his room "listening to the rain and thinking about the water that separates me from everyone" (3:97).

The primary enclosure filled with water that separates one from the world is the amnion, and Hernández's canon is replete with imagery suggesting repair to an unconscious wallow in the cushioned, secure, warm, womb water of the prenatal mother. If appreciated for its poetics rather than its science, Sandor Ferenczi's theory of the "Thalassal Regressive Trend" is instructive in this context. The backdrop is established by the "oceanic feeling" of eternity, also recognized by Freud as an "oceanic reunion," that is based in the merging sensation experienced by the infant in the earliest relations with the mother's body.[150] The thalassal regressive trend as "the striving towards the aquatic mode of existence abandoned in primeval times" endeavors "to restore the lost mode of life in a moist *milieu* which at the same time provides a supply of nourishment; in other words, to bring about *the reestablishment of the aquatic mode of life in the form of an existence within the moist and nourishing interior of the mother's body.*"[151] The mother as "the symbol and partial substitute for the sea," then takes a decided turn toward the themes in *The Hortensias* when copulation itself is understood as "nothing but the expression of the striving to return to the mother's womb."[152] Coitus is "the gratification of the impulse towards regression to the maternal womb and to the prototype of everything maternal, the sea."[153] Horacio's sexual penetration of dolls containing maternal water is by these lights a symbolic restitution of "the pleasure of intrauterine existence," and more, "the expression of the fantasy of veritably merging one's self with the body of the partner or perhaps of forcing one's way *in toto* into it (as a substitute for the mother's womb)."[154] The *in toto* is generally provided for metonymically: "The fantasy originates in the intrauterine (mother's body) complex and usually has the content of the man's desire to creep completely into the genital from which he came"; "The entire individual is in this case a penis."[155]

From another angle the reabsorption into the mother is not desirable but dreaded. According to Janine Chasseguet-Smirgel, incestuous fantasies of a boy's oedipal complex are complicated by "fears of being reabsorbed by the womb." "The penis represents as it were a stop, which protects from symbiosis, from the melting of boundaries between the ego and non-ego" or mother and son, and therefore the "horror of incest" to which Freud makes reference carries castration anxieties because a boy fears "losing his identity and what forms its basis, maleness, in a return to the place from which we all stem, 'the former home of all human beings,' the mother's womb."[156]

Horacio's fusion with the womb-water doll at the conclusion of *The Hortensias* can in this context be understood as the consequence of an "incest" that sucked him back up definitively into the vacuum of a mother-infant symbiosis that seems never to have been adequately resolved. He is absorbed, he is pulled under the skin that covers undulating muscles, he drowns again and again, he loses his body in a "radical dampness."[157] But the fact that the dolls are of his own design and that he gladly (if compulsively) rehearses his passion on their water-logged bodies suggests not so much a dread of losing his autonomy as a need for fusion, a need to mingle his own Dionysian overflow with the "oceanic feeling" that the dolls afford him. "If there is a struggle against the invading intrusion it is because there is a secret desire to be completely invaded by the object; not only to be united with it but also to be reduced to total passivity, like a baby in his mother's womb."[158]

In the most severe cases (and Horacio's is rather severe) the symbolic actions dramatizing this desire are readily legible. Ferenczi relates the unambiguous example of a young homosexual with "an indissoluble fixation upon his mother" who "lay on the bottom of a bathtub filed with warm water" and maintained "this archaic aquatic status of foetal situation" by breathing through a tube.[159] While Hernández's own uterine longings never came to such an extreme, he did in his later years confine himself by choice to a basement room in the house of Reina Reyes, his matronly wife at the time. The feel of that ambience—dark, damp, enclosed, tight—had its cavernesque wombishness further enhanced by a small entryway, by descriptions of plumbing (suggesting the uterotubal sort), and by its comparison to a boat and a ship (3:186). Hernández was at this point in his life almost as obese as Margarita was in her flooded house, and with a stretch of the imagination one can envision him situated in a room that seemed almost an extension of his body, as though it were the womb from which he would be reborn, from himself, via the Raskolnikovian self-analysis that he conducted there in the "Diary of Shamelessness."

A more pronounced and pathological "thalassal regressive trend" is recorded in the case of a voyeur who, upon seeing the vulva, immediately fantasized "that he could climb back into the vagina, become a baby, have no need for worry and acquire peace."[160] This urge for absolute prenatal tranquility differs little from the urge for death itself—the floating stillness of death—and reminds one of the eerie suicides committed by walking into the ocean. Ferenczi is quite aware of the semblance between nonexistence at both ends of the spectrum, and his comments are particularly suggestive when we recall that the mother-lover in *The Hortensias* is herself an inanimate surrogate: "We have represented in the sensation of orgasm not only *the repose of the intrauterine state*, the tranquil existence in a more friendly environment, but also *the repose of the era before life originated*, in other words, *the deathlike repose of the inorganic world*."[161] The dreaded death of himself and of the María-mother instigates Horacio's compulsion to mount "dead" dolls standing in for the womb, but then via a cruel circularity this very ritual summoned forth to transcend death—to mock it with complicated, tragicomic humping—turns back against Horacio and compels him down a tumultuous course toward his own symbolic death in madness. The dark water glossing Hernández's entire canon mediates a relation not merely between ritualized sexuality and death, but also between the womb as locus of life-giving fecundity and the womb as tomb, as the black hole that absorbs all into oblivion.

Consequently the eroticized tunnel in "Except Julia" is linked to a tomb by dream imagery (2:80); the piano—equated elsewhere with women—is a "sarcophagus" and a "coffin" (2:97, 2:99); and the house of Muñeca (= doll) is a "sacred tomb that had been hastily abandoned" (2:108). "Just as the Great Mother [not to mention the everyday one] can be terrible as well as good, so the Archetypal Feminine is not only a giver and protector of life but, as container, also holds fast and takes back; she is the goddess of life and death at once." The vessel of the female body gestates and gives birth but also—notably in Mother Earth and sea imagery—"takes back the dead into the vessel of death, the cave or coffin, the tomb or urn."[162] The "tomb" in which Horacio buries himself alive resembles the megalithic graves that take the shape of an anthropomorphic goddess or, even more explicitly, of a vagina and uterus covered with a triangular stone representing the pubic bush.[163] "Womblike caves" and "vagina-uterus-shaped caves" are utilized as tombs, sanctuaries, sacrificial alters, and crypts where death-defying rituals are rehearsed. In initiation rites the neophytes who enter such confines (tunnels, flooded houses, memories, dolls) return to the womb to ritualize a death that affords a certain perpetuity.[164]

Notes

INTRODUCTION

1. Felisberto Hernández, *Obras completas*, introducción, ordenación y notas de José Pedro Díaz (Montevideo: Arca Editorial, 1981), 1:78. Further references to this work, abbreviated *OC,* will appear in the text with volume number and page number. Translations are mine.

The term "exhibitionist modesty" is from Lisa Block de Behar, "Los límites del narrador: un estudio sobre Felisberto Hernández," *Studi di letteratura ispano-americana* 13–14 (1983): 17. Roland Barthes also refers to "an introduction to what will never be written" in *The Pleasure of the Text*, trans. Richard Miller (New York: Hill and Wang, 1975), 18.

2. Referring to one of these coverless chapbooks, *La envenenada* (The poisoned girl), Juan Carlos Onetti remarked that the paper looked like that used to wrap noodles, and that the binding was stitched with leftover pieces of wire. See Onetti's "Felisberto, el 'naif'," in *Felisberto Hernández: valoración crítica,* ed. Walter Rela (Montevideo: Editorial Ciencias, 1982), 32.

3. Note that on *OC,* 2:161 the word *libre* is used to mean "uncovered." Horacio's mirrors in *The Hortensias* are usually covered with curtains, but on one occasion the twin maids "had left the mirrors *libres*."

4. The title "Book Without Covers" "is already in itself a true dedication and homage to Vaz Ferreira." See Luis Victor Anastasía, "Sobre la filosofía de Felisberto Hernández," *Prometeo: Revista Uruguaya de Cultura* 1, no. 1 (1979): 31.

A formatting error in the *Book Without Covers* further contributes to the intermixing of the "before and after." The word "Prologue" seems to be the title of the entire opening piece, but a reading of the text reveals that the "Prologue" heading corresponds only to the first paragraph, which introduces the diary pages that follow it in a second ("madman") narrative voice. See Díaz's note to page 79 in *OC,* 1:209.

5. Henri Bergson, *Mind-Energy*, trans. H. Wildon Carr (New York: Henry Holt, 1920), 6 and 55–57, respectively. Cf. Lacanian interpretation, in which meaning is produced in a slide between signifiers, in a relation and a movement rather than in an a priori truth preceding them.

6. Carlos Vaz Ferreira, *Lógica viva*, in *Obras completas* (Montevideo: Cámara de Representantes de la República Oriental del Uruguay, 1963), 172. See Ana Inés Larre Borges, "Felisberto Hernández: una conciencia filosófica," *Revista Biblioteca Nacional* 22 (1983): 13–14. See also Roberto Echavarren, *El espacio de la verdad* (Buenos Aires: Editorial Sudamericana, 1981), 10–11.

7. The Robert Penn Warren passage is in Elaine Barry, ed., *Robert Frost on Writing* (New Brunswick, N.J.: Rutgers University Press, 1973), 160.

8. One of Knut Hamsun's narrators similarly describes an associative creative process as "like being awake while you talk in your sleep." Knut Hamsun, *Hunger*, trans. Robert Bly (New York: Farrar, Straus, and Giroux, 1967), 85.

9. See also *OC*, 1:153, 1:184, and, regarding footprints, 3:77. In an unpublished letter sent by Hernández to Amalia Nieto in May 1936, Hernández writes: "In regard to mystery I will tell you that I believe in it blindly, that I love it and that it is the God that moves the greatest spirits."

10. The first quoted passage is from Friedrich Nietzsche, *The Will to Power*, ed. Walter Kaufmann (New York: Vintage Books, 1968), 428.

11. In *Las Hortensias* the dolls that "get under Horacio's skin" are also related to advertising, as their material prototype is the shopwindow mannequin.

12. The Barthes quotes are from *The Pleasure of the Text*, 40, and *Roland Barthes by Roland Barthes*, trans. Richard Howard (New York: Hill and Wang, 1977), 152, respectively.

13. See also *OC*, 1:78, 1:190, 3:175. In regard to *lo otro*, Dostoevsky noted that "Reality is not limited to the familiar, the commonplace, for it consists in huge part of a *latent, as yet unspoken future word.*" Quoted in Rosemary Jackson, *Fantasy: The Literature of Subversion* (London: Methuen, 1981), 19.

14. From a Hernández lecture, "Some Ways of Thinking about Reality," dictated to Reina Reyes and appended to Larre Borges, "Felisberto Hernández," 40.

15. Ana María Hernández, "Mis Recuerdos," *Escritora* 7, no. 13–14 (1982): 339. See also *OC*, 2:98, 3:216.

16. See J. Hillis Miller, *Versions of Pygmalion* (Cambridge: Harvard University Press, 1990), 8–9.

17. Jean-Philippe Barnabé, "Tanteos e ilaciones," unpublished essay.

18. Roberto Echavarren, "La ética de la escritura," presented at the conference "Felisberto Hernández: An International Homage," The American University, April 1993.

19. In Paulina Medeiros, *Felisberto y yo* (Montevideo: Libros del Astillero, 1982), 119. Vaz Ferreira called for books that leave more to be said than they themselves actually express. See Anastasía, "Sobre la filosofía," 31. In Hernández's *ars poetica*, nothing-to-say is often thematized through metafictional preoccupations. See *OC*, 3:79, 3:175.

20. Barnabé, "Tanteos e ilaciones," 23. José Miguel Oviedo notes that in Hernández stories "the words are evasive [*dan rodeos*] and the conversations are a dialogue among the deaf." In "Felisberto en el balcón: una relectura," presented at the conference "Felisberto Hernández: An International Homage," The American University, April 1993.

21. Jean-Philippe Barnabé, "El cuento de nunca acabar," presented at the conference "Felisberto Hernández: An International Homage," The American University, April 1993.

22. Gérard Genette, *Figures of Literary Discourse*, trans. Alan Sheridan (New York: Columbia University Press, 1982), 226.

23. See also *OC*, 1:162, 1:171, 3:39. On 3:147: "I loved seeing them delivered to their 'Silence'."

24. The Proust quotes in this and the previous sentence are from Philippe Sollers, *Writing and the Experience of Limits*, ed. David Hayman (New York: Columbia University Press, 1983), 196.

25. Barthes, *Pleasure*, 16. These poetics of the "unfinished" have a long history. In *Tristram Shandy* Laurence Sterne remarks of writing: "The truest respect which you can pay to the reader's understanding, is to halve this matter amicably, and leave him something

to imagine." Wolfgang Iser adds, "A literary text must therefore be conceived in such a way that it will engage the reader's imagination in the task of working things out for himself." See Wolfgang Iser, *The Implied Reader* (Baltimore: Johns Hopkins University Press, 1974), 275. For discussion of how humans need "a little satisfied curiosity and a little doubt," see *OC,* 1:88–91. In the letter to Nieto dated May 1936, Hernández notes that "mystery" tempts writers to destroy it.

26. Genette, *Figures of Literary Discourse,* 70.

27. For more on silence in this context, see *OC,* 3:145.

28. For an example, see ibid., 1:31.

29. Bergson, *Mind-Energy,* 57. On the same page he stresses that "the words, taken individually, no longer count" and that "the writer's art consists above everything in making us forget that he is using words." For additional Hernández passages on silence, see *OC,* 3:145–47.

30. Hillis Miller, *Versions of Pygmalion,* 240.

31. Bergson, *Mind-Energy,* 92. See also 52–58.

32. Umberto Eco, *The Open Work,* trans. Anna Cancogni (Cambridge: Harvard University Press, 1989), 21. The term "field of possibilities" is Henri Pousseur's, cited by Eco on 14. The second quoted passages is from Roland Barthes, *The Semiotic Challenge,* trans. Richard Howard (New York: Hill and Wang, 1988), 292. The last two quoted passages are from Tzvetan Todorov, *Mikhail Bakhtin: The Dialogical Principle,* trans. Wlad Godzich (Minneapolis: University of Minnesota Press, 1984), 48, 56. For intertextuality as adherence to different sign systems, see Julia Kristeva, *Revolution in Poetic Language,* trans. Margaret Waller (New York: Columbia University Press, 1984), 59–60.

33. Hernández's edition, in the possession of his widow Reina Reyes, is Alfred North Whitehead, *Modos de pensamiento* (Buenos Aires: Losada, 1944). The passage in question is on 45; see Anastasía, "Sobre la filosofía," 35. The English version cited in the text is from Alfred North Whitehead, *Modes of Thought* (New York: Capricorn Books, 1958), 46. Note that in the Spanish version read by Hernández the word "increased" is translated as *enriquecida* (enriched). See also *OC,* 3:200.

34. Genette, *Figures of Literary Discourse,* 73.

35. The Reyes observation is from Ricardo Pallares and Reina Reyes, *¿Otro Felisberto?* (Montevideo: Casa del Autor Nacional, 1983), 27. The Medeiros remark is quoted in Franciso Lasarte, *Felisberto Hernández y la escritura de "lo otro"* (Madrid: Insula, 1981), 18. The university comment is in a letter from Hernández to Medeiros in the latter's *Felisberto Hernández y yo,* 44. "Felisberto did not pass the Liceo entrance exam and returned to repeat the last year of primary school, which would be the last year of his regular studies." Norah Giraldi Dei Cas, "Música y estructura narrativa en la obra de Felisberto Hernández" (diss., The Sorbonne, 1992), 44.

36. Hernández's marginalia terminates well before the conclusion of most extant books from his collection. In conversation his daughter Ana María Hernández de Elena related to me that Hernández lost interest and preferred to go on to something new once he had understood an author's technique and derived what he could from it. The partially read books also interrelate with the "unfinished" concept in Hernández's writing in its most literal application: "And to tell the truth I'd like to begin another novel; but I won't begin it, because I fear that I'll abandon this one" (*OC,* 1:208). The tendency to leave behind the "known" and to gravitate toward "mystery" is also expressed in the disposable love objects and in voyeurism, as described in later chapters.

The phrase on Vaz Ferreira is from José Pedro Díaz, *Felisberto Hernández: el espectáculo imaginario* (Montevideo: Arca, 1991), 86. See also 85, 88.

Regarding "osmosis," see Esther de Cáceres, "Testimonio sobre Felisberto Hernández," in *Felisberto Hernández: notas críticas* (Montevideo: Cuadernos de Literatura, Fundación de Cultura Universitaria, 1970), 9. The same author, a lifelong friend of Hernández, notes that his relation with Vaz Ferreira was characterized by "extremely intense admiration, respect, and fidelity" (ibid.).

37. The quoted phrase is from Pallares and Reyes, *¿Otro Felisberto?*, 23. Hernández's socially marginal characters tending to their idiosyncratic obsessions likewise evidence a need for isolation; see, for example, *OC*, 2:75, 2:80. Elsewhere we read: "he was sufficient to himself and had no communication with the rest of the world" (2:116). According to Medeiros, Hernández's father shut himself away in an unlit room when problems overwhelmed him. See Giraldi Dei Cas, "Música," 40.

38. Genette, *Figures of Literary Discourse*, 66.

39. Thomas H. Ogden, "On Potential Space," *International Journal of Psycho-Analysis* 66 (1985): 134. This psychoanalytic perspective is closely related to the original term used by Jacques Derrida to describe his methodology: "de-sedimentation" as the "tracing of a path among textual strata in order to stir up dormant sediments of meaning which have accumulated and settled into the text's fabric." See Josué V. Harari, ed., *Textual Strategies: Perspectives in Post-Structuralist Criticism* (Ithaca: Cornell University Press, 1979), 37.

40. Peter Brooks, *Reading for the Plot* (New York: Vintage Books, 1984), xiv.

41. Ibid., 283.

42. Saúl Yurkievich, "Mundo moroso y sentido errático en Felisberto Hernández," in *Felisberto Hernández ante la crítica actual*, ed. Alain Sicard (Caracas: Monte Avila Editores, 1977), 369. Under the influence of Vaz Ferreira the young Hernández argued much the same; see *OC*, 1:168. See also 3:208.

43. The quoted passages is from Jean-Paul Sartre; see Tzvetan Todorov, *The Fantastic: A Structural Approach to a Literary Genre*, trans. Richard Howard (Cleveland, Ohio: The Press of Case Western Reserve University, 1973), 173–74. Todorov notes that psychoanalysis has replaced the literature of the fantastic because "There is no need today to resort to the devil in order to speak of an excessive sexual desire, and none to resort to vampires in order to designate the attraction exerted by corpses; psychoanalysis, and the literature which is directly or indirectly inspired by it, deal with these matters in undisguised terms" (160–61).

44. See Jean Pierrot, *The Decadent Imagination* (Chicago: University of Chicago Press, 1981), 147. The decadents placed the emphasis "less on miraculous distortions of objective reality than upon the human truth of the psychological states involved," with "the desire to renew the setting of fantastic fiction by using everyday modern life as its background" (148).

45. Rosemary Jackson, "Narcissism and Beyond: A Psychoanalytic Reading of *Frankenstein* and Fantasies of the Double," in *Aspects of Fantasy*, ed. William Coyle (Westport, Conn.: Greenwood Press, 1981), 43. The refraction trope was also used by Franciso Lasarte in reference to Hernández's use of "mystery" and "memory" "as prisms that refract the narrator's perceptions." See Francisco Lasarte, "Función de 'misterio' y 'memoria' en la obra de Felisberto Hernández," *Nueva revista de filología hispánica* 27 (1978): 59.

46. The first quoted phrase is from Hugo Verani, "Felisberto Hernández: la inquietante extrañeza de lo cotidiano," *Anales de literatura hispanoamericana* 16 (1987): 127–44; and the second is from Julio Cortázar in his prologue to Felisberto Hernández, *La casa inundada y otros cuentos*, ed. Cristina Peri Rossi (Barcelona: Editorial Lumen, 1975), 9.

47. Verani, "Felisberto Hernández," 129. The division of literature into broad generic classes—those that are "supernatural" and those that choose their subjects from "ordinary

life"—led Coleridge to observe that the latter "excite a feeling analogous to the supernatural, by awakening the mind's attention from the lethargy of custom." These texts, further, break through "the film of familiarity" and lead the reader to "the loveliness and wonders" of the world as an "inexhaustible treasure." See *Biographia Literaria*, vol. 7 of *The Collected Works of Samuel Taylor Coleridge*, ed. James Engell and W. Jackson Bate (Princeton: Princeton University Press, 1983), 6–7.

48. Lasarte, *"Lo otro,"* 156.

49. See José Bleger, *Simbiosis y ambigüedad* (Buenos Aires: Editorial Paidós, 1967), 167. See also 168.

50. Lasarte, *"Lo otro,"* 16.

51. For Hernández comments on psychoanalysis, see *OC*, 1:193, 1:196–97. In an unpublished letter sent by Hernández to Amalia Nieto from Ignacio Villegas/Gran Hotel España on 12 May 1940, Hernández described how in the provincial town of Pico he lectured on the principles of psychology to a group of medical doctors and then had the "audacity" to attend a patient. On his deathbed Hernández proposed to Nieto's sister—a psychologist close to Waclaw Radecki—that he and she collaborate on a project.

52. See Waclaw Radecki, *Tratado de psicología*, trans. Camilo Payssé and Víctor Delfino (Buenos Aires: Casa Editora Jacobo Peuser, 1933). The work includes illustrations indicating the *foco* and *franja*. In a copy of *Clemente Colling* inscribed for Radecki, Hernández called him "one of the greatest men of our time" and thanked him for "the highest honor of his friendship." The inscription is dated January 1943; the book is in the archives of Ana María Hernández de Elena.

Cf. the following observation by another of Hernández's major influences, Henri Bergson: "To live is to be inserted in things by means of a mechanism which draws from consciousness all that is utilizable in action, all that can be acted on the stage, and darkens the greater part of the rest." *Mind-Energy*, 71.

53. José Ortega y Gasset, *The Dehumanization of Art* (Princeton: Princeton University Press, 1948), 36.

54. Cortázar, "Prólogo," in Hernández, *La casa inundada*, 7.

55. David Sylvester, *The Brutality of Fact: Interviews with Francis Bacon* (London: Thames and Hudson, 1987), 134.

56. The first-quoted passage was later revised out of this text in the *Book Without Covers*; see *OC*, 1:84.

57. The quoted phrases are from the letter sent to Amalia Nieto in May 1936.

58. The quoted passage is from Pierrot, *Decadent Imagination,* 155.

59. Lasarte, *"Lo otro"*, 27. See also Ana María Barrenechea, "Ex-centricidad, divergencias y con-vergencias en Felisberto Hernández," *MLN* 91 (1976): 327.

60. Sigmund Freud, "The Uncanny," in *Standard Edition,* ed. James Strachey, vol. 15 (London: Hogarth Press, 1955), 241. The *unheimlich* quality of the idealized world in the memory-based fictions is suggestive in light of another comment made by Freud: "What he projects before him as his ideal is the substitute for the lost narcissism of his childhood in which he was his own ideal." Sigmund Freud, "On Narcissism: An Introduction," in *Standard Edition,* ed. James Strachey, vol. 14 (London: Hogarth Press, 1957), 94.

61. Anthony Vidler, *The Architectural Uncanny* (Cambridge: MIT Press, 1992), 7.

62. Hillis Miller, *Versions of Pygmalion,* 238. Prosopopoeia is the trope that "ascribes a face, a name, or a voice to the absent, inanimate, or the dead" (4). See also Christian Metz, *The Imaginary Signifier: Psychoanalysis and the Signifier,* trans. Celia Britton and Annwyl Williams (Bloomington: Indiana University Press, 1982), 70, where a former belief is held to be beneath a new one, while the latter is disavowed on another level.

63. Cited in Mario Praz, *Mnemosyne: The Parallel Between Literature and the Visual Arts* (Princeton: Princeton University Press, 1970), 36.

64. Ginette Paris, *Pagan Grace: Dionysos, Hermes, and Goddess Memory in Daily Life*, trans. Joanna Mott (Dallas, Tex.: Spring Publications, 1990), 121.

65. Ivan Illich, *H_2O and the Waters of Forgetfulness: Reflections on the Historicity of "Stuff"* (Dallas, Tex.: Dallas Institute of Humanities and Culture, 1985), 31. In "The Poisoned Girl" the victim dies beside an arroyo, which on *OC*, 1:127 is depicted as a river dividing the dead from the living.

66. Eco, *Open Work*, 3

67. Todorov, *Fantastic*, 25.

68. Whitehead, *Modos de pensamiento*, 45; see Anastasía, "Sobre la filosofía," 5. English version from Whitehead, *Modes of Thought*, 46.

69. Echavarren, *El espacio de la verdad*, 75. Elsewhere the narrator thinks about "the mystery of a woman" and the result is a similar "confusion" (*OC*, 1:171).

70. Much the same simultaneity of opposites is accomplished by oxymorons: "death had a special life" (*OC*, 1:130).

71. For a word from Ferdinand de Saussure, see his *Course in General Linguistics*, trans. Wade Baskin (London: Fontana, 1974), 11–121. The passage quoted in the text is from Tzvetan Todorov, *Theories of the Symbol*, trans. Catherine Porter (Ithaca: Cornell University Press, 1982), 20. There are exceptions to Todorov's assertion; the names of fictional characters, for example. Later in the text Todorov reminds us that "arbitrariness is not, for Saussure, merely one of the sign's various features, but its fundamental characteristic" (268). See also a summary of Lacan's seminar comments on the infant's name in Michael Clark, *Jacques Lacan: An Annotated Bibliography*, vol. 1 (New York: Garland Publishing, 1988), 31.

For Hernández on arbitrariness and proper nouns, see *OC*, 1:153, 1:160, 1:197.

72. See also *OC*, 3:19. Other words, however, seem to the narrator to have an intrinsic bond to their referents: a round face, for example, seems a requisite for proper application of the word *abuela* (grandmother) (2:16).

73. Michel Foucault, *The Order of Things* (New York: Vintage Books, 1970), 9. Lacan similarly observed that "The power of naming objects structures the perception itself." *The Seminar of Jacques Lacan, Book II*, ed. Jacques-Alain Miller (New York: W. W. Norton, 1988), 169.

74. Rudolph Binion, *After Christianity: Christian Survivals in Post-Christian Culture* (Durango, Colo.: Logbridge-Rhodes, 1986), 100. See the entire chapter "True Seeming" for a cultural overview of *seems* motifs.

75. Norah Giraldi Dei Cas and Frank Graziano, unpublished interview with María Isabel ("Mabel") Hernández Guerra, April 1993.

76. David Lean, director, *Lawrence of Arabia*, Columbia Pictures, 1962. Philippe Sollers offered another dictum in this line: *"Whoever does not write is written"* (*Writing*, 199). Note that *Lawrence of Arabia* and another of Hernández's favorites, *Ben Hur* (directed by William Wyler, 1959), have in common with one another and with Hernández's canon the thematic centrality of water.

77. Lasarte, *"Lo otro,"* 28. See Bleger, *Simbiosis y ambigüedad,* 178, on "as if."

78. The de-specification of plot settings was calculated by Hernández. Barnabé notes, for example, that a draft manuscript of "On Tour with Yamandú Rodríguez" includes the crossed-out phrase "Upon arriving at Melo," which is replaced in the later version by "We arrived at a small city." "Tanteos," 17. A similar example is presented on 28 of the same work.

79. Quoted passages are from Eco, *Open Work*, 9.

80. Todorov, *Fantastic*, 38.

81. The quoted phrase is from Italo Calvino, "Las zarabandas mentales de Felisberto Hernández," in Felisberto Hernández, *Novelas y cuentos*, ed. José Pedro Díaz (Caracas: Biblioteca Ayacucho, 1985), 3.

82. The quoted passages are from Yurkievich in Sicard, *Felisberto Hernández;* see 124–25, 363–64, 381, 382.

83. For a "love scene" example, see Horacio's first escapade with Hortensia on *OC,* 2:158.

84. Cf: "I want to say what is happening to me . . . in order to see if by saying what happens to me, it stops happening to me" (*OC*, 1:140).

85. Sheldon Bach, "On Sadomasochistic Object Relations," in *Perversions and Near-Perversions in Clinical Practice: New Psychoanalytic Perspectives,* ed. Gerald I. Fogel and Wayne A. Myers (New Haven: Yale University Press, 1991), 87.

86. The quoted passage is from Robert J. Stoller, "Hostility and Mystery in Perversion," *International Journal of Psychoanalysis* 55 (1974): 429.

87. From Théophile Gautier's preface ("the first entirely approbative and widely influential view of decadence as a *style*") written in 1868 for Baudelaire's *Fleurs du Mal.* Cited in Matei Calinescu, *Five Faces of Modernity* (Durham, N.C.: Duke University Press, 1987), 164.

88. D. W. Winnicott, *Playing and Reality* (London: Tavistock Publications, 1971), 2.

89. Ibid., 3.

90. Ibid., 89.

91. Both passages from ibid., 51.

92. Winnicott, *Playing and Reality,* 13.

93. See *OC,* 3:175 for an additional examples. The study of English and shorthand provided other sign systems into which Hernández "escaped."

94. Giraldi Dei Cas and Graziano, interview with Hernández Guerra.

95. See Michael Riffaterre, *Fictional Truth* (Baltimore: Johns Hopkins University Press, 1990), xv. The text continues: "Furthermore, verisimilitude is an artifact, since it is a verbal representation of reality rather than reality itself: verisimilitude itself, therefore, entails fictionality."

96. Tzvetan Todorov, *Introduction to Poetics*, trans. Richard Howard (Sussex, U.K.: Harvester Press, 1981), 18. See also Metz, *Imaginary Signifier,* 72.

97. Winnicott, *Playing and Reality,* xii. Rosemary Jackson employs the optical concept "paraxis" to describe this fantastic area where "object and image seem to collide." See her *Fantasy*, 19.

98. See André Green, *On Private Madness* (Madison, Conn.: International Universities Press, 1986), 274. See also Bleger, *Simbiosis y ambigüedad,* 167–68, on the absence of demarcation and discrimination.

99. Note that Vaz Ferreira wanted "to teach to hesitate." See Larre Borges, "Felisberto Hernández," 12.

100. On *OC,* 2:127, "my head was like a huge room in which my thoughts did gymnastics."

101. Marcel Proust, *Swann's Way,* in *Remembrance of Things Past,* trans. C. K. Scott Moncrieff (New York: Random House, 1934), 1:10. In light of the coming chapters' discussion of Hernández's relation to his mother, it is interesting to note that the Mamma of Proust's text winds up spending the night in his room, with the father going off to bed alone.

102. For another vivid example of the subject scripting discourse for a girl (in this case

absent), see *OC,* 3:31–32. See also 3:91 for an additional example of the ritual prolongation of time.

103. See also the use of the balcony in "Mamma's Tree" (*OC*, 2:184, 2:194).

104. Ogden, "On Potential Space," 133.

105. The quoted passage is from ibid., 134. For another case study, see Simon Hatcher, "A Case of Doll Phobia," *British Journal of Psychiatry* 155 (1989): 255–57.

Chapter 1. Narcissus and Hernández

1. See *The Metamorphoses of Ovid*, trans. Mary M. Innes (Harmondsworth: Penguin Books, 1986), 83–87. Modern Ovid translations in the text are from Louise Vinge, *The Narcissus Theme in Western European Literature up to the Early Nineteenth Century* (Lund, Sweden: Gleerups, 1967), 7–12.

2. On Nemesis, see Tony Siebers, *The Mirror of Medusa* (Berkeley: University of California Press, 1983), 81.

3. This and all Old English passages are from Ovid, *Metamorphoses*, trans. Arthur Golding, ed. John Frederick Nims (New York: Macmillan, 1965), 73–77.

4. Vinge, *Narcissus Theme,* 16–17.

5. Siebers, *Mirror of Medusa,* 71–72.

6. In psychoanalytic usage "object" refers to people as well as to things. The term is used in contradistinction to "subject" (subject versus object) rather than to distinguish between the living and the inanimate. This usage of "object"—employed throughout *The Lust of Seeing*—is fortuitous in the context of fictions in which love objects (normally people) are often things (such as Hortensia dolls).

7. When Hernández says in a letter to a lover "I cover your mouth with kisses" the silencing of the woman and the loving of the woman are likewise registered simultaneously. Paulina Medeiros, *Felisberto y yo* (Montevideo: Libros del Astillero, 1982), 93.

8. Christine Brooke-Rose, "Woman as a Semiotic Object," in *The Female Body in Western Culture,* ed. Susan Rubin Suleiman (Cambridge: Harvard University Press, 1986), 310. In a different perspective, Ksenija Bilbija follows talmudic interpretations in pointing out that a golem is mute not inherently but by virtue of the "impurity" of its creator. The female golem (Hortensia) is never empowered with speech because her creation was preceded by the desire for sexual exploitation. Ksenija Bilbija, *"Las Hortensias:* The Fabrication of Desire," presented at the conference "Felisberto Hernández: An International Homage," The American University, April 1993.

9. Quoted phrase is from Brooke-Rose, "Woman as a Semiotic Object," 310.

10. Jean Cocteau, *Cocteau's World: An Anthology of Writings by Jean Cocteau,* ed. Margaret Crosland (New York: Dodd, Mead, & Company, 1972), 475.

11. *Diagnostic and Statistical Manual of Mental Disorders*, 3d ed., rev. (Washington, D.C.: American Psychiatric Association, 1987), 350–51. Cited later as *DSM-III-R.*

12. Salman Akhtar, "Narcissistic Personality Disorder," *Narcissistic Personality Disorder, The Psychiatric Clinics of North America* 12, no. 3 (September 1989): 520. In a 1919 paper Freud remarked, "As is well known, this neurotic delusion of inferiority is only a partial one, and is completely compatible with the existence of a self-overvaluation derived from other sources." See "A Child is Being Beaten," in *Standard Edition*, ed. James Strachey, vol. 17 (London: Hogarth Press, 1955), 193.

13. Otto Kernberg, *Borderline Conditions and Pathological Narcissism* (New York: Aronson, 1975), 227.

14. The quoted passages are from Ana María Hernández, "Mis recuerdos," *Escritura* 7, nos. 13–14 (1982): 337–38; with the exception of the passage between dashes, which is from M. Masud R. Khan, *Alienation in Perversions* (New York: International Universities Press, 1979), 14.

15. Norah Giraldi Dei Cas, *Felisberto Hernández, del creador al hombre* (Montevideo: Ediciones de la Banda Oriental, 1975), 26.

16. The first quoted passage is from Medeiros, *Felisberto y yo,* 23.

17. Mary Ann Caws, *The Eye in the Text: Essays on Perception, Mannerist to Modern* (Princeton: Princeton University Press, 1981), 64.

18. Giraldi Dei Cas, *Felisberto Hernández,* 60.

19. In Francisco Lasarte, *Felisberto Hernández y la escritura de "lo otro"* (Madrid: Insula, 1981), 18–19.

20. José Pedro Díaz, *Felisberto Hernández: el espectáculo imaginario,* vol. 1 (Montevideo: Arca, 1991), 11.

21. Ibid., 87.

22. Medeiros, *Felisberto y yo,* 17.

23. Ibid., 19–20.

24. Kernberg, *Borderline Conditions and Pathological Narcissism,* 233. See also 236, where "they experience themselves as part of that outstanding person . . . ; the admired individual is merely an extension of themselves."

25. From an unpublished letter sent by Hernández to Amalia Nieto from Las Flores on 21 August 1940.

26. The passages are frequently cited. For the Vaz Ferreira passage, see Giraldi Dei Cas, *Felisberto Hernández,* 47; for the Supervielle, Tomás Eloy Martínez, "Para que nadie olvide a Felisberto Hernández," *La opinión cultural,* 31 March 1974, 4; and for the Gómez de la Serna, Lasarte, *"Lo otro,"* 24. Another of the cornerstone passages came later from Italo Calvino, commenting on Hernández's originality: "Felisberto Hernández is a writer who resembles no one." See Calvino's introduction, "Las zarabandas de Felisberto Hernández," in Felisberto Hernández, *Novelas y cuentos,* ed. José Pedro Díaz (Caracas: Biblioteca Ayacucho: 1985), 3.

27. The quoted phrase is from Juan Carlos Onetti, "Felisberto, el 'naif'," in *Felisberto Hernández: valoración crítica,* ed. Walter Rela (Montevideo: Editorial Ciencias, 1982), 31.

28. Much of this text, written in French, is adapted from the Amigos del Arte talk on *OC,* 3:216–17.

29. The quoted phrase is from Lasarte, *"Lo otro,"* 25; I am also following Giraldi Dei Cas, *Felisberto Hernández,* 27. Rodríguez Monegal's misreading of *No One Lit the Lamps* was published in *Clinamen* 2 (May–June 1948): 51–52.The quoted phrase in the next sentence is from Akhtar, "Narcissistic Personality Disorder," 520.

30. The quoted phrase is from Kernberg, *Borderline Conditions and Pathological Narcissism,* 229.

31. Quoted passages in this and the previous sentence are from Medeiros, *Felisberto y yo,* 21, 23, and 27, respectively.

32. The quoted passage is from Reina Reyes, in Ricardo Pallares and Reina Reyes, *¿Otro Felisberto?* (Montevideo: Editorial Imago, 1983), 22.

33. Reyes quoted in Eloy Martínez, "Para que nadie olvide," 6.

34. Medeiros, *Felisberto y yo,* 25, and Reyes in Reyes and Pallares, *¿Otro Felisberto?,* 22, respectively.

35. Giraldi Dei Cas, *Felisberto Hernández,* 27.

36. Medeiros, *Felisberto y yo,* 23–24.

37. Anatole Baju, cited in Matei Calinescu, *Five Faces of Modernity* (Durham, N.C.: Duke University Press, 1987), 176.

38. Medeiros, *Felisberto y yo*, 24.

39. The quoted phrases are from Norah Giraldi de Dei Cas, "Las seis viudas," *La opinión cultural*, 31 March 1974, 9 and Eloy Martínez, "Para que nadie olvide," 2, respectively. Note that one of Hernández's major influences, Marcel Proust, had a similar relation with his mother. When at the age of thirteen or fourteen Proust was asked on a questionnaire, "Your idea of misery?," he responded, "Being separated from Mother." Quoted in J. E. Rivers, *Proust and the Art of Love* (New York: Columbia University Press, 1980), 15.

40. Ben Burnsten, "Some Narcissistic Personality Types," in *Essential Papers on Narcissism*, ed. Andrew P. Morrison (New York: New York University Press, 1986), 394.

41. First quoted phrase is from Deolinda Hernández, sister of Felisberto, in Luis Neira, "El Felisberto de la calle cortada," interview with Deolinda Hernández, *El Día*, 5 April 1981, 3; the second is from Medeiros, *Felisberto y yo*, 9.

42. Norah Giraldi Dei Cas and Frank Graziano, interview with María Isabel ("Mabel") Hernández Guerra, April 1993.

43. The quoted phrases are from Giraldi Dei Cas, *Felisberto Hernández*, 20–21 and 98, respectively.

44. Reyes, cited in Eloy Martínez, "Para que nadie olvide," 6. In an interview with Giraldi Dei Cas, Reyes commented that Calita was responsible for the failure of the Hernández-Reyes marriage. See Norah Giraldi Dei Cas, "Música y estructura narrativa en la obra de Felisberto Hernández" (diss., La Sorbonne, 1992), 42.

45. Khan, *Alienation in Perversions*, 12.

46. In Neira, "El Felisberto de la calle cortada," 3.

47. Giraldi Dei Cas and Graziano, interview with Hernández Guerra.

48. Quoted phrase is from Kernberg, *Borderline Conditions and Pathological Narcissism*, 235.

49. In this and the previous sentences I am following Giraldi Dei Cas, "Música," 41.

50. Kernberg, *Borderline Conditions and Pathological Narcissism*, 235.

51. Khan, *Alienation in Perversions*, 12.

52. Arnold M. Cooper, "The Unconscious Core of Perversion," in *Perversions and Near-Perversions in Clinical Practice: New Psychoanalytic Perspectives*, ed. Gerald I. Fogel and Wayne A. Myers (New Haven: Yale University Press, 1991), 23.

53. Burnsten, "Some Narcissistic Personality Types," 387.

54. Robert S. Wallerstein, *Forty-Two Lives in Treatment: A Study of Psychoanalysis and Psychotherapy* (New York: Guilford Press, 1986), 334. See also Khan, *Alienation in Perversions*, 13, where separation trauma results in panic, threat of annihilation, and an unconscious sense of abandonment.

55. Giraldi Dei Cas, *Felisberto Hernández*, 21.

56. Eloy Martínez, "Para que nadie olvide," 3.

57. Giraldi Dei Cas, *Felisberto Hernández*, 26.

58. For examples of this confusion, see ibid. and Eloy Martínez, "Para que nadie olvide," 3. Hernández's adult life evidences a pronounced concern to secure such approval from other "authorities."

59. In *Clemente Colling* a frog incident and other "cruel jokes" are attributed to another "distant aunt," Petrona (*OC*, 1:33–34).

60. Giraldi Dei Cas, *Felisberto Hernández*, 24. Other details regarding Deolinda in the preceding sentences are from Giraldi Dei Cas, "Música," 42–43.

61. The first quoted phrase is from Medeiros, *Felisberto y yo*, 10; the second is from

Deolinda Hernández in Neira, "El Felisberto de la calle cortada," 3; others are from Giraldi Dei Cas, *Felisberto Hernández,* 20 (see also 24).

62. D. W. Winnicott, *Playing and Reality* (London: Tavistock Publications, 1971), 17. See *OC,* 3:52.

63. Winnicott, *Playing and Reality,* 17. See also 108, where in the paradox characteristic of potential space the objects are "both *joined and separated* by the string."

64. Ibid., 19.

65. This and the previous quoted passage are from ibid., 43.

66. The quoted passage is from ibid., 19. See also 97.

67. Ibid., 46 and 20, respectively.

68. Ibid., 20.

69. For textual examples of frustrated hope in the quest to "be someone," see *OC,* 1:38, 2:199, 3:39.

70. The book is in the archive of Ana María Hernández de Elena.

71. M. Mahler, quoted in Malcolm Pines, "Mirroring and Child Development," *Psychoanalytic Inquiry* 5, no. 2 (1985): 217.

72. Khan, *Alienation in Perversions,* 12.

73. Ibid., 13.

74. Christopher Bollas, *The Shadow of the Object: Psychoanalysis of the Unthought Known* (London: Free Association Books, 1987), 18–22.

75. All passages from the letter are from Pallares and Reyes, ¿*Otro Felisberto?,* 9–13. In an unpublished essay entitled "Money: The Great Test of Human Action," Hernández laments society's "injustice" in "not economically saving the life of the creator" (p. 1).

A psychiatrist introduced, though not convincingly, a new nosological entity termed "the Nobel Prize Complex." The majority of individuals with this complex are firstborn, and they present with fantasies including one clearly evidenced in the Hernández letter: "the passive fantasy of being the 'special one' chosen by virtue of exceptional gifts." See Helen H. Tartakoff, "The Normal Personality in Our Culture and the Nobel Prize Complex," in *Psychoanalysis—A General Psychology,* ed. Rudolph M. Loewenstein et al. (New York: International Universities Press, 1966), 222–52. The quoted passage is on 237.

76. The quoted passage is from Giraldi Dei Cas, "Las seis viudas," 9.

77. Thomas Freeman, "Narcissism and Defensive Processes in Schizophrenic States," in *Essential Papers on Psychosis,* ed. Peter Buckley (New York: New York University Press, 1988), 79.

A curious polarity is established by Hernández's relation with his first wife and her family. They perceived Hernández-the-suitor as a cultured intellectual from the capital, but Hernández's later, more relaxed demeanor led them to believe that he was "an impostor" (Giraldi Dei Cas and Graziano, interview with Hernández Guerra).

78. The quoted phrase is from Kernberg, *Borderline Conditions and Pathological Narcissism,* 227.

79. Thomas H. Ogden, "On Potential Space," *International Journal of Psycho-Analysis* 66 (1985): 138.

80. Kernberg, *Borderline Conditions and Pathological Narcissism,* 228. See also the same author's *Object-Relations Theory and Clinical Psychoanalysis* (New York: Jason Aronson, 1976), 187.

81. Washington Lockhart, *Felisberto Hernández: una biografía literaria* (Montevideo: Arca, 1991), 40.

82. Giraldi Dei Cas, "Las seis viudas," 8.

83. Medeiros, *Felisberto y yo,* 8.

84. James L. Sacksteder, "Psychoanalytical Conceptualizations of Narcissism from Freud to Kernberg and Kohut," in *New Perspectives on Narcissism,* ed. Eric M. Plakun (Washington, D.C.: American Psychiatric Press, 1990), 48.

85. The quoted passages are from *DSM-III-R*, 350–51, and Akhtar, "Narcissistic Personality Disorder," 520, respectively.

86. Kernberg, *Borderline Conditions and Pathological Narcissism*, 228.

87. In Neira, "El Felisberto de la calle cortada," 3.

88. Reyes, in Pallares and Reyes, *¿Otro Felisberto?,* 31 .

89. Bleger, *Simbiosis y ambigüedad,* 219. The sincerity of crying in "The Crocodile" is perhaps recontextualized by the following passage from a letter send by Hernández to Amalia Nieto from Fray Bentos on 8 June 1936. Hernández was at a dinner at which all "was going very well" and "with great cordiality" when suddenly, he says, "I was overcome by the uncontainable desire to cry, to break out in sobs; I took out my handkerchief with the pretext of bringing it to my nose, turned around in the chair, and squeezed my face as hard as I could; I don't think anyone noticed anything. . . ." The desire to cry here, as in "The Crocodile," was catalyzed by a memory, in the present case a memory of the love left behind while Hernández was touring as a concert pianist.

90. Reyes, quoted in Eloy Martínez, "Para que nadie olvide," 4. In Pallares and Reyes, *¿Otro Felisberto?,* the latter recalls the phrase as follows: "I wrote a story: Other People's Feelings" (31).

91. Reyes, in Pallares and Reyes, *¿Otro Felisberto?,* 31.

92. The quoted passage is from *DSM-III-R*, 347. In describing the "doubled" protagonists of romantic literature, Rank identifies much the same: "the direct inability to love" alternating with "an exorbitantly strained longing for love," these being "the two poles of this overexaggerated attitude toward one's own ego." See Otto Rank, *The Double*, trans. and ed. Harry Tucker Jr. (Chapel Hill: University of North Carolina Press, 1971), 48.

93. André Green, *On Private Madness* (Madison, Conn.: International Universities Press, 1986), 27. See *OC,* 3:175 for "the contradictory states that he discovers in himself."

94. Green, *On Private Madness,* 27. The "pathological devaluation of women" also returns to the maternal imago as, "in the final analysis, devaluation of mother." See Kernberg, *Object-Relations Theory,* 195.

95. In *Object-Relations Theory* Kernberg says of one narcissist: "On the surface he treated her [his wife] in a gentle, friendly, detached manner, but he ruthlessly neglected her deeper needs" (196).

96. The quoted phrase is from Sacksteder, "Psychoanalytical Conceptualizations," 48. The apparent exception to the idealization/devaluation cycle seems to be Hernández's first wife, María Isabel Guerra. Perhaps because she was his first wife, and certainly because her withdrawal from the marriage devastated him and foreclosed the cycle's continuation, María Isabel was overidealized but never devalued. Well after she broke the marriage and his heart, Hernández was unable to relinquish his love for her, and "even cried of emotions at the movies . . . comparing her beauty with that of the actresses that appeared on the screen." Giraldi Dei Cas, following testimony of Alfredo and Esther Cáceres, in "Música," 54.

97. Quotes phrases are from Brooke-Rose, "Woman as a Semiotic Object," 314.

98. Kernberg, *Borderline Conditions and Pathological Narcissism*, 231. Freud observed: "What possesses the excellence which the ego lacks for making it an ideal, is loved." Sigmund Freud, "On Narcissism: An Introduction," in *Standard Edition*, ed. James Strachey, vol. 14 (London: Hogarth Press, 1957), 101.

99. The quoted passage is from Green, *On Private Madness,* 94.

100. Ibid., 95.

101. The quoted phrase is from Bollas, *Shadow of the Object,* 63.

102. The quoted passage is from Medeiros, *Felisberto y yo,* 9. See the same page for related comments.

103. Khan, *Alienation in Perversions,* 15.

104. Friedrich Nietzsche, *The Will to Power,* ed. Walter Kaufmann (New York: Vintage Books, 1968), 424. For an example of the son as a doll, see Françoise Dolto, *La imagen inconsciente del cuerpo* (Barcelona: Ediciones Paidós, 1986), 216.

105. In an unpublished letter sent by Hernández to Amalia Nieto from Treinta y Tres on 9 May 1941, Hernández refers to "the desire to begin greater things" without pausing to "concretize what I have already worked on." See also *OC,* 3:36. As mentioned earlier, most of the remaining books that belonged to Hernández are annotated in his hand only through approximately the first third of the text. Ana María Hernández de Elena told me that her father would read until he discovered the author's method and would then abandon the book, preferring to go on to something new.

106. Arnold Cooper, "Narcissism and Masochism," in *Narcissistic Personality Disorder, The Psychiatric Clinics of North America* 12, no. 3 (September 1989): 543. See also Kernberg, *Borderline Conditions and Pathological Narcissism,* 231.

107. Cooper, summarizing Khan and Stoller in "The Unconscious Core," 24.

108. Sigmund Freud, *Introductory Lectures on Psycho-Analysis,* in *Standard Edition,* ed. James Strachey, vol. 16 (London: Hogarth Press, 1963), 416.

109. The quoted passage is from Heinz Kohut, *The Analysis of the Self* (New York: International Universities Press, 1971), 3.

110. The quoted passage is from Reyes, in Pallares and Reyes, *¿Otro Felisberto?,* 30.

111. Reyes, in ibid., 32; Medeiros, *Felisberto y yo,* 24; Giraldi Dei Cas, following Deolinda Hernández, in "Música," 39; and Reyes in Pallares and Reyes, *¿Otro Felisberto?,* 32, respectively.

112. Ester de Cáceres, "Testimonio sobre Felisberto Hernández," in *Felisberto Hernández: notas críticas,* ed. Lídice Gómez Mango (Montevideo: Cuadernos de Literatura 16), 6 and 7, respectively.

113. The quoted passage is from Akhtar, "Narcissistic Personality Disorder," 520.

114. Pallares and Reyes, *¿Otro Felisberto?,* 11.

115. Arnold H. Modell, *Object Love and Reality* (New York: International Universities Press, 1968), 39.

116. The quoted phrase is from Kernberg, *Borderline Conditions and Pathological Narcissism,* 230. For a fine example of "splendid isolation," see *OC,* 3:37.

117. The first quoted passage is from Modell, *Object Love and Reality,* 39; the second is from Brian Ackner, "Depersonalization II: Clinical Syndromes," *Journal of Mental Science* 100 (1954): 867; and the third is from ibid., 871.

118. Quoted passages are from Reyes in Pallares and Reyes, *¿Otro Felisberto?,* 24 and 26, respectively.

119. Cooper, summarizing Kohut, in "Narcissism and Masochism," 543.

120. For other examples, see *OC,* 2:141, 2:145.

121. Kernberg, *Borderline Conditions and Pathological Narcissism,* 233.

122. Burnsten, "Some Narcissistic Personality Types," 379.

Chapter 2. The Poetics of Reflection

1. The quoted phrase is from Herbert Grabes, *The Mutable Glass: Mirror Imagery in Titles and Texts of the Middle Ages and the English Renaissance,* trans. Gordon Collier (Cambridge: Cambridge University Press, 1982), 83.

2. Ovid, *Metamorphoses*, trans. Arthur Golding, ed. John Frederick Nims (New York: Macmillan, 1965), 77.

3. Christian Metz, *The Imaginary Signifier: Psychoanalysis and the Signifier*, trans. Celia Britton and Annwyl Williams (Bloomington: Indiana University Press, 1982), 97.

4. Wim Wenders, director, *Paris, Texas*, written by Sam Shepard, Twentieth Century Fox, 1984. For an interesting hagiographical example of a similar phenomenon, see John Coakley, "Friars as Confidants of Holy Women in Medieval Dominican Hagiography," in *Images of Sainthood in Medieval Europe*, ed. Renate Blumenfeld-Kosinski and Timea Szell (Ithaca: Cornell University Press, 1991), 237. Raymond, the confessor of Catherine of Siena, relates that "Suddenly her face was transformed into the face of a bearded man" who turned out to be Christ (237).

5. The quoted passage is in John Russell, *Francis Bacon* (New York: Oxford University Press, 1979), 90. Referring to his own paintings, Bacon remarked: "What I want to do is to distort the thing far beyond the appearance, but in the distortion to bring it back to a recording of the appearance." David Sylvester, *The Brutality of Fact: Interviews with Francis Bacon* (London: Thames and Hudson, 1987), 40. For images in Hernández perceived as though in a distorting mirror, see *OC*, 3:79, 3:178.

6. Jacqueline Rose, *Sexuality in the Field of Vision* (New York: Verso, 1986), 228.

7. See Benjamin Goldberg, *The Mirror and Man* (Charlottesville: University of Virginia Press, 1985), 246–47, for a summary of the 1964 Traub and Orbach experiment concerning reflection distortions.

8. The quoted passage is from José Bleger, *Simbiosis y ambigüedad* (Buenos Aires: Editorial Paidós, 1967), 221.

9. See, for example, *OC*, 2:48, 2:55.

10. The fragment "The Mirrors" (which served as raw material for *The Hortensias*) states the same on *OC*, 2:211–12.

11. Cf. *OC*, 3:86, where a framed picture doubles as a doorway.

12. For the Indian and Chinese examples, see B. A. Litvinskii in *Encyclopedia of Religion*, s.v. "Mirrors." In "Except Julia," tactile (rather than visual) contact results from the inability to distinguish a glass-covered portrait from a vanity mirror (*OC*, 2:82). Regarding the Chinese example, cf. Umberto Eco, *Semiotics and the Philosophy of Language* (London: Macmillan, 1984), 211: As long as he looks at the mirror, he says, "It gives me back my facial features, but if I mailed a mirror which I have long looked at to my beloved, so that she may remember my looks, she could not see me (and would instead see herself)."

13. Frederick Goldin, *The Mirror of Narcissus in the Courtly Love Lyric* (Ithaca: Cornell University Press, 1967), 78 and 258, respectively. Grabes remarks that "the lover as a mirror of the beloved (or vice versa)" had great currency in the Middle Ages and English Renaissance (*Mutable Glass*, 78).

14. Cf. the "lighted fishtank" on *OC*, 3:124.

15. On *OC*, 2:164 flames appear on a mirror and then on a windowpane "like on a movie screen."

16. See the notebook draft of this image on *OC*, 3:170. For other inversion images, see 3:87 (walking backwards), 3:88 (fountain turned into island), and 3:137 (pants on backwards). Cf. the curious auditory hallucination of a sailor on a solo voyage between Massachusetts and England: "The trouble is that you are sailing clockwise. You have to sail counterclockwise to get out." See Arnold H. Modell, *Object Love and Reality* (New York: International Universities Press, 1968), 109.

17. For discussion of the mirror as prosthesis, see Eco, *Semiotics*, 208–11.

18. In D. W. Winnicott, *Playing and Reality* (London: Tavistock Publications, 1971), 117.

19. Oscar Wilde, quoted in M. H. Abrams, *The Mirror and the Lamp: Romantic Theory and the Critical Tradition* (New York: Oxford University Press, 1953), 30.

20. In Sylvester, *Brutality of Fact,* 87.

21. For a distinct example of ritual distancing in Hernández's work, see Margarita's use of the telephone on *OC,* 3:88.

22. Victoria Hamilton, *Narcissus and Oedipus* (London: Routledge & Kegan Paul, 1982), 133.

23. The second quoted passage is from Heinz Kohut, *The Analysis of the Self: A Systematic Approach to the Psychoanalytic Treatment of Narcissistic Personality Disorders* (New York: International Universities Press, 1971), 6. See also *OC,* 2:187, where a peek-a-boo that violates ritual distance is presented through a figurative curtain.

24. For a discussion of the ideal mother—in this case the Virgin Mary—behind glass, see Carla Gottlieb, "The Window as a Token of Maidenhood" in *The Window in Art: From the Window of God to the Vanity of Man* (New York: Abaris Books, 1981).

25. The relationship between Hernández and Medeiros is itself referred to as "our daughter" in their correspondence. See Paulina Medeiros, *Felisberto Hernández y yo* (Montevideo: Libros del Astillero, 1982), 43.

26. Sigmund Freud, "Thoughts for the Times on War and Death," *Standard Edition,* ed. James Strachey, vol. 14 (London: Hogarth Press, 1957).

27. See also *OC,* 2:203. The protagonist of "The Crocodile" refers to himself as a "toy" on 3:92.

28. Note that Igor Stravinsky's *Petrushka,* played in its solo piano version by Hernández at the climax of his piano career, concerns a puppet that is brought to life, entangled in a love triangle, and murdered by his rival, and that then returns as a ghost (= double).

29. See Louise Vinge, *The Narcissus Theme in Western European Literature up to the Early Nineteenth Century* (Lund, Sweden: Gleerups, 1967), 22. Note that the Narcissus myth incorporated into Edenic themes has Milton's Eve in *Paradise Lost* more fond of her own reflection than of Adam.

On *OC,* 3:101–2 the protagonist of "The Crocodile" alternates between a caricature of himself, a mirror image of his face, and this image compared to a sister. Margarita of "The Flooded House" is throughout the text a kind of female Narcissus, and elsewhere we find a male subject's double (his head) compared to a woman who is leaving (2:209), and a "drowned" girl remembered in commensal ceremonies in which men behave "as if they wanted to rise up from the center of the river and get out of the water" (2:61).

30. Quoted in Grabes, *Mutable Glass,* 119.

31. Hegel, *Phenomenology of Mind* (1807), 86. See also Eric Alliez and Michel Feher, "Reflections of a Soul," in *Fragments for a History of the Human Body,* ed. Michel Feher et al., pt. 2 (New York: Zone, 1989), 68: "There is no longer a point at which one can fix the limits of oneself and say, 'Up to this point, it is me.'"

32. The quoted passage is from Sigmund Freud, "On Narcissism: An Introduction," *Standard Edition,* ed. James Strachey, vol. 14 (London: Hogarth Press, 1957), 100.

33. Ibid., 88. On the same page: Object-love of the attachment type "displays the marked sexual overvaluation which is doubtless derived from the child's original narcissism and thus corresponds to a transference of that narcissism to the sexual object."

The breakdown of differentiation is patent in one patient's discourse, which evidenced no clear distinction between himself, his wife, and his children; "when he spoke of them he was speaking of himself" (Bleger, *Simbiosis y ambigüedad,* 170).

34. Grabes, *Mutable Glass,* 112.

35. Ibid., 131.

36. The quoted passage is from André Green, *On Private Madness* (Madison, Conn.: International Universities Press, 1986), 95. Tony Siebers notes that Echo "plays the mirror" of Narcissus's words. See his *The Mirror of Medusa* (Berkeley: University of California Press, 1983), 66.

37. The quoted phrase is from Green, *On Private Madness*, 257.

38. Elsewhere in Hernandez's canon, in "Spanish Dance", a metaphor establishes a male as the flower bound in the dramatic movement of a female: "You will carry me between your teeth" (*OC,* 1:177). Note that Hernández's grandfather was a gardener and that his second daughter was, for a period, a flamenco dancer. In Gutierre Tibón, *Diccionario de nombres propios* (Mexico: Editorial Fournier, 1956), "Hortensia" means "a female gardener" (261).

39. For a discussion of the etymology of "Narcissus" and of the narcotic poetics, see Siebers, *Mirror of Medusa,* 59–61.

40. Thomas H. Ogden, "The Concept of Internal Object Relations," *International Journal of Psycho-Analysis* 64 (1983): 227. In the sentences above I am closely following ibid., 228.

41. Hanna Segal, quoted in Green, *On Private Madness,* 89.

42. Ogden (summarizing Bion), "Internal Object Relations," 233.

43. Ibid., 234. Green likewise summarizes that "projection arises simultaneously with splitting" (*On Private Madness,* 89).

44. Claire Rosenfield, "The Shadow Within: The Conscious and Unconscious Use of the Double," in *Stories of the Double,* ed. Albert J. Guerard (Philadelphia: J. B. Lippincott, 1967), 314. In the literature of the Río de la Plata, Jorge Luis Borges's "Tlön, Uqbar, Orbis Tertius" is an interesting example, depicting a world in which external objects are whatever each individual wishes them to be.

45. See Modell, *Object Love and Reality,* 39.

46. Ogden, "Internal Object Relations," 232. On 234: "there is an attempt to make the recipient's experience congruent with the way in which the internal object (aspect of the ego) *experiences itself* and perceives the self-component of the internal relationship." For a textual example see *OC,* 2:165, where Hortensia "dead" in the piano-casket is associated with Horacio's fear of death. Fear of death is expressed in context of the self/body duality on 3:194.

47. The quoted word is from Bion in Ogden, "Internal Object Relations," 232.

48. Jorge Luis Borges, *Ficciones* (Madrid: Alianza; Buenos Aires: Emecé Editores, 1982), 14. Translation from *Ficciones,* ed. Anthony Kerrigan (New York: Grove Press, 1962), 17.

49. Jean Pierrot, *The Decadent Imagination, 1880–1900* (Chicago: University of Chicago Press, 1981), 212.

50. See also Reyes, in Ricardo Pallares and Reina Reyes, *¿Otro Felisberto?* (Montevideo: Editorial Imago, 1983), 27, where a paraphrase of Hernández's discussion of this point is included. Cf. *OC,* 3:86, 3:88, where the ritual's similarity to a wake is denied, underscoring the fear of death that it dramatizes. Margarita's ritual says *wake,* while her discourse of denial facilitates the wake's repetition.

51. Goldberg, *Mirror and Man,* 5.

52. Siebers, *Mirror of Medusa,* 57–58.

53. The second passage is quoted in Alan Dundes, "Wet and Dry, the Evil Eye," in *The Evil Eye: A Folklore Casebook,* ed. Alan Dundes (New York: Garland Publishing, 1981), 269.

54. Horacio's privileged Hortensia doll "could also transmit omens and receive messages from other dolls" (*OC,* 2:145). See also 2:146, where Horacio sends ideas to María

and where Horacio fears "transmittal" of María's illness to him through her cheek. The passage at the bottom of 2:176 and top of 2:177 is also exemplary in this context.

55. This notebook fragment was used, in revised form, in *Lands of Memory* (*OC*, 3:30).

56. Robert Eisler has traced the broken-mirror superstition "back to the Greek Mysteries, specifically as it manifested itself in the association of the mirror of the eye with the window of the soul: 'The eye breaks at death'" (Grabes, *Mutable Glass*, 107).

57. For these last three examples in context of others, see Sir James George Frazer, *The Golden Bough* (New York: Macmillan, 1969), 223.

58. Ibid. For other examples, see Otto Rank, *The Double*, trans. and ed. Harry Tucker Jr. (Chapel Hill: University of North Carolina Press, 1971), 64.

59. The quoted phrase is from Grabes, *Mutable Glass*, 5. See plate 31 (p. 138), plate 32 (p. 140), and plate 38 (p. 157) for fine Etruscan examples.

60. Ibid., 150.

61. Ibid., 151.

62. Litvinskii, "Mirrors," 559.

63. Regarding the Jewish traditions, see Goldberg, *Mirror and Man,* 5–6. Regarding Shakespeare, see Grabes, *Mutable Glass,* 107. On the Greek island of Andros, girls look for the reflection of their future husbands in a mirror held over a well; see Goldberg, *Mirror and Man,* 10.

64. For other examples of covered mirrors in literature, see Rank, *Double,* 6, 9, 15.

65. Frazer, *Golden Bough,* 223. See also Ruth Richardson, *Death, Dissection and the Destitute* (London: Routledge and Kegan Paul), 27.

66. 1 Cor. 13:12. See also the smoky or smoke-screened mirror in "Mur" on *OC,* 3:128–30, 3:134. See also drafts of these passages on 3:170.

67. See Louis-Vincent Thomas, *Antropología de la muerte*, trans. Marcos Lara (Mexico: Fondo de Cultura Económica, 1983), 33.

68. Cf. Ovid's description of Narcissus's death with a melting wax trope. On *OC,* 2:166 Horacio wears yellow gloves. See also 3:185, where the narrator's hands—"confused" with the imagined fragmented hand of someone else—are "the hands of a digger [*cavador*]," the last word carrying a suggestive echo: *cadáver* (cadaver). For other wax examples, see Rank, *Double,* 14. For "life-sized dolls of necromancy" related to "the wax images of witchcraft" see also Ralph Tymms, *Doubles in Literary Psychology* (Cambridge: Bowes and Bowes, 1949), 23.

69. For a tour through the eerie world of wax museums, see Marie-Helene Huet, *Monstrous Imagination* (Cambridge: Harvard University Press, 1993), 188–218. When the protagonist of "The Poisoned Girl" lets his thoughts wander, he too associates the mirror with death; see *OC,* 1:131.

70. The light-bedazzled image recalls a similar scene in "The Usher," in which the protagonist faints upon seeing his glowing eyes reflected in a mirror (*OC,* 2:62). See also 1:93, where the narrator and his Marisa are entombed between a balcony and window-mirrors.

71. The image of confusing reflections on a stairway is also in the draft entitled "The Mirrors"; see *OC,* 2:211.

72. The quoted phrase is from Joseph Beaumont in Grabes, *Mutable Glass,* 105. Note that in the showcase as a surrogate mirror Horacio "hides" in the "confusion" of reflections. Cf. also the remark by Theodore Roethke regarding a woman "who expends herself in mirrors, like a whore." See Jenijoy La Belle, *Herself Beheld: The Literature of the Looking Glass* (Ithaca: Cornell University Press, 1988), 73.

73. Michel Foucault, *The Order of Things* (New York: Vintage Books, 1970), 5.

74. On *OC*, 3:109 an old man's eyes are covered with walnut shells; looking through the tiny holes in them "adjusted his point of view and corrected I don't know what defect."

75. See Pierrot, *Decadent Imagination*, 210.

76. A similar trope regarding the courtesy of inclined mirrors is on *OC*, 3:164.

77. Cited in Siebers, *Mirror of Medusa*, 57. For additional examples, see 58. See also 68.

78. Eugene S. McCartney, "Praise and Dispraise in Folklore," in Dundes, *Evil Eye*, 19. See Siebers, *Mirror of Medusa*, 82, for other examples. Envy is generally the motivator of the evil eye, and in Giotto's early fourteenth-century virtues and vices frescoes (Arena Capella, Padua) self-fascination is suggested as Envy is a demonic hag with a snake curling out of her mouth and hissing into her own eyes.

79. McCartney, "Praise and Dispraise in Folklore," 19.

80. Elizabeth A. Waites, "Fixing Women: Devaluation, Idealization, and the Female Fetish," *Journal of the American Psychoanalytic Association* 30, no. 2 (1982): 442.

81. From Cocteau's *Orphée*, cited in Goldberg, *Mirror and Man*, 243.

82. Grabes, *Mutable Glass*, 156. For examples see plate 45 (p. 191) and plate 21 (p. 106).

83. All passages regarding this female patient are from Gustav Bychowski, "Disorders in the Body-Image in the Clinical Pictures of Psychoses," *Journal of Nervous and Mental Disease* 97 (1943): 320. Cf. *OC*, 1:199, "a new toy like the one I would be."

84. Bychowski, "Disorders," 322. For a similar example of a narcissist for whom people and situations "had a bizarre, almost lifeless quality," see Otto F. Kernberg, *Object-Relations Theory and Clinical Psychoanalysis* (New York: Jason Aronson, 1976), 165.

85. Winnicott, *Playing and Reality*, 111.

86. Ibid., 111–12.

87. See Paula Elkisch, "The Psychological Significance of the Mirror," *Journal of the American Psychological Association* 5 (1957): 241 n. 9. For examples of the eye as reflector, see *OC*, 1:54–55, 2:86, 3:16, 3:29. For discussion of the eye as mirror, see Grabes, *Mutable Glass*, 83–85.

88. Winnicott, *Playing and Reality*, 112.

89. Malcolm Pines, "Mirroring and Child Development," *Psychoanalytic Inquiry* 5, no. 2 (1985): 216.

90. S. J. Pawlby, quoted in ibid., 215.

91. Ibid.

92. Winnicott, *Playing and Reality*, 114.

93. See also *OC*, 2:106, where the character Muñeca is described as though through a distorting mirror.

94. Cf. *OC*, 3:180, where lips are also compared to intestines.

95. Both quoted passages are from Sylvester, *Brutality of Fact*, 40.

96. Winnicott, *Playing and Reality*, 112–13.

97. D. E. Scharff quoted in Pines, "Mirroring and Child Development," 220.

98. See Hamilton, *Narcissus and Oedipus*, 62.

99. Metz, *Imaginary Signifier*, 4.

100. Winnicott, *Playing and Reality*, 114.

101. La Belle, *Herself Beheld*, 80.

102. James Joyce, *A Portrait of the Artist as a Young Man* (New York: Viking Press, 1964), 71.

103. The quoted phrase is from Beatrice Priel, "On Mirror-Image Anxiety," *Journal of Genetic Psychology* 151 (December 1990): 191. Insofar as the screen and the mirror can be

related, Hernández's preferred angle of perspective in movie theaters ("In addition to being in the front, I like to sit alone and a little to the left") (*OC*, 2:206) could be interpreted metaphorically as a gesture to view the self in the mirror without seeing mother, to view mother voyeuristically without seeing oneself (doing so), or to view oneself without being seen by the mother.

104.   J. Grimm, cited by A. E. Crawley in *Encyclopaedia of Religion and Ethics* (1912), s.v. "Doubles."

105.   Infants begin reacting to mirrors at eighteen weeks, and over 60 percent of them try to look at the back of a small mirror to find the "other." See Pines, "Mirroring and Child Development," 211.

106.   Maurice Merleau-Ponty, *The Primacy of Perception*, ed. James M. Edie (Evanston, Ill.: Northwestern University Press, 1964), 127–28. Merleau-Ponty is following Henri Wallon's argument.

107.   Ibid., 129. Between eighteen months and two years "the child can identify his mirror image by his proper name; e.g., answers 'Johnnie' to the question 'Who is that you see in the mirror?' whereas when asked who he himself is, he is unable to use his own name and replies, 'Me'" (Pines, "Mirroring and Child Development," 225).

108.   Priel, "On Mirror-Image Anxiety," 190.

109.   The quoted phrase is from *Roland Barthes by Roland Barthes*, trans. Richard Howard (New York: Hill and Wang, 1977), 153.

110.   Goldberg, *Mirror and Man,* 10.

111.   Ibid., 19.

112.   The examples are from Grabes, *Mutable Glass,* 125–30.

113.   The examples are from Litvinskii, "Mirrors," 559.

114.   Note that Horacio's extramarital "affairs" in the rented Las Acacias house are finally revealed through a link with a mother-imago capable of "seeing" him even where he hides. See *OC,* 2:178.

115.   The Shelley incident is cited in John Todd and Kenneth Dewhurst, "The Double: Its Psycho-Pathology and Psycho-Physiology," *Journal of Nervous and Mental Disease* 12 (1955): 51. For examples from Georges Bataille, see *The Story of the Eye* (London: Penguin Modern Classics), 54, 66. In some traditions there is a direct causal relation between returning to the mother's breast after weaning and having the evil eye. (See Howard F. Stein, "Envy and the Evil Eye Among Slovak-Americans: An Essay in the Psychological Ontogeny of Belief and Ritual" in Dundes, *Evil Eye,* esp. 228–32. See also Dundes, "Wet and Dry," 277–78.) In India, for example, an invisible spirit, a double, is born with each child. If the mother does not keep one breast tied for forty days (to starve the double) while she feeds the child with the other, then this child will grow up with the evil eye (ibid., 270–71). See also Marija Gimbutas, *The Language of the Goddess* (San Francisco: Harper & Row, 1989), 51, where a relation is established between the eyes and breasts of goddesses.

116.   See Ernesto Sábato, *Sobre héroes y tumbas* (Barcelona: Seix Barral, 1981), 436–40.

117.   See Ernesto Sábato, *Abaddón: el exterminador* (Barcelona: Seix Barral, 1982), 419–20.

118.   A patient prone to autoscopic images similarly remarked, "I knew that I was alone, yet suddenly I felt surrounded by hordes of people." See Todd and Dewhurst, "The Double," 52.

119.   See also *OC,* 3:169, where the dead father hears from his grave.

120.   For further discussion of this scene, see Roberto Echavarren, *El espacio de la verdad* (Buenos Aires: Editorial Sudamericana, 1981), 75–79. Cf. *OC,* 2:105, where under separate circumstances the mirrors themselves (rather than the eyes) are lowered.

121. The quoted phrases are from M. Masud R. Khan, *Alienation in Perversions* (New York: International Universities Press, 1979), 22.

122. Tzvetan Todorov, *Mikhail Bakhtin: The Dialogical Principle*, trans. Wlad Godzich (Minneapolis: University of Minnesota Press, 1981), 96.

123. Quoted in Todd and Dewhurst, "The Double," 49.

124. Karl Jaspers, cited in Clive S. Mellor, "Depersonalisation and Self Perception," *British Journal of Psychiatry* 153 (1988): 16 (supp. 2).

125. The quoted phrases in this and the previous sentences are from an unpublished letter sent by Hernández to Amalia Nieto from Treinta y Tres on 5 May 1941.

126. From an unpublished letter sent by Hernández to Amalia Nieto from Treinta y Tres on 20 October 1941. In earlier letters, and again later in this one, Hernández expresses his need for social withdrawal until he can "wake up."

127. The quoted phrase was related to me by Hernández's friend Jorge Sclavo in August 1991.

128. From an unpublished letter sent by Hernández to Amalia Nieto from Treinta y Tres on 9 May 1941.

129. From an unpublished letter sent by Hernández to Amalia Nieto from Las Flores on 21 August 1940.

130. From an unpublished letter sent by Hernández to Amalia Nieto from provincial Uruguay in April 1936.

131. Horacio sees his signed name as though it were on "a check without funds" (*OC*, 2:158).

132. The quoted passage is from Fredric Jameson, "The Politics of Theory: Ideological Positions in the Post-Modern Debate," *New German Critique* 33, p. 63.

133. From the letter to Nieto, April 1936.

134. Norah Giraldi Dei Cas and Frank Graziano, interview with María Isabel ("Mabel") Hernández Guerra, April 1993.

135. Rank, *Double*, 77.

136. Donald Moss, "Brain, Body and World: Perspectives on Body-Image," in *Existential-Phenomenological Alternatives for Psychology*, ed. Ronald S. Valle and Mark King (New York: Oxford University Press, 1978), 87–88.

137. From the letter to Nieto, 9 May 1941. The comment is made by Hernández in regard to his having to continually report bad news to Amalia Nieto about his career and financial difficulties, but it more generally speaks to the "confessional" dimension of Hernández's writing.

138. See also *OC*, 2:125.

139. One patient's imaginary childhood playmate took on definitive personality attributes and was titled the "Advisor." See James S. Grotstein, "Autoscopy: The Experience of Oneself as a Double," *Hillside Journal of Clinical Psychology* 5, no. 2 (1983): 284.

140. The Whitman phrase is quoted in Robert Rogers, *The Double in Literature* (Detroit, Mich.: Wayne State University Press, 1970), 2.

141. See Bychowski, "Disorders," 331, and Tymms, *Doubles in Literary Psychology*, 26.

142. See also *OC*, 3:193 and the related experience described by Rank in *The Double*, 39.

143. The examples in the text are from Todd and Dewhurst, "The Double," 48–51.

144. Paul Schilder, cited in Mellor, "Depersonalization," 15. See also Ogden, "Internal Object Relations," 231, where they are "'going through the motions,' detached, mechanical, and lacking spontaneity."

145. The first passage is quoted in Brian Ackner, "Depersonalization II: Clinical Syndromes," *Journal of Mental Science* 100 (1954): 867, 868. Ackner notes that this type of patient "feels like an automaton, with no personality, whose body feels dead and unresponsive, or for whom the outside world appears strangely flat and still" (855). The other passages quoted in this sentence are from Paul Schilder, *The Image and Appearance of the Human Body* (New York: International Universities Press, 1970), 159.

146. The quoted passage is from a patient in Lara H. Maack and Paul E. Mullen, "Doppelganger, Disintegration and Death: A Case Report," *Psychological Medicine* 13 (1983): 652.

147. Grotstein, "Autoscopy," 288.

148. W. J. K. Cumming, "The Neurobiology of the Body Schema," *British Journal of Psychiatry* 153 (1988): 7 and 10 (supp. 2), respectively. See also Bychowski, "Disorders," 314.

149. Bychowski, "Disorders," 321.

150. Ibid., 322.

151. Ackner, "Depersonalization II," 870. See also 871: "The top part of my head often seems to disappear."

152. Schilder, *Image and Appearance of the Human Body*, 139.

153. All passages are from ibid., 159. On 160 a patient "is always afraid that somebody will step on her limbs."

154. Todd and Dewhurst, "The Double," 54. Another patient mentioned on the same page would repeatedly look into a mirror to assure herself that she was indeed present. In Ackner, a patient remarks, "Sometimes I lie in bed and feel so unreal that I move just to see if I am" ("Depersonalization II," 866).

155. Quoted in Ackner, "Depersonalization II," 871.

156. Todd and Dewhurst, "The Double," 50. See also Victor Tausk, "On the Origin of the 'Influencing Machine' in Schizophrenia," in *Essential Papers on Psychosis*, ed. Peter Buckley (New York: New York University, 1988), where the "influencing machine" "has the form of a human body, indeed, the patient's own form" (56).

157. The quoted passages are in Thomas Freeman, "Narcissism and Defensive Processes in Schizophrenic States," in Buckley, *Essential Papers*, 82.

158. For similar examples, see *OC*, 2:131, 3:204.

159. See also *OC*, 3:69, 3:104.

160. On *OC*, 3:112 a soldier in uniform and then out of it seems "a double."

161. Rank, *Double*, 86.

162. Crawley, "Doubles," 856.

163. Rank, *Double*, 86 and 6–7, respectively.

164. Ibid., 7.

165. Sigmund Freud, "On the Universal Tendency to Debasement in the Sphere of Love," in *Standard Edition*, ed. James Strachey, vol. 11 (London: Hogarth Press, 1957), 179.

166. Simultaneous death of the self and wayward shadow or reflection is a common theme in the literature of the double. Classic examples include Edgar Allan Poe's *William Wilson* and Robert Louis Stevenson's *The Strange Case of Dr. Jekyll and Mr. Hyde*.

167. Paul Coates, *The Double and the Other: Identity as Ideology in Post-Romantic Fiction* (New York: St. Martin's Press, 1988), 1 and 2, respectively.

168. The quoted phrase is in J. M. R. Damas Mora et al., "On Heautoscopy or the Phenomenon of the Double: Case Presentation and Review of the Literature," *British Journal of Medical Psychology* 53 (1980): 77.

169. The quoted passage is from Rosemary Jackson, "Narcissism and Beyond: A

Psychoanalytical Reading of *Frankenstein* and Fantasies of the Double," in *Aspects of Fantasy,* ed. William Coyle (Westport, Conn.: Greenwood Press, 1981), 47.

170. Khan, *Alienation in Perversions,* 16.

171. See Grotstein, "Autoscopy," 260–61.

172. See James H. Matinband and Charles E. Passage, trans., *Amphitryon: Three Plays in New Verse Translations* (Chapel Hill: University of North Carolina Press, 1974), 27–110. For a summary of various literary adaptations of the Amphitryon theme, see Tymms, *Doubles in Literary Psychology,* 20–21.

173. Gutierre Tibón, *Diccionario de nombres propios* (Mexico: Editorial Fournier, 1956), 261.

174. Bychowski, "Disorders," 328–29. On 331 van Bogaert is quoted: "The phantom image is nothing else but a projection of the person's own body." One of Hernández's grandsons suffers from schizophrenia, and his symptoms include imaginary companions. One of these is an evil figure named Peter with whom he converses, and another a European girlfriend for whom he lavishly buys gifts.

175. The quoted passages are from Annemarie de Waal Malefijt, *Images of Man: A History of Anthropological Thought* (New York: Alfred A. Knopf, 1974), 4.

176. Jackson, "Narcissism and Beyond," 46.

177. Michael Clark, summarizing Jane Gallop in his *Jacques Lacan: An Annotated Bibliography,* vol. 2 (New York: Garland Publishing, 1988), 283. For discussion of the point, see Jane Gallop, *Reading Lacan* (Ithaca: Cornell University Press, 1985), 79–86. "The image of the body in bits and pieces is fabricated retroactively from the mirror stage" (86).

178. The quoted passages in this and the previous sentence are from Jacques Lacan, *Ecrits,* trans. Alan Sheridan (New York: W. W. Norton, 1977), 4.

179. Ibid.

180. Anthony Elliott, *Social Theory and Psychoanalysis in Transition: Self and Society from Freud to Kristeva* (Oxford: Blackwell, 1992), 128.

181. Lacan, *Ecrits,* 2.

182. Elliott, *Social Theory and Psychoanalysis,* 128.

183. The quoted phrase is from Jacques Lacan, *The Seminar of Jacques Lacan, Book II,* ed. Jacques-Alain Miller, trans. Sylvana Tomaselli (New York: W. W. Norton, 1991), 54.

184. The quoted passages in this sentence and the previous one are from ibid., 50 and 54, respectively.

185. Bychowski, "Disorders," 318.

186. All quotations in this paragraph are from Lacan, *Seminar II,* 166.

187. See Clark, *Lacan Bibliography,* 34. Gilles Deleuze worded it aptly: "Each of us is a group." See Michel Foucault, *Microfísica del poder* (Madrid: Las Ediciones de la Piqueta, 1980), 78. Multiplication is common in the literature of the double; for an example, see Rank, *Double,* 6.

188. Harold F. Searles, "Sources of Anxiety in Paranoid Schizophrenia," in Buckley, *Essential Papers,* 100. On the same page another woman remarks, "These people are in my bowels and in my stomach and in my heart!"

189. Tymms, *Doubles in Literary Psychology,* 33.

190. Lacan, *Seminar II,* 169.

191. The quoted passage is from J. Hillis Miller, *Versions of Pygmalion* (Cambridge: Cambridge University Press, 1990), 234.

192. Rogers, *Double in Literature,* 2.

193. Miller, *Versions of Pygmalion,* 222. The definition given parenthetically in the

previous sentence is from ibid., 4. The endurance of Horacio-type erotic attraction to the nexus of fragmentation and voyeurism is suggested, for example, by a man who "Likes to watch X-rated cable TV movies without paying the $3 to have them unscrambled. 'When they're scrambled like that, you see bits and pieces. Sometimes you can't even tell if they're male or female. It's like peeking through somebody's window.'" See Fred Tasker, "A Serious and Semi-Serious Look at Sex Fantasies." *Miami Herald,* 19 July 1995, 2E.

194. Bychowski, "Disorders," 318. Another psychiatric patient often felt something lying on her arm: "When she looked to see what it was, she would observe an extra arm and hand lying on top of the real one." Todd and Dewhurst, "The Double," 54.

195. Clark (summarizing Lacan), *Lacan Bibliography,* 141.

196. The quoted passage is from Francisco Lasarte, *Felisberto Hernández y la escritura de "lo otro"* (Madrid: Insula, 1981), 162.

197. This case is described in Rank, *Double,* 73 n. 8.

198. As paraphrased by Lacan in *Ecrits,* 138.

199. Edward Peter Nolan, *Now Through a Glass Darkly: Specular Images of Being and Knowing from Virgil to Chaucer* (Ann Arbor: University of Michigan Press, 1990), 292.

200. Ibid., 292 and 293, respectively.

201. The quoted passage is from Giraldi Dei Cas and Graziano, interview with Hernández Guerra.

202. Todd and Dewhurst, "The Double," 53.

203. For other examples see *OC,* 3:25, 3:57, 3:94, 3:109, 3:185. The first quoted passages is from Bychowski, "Disorders," 317.

204. The quoted phrase is from Todd and Dewhurst, "The Double," 49.

205. "Frankenstein's monster is a fantastic example of the idea of '*le corps morcelé,*' the body-in-pieces, for it is actually made up of dismembered, disjointed bodies, not one but many." Jackson, "Narcissism and Beyond," 49.

206. In *The Lost Horse* Celina is also described in a black-and-white contrast. Note that *araña* means spider, recalling the showcase-scene doll with multiple legs.

207. See the similar arm imagery on *OC,* 2:202, and the arm-related discussion on 3:54–55.

208. "This phenomenon was exploited to illustrate the doctrine of transubstantiation: just as the fragments of a broken mirror each furnish a complete image of an object, Christ is wholly present in each fragment of broken bread (the Host). . . . " Grabes, *Mutable Glass,* 107. See *OC,* 1:26 for reflections off a broken bottle's fragments.

209. In this and the previous sentence I am following Lisa Block de Behar, *Una retórica del silencio* (Mexico: Siglo Veintiuno Editores, 1984), 159–60.

210. Metz, *Imaginary Signifier,* 4. Cinema "is a new kind of mirror" (45).

211. The quotations are from Eco, *Semiotics,* 222, 224, and 216, respectively.

212. Metz, *Imaginary Signifier,* 45–46. See also 48–49.

213. Regarding the machine noises, the schizophrenic's "influencing machine" counts among its forms the cinematograph that "makes the patients see pictures." See Tausk, "Origin of the Influencing Machine," 50.

214. Metz, *Imaginary Signifier,* 75.

215. Vinge, *Narcissus Theme,* 17.

216. Kernberg, *Object-Relations Theory,* 192–93. Another patient had the sensation that "some physical change had taken place in his forehead, as if a Chinese wall separating him from the world had toppled"; Bychowski, "Disorders," 322.

217. Coates, *Double and the Other,* 194.

CHAPTER 3. THE TACTILITY OF SIGHT

1. Plato, *Timaeus*, edited, translated, and with an introduction by John Warrington (London: Dent; New York: Dutton, 1965), 44.

2. A separate tradition rejected the light-emission theory, arguing instead for intromission of rays emitted by objects. For a useful historical overview, see David C. Lindberg, *Theories of Vision From Al-Kindi to Kepler* (Chicago: University of Chicago Press, 1976). The Theophrastus passage is cited on 4.

3. See Herbert Grabes, *The Mutable Glass: Mirror-Imagery in Titles and Texts of the Middle Ages and English Renaissance*, trans. Gordon Collier (Cambridge: Cambridge University Press, 1982), 136. The Yeats phrase was extracted from the same book's epigraph. See also Eric Alliez and Michel Feher, "Reflections of a Soul," in *Fragments for a History of the Human Body*, ed. Michel Feher et al., pt. 2 (New York: Zone, 1989), 64, where the subject "turns not simply away from this dark mirror but right around and converts itself to the source of light from which it proceeds and which it now discovers deep inside itself."

4. Also suggested are refined perceptive capabilities as punishment for narcissism (see *OC*, 1:79–84 for explicit treatment) and a reaction formation masquerading the eye light as emblem of grandeur when it ultimately represents inferiority (see 1:37, where an embarrassed face lights up and "a very strong light" emits from it).

5. See, for example, Gen. 19:26 and the suggestive Lev. 18 prohibitions against viewing the nakedness of family members.

6. For bibliography on eye imagery in dreams, see Sigmund Freud, *The Interpretation of Dreams*, in *Standard Edition*, ed. James Strachey, vol. 5 (London: Hogarth Press, 1958), 398.

7. Otto. F. Kernberg, *Object-Relations Theory and Clinical Psychoanalysis* (New York: Jacob Aronson, 1976), 187.

8. Robert J. Stoller, *Perversion: The Erotic Form of Hatred* (New York: Dell, 1975), 96. On 116 "sexual boredom" is described as the loss of a sense of risk in lovemaking.

9. For discussion see Alexandre Kojève, *Introduction to the Reading of Hegel*, trans. James H. Nichols Jr. (New York: Basic Books, 1969). René Girard, in *Violence and the Sacred*, trans. Patrick Gregory (Baltimore: Johns Hopkins University Press, 1977), demonstrates how *"the subject desires the object because the rival desires it"* (145). Serge Viderman pursues this line of thought—"that the object of desire is desired only because it is the object of desire of the other" (195)—in "The Subject-Object Relation and the Problem of Desire," in *Psychoanalysis in France*, ed. Serge Lebovici and Daniel Widlöcher (New York: International Universities Press, 1980).

10. J. L. Rubins, cited in R. Spencer Smith, "Voyeurism: A Review of Literature," *Archives of Sexual Behavior* 5, no. 6 (1976): 597.

11. Christian Metz, *The Imaginary Signifier: Psychoanalysis and the Cinema*, trans. Celia Britton et al. (Bloomington: Indiana University Press, 1977), 60. Note that voyeurs say "The major and most consistent quality" of their parents is "emotional distance." See Smith, "Voyeurism," 591.

12. The second quoted phrase is from B. Karpman, cited in Smith, "Voyeurism," 594.

13. The quoted phrase is from Grabes, *Mutable Glass*, 85.

14. Robert J. Stoller, "Hostility and Mystery in Perversion," *International Journal of Psycho-Analysis* 55 (1974): 430.

15. Irvin D. Yalom, "Aggression and Forbiddenness in Voyeurism," *Archives of General Psychiatry* 3 (1960): 316.

16. The quoted passage is from ibid., 310. Another voyeur remarked that the ritual

"has to be clandestine—she must be a stranger and she mustn't see me watching" (314). Erotic pleasure in clinical cases as much as for Hernández characters "seems to increase when the voyeur observes without detection" (317).

17. Ibid., 312.

18. The quoted passage is from William Shakespeare, *Richard III* 1.4.31.

19. Cf. the empty eyes on *OC,* 2:41, refilled on 2:42.

20. On another occasion the heart exits through the eyes; see *OC,* 3:35.

21. Cf. *OC,* 2:167, where the reading of poetry is compared to a peek through a partially opened door.

22. From a letter by Hernández to Paulina Medeiros in her *Felisberto y yo* (Montevideo: Libros del Astillero, 1982), 40.

23. Yalom, "Aggression," 310.

24. The quoted phrase is from Julia Kristeva, *Tales of Love,* trans. Leon S. Roudiez (New York: Columbia University Press, 1987), 349.

25. The quoted passage is from Yalom, "Aggression," 309. See also 318.

26. The quoted phrase is from John Money, "Paraphilias: Phenomenology and Classification," *American Journal of Psychotherapy* 38, no. 2 (April 1984): 175.

27. The quoted phrases are from Jonathan Z. Smith, *Imagining Religion: From Babylon to Jonestown* (Chicago: University of Chicago Press, 1982), 54.

28. Grimm's dictionary and Schelling, respectively, quoted in Sigmund Freud, "The Uncanny," in *Standard Edition,* ed. James Strachey, vol. 17 (London: Hogarth Press, 1955), 225 and 224, respectively.

29. See also the draft of this text on *OC,* 2:197. The *ars poetica* statement on 1:125 is also interesting in this context.

30. For additional examples see *OC,* 1:97, 1:110, 1:118, 3:28, 3:44, 3:47.

31. Otto Fenichel, *The Psychoanalytic Theory of Neurosis* (New York: W. W. Norton, 1945), 491. The link between gluttony and "voracious looking" is particularly resonant when one recalls that Hernández was obese in his later years. The figurative eating of light is mentioned in "Lucrecia" (*OC,* 3:108).

32. The phrase "the lust of seeing" is also found in an expanded version in *Clemente Colling* (*OC,* 2:43).

33. Hermann von Helmholtz, cited in "Perception as Hypotheses," in *The Oxford Companion to the Mind,* ed. Richard L. Gregory (New York: Oxford University Press, 1987), 608.

34. André Green, *On Private Madness* (Madison, Conn.: International Universities Press, 1986), 96.

35. The quoted phrase is from artist Josef Albers, cited in Stanley Rosner and Elisa Rosner, "The Eye and the Camera: A Psychoanalytical Note," *Dynamic Psychotherapy* 3, no. 2 (Winter 1985): 183. Metz remarked, "I must perceive the photographed object as absent, its photograph as present, and the presence of this absence as signifying" (*Imaginary Signifier,* 57).

36. Quoted passages are from Yalom, "Aggression," 314, 315. Referring to one of these cases, Yalom notes: "About one-fourth of the evenings he went out he only peeped; one-half of the evenings he burglarized; and one-fourth of the time he did both" (315).

37. See *OC,* 2:25, where recollection is compared to watching a film. Note the play on *acomodar* in that passage and on 3:53.

38. The quoted phrase is from Metz, *Imaginary Signifier,* 65.

39. Ibid., 66.

40. See also *OC,* 2:137.

41. Metz, *Imaginary Signifier,* 49.

42. Ibid., 63.

43. Ibid., 49.

44. Ibid., 50–51.

45. The quoted phrase is from Rev. 1:14. The same phrase is repeated in Rev. 2:18, 19:12.

46. For a discussion see Yi-Fu Tuan, *Space and Place: The Perspective of Experience* (Minneapolis: University of Minnesota, 1977), 41.

47. For another robbed vision, see *OC,* 3:75.

48. Quoted phrase is from Green, *On Private Madness,* 95.

49. In a letter to Paulina Medeiros, Hernández describes how passion is undone if the absent lover reappears. See Medeiros, *Felisberto y yo,* 91.

50. Cf. *OC,* 2:205, where the narrator's shoes shine in the light of a movie usher's flashlight.

51. See also *OC,* 1:126, 1:159, 2:119–20, 3:106, 3:138, 3:74. Note that the Spanish expression for having nothing to do with someone or something is *nada que ver,* literally "nothing to see."

52. See also *OC,* 1:158, where the superiority is reaffirmed, and 1:131, where the writer is "one more human thing in the heap." Other examples are on 2:96, and in the circumstances around the phrase "poor pianist" on 2:115. On 3:41 a causal relation is established between being a failure (playing the piano poorly) and intrusion into other peoples' privacy.

53. The ambiguity of this inflated sense of self-importance is particularly resonant in an autobiographical reading. When in financial desperation Hernández toured grim provincial theaters or offered his subordinate courtesy working demeaning bureaucratic jobs, he no doubt had to remind himself constantly of the unrecognized qualities that he believed himself to hold in reserve. In one job Hernández's supervisors recognized his insubordinate air of superiority; in response they assigned him the most demeaning tasks (including sending him out to buy their cigarettes) "to tame his pride." See Tomas Eloy Martínez, "Para que nadie olvide a Felisberto Hernández," *La opinión cultural,* 31 March 1974, 6.

54. See also *OC,* 2:61, 2:62, 2:63, 2:69.

55. See, for example, Money, "Paraphilias," 174, and Yalom, "Aggression," 312.

56. Yalom, "Aggression," 312. Shortly after he yelled to one of his peep victims, "My, you have big breasts" and barely escaped capture by the police (312).

57. Rosner and Rosner, "The Eye and the Camera," 184. For discussion of these themes as they relate to other literary works, see Beth Newman, "'The Situation of the Looker-on': Gender, Narration, and Gaze in *Wuthering Heights,*" *PMLA* 105 (October 1990): 1034.

58. In "Except Julia," Alejandro is subordinated by a similar eye aversion (*OC,* 2:73).

59. This and the quoted passage in the previous sentence are from D. W. Winnicott, *Playing and Reality* (London: Tavistock Publications, 1971), 114. When these dynamics are applied to Hernández as author rather than to his characters, one can note with Peter Brooks that "Seduction appears as a predominant motive" for the writing of fiction, "be it specifically erotic and oriented toward the capture of the other, or more nearly narcissistic, even exhibitionistic, asking for admiration and attention." See Peter Brooks, *Reading for the Plot: Design and Intention in Narrative* (New York: Vintage Books, 1984), 236.

60. François Hartog, *The Mirror of Herodotus: The Representation of the Other in the Writing of History,* trans. Janet Lloyd (Berkeley: University of California Press, 1988), 268.

Hartog clarifies this: "The point is, precisely, that to have had a vision is not to have seen." For seems/is ambiguity as a fundamental characteristic of fantastic literature, see Tzvetan Todorov, *Introducción a la literatura fantástica* (Buenos Aires: Editorial Tiempo Contemporaneo, 1972), 44, 56, 101, for example.

61. For Plotinus, the work of art is "the reflection of a luminous source rather than a copy of an ideal model." See Alliez and Feher, "Reflections of a Soul," 73, 75. See also Balzac's *Sarrasine* and Roland Barthes's discussion of it in the latter's *S/Z* (New York: Hill and Wang, 1974), esp. 238, where "This was more than a woman, this was a masterpiece!" (discussion on 114), and 239, where the mistress is "sketched in every pose."

62. See *OC*, 1:113 for the candlelight on another girl's face. See also 1:165 for a similar image. In "Except Julia," the girls along the wall flash lights to call the tunnel owner (2:81, 2:84).

63. Yalom, "Aggression," 306. Metz notes, "the point is to gamble simultaneously on the excitement of desire and its non-fulfillment" (*Imaginary Signifier,* 77).

64. For other instances concerning the *pollera*, see *OC*, 3:16, 3:79, 3:92, 3:93, 3:101, 3:154. Lucrecia and her dress are melded to a chair on 3:110. In the chapters deleted from *The Hortensias,* "some white tablecloths covered some round tables with iron legs," and the result is compared to "skinny black girls in *polleras.*" Manuscript of *The Hortensias,* collection of Ana María Hernández de Elena, page numbered 2 (also numbered 32).

65. Sigmund Freud, "Notes Upon a Case of Obsessional Neurosis," in *Standard Edition,* ed. James Strachey, vol. 10 (London: Hogarth Press, 1955), 160. The quoted words are the Rat Man's.

66. Freud, *Dreams,* 355. See also the desperate climb up stairs to the *paraíso* on *OC,* 3:9.

67. See also *OC,* 3:74, 3:89. The eroticization of piano playing includes additional *cola* puns, including *piano de cola* (grand piano) and *cola del frac* (tuxedo tail).

68. Yalom, "Aggression," 318.

69. Stoller, "Hostility and Mystery," 431. See also 429.

70. From an unpublished letter sent by Hernández to Amalia Nieto from Paysandú on 23 June 1936. See *OC,* 2:203.

71. Sigmund Freud, "A Special Type of Object-Choice," in *Standard Edition,* ed. James Strachey, vol. 11 (London: Hogarth Press, 1957), 174.

72. Marie-Henri Beyle [Stendhal, pseud.], *The Life of Henry Brulard,* trans. Catherine A. Phillips (London, 1925), 27–28. For discussion, see Gérard Genette, *Figures of Literary Discourse,* trans. Alan Sheridan (New York: Columbia University Press, 1982), 149. In Hernández's "Ursula" a similar low-bed perspective is registered, with the narrator visited by a woman loaded with mother attributes. See *OC,* 3:121.

73. The quoted phrase is from Green, *On Private Madness,* 256.

74. This dream text was extracted from a text published posthumously, "My First Concert in Montevideo." See *OC,* 2:201.

75. The usher as cuckold *(cornudo)* is further suggested in the text by a play between *cornudo* and *cornetazo;* see *OC,* 2:68. For a similar *cornetazo,* see 2:175.

76. See Richard C. Coss, "Reflections on the Evil Eye," in *The Evil Eye: A Folklore Casebook,* ed. Alan Dundes (New York: Garland Publishing, 1981), 182. For a multicultural overview of the evil eye, see Clarence Maloney, ed., *The Evil Eye* (New York: Columbia University Press, 1976). For a useful study of the evil eye in a Latin American context, see Richard N. Adams, *Un análisis de las creencias y prácticas médicas en un pueblo indígena de Guatemala* (Guatemala: Editorial del Ministerio de Educación Pública, 1952).

77. Alan Dundes, "Wet and Dry, the Evil Eye: An Essay in Indo-European and Semitic Worldview," in Dundes, *Evil Eye,* 258.

78. Ibid., 263.

79. Cited in Armando F. Favazza, *Bodies Under Siege: Self-Mutilation in Culture and Psychiatry* (Baltimore: Johns Hopkins University Press, 1987), 75.

80. For the Scythia example, see Lindberg, *Theories of Vision,* 88. Regarding the Black Death, see Frederick Thomas Elworthy, *The Evil Eye: The Origins and Practices of Superstition,* introduction by Louis S. Barron (New York: Julian Press, 1958), 34. Willa Appel notes that "The evil eye is in some respects like a virus, and the village lies in constant threat of an imminent plague." See her "The Myth of the *Jettatura,*" in Maloney, *Evil Eye,* 17. For several other examples, see Garfield Tourney and Dean J. Plazak, "Evil Eye in Myth and Schizophrenia," *Psychiatric Quarterly* 28 (1954): 478–85.

81. Favazza, *Bodies Under Siege,* 77 and 88, respectively.

82. See Tobin Siebers, *The Mirror of Medusa* (Berkeley: University of California Press, 1983), 33.

83. Gerald Mast, *A Short History of the Movies* (New York: Macmillan, 1986), 13.

84. Appel, "Myth," 24. Examples of the erotic-destructive properties of the eye are plentiful. Tourney and Plazak cite a particularly explicit case: "The natives of the New Hebrides believe the evil eye readily pierces the openings of the body in a destructive fashion, particularly those of the genitalia, and hence men are very careful to keep the penis, and women the vulva, well protected" ("Evil Eye in Myth and Schizophrenia," 484).

85. Stephen Langdon, "An Incantation in the 'House of Light' Against the Evil Eye," in Dundes, *Evil Eye,* 40.

86. Géza Róheim, "The Evil Eye," in Dundes, *Evil Eye,* 218. See also Dundes, "Wet and Dry," 264.

87. Dundes, "Wet and Dry," 265.

88. Ibid., 285.

89. The quoted phrase is from Sandor Ferenczi, cited in Fenichel, *Psychoanalytic Theory of Neurosis,* 227.

90. Dundes, "Wet and Dry," 274.

91. Tourney and Plazak, "Evil Eye in Myth and Schizophrenia," 488.

92. Victor Tausk, "On the Origin of the 'Influencing Machine' in Schizophrenia," in *Essential Papers on Psychosis,* ed. Peter Buckley (New York: New York University, 1988), 50. In male cases it produces "erections and seminal emissions" that are "intended to deprive the patient of his male potency and weaken him" (50).

93. Harold F. Searles, "Sources of Anxiety in Paranoid Schizophrenia," in Buckley, *Essential Papers,* 100.

94. Elworthy, *Evil Eye,* 243.

95. Regarding the hard eye, see Siebers, *Mirror of Medusa,* 33.

96. In this paragraph I am closely following Dundes, "Wet and Dry," 279.

97. The first quoted phrase is from Fenichel, *Psychoanalytic Theory of Neurosis,* 201, and the second from Heliodorus of Emesa (third century B.C.), cited in Tourney and Plazak, "Evil Eye in Myth and Schizophrenia," 480.

98. See *OC,* 2:213 for another hat with ominous qualities.

99. Yalom, "Aggression," 316.

100. Regarding the "black lantern" *(farol negro),* note that in South American figurative usage the eyes are sometimes referred to as *faroles.*

101. See Jonathan P. Rossman and Phillip J. Resnick, "Sexual Attraction to Corpses: A

Psychiatric Review of Necrophilia," *Bulletin of the American Academy of Psychiatry and the Law* 17, no. 2 (1989): 153.

102. Paul Lelliott and Isaac Marks, "Management of Obsessive-Compulsive Rituals Associated with Delusions, Hallucinations and Depression: A Case Report," *Behavioural Psychotherapy* 15, no. 1 (January 1987): 78.

Many voyeurs have demonstrated that their ritual is compensatory: the lust of seeing "steals the spotlight" by displacing genuine sexual relations, but at the same time it provides the peeper with an "auxiliary power" that may help his performance in the marriage bed." See Money, "Paraphilias," 174.

103. Cf. the light and breast image on *OC*, 2:154.

104. It also reads: "I am humiliated; I discover revenge; I humiliate; I have mastered the past." See Robert J. Stoller, "The Term *Perversion*," in *Perversions and Near-Perversions in Clinical Practice*, ed. Gerald I. Fogel and Wayne A. Myers (New Haven: Yale University Press, 1991), 47.

105. Yalom, "Aggression," 316. Another voyeur entered a home quite uncertain of what he was going to do: "I was probably going to choke her into unconsciousness and then disrobe her and probably feel her breasts" (312).

106. Use of the verb *apagar* (to extinguish) earlier in the text is resonant in this context; see *OC*, 2:59.

107. See Carla Gottlieb, *The Window in Art: From the Window of God to the Vanity of Man* (New York: Abaris Books, 1981), 67 .

108. See ibid., 163–65.

109. From the unpublished chapters of *The Hortensias* manuscript, page 11 (also numbered 90), archive of Ana María Hernández de Elena.

110. Kojève, *Introduction to the Reading of Hegel,* 4.

111. Stoller, "Hostility and Mystery," 428.

112. Ibid., 429. Regarding revenge, see also Green, *On Private Madness*, 22. Stoller's extension of separation anxiety into "symbiosis anxiety" is also suggestive in Hernández's case.

113. Stoller, "Hostility and Mystery," 431–32.

114. The first quote is from Thomas N. Wise, following Stoller in "Fetishism—Etiology and Treatment: A Review from Multiple Perspectives," *Comprehensive Psychiatry* 26, no. 3 (May/June 1985): 251. The second quote is from a patient in Yalom, "Aggression," 316.

115. Winnicott, *Playing and Reality,* 90.

116. Both quoted passages are from Fenichel, *Psychoanalytic Theory of Neurosis*, 71.

117. Yalom, "Aggression," 318.

118. Wilfred Bion, cited in Thomas H. Ogden, "The Concept of Internal Object Relations," *International Journal of Psycho-Analysis* 64 (1983): 232.

119. Thomas H. Ogden, "On Potential Space," *International Journal of Psycho-analysis* 66 (1985): 138. See also Ogden, "Internal Object Relations," 232.

120. Montaigne quoted in Favazza, *Bodies Under Siege,* 75.

121. Luis-Vincent Thomas, *El cadáver: de la biología a la antropología*, trans. Juan Damonte (Mexico: Fondo de Cultura Económica, 1989), 30. The next sentence in the text follows the same source.

In the usher's earlier image of the girl's drowning he casts a yellowed moonlight on her (*OC*, 2:60). On his deathbed Hernández feared that his corpse would be discolored (empurpled) and consequently would not be made available to the gaze of mourners.

122. The first two quoted phrases are from Kristeva, *Tales of Love*, 350, and the other is from Siebers, *Mirror of Medusa*, 68. "The image of turning to stone, of genuine physical petrifaction at the hands [or eyes] of another recurs throughout Western literature, and especially in Ovid. We need only turn to the battle scene of Perseus's wedding to Andromeda in Book Five for an example. To combat Phineus and his allies, Perseus unveils the Gorgon's evil eye, creating a gallery of stone figures" (68).

123. Kristeva, *Tales of Love*, 349.

124. The quoted phrase is borrowed from W. R. Bion, who uses it in reference to one of his patients in *Second Thoughts: Selected Papers on Psycho-Analysis* (New York: Jason Aronson, 1977), 17.

125. I am following Roland Barthes, *A Lover's Discourse*, trans. Richard Howard (New York: Hill and Wang, 1978), 71. For Horacio and the usher, the body is "a vitrified figurine in which I could read, without understanding anything about it, *the cause of my desire*" (72).

126. See *OC*, 3:19 where the eyes are also out of control, and 3:177, where the narrator desires blinders like those worn by horses.

127. The first quoted passage is from Deut. 25:12. See also Ezek. 5:11.

128. See Marija Gimbutas, *The Civilization of the Goddess*, ed. Joan Marler (San Francisco: HarperSanFrancisco, 1991), 240; and Marija Gimbutas, *The Language of the Goddess* (San Francisco: Harper & Row, 1989), 209.

129. The fusion of narrator/daughter identities accumulates in traces throughout "The Usher." Dressed in his tailed tuxedo, for example, the usher provides an inverted complement for the daughter in her training negligee (*cola* is used in Spanish for both of the "tails"). The usher, like many of Hernández's characters, also shares with the daughter distinct qualities as a "sleepwalker." Hernández himself provides the model: "I go through life like a sleepwalker." See Ana María Hernández, "Mis recuerdos," *Escritura* 7, nos. 13–14 (1982): 338.

130. Flaubert describing the death of Emma Bovary. For description of the eye after death, see Louis-Vincent Thomas, *Antropología de la muerte* (Mexico: Fondo de Cultura Económica, 1983), 37, and the same author's *El cadáver*, 26.

More broadly, the empty eyes epitomize the blankness of the corpse's face. "When a human being disappears in death, he loses his face at the same instant that he loses his life. The dead, their heads covered with darkness, drowned in shadow, are 'faceless' as they are 'without *menos*.'" See Jean-Pierre Vernant, "Dim Body, Dazzling Body," in Feher et al., *Fragments for a History*, pt. 1, 38.

131. The quoted phrase is from Siebers, *Mirror of Medusa*, 68. Ovid compares Narcissus to "a statue carved from Parian marble."

The Malayan syndrome "Amok"—which, as in "The Usher," mingles homicidal and suicidal violence—is also referred to as *mata gelap*, which means "darkened eye." See Harold I. Kaplan and Benjamin J. Sadock, *Modern Synopsis of Comprehensive Textbook of Psychiatry* (Baltimore: Williams & Wilkins, 1981), 658.

132. Luke 11:34. See also Matt. 6.22–23. The parallels of "The Usher" and Alfred Hitchcock's 1954 film *Rear Window* are striking. Hitchcock's protagonist is an injured, wheelchair-bound photographer who spends his time voyeuristically monitoring the neighborhood from the rear window of his apartment. His fantasies intermingle with the realities that they begin to displace (including the girlfriend), until finally the imagined murder with which the voyeur is obsessed turns out to be an actual one. When the murderer pursues the voyeur himself (now "the man who knew too much"), the latter defends himself with light from flashbulbs on his camera.

CHAPTER 4. THE MATERNAL BODY

1. For additional examples, see *OC,* 3:106–7, 3:157.

2. For additional examples, see *OC,* 1:67, 1:97–98, 1:139, 2:9, 2:110, 2:111, 2:129, 3:20, 3:21, 3:68, 3:97, 3:133.

3. Rubén Darío, "Era un aire suave," in *Antología crítica de la poesía modernista hispanoamericana,* ed. J. O. Jiménez (Madrid: Hiperión, 1985), 183–84. When Eulalia looks, her blue eyes "spill a strange living light."

4. For additional examples, see *OC,* 2:11, 2:31, 2:67, 2:80, 3:31, 3:170.

5. Gaston Bachelard, *The Poetics of Space,* trans. Maria Jolas (New York: Orion Press, 1964), 68.

6. A similar arrangement is found on *OC,* 2:18, where Celina has a closer relation with the boy's piano-playing hands than the boy himself does. See also 3:79.

7. See also *OC,* 1:165, where the speaking narrator did not hear himself but rather "kept hearing what you were saying with your gestures"; and "The Balcony," where the dead mother's presence "lives" in the piano (2:54, for example).

8. The black-and-white clothing is also nunlike. See the similar image in the convent setting of "Lucrecia" (*OC,* 3:105).

For a clinical case in which women, dolls, and furniture are linked, see Francoise Dolto, *La imagen inconsciente del cuerpo* (Barcelona: Paidós, 1984), 238.

9. See also *OC,* 1:109.

10. The first quote is from a letter to Paulina Medeiros in her *Felisberto y yo* (Montevideo: Libros del Astillero, 1982), 49. See also *OC,* 3:38, 3:93.

11. On *OC,* 2:154 Hortensia appears in a tree. For additional vegetation examples see 1:133, 2:41, 2:81, 2:139, 2:184. On 3:195 plant, memory, and cinema images are combined. Note that green was the color that Hernandez found most pleasing. He held this in common with Waclaw Radecki, a psychologist who had significant influence on Hernández.

12. See *OC,* 2:205, where an image combines cow/milk (= mother), cinema, and piano themes. Plant images are common in archetypal maternal imagery. For a woman "like a motionless plant" that bears fruit, for example, see Erich Neumann, *The Great Mother: An Analysis of the Archetype,* trans. Ralph Manheim (Princeton: Princeton University Press, 1963), 129. Elsewhere "The Great Mother Earth who brings forth all life from herself is eminently the mother of all vegetation" (48).

13. When María is upset over the later dolls of *The Hortensias* she bumps into "innocent flowerpots and plants" (*OC,* 2:169).

14. Note that Hernández's grandfather was a gardener.

15. Janine Chasseguet-Smirgel, *Sexuality and Mind: The Role of the Father and the Mother in the Psyche* (New York: New York University Press, 1986), 139.

16. According to one of his friends, Hernández at least once ejaculated while writing. He was on a bus at the time, overtaken by the coincidence of his creative excitement and the rhythmic rocking that moved him down the road. Whether the story is fact or folklore is unimportant; the poetics obtain. As Balzac is reputed to have remarked after intercourse, "There goes another novel."

17. *Porrón* as an adjective means slow or stupid, thereby carrying another quality of the mindless dolls and the devalued female.

18. All passages quoted from the Pygmalion tale are from Ovid, *Metamorphoses,* trans. Mary M. Innes (New York: Penguin Books, 1955), 231–32.

19. The quoted passage is from John Berger et al., *Ways of Seeing* (London: Penguin Books, 1972), 62. One is reminded of the toy "Mr. Potatohead," which affords the same luxury.

20. G. Karl Galinsky, *Ovid's* Metamorphoses (Berkeley: University of California Press, 1975), 87.

21. See Françoise Héritier-Augé, "Older Women, Stout-Hearted Women, Women of Substance," in *Fragments for a History of the Human Body*, ed. Michel Feher et al., pt. 3 (New York: Zone, 1989), 290, where men are dry and hot, women are wet, and "the male's sperm permeates the woman's organism, vivifies all of its functions and *heats* them up."

22. All quoted passages concerning the *Tristrams saga* are from Paul Schach, trans., *The Saga of Tristram and Isönd*, introduced by Paul Schach (Lincoln: University of Nebraska Press, 1973), 120–30. I am very grateful to Professor Rudolph Binion for calling the *Tristrams saga* to my attention.

23. This and the previous quotation are from Elizabeth A. Waites, "Fixing Women: Devaluation, Idealization, and the Female Fetish," *Journal of the American Psychoanalytic Association* 30, no. 2 (1982): 437.

24. Ibid., 445–46.

25. The quoted passages are from Thomas N. Wise, "Fetishism—Etiology and Treatment: A Review from Multiple Perspectives," *Comprehensive Psychiatry* 26, no. 3 (May/June 1985): 253.

26. Regarding the relics, see Patrick J. Geary, *Furta Sacra: Thefts of Relics in the Central Middle Ages* (Princeton: Princeton University Press, 1978), 39. See also 37.

27. See James S. Grotstein, "Autoscopy: The Experience of Oneself as Double," *Hillside Journal of Clinical Psychology* 5, no. 2 (1983): 260.

28. Arnold Goldberg, "Narcissism and the Readiness for Psychotherapy Termination," *Archives of General Psychiatry* 32 (June 1975): 695.

29. The quoted passages are from M. Masud R. Khan, *Alienation in Perversions* (New York: International Universities Press, 1979), 14.

30. Ibid., 16–17.

31. Ibid., 43.

32. Peter Brooks, *Body Work: Objects of Desire in Modern Narrative* (Cambridge: Harvard University Press, 1993), 24.

33. André Green, *On Private Madness* (New York: International Universities Press, 1986), 142. See also Goldberg, "Narcissism," 697, where the "loss (in the psychological sense) of an omnipotent parent allows the child to assume for himself the functions managed by the parent."

34. Rosemary Jackson, "Narcissism and Beyond: A Psychoanalytic Reading of *Frankenstein* and Fantasies of the Double," in *Aspects of Fantasy*, ed. William Coyle (Westport, Conn.: Greenwood Press, 1981), 48.

35. See Emily D. Bilski and Moshe Idel, "The Golem: An Historical Overview," in *Golem! Danger, Deliverance and Art*, ed. Emily Bilski (New York: Jewish Museum, 1988), and Moshe Idel, *Golem: Jewish Magical and Mystical Traditions on the Artificial Anthropoid* (New York: State University of New York Press, 1990).

36. In popular etymology "Horacio" is attributed to a Greek root meaning "spectator." See Gutierre Tibón, *Diccionario de nombres propios* (Mexico: Editorial Fournier, 1956), 261.

37. Ricardo Pallares and Reina Reyes, *¿Otro Felisberto?* (Montevideo: Casa del Autor Nacional, 1983), 33.

38. In the Marquis de Sade's novella *Justine*, a character shows Justine a wax effigy in the posture of the crucified Christ and remarks: "This statue is the representation of my former mistress, who died nailed to this wall. I had it constructed to replace her real body when it began to decompose."

39. See the similar "crisis of tears" on *OC,* 3:80.

40. Crying and a "keyhole" peeking effect are also combined on *OC,* 3:92.

41. The quoted phrase is from the Song of Sol. 4:12.

42. For a showcase scene suggesting the triumph of Hortensia over Maria, see *OC,* 2:170.

43. Note that the Latin *dulia* is "veneration."

44. The book is in the archive of Ana María Hernández de Elena.

45. In an interview conducted with Ismael Hernández by A. Salsamendi in 1964. The typescript is in the archives of Ana María Hernández de Elena.

46. In a conversation with me in August 1991, Ana María Hernández de Elena observed, "Those legs are Calita's." Another biographical link is suggested in "Mamma's Tree" by the cousin-lover's work as a movie-theater musician (*OC,* 2:184). Note also that Ana María Hernández married her first cousin, Sergio Elena.

In "Mamma's Tree" the "difficult steps" of the daughter are also recaptured in her mother's feet "as blind animals, already close to death, moving with difficulty" (2:192). See also the thin and heavy columns on 3:104.

47. *Pollera* is mentioned in passing in "Mamma's Tree" (*OC,* 2:189). The multiple identities consolidating on the fat legs might be the source of the peculiar compromise offered by this image: "I saw from behind a girl who had one leg fatter than the other" (3:169).

48. Ana María Hernández, "Mis recuerdos," *Escritura* 7, nos. 13–14 (1982): 343.

49. Medeiros, *Felisberto y yo,* 31, 9, 52, 56, 72, and 41, respectively. See also 37.

50. Luis Neira, "El Felisberto de la calle cortada," *El día* (4 April 1981): 3.

51. The quoted phrase is from Otto F. Kernberg, *Object Relations Theory and Clinical Psycho-Analysis* (New York: Jason Aronson, 1976), 196.

52. Irvin D. Yalom, "Aggression and Forbiddenness in Voyeurism," *Archives of General Psychiatry* 3 (1960): 310. One voyeur at the age of nine "made a hole in the floor which permitted him to look into the bathroom below." From this vantage point "he would observe his mother, sister and aunt in the bathroom." In later years the patient "was bashful and withdrawn and went about with his eyes directed to the floor." See Harry H. Nierenberg, "A Case of Voyeurism," *Annual Survey of Psychoanalysis* 1 (1951): 174.

53. Yalom, "Aggression," 310.

54. Ibid., 312.

55. The first quoted passage is from a narcissistic analysand discussed in Robert S. Wallerstein, *Forty-Two Lives in Treatment: A Study in Psychoanalysis and Psychotherapy* (New York: Guilford Press, 1986), 323.

56. The quoted phrase is from Neumann, *Great Mother,* 129.

57. Roland Barthes, *S/Z,* trans. Richard Miller (New York: Hill and Wang, 1974), 238.

58. See *The Hortensias* manuscript, archive of Ana María Hernández de Elena, 90–98. The quoted words regarding the countess are on 3 (also numbered 33).

59. Cited in Otto Fenichel, *The Psychoanalytic Theory of Neurosis* (New York: W. W. Norton, 1945), 348.

60. See *OC,* 3:70, where a piece of bread floating through the door between bedroom and dining room "joins" the narrator's wife and Margarita.

61. Norah Giraldi Dei Cas and Frank Graziano, interview with María Isabel ("Mabel") Hernández Guerra, April 1993.

62. Lisa Block de Behar, "Los límites del narrador," *Studi di letteratura ispano-americana* 13–14 (1983): 28.

63. Christopher Bollas, *The Shadow of the Object: Psychoanalysis of the Unthought Known* (London: Free Association Books, 1987), 40.

64. Sigmund Freud, "A Special Type of Object-Choice," in *Standard Edition*, ed. James Strachey, vol. 11 (London: Hogarth Press, 1957), 169.

65. The quoted phrases are from Sigmund Freud, "On the Universal Tendency to Debasement in Love," in *Standard Edition*, ed. James Strachey, vol. 11 (London: Hogarth Press, 1957), 189.

66. Freud, "A Special Type of Object Choice," 169.

67. Ibid., 168.

68. The last quoted passage is from Wallerstein, *Forty-Two Lives,* 337.

69. The quoted words are Thomas H. Ogden's, summarizing Klein, in his "The Concept of Internal Object Relations," *International Journal of Psycho-Analysis* 64 (1983): 229.

70. Ibid.

71. See Heinz Kohut, *The Analysis of Self* (New York: International Universities Press, 1971).

72. José Bleger, *Simbiosis y ambigüedad* (Buenos Aires: Editorial Paidós, 1967), 176.

73. See also *OC,* 2:107 regarding a similar play with Dolly's name.

74. See Norah Giraldi Dei Cas, *Felisberto Hernández: del creador al hombre* (Montevideo: Ediciones de la Banda Oriental, 1975), 19.

75. Julia Kristeva, "Stabat Mater," in *The Female Body in Western Culture,* ed. Susan Rubin Suleiman (Cambridge: Harvard University Press, 1986), 116.

76. Christian Metz, *The Imaginary Signifier: Psychoanalysis and the Cinema*, trans. Celia Britton et al. (Bloomington: Indiana University Press, 1977), 59.

77. See Alain Sicard, ed., *Felisberto Hernández ante la crítica actual* (Caracas: Monte Avila, 1977), 151, 162, 165–66.

78. See Francisco Lasarte, *Felisberto Hernández y la escritura de "lo otro"* (Madrid: Insula, 1981), 147.

79. A piano-woman pun similar to *tocar* is established at the beginning of "The Crocodile"; see *OC,* 3:90.

80. See also *OC,* 3:10.

81. See *OC,* 1:110 for a similar example.

82. For the Mahler passage, see Theodor Reik, "En el principio es el silencio," in *El silencio en psicoanálisis,* ed. Juan David Nasio (Buenos Aires: Amorrortu Editores, 1988), 26.

83. In a different perspective, the sexual promiscuity with mass-produced love objects can also be understood as a counterphobic defense, designed to create the illusion of control and to allay the fear of oneself becoming the doll-thing of the mother and her surrogates.

84. The quoted phrase is from Otto F. Kernberg, "Aggression and Love in the Relationship of the Couple," in *Perversions and Near-Perversions in Clinical Practice,* ed. Gerald I. Fogel and Wayne A. Myers (New Haven: Yale University Press, 1991), 155. An example of this type of analysand is found on the same page.

85. Freud, "On the Universal Tendency to Debasement," 183. The passage in the next sentence is from the same source, 189. In François Truffaut's film *The Bride Wore Black* a character comments, "All women are whores except my mother, who is a saint" (Films du Carrosse, 1968).

86. In these last two sentences I am following John Money, "Paraphilias: Phenom-

enology and Classification," *American Journal of Psychotherapy* 38, no. 2 (April 1984): 174. The quoted passage is from the same page.

87. Waites, "Fixing Women," 451.

88. Freud, "A Special Type of Object-Choice," 171.

89. Victoria Hamilton, *Narcissus and Oedipus* (London: Routledge & Kegan Paul, 1982), 133. For discussion of the corpse as a present absence, see Louis-Vincent Thomas, *El cadáver*, trans. Juan Damonte (Mexico: Fondo de Cultura Económica, 1989), 216.

90. The quoted passage is cited in Rafael E. Lopez, "Libido Adhesiveness and Working Through during Pathological Mourning," *Scandinavian Psychoanalytic Review* 7, no. 1 (1984): 38.

91. Money, "Paraphilias," 171. Money also mentions another Hernández trademark—fatness—as a factor of devaluation.

92. Ibid.

93. The quoted phrases are from Julia Kristeva, *Tales of Love*, trans. Leon S. Soudiez (New York: Columbia University Press, 1987), 356.

94. Jonathan P. Rosman and Phillip J. Resnick, "Sexual Attraction to Corpses: A Psychiatric Review of Necrophilia," *Bulletin of the American Academy of Psychiatry and the Law* 17, no. 2 (1989): 159.

95. Ibid., 161.

96. The quoted phrase is from Kernberg, *Object Relations Theory*, 195.

97. As Ernest Jones put it, "The dead person who loves will love forever and will never be weary of giving and receiving caresses." Quoted in Rosman and Resnick, "Sexual Attraction to Corpses," 161.

98. Kernberg, *Object Relations Theory*, 193.

99. D. W. Winnicott, *Playing and Reality* (New York: Tavistock Publications, 1971), 22.

100. The parenthetically quoted passage is Robert J. Stoller's concept, developed in his *Perversion: The Erotic Form of Hatred* (New York: Delta Books, 1975).

101. Kernberg, *Object Relations Theory*, 193.

102. The mirror is a "symbol of the female sex" referred to in Chinese as the "secret place." B. A. Litvinskii, in *The Encyclopedia of Religion*, s.v. "Mirrors."

103. All quoted passages in this and the previous paragraph are from Arnold M. Cooper, "The Unconscious Core of Perversion," in Fogel and Myers, *Perversions and Near-Perversions*, 24.

104. The quoted passages in this and the previous sentence are from Kristeva, *Tales of Love*, 356 and 357, respectively.

105. Neumann, *Great Mother,* 39.

106. Ibid., 42.

107. Ibid., 128.

108. The first quoted passage is from the Song of Sol. 4:12 and the second from Prov. 23:27. See also Northrop Frye, *Anatomy of Criticism* (Princeton: Princeton University Press, 1973), 146.

109. The first quoted passage is from Elizabeth Robertson, "The Corporeality of Female Sanctity in *The Life of Saint Margaret*," in *Images of Sainthood in Medieval Europe*, ed. Renate Blumenfeld-Kosinski and Timea Szell (Ithaca: Cornell University Press, 1991), 281. The second passage in this sentence and the passages in the next are from Clarissa W. Atkinson, "'Precious Balsam in a Fragile Glass': The Ideology of Virginity in the Later Middle Ages," *Journal of Family History,* summer 1993, 137–38.

Note that in medieval *contemptus mundi* literature Death compares woman to a vessel in grotesque imagery, including "a bag of filth," "a repulsive bucket," "a mildewed coffer," "a threadbare sack," and "a pocket with a hole." See Jean Delumeau, *Sin and Fear: The Emergence of a Western Guilt Culture*, trans. Eric Nicholson (New York: St. Martin's Press, 1991), 47.

110. In Herbert Grabes, *The Mutable Glass* (Cambridge: Cambridge University Press, 1982), 161. See also Neumann, where "as uterus she is the vessel that is 'broken' at birth" (*Great Mother,* 128).

111. The longer passage is from Neumann, *Great Mother,* 124, and the fragmented quotations later in the sentence from C. G. Jung, *Symbols of Transformation: An Analysis of the Prelude to a Case of Schizophrenia*, trans. R. F. C. Hull (Princeton: Princeton University Press, 1967), 240.

112. Marija Gimbutas, *The Civilization of the Goddess* (San Francisco: HarperSanFrancisco, 1991), 234.

113. Cushing, cited in Neumann, *Great Mother,* 123.

114. Ibid., 122.

115. Ibid., 122–23.

116. Ibid., 121.

117. Ibid., 129.

118. Ibid., 25. See also 42.

119. Bollas, *Shadow of the Object,* 56.

120. This and the quoted passage in the previous sentence are from Bleger, *Simbiosis y ambigüedad,* 192. For another example of "a shell of a person," see Anthony B. Joseph and Daniel H. O'Leary, "Brain Atrophy and Interhemispheric Fissure Enlargement in Cotard's Syndrome," *Journal of Clinical Psychiatry* 47 (1986): 519.

121. Brian Ackner, "Depersonalization II: Clinical Syndromes," *Journal of Mental Science* 100 (1954): 868–69.

122. Bleger, *Simbiosis y ambigüedad,* 192.

123. This and the quoted passage in the previous section are from ibid., 191.

124. The quoted passage is from Neumann, *Great Mother,* 132. See also Bleger, *Simbiosis y ambigüedad,* 219.

125. Norah Giraldi Dei Cas and Frank Graziano, interview with María Isabel ("Mabel") Hernández Guerra, April 1993.

126. Note that the Spanish *margarita* means "daisy"; this last image therefore delivers a flower and its vase all in one, like the Hortensias.

127. See also *OC,* 2:16. On 2:44 another pitcher or vase is the centerpiece for a quasi-erotic encounter. Note the similarity of the Spanish words used by Hernández in all of these cases: *jarra, jarro,* and *jarrón.*

128. Frye, *Anatomy of Criticism,* 198.

129. See Clyde Kluckhorn, "Recurrent Themes in Myth and Mythmaking," in *Myth and Mythmaking,* ed. Henry A. Murray (Boston: Beacon Press, 1968), 50.

130. Freud, *Dreams,* 354. See also Chasseguet-Smirgel, *Sexuality and Mind,* 63, where a patient's fear of entering a room relates to the fear of entering mother's body sexually. Suggestive room and stairway imagery are also found in the opening of "Ursula" (*OC,* 3:118).

131. Neumann, *Great Mother,* 137. See *OC,* 2:23 for an inversion of "The Flooded House" trope (Celina's house is an island). See also 2:37.

In classical theory "the (idealized) body was, so to speak, directly projected onto the building." Leon Battista Alberti made the proposition that "the building is in its entirety like a body composed of its parts," and "Francesco di Giorgio showed a figure superimposed literally on the plan of a cathedral and of a city, while [Antonio di Piero Averlino] Filarete compared the buildings's cavities and functions to those of the body, its eyes, ears, nose, mouth, veins, and viscera." See Anthony Vidler, *The Architectural Uncanny* (Cambridge: MIT Press, 1992), 70–71.

For the Pueblo Indians, the structure housing the entire community is a monolithic extension of the earth as mother. See Tito Naranjo and Rina Swentzell, "Healing Spaces in the Tewa Pueblo World," *American Indian Cultural and Research Journal* 13, nos. 3 and 4 (1989): 263–64.

132. O. V. de Milosz, cited in Bachelard, *Poetics of Space,* 45.

133. Neumann, *Great Mother,* 46. The feminized city is linked with eye themes in a notable pun from *Lands of Memory*; see *OC,* 3:16.

See also Giulia Sissa, "Subtle Bodies," in Feher et al., *Fragments for a History,* pt. 3, 149: "Mary is the gate through which Christ entered this world, in a virginal birth, without undoing the genital locks"

134. Jung, *Symbols of Transformation,* 208.

135. See Gimbutas, *Civilization,* 256–59.

136. Frye, *Anatomy of Criticism,* 150.

137. For another potential suicide-by-water, see *OC,* 3:14.

138. Green, *On Private Madness,* 90.

139. Ogden, "Internal Object Relations," 232.

140. Françoise Héritier-Augé, "Semen and Blood: Some Ancient Theories Concerning their Genesis and Relationship," in Feher et al., *Fragments for a History,* 171. The author is following S. Sauneron.

141. Bruce M. Knauft, "Bodily Images in Melanesia: Cultural Substances and Natural Metaphors," in Feher et al., *Fragments for a History,* pt. 3, 204.

142. Luce Irigaray, *Speculum of the Other Woman,* trans. Gillian C. Gill (Ithaca: Cornell University Press, 1985), 18.

143. Jung, *Symbols of Transformation,* 218 and 267, respectively. For some Latin American examples of water myths with maternal aspects, see Javier Ocampo López, "Mitos y creencias en los procesos de cambio en América Latina," in *América Latina en sus ideas,* ed. Leopoldo Zea (Mexico: Siglo Ventiuno Editores, 1986), 408.

144. Richard Broxton Onians, *The Origins of European Thought about the Body, the Mind, the Soul, the World, Time, and Fate* (Cambridge: Cambridge University Press, 1954), 247.

145. Neumann, *Great Mother,* 47.

146. See also *OC,* 3:173. On 2:67 a beach and sea-foam image emerges in a context intermingling mother and lover.

147. The quoted passages in this and the previous sentence are from Wallerstein, *Forty-Two Lives,* 335.

148. This "represented her mother destroyed by oral, anal, and urethral means." Melanie Klein, "The Oedipus Complex in the Light of Early Anxieties," in *Essential Papers on the Psychology of Women,* ed. Claudia Zanardi (New York: New York University Press, 1990), 73.

149. Hyman Spotnitz and Philip Resnikoff, "The Myths of Narcissus," *Psychoanalytic Review* 14 (1954): 174.

150. See Sigmund Freud, *Civilization and Its Discontents, Standard Edition,* ed. James Strachey, vol. 11 (London: Hogarth Press, 1961), 66–68. See also Fenichel, *Psychoanalytic Theory of Neurosis,* 39 and 420; Chasseguet-Smirgel, *Sexuality and Mind,* 135; and Arnold H. Modell, *Object Love and Reality* (New York: International Universities Press, 1968), 38.

151. Sandor Ferenczi, *Thalassa: A Theory of Genitality*, trans. Henry Alden Bunker (New York: W. W. Norton, 1968), 52 and 54, respectively.

152. Ibid., 19.

153. Ibid., 60.

154. Ibid., 34 and 49, respectively.

155. Victor Tausk, "On the Origin of the 'Influencing Machine' in Schizophrenia," in *Essential Papers on Psychosis,* ed. Peter Buckley (New York: New York University Press, 1988), 72. In the context of "The Usher," cf. 1 Cor. 12.15, where the whole body is an eye.

156. Chasseguet-Smirgel, *Sexuality and Mind,* 66.

157. The quoted phrase is a trope for death in Delumeau, *Sin and Fear,* 59.

158. Green, *On Private Madness,* 27.

159. Ferenczi, *Thalassa,* 48.

160. Cited in Yalom, "Aggression," 307.

161. Ferenczi, *Thalassa,* 63. See also Louis-Vincent Thomas, *El cadáver: de la biología a la antropología,* trans. Juan Damonte (Mexico: Fondo de Cultura Económica, 1989), 100–102.

162. Neumann, *Great Mother,* 45.

163. See Gimbutas, *Civilization,* 243, 299.

164. See Marija Gimbutas, *The Language of the Goddess* (San Francisco: Harper & Row, 1989), 223.

Select Bibliography

RECENT MAJOR EDITIONS OF WORKS BY FELISBERTO HERNÁNDEZ

Hernández, Felisberto. *Obras completas*. Edited and introduced by José Pedro Díaz. 3 vols. Montevideo: Arca-Calicanto Editoriales, 1981, 1982, 1988.

———. *Obras completas*. With a preface by David Huerta. 3 vols. Mexico: Siglo XXI, 1983.

———. *Novelas y cuentos*. Edited by José Pedro Díaz. Caracas: Biblioteca Ayacucho, 1985.

———. *Narraciones incompletas*. Madrid: Ediciones Siruela, 1990.

SECONDARY BOOKS ON THE LIFE AND WORK
OF FELISBERTO HERNÁNDEZ

Antúnez, Rocío. *Felisberto Hernández: el discurso inundado*. Mexico: Instituto Nacional de Bellas Artes, 1985.

Blengio Brito, Raúl. *Felisberto Hernández: el hombre y el narrador*. Montevideo: Ediciones de la Casa del Estudiante, 1981.

Canepa, Aldo L. *Felisberto Hernández*. Montevideo: Editorial Técnica, 1979.

Cánova, Virginia. *La creación literaria en Felisberto Hernández como arma contra la alienación*. Montevideo: Puntosur Editores, 1990.

Díaz, José Pedro. *Felisberto Hernández: el espectáculo imaginario*. Montevideo: Arca Editorial, 1991.

Echavarren, Roberto. *El espacio de la verdad: práctica del texto en Felisberto Hernández*. Buenos Aires: Editorial Sudamericana, 1981.

Escritura: revista de teoría y crítica literarias 7, no 13–14 (1982). Special issue dedicated to Felisberto Hernández.

Ferré, Rosario. *El acomodador: una lectura fantástica de Felisberto Hernández*. Mexico: Fondo de Cultura Económica, 1986.

Giraldi Dei Cas, Norah. *Felisberto Hernández: del creador al hombre*. Montevideo: Ediciones de la Banda Oriental, 1975.

Gómez Mango, Lídice, ed. *Felisberto Hernández: notas críticas*. Montevideo: Cuadernos de Literatura, Fundación de Cultura Universitaria, 1970.

Lasarte, Francisco. *Felisberto Hernández y la escritura de "lo otro."* Madrid: Insula, 1981.

Lockhart, Washington. *Felisberto Hernández: una biografía literaria.* Montevideo: Arca Editorial, 1991.

Medeiros, Paulina. *Felisberto y yo.* Montevideo: Libros del Astillero, 1982.

Rela, Walter, ed. *Felisberto Hernández: valoración crítica.* Montevideo: Editorial Ciencias, 1982.

Pallares, Ricardo. *Felisberto Hernández y las lámparas que nadie encendió.* Montevideo: Instituto de Filosofía, Ciencias y Letras, 1980.

Pallares, Ricardo, and Reina Reyes, *¿Otro Felisberto?* Montevideo: Casa del Autor Nacional, 1983.

Sicard, Alain, ed. *Felisberto Hernández ante la crítica actual.* Caracas: Monte Avila, 1977.

OTHER SECONDARY BOOKS

Barthes, Roland. *The Pleasure of the Text.* Translated by Richard Miller. New York: Hill and Wang, 1975.

———. *Roland Barthes by Roland Barthes.* Translated by Richard Howard. New York: Hill and Wang, 1977.

Bergson, Henri. *Mind-Energy.* Translated by Wildon Carr. New York: Henry Holt, 1920.

Bleger, José. *Simbiosis y ambigüedad.* Buenos Aires: Editorial Paidós, 1967.

Brooks, Peter. *Reading for the Plot.* New York: Vintage Books, 1984.

Buckley, Peter, ed. *Essential Papers on Psychosis.* New York: New York University Press, 1988.

Clark, Michael. *Jacques Lacan: An Annotated Bibliography.* Vol. 1. New York: Garland Publishing, 1988.

Diagnostic and Statistical Manual of Mental Disorders. 3d ed., rev. Washington, D.C.: American Psychiatric Association, 1987.

Dundes, Alan. *The Evil Eye: A Folklore Casebook.* New York: Garland Publishing, 1981.

Eco, Umberto. *The Open Work.* Translated by Anna Cancogni. Cambridge: Harvard University Press, 1989.

———. *Semiotics and the Philosophy of Language.* London: Macmillan, 1984.

Favazza, Armando F. *Bodies Under Siege: Self-Mutilation in Culture and Psychiatry.* Baltimore: Johns Hopkins University Press, 1987.

Fogel, Gerald I., and Wayne A. Meyers. *Perversions and Near-Perversions in Clinical Practice: New Psychoanalytical Perspectives.* New Haven: Yale University Press, 1991.

Freud, Sigmund. "A Special Type of Object Choice" and "On the Universal Tendency to Debasement in the Sphere of Love." In *Standard Edition,* edited by James Strachey, vol. 11. London: The Hogarth Press, 1957.

———. "On Narcissism." In *Standard Edition,* edited by James Strachey, vol. 14. London: The Hogarth Press, 1957.

———. "The Uncanny." In *Standard Edition,* edited by James Strachey, vol. 15. London: The Hogarth Press, 1955.

———. "A Child is Being Beaten." In *Standard Edition,* edited by James Strachey, vol. 17. London: The Hogarth Press, 1955.

Gimbutas, Marija. *The Language of the Goddess*. San Francisco: Harper and Row, 1989.

————. *The Civilization of the Goddess*. Edited by Joan Marler. San Francisco: HarperSanFrancisco, 1991.

Grabes, Herbert. *The Mutable Glass: Mirror Imagery in Titles and Texts of the Middle Ages and the English Renaissance*. Translated by Gordon Collier. Cambridge: Cambridge University Press, 1982.

Green, André. *On Private Madness*. Madison, Conn.: International Universities Press, 1986.

Hillis Miller, J. *Versions of Pygmalion*. Cambridge: Harvard University Press, 1990.

Kernberg, Otto F. *Borderline Conditions and Pathological Narcissism*. New York: Jason Aronson, 1975.

————. *Object-Relations Theory and Clinical Psychoanalysis*. New York: Jason Aronson, 1976.

————, ed. *Narcissistic Personality Disorder, The Psychiatric Clinics of North America* 12, no. 3 (September 1989).

Khan, Masud R. *Alienation in Perversions*. New York: International Universities Press, 1979.

Kohut, Heinz, *The Analysis of the Self*. New York: International Universities Press, 1971.

Lacan, Jacques. *Ecrits*. Translated by Alan Sheridan. New York: W. W. Norton, 1977.

————. *The Seminar of Jacques Lacan, Book II*. Edited by Jacques-Alain Miller. Translated by Sylvana Tomaselli. New York: W. W. Norton, 1991.

Lindberg, David C. *Theories of Vision from Al-Kindi to Kepler*. Chicago: University of Chicago Press, 1982.

Merleau-Ponty, Maurice. *The Primacy of Perception*. Edited by James M. Edie. Evanston, Ill.: Northwestern University Press, 1964.

Metz, Christian. *The Imaginary Signifier: Psychoanalysis and the Signifier*. Translated by Celia Britton and Annwyl Williams. Bloomington: Indiana University Press, 1982.

Morrison, Andrew P., ed. *Essential Papers on Narcissism*. New York: New York University Press, 1986.

Neumann, Eric. *The Great Mother: An Analysis of the Archetype*. Translated by Ralph Manheim. Princeton: Princeton University Press, 1963.

Nietzsche, Friedrich. *The Will to Power*. Edited by Walter Kaufmann. New York: Vintage Books, 1968.

Pierrot, Jean. *The Decadent Imagination, 1880-1900*. Chicago: University of Chicago Press, 1981.

Rank, Otto. *The Double*. Edited and translated by Harry Tucker Jr. Chapel Hill: University of North Carolina Press, 1971.

Siebers, Tony. *The Mirror of Medusa*. Berkeley: University of California Press, 1983.

Suleiman, Susan Rubin, ed. *The Female Body in Western Culture*. Cambridge: Harvard University Press, 1986.

Sylvester, David. *The Brutality of Fact: Interviews with Francis Bacon*. London: Thames and Hudson, 1987.

Todorov, Tzvetan. *The Fantastic: A Structural Approach to a Literary Genre*. Translated by Richard Howard. Cleveland: The Press of Case Western Reserve University, 1973.

Vaz Ferreira, Carlos. *Obras completas*. Montevideo: Cámara de Representantes de la República Oriental del Uruguay, 1963.

Vinge, Louise. *The Narcissus Theme in Western European Literature up to the Early Nineteenth Century.* Lund, Sweden: Gleerups, 1967.

Whitehead, Alfred North. *Modes of Thought.* New York: Capricorn Books, 1958.

Winnicott, D. W. *Playing and Reality.* London: Tavistock Publications, 1971.

Index